The
Compleat
Academic

The
Compleat
Academic

A Career Guide

Second Edition

Edited by

John M. Darley, Mark P. Zanna, and Henry L. Roediger III

American Psychological Association • Washington, DC

First printing, June 2003
Second printing, November 2003
Third printing, June 2004

Published by
American Psychological Association
750 First Street, NE
Washington, DC 20002
www.apa.org

To order
APA Order Department
P.O. Box 92984
Washington, DC 20090-2984
Tel: (800) 374-2721
Direct: (202) 336-5510
Fax: (202) 336-5502
TDD/TTY: (202) 336-6123
Online: www.apa.org/books/
Email: order@apa.org

In the U.K., Europe, Africa, and the
Middle East, copies may be ordered from
American Psychological Association
3 Henrietta Street
Covent Garden, London
WC2E 8LU England

Typeset in Goudy by World Composition Services, Inc., Sterling, VA

Printer: Port City Press, Inc., Baltimore, MD
Cover Designer: Naylor Design, Washington, DC
Project Manager: Debbie Hardin, Carlsbad, CA

The opinions and statements published are the responsibility of the authors, and such opinions and statements do not necessarily represent the policies of the American Psychological Association. Any views expressed herein do not necessarily represent the views of the United States government and an author's participation is not meant to serve as an official endorsement or position of the United States government.

Library of Congress Cataloging-in-Publication Data
The compleat academic : a career guide / edited by John M. Darley, Mark P. Zanna, and Henry L. Roediger, III.—2nd ed.
    p. ; cm.
Includes bibliographical references and index.
ISBN 1-59147-035-8 (alk. paper)
    1. Social sciences—Study and teaching. 2. Social sciences—Vocational guidance. 3. College teaching—Vocational guidance. I. Darley, John M. II. Zanna, Mark P. III. Roediger, Henry L.

H62.C584824 2003
300 .71 1—dc21   2003041830

British Library Cataloguing-in-Publication Data
A CIP record is available from the British Library.

Printed in the United States of America

CONTENTS

CONTRIBUTORS

Jonathan R. Alger, University of Michigan, Ann Arbor
David A. Balota, Washington University, St. Louis, MO
Daryl J. Bem, Cornell University, Ithaca, NY
Douglas A. Bernstein, University of South Florida, Tampa
Deborah L. Best, Wake Forest University, Winston-Salem, NC
Richard R. Bootzin, University of Arizona, Tucson
Todd S. Braver, Washington University, St. Louis, MO
Elizabeth D. Capaldi, University of Buffalo, State University of New York
Kevin M. Carlsmith, Colgate University, Hamilton, NY
John M. Darley, Princeton University, Princeton, NJ
John F. Dovidio, Colgate University, Hamilton, NY
James L. Hilton, University of Michigan, Ann Arbor
James M. Jones, University of Delaware, Newark
Patrick C. Kyllonen, Educational Testing Service, Princeton, NJ
Charles G. Lord, Texas Christian University, Fort Worth
Sandra Goss Lucas, University of Illinois at Urbana–Champaign
Joanne Martin, Stanford University, Stanford, CA
Kathleen B. McDermott, Washington University, St. Louis, MO
Susan Nolen-Hoeksema, University of Michigan, Ann Arbor
Denise C. Park, University of Illinois at Urbana–Champaign
Louis A. Penner, University of South Florida, Tampa
Eun Rhee, University of Delaware, Newark
Henry L. Roediger III, Washington University, St. Louis, MO
David A. Schroeder, University of Arkansas, Fayetteville
Jane Steinberg, National Institute of Mental Health, Bethesda, MD
Robert J. Sternberg, Yale University, New Haven, CT
Shelley E. Taylor, University of California, Los Angeles
Jeffrey M. Zacks, Washington University, St. Louis, MO
Mark P. Zanna, University of Waterloo, Ontario, Canada

FOREWORD

Angling may be said to be so like the mathematics that it can never be fully learnt.

Izaak Walton, 1653

It is a truism that such high-skill activities as angling or academics require similarly skillful instruction. Mentors have taught their apprentices since the beginning of time, but only recently have mentors invented systematic tools to convey these skills. And so it was in academics prior to the publication of the first edition of *The Compleat Academic* in 1987. Many unwritten norms and guidelines for academic behavior were passed down from generation to generation, but these were generally discussed behind closed doors and not necessarily explicated in public. This meant that students and junior faculty were crucially dependent on their supervisors and senior colleagues to "show them the ropes." Even when they were willing, of course, this did not necessarily translate into clear and easy-to-follow advice. The first edition of *The Compleat Academic* changed all this, presenting information about many of the field's unwritten norms and guidelines and providing clear and diverse practical advice for new, and not-so-new, academics.

The first edition of the book helped mentors train their students and other students to train themselves in the no longer so inscrutable ways and wiles of the life academic. The wisdom contained there in nine chapters spanning a mere 225 pages helped many fledgling scholars thrive, and, we may dare add, provided good advice for the more experienced scholar as well. In short, *The Compleat Adademic* has been a compleat success.

Given the first edition's remarkable compleatness, one might question the value of a new edition; why not simply keep the first edition in print? A quick scan of this new edition is ample testimony to the contrary. Despite such seemingly eternal constants as the venerable edict to "publish-or-perish," the academy can never be regarded as in stasis, only flux. This new edition reflects the many changes that the academy has faced in the sixteen-odd years since the first edition was published, including the growing use of computers in research and teaching and the roles of academics in consulting and working for industry and government. In addition, issues that were just beginning to be discussed in the 1980s, such as political correctness, are now front and center in the life of academics. Thus, the second edition has expanded to 20 chapters spanning 422 pages.

For their contributions to psychology through the wisdom contained in this new edition of *The Compleat Academic*, we are deeply indebted to editors John M. Darley, Mark P. Zanna, Henry L. Roediger III, and the authors who contributed to this volume. But their contributions do not stop there. As with the first edition, this volume is sponsored by the Society for the Psychological Study of Social Issues (SPSSI). As such, the royalties from sales will go to SPSSI to further its educational and scientific endeavors.

We invite psychologists and other social scientists who are interested in social issues to learn more about SPSSI (www.spssi.org). We have over 3,000 members from around the world, and we publish print and electronic journals, hold a biennial conference and sponsor theme conferences, and provide grants and awards for research on social issues.

We may not be compleat academics all, but we can and should continue to strive to be.

Blair T. Johnson
Victoria M. Esses

PREFACE

Academia in general and academic psychology in particular have formal and informal rules of operation, as do all institutions. Formal rules are codified in faculty handbooks and exist for special purposes, such as for publication (e.g., the *Publication Manual of the American Psychological Association*). Those written rules are available for everyone to read. However, the unwritten rules that govern the field are harder to discover. The contributors to *The Compleat Academic: A Career Guide* go beyond the written rules that everybody should know to provide the usually unwritten rules of the academic game that are also critical. Many seasoned academics have learned these implicit rules through experience, and they sometimes take them for granted. We hope that we can make this tacit knowledge explicit for graduate students, postdoctoral fellows, and assistant professors beginning their careers. However, we believe that these chapters have a great deal to offer all academic psychologists. In editing this volume, we have learned much ourselves about how others think and how they operate within the field.

Readers of the first edition will find many of the same chapters in this second edition, although they have been revised thoroughly and updated in light of many comments received over the years. The editors of the first edition (Mark P. Zanna and John M. Darley) asked Henry Roediger III to come aboard as third editor. Together, we have reorganized and revamped the book, adding many new chapters in the process. (The first edition contained 9 chapters; this edition contains 20.)

We have avoided the temptation to review the contents and organization of the book; reading the Contents shows you the result of our thinking through the titles of the chapters and their ordering. Suffice it to say that *The Compleat Academic* is, we feel, even more complete in its second edition. Still, there is always room for improvement. We hope for a third edition

This book is published under the auspices of the Society for the Psychological Study of Social Issues, an organization with a long and honorable tradition of societal concern. Proceeds from the publication of this book go to that organization.

some day, so we welcome suggestions, reflections, additions, and—yes—criticisms from readers.

This book says something, but not everything, about a number of problems a beginning academic will face. Many suggestions throughout the book need to be qualified in the context in which the reader finds him- or herself. It would be a mistake to consider this book the source of definitive advice. Rather, we hope that it will initiate discussion among faculty and graduate students about the topics on which we touch. Indeed, often authors of different chapters disagree themselves. Should you consider writing a textbook relatively early in your career? Or at all? You will read various opinions in separate chapters. Keep in mind that the authors are individuals offering advice that has worked for them. Like all advice, you will hear conflicting opinions, and you will need to factor your own personality and proclivities into the equation to decide which pieces of advice make sense for you.

Every book has a list of authors and editors. However, many others need to be thanked for their efforts, without which publication of this book would not have been possible. Kevin M. Carlsmith, at first a graduate student at Princeton and then a faculty member at the University of Virginia, has helped our cause in many ways, riding herd on the entire project. Carlsmith is preparing a companion volume to accompany this one, titled *The Compleat Graduate Student*, which will provide advice to beginning graduate students much as this volume does for assistant professors. Several people at the American Psychological Association have stewarded this volume through the production process. We thank especially Phuong Huynh, our developmental editor, who read the entire volume and made astute comments on each chapter.

We hope readers will find *The Compleat Academic* rewarding. May your careers go far and your discoveries be great.

I

STARTING A CAREER

1

A GUIDE TO PHD GRADUATE SCHOOL: HOW THEY KEEP SCORE IN THE BIG LEAGUES

CHARLES G. LORD

Imagine an alternate universe in which you play college baseball, spend a few years in the minor leagues, and then get your big chance in the majors. In your first time at bat, you hit a towering drive. As the ball easily clears the center field wall, you nonchalantly toss aside your bat and prepare to jog around the bases to wild applause. Instead, the crowd moans and the umpire bellows "YER OUT!" Someone forgot to tell you that the rules are different in the major leagues. They play by a different scorecard.

This imaginary scenario would never happen in baseball, because the important rules of the game stay the same from the sandlot to the big leagues. The central message of this chapter, though, is that academic doctoral programs are not playing baseball but hardball. When you move from being an undergraduate (or even from many master's programs) to being a graduate student in a doctorate program, they change the rules! They use a different scorecard. If you understand how you got admitted to your PhD program, what the faculty want from you, and how to keep score, you have a good chance of going on to a successful academic career. You will not be getting a letter from the chair of your department saying, in effect, "YER OUT!"

HOW YOU GOT ADMITTED

I remember being surprised a few years after getting my PhD when, over refreshments at a convention, several of my former fellow students from graduate school acknowledged that they initially had the same doubts I had. Although none of us ever admitted it at the time, we had each harbored the same unspoken fear during our first year of graduate school. "Any day now," I remember suspecting, "they're going to realize that I don't belong here with all these brilliant people. The admissions committee made a serious mistake."

Years later, I realized that my suspicions were all too true! After serving on graduate admissions committees for many years, I can tell you from first-hand experience that PhD admissions committees make serious mistakes. The problem is that they are forced to use performance data from one set of tasks to predict subsequent performance on an entirely different set of tasks. The admissions committees for PhD programs are like sports teams that try to predict from performance at professional basketball to performance in major league baseball. They select a Michael Jordan on the assumption that the greatest basketball player of all time must be an all-around athlete who will also excel in the big leagues of baseball. They are frequently wrong.

Unfortunately, undergraduates are graded primarily on how well they acquire facts—on knowing the periodic table of elements, reciting from memory the central arguments in Plato's dialogues, and listing the primary causes of the Civil War. When admissions committees examine an applicant's undergraduate straight-A transcript, what have they learned about the applicant? Not much! They have learned primarily that the applicant knows many facts.

Most PhD programs do not teach students to know *that*; instead, they teach students to know *how*. Admittedly, PhD programs teach some facts. The required courses in a PhD program are usually designed to make sure that all entering students have the same knowledge base. Learning facts, though, is far from the central goal in graduate school. Faculty members are not as concerned with your learning *that* as they are with your learning *how* to do top-notch research in your discipline.

People who are brilliant at learning facts are sometimes surprisingly poor at learning how to do research. I have been keeping records in my institution's PhD program for the past 12 years. Each year and across years, I try to predict from the admitted applicants' undergraduate grades and their scores on the graduate record exam (GRE) to various outcomes such as

TABLE 1.1
Success of Nine Variables at Predicting Who Gets a Stipend, Who Gets Good Grades in Graduate Courses, and Who Gets a PhD ($N = 90$)

Predictor	Stipend	Graduate grades	PhD
Undergraduate GPA	.26*	.38*	.14
Last 60 hours GPA	.27*	.42*	.11
GPA in major	.28*	.30*	.18
GRE-V	.21*	.25*	.03
GRE-Q	.33*	.03	−.07
GRE-A	.40*	.23*	.02
Graduate research competence			.83*
Number of publications			.63*

Note. *$p < .05$.

finishing the PhD or publishing in top journals. Each year and across years, I have had little success.

To understand why I have been unable to predict who succeeds in graduate school, look at Table 1.1, which reflects information about 90 students who entered the PhD program at my institution from 1987 through 1995. The admissions committee, which has different faculty members from one year to the next, must decide not only who gets accepted to the program but also which of the admitted applicants have the most potential. They rank-order the admitted candidates and offer the "best" a departmental fellowship that includes both a tuition waiver and a sizable stipend. Of the 90 students who were admitted to the PhD program from 1987 through 1995, the committee awarded fellowships to 51 of them and told the other 39 that they could enter the program, but only if they agreed to pay their own way. The difference between getting a fellowship and not getting one at my university is worth approximately $80,000 across four years. At many universities, the dollar difference is even greater.

If you examine the leftmost column of Table 1.1, you will understand why your undergraduate advisers kept telling you to get good grades and study hard for the GRE if you wanted to be admitted to graduate school, and especially if you wanted funding. Admissions committee members typically see three undergraduate grade point averages: your overall average for four years, your average in the last 60 hours, and your average in your major. They also see three GRE scores: the verbal score, the quantitative score, and the analytical score. Every one of these six variables is significantly correlated with whether the admissions committee will award a fellowship. The higher a student's undergraduate grades and GRE scores, the more likely that student was to get a coveted stipend.

Now examine the middle column of Table 1.1. Five of the six variables were significantly correlated with grades in graduate courses. If faculty members had been interested in predicting which of the entering students would get the best grades in graduate courses, they would have been very pleased with themselves. It is not surprising that undergraduate grades predicted graduate grades, because many required graduate courses are little more than advanced versions of the courses you took as an undergraduate. They emphasize learning *that* more than learning *how*. The correlations with undergraduate grade point average might have been even higher, except that some of our graduate courses require students to show that they are learning *how* to do what they will later be required to do in their professional careers.

The significant correlations between graduate grades and two of the three GRE scores are surprising, given that other researchers have found little relationship between GRE scores and graduate course grades (e.g., Sternberg & Williams, 1997). One possible explanation is that in my institution's program we admit students with a much wider range of GRE scores (all the way from 800 to 1450 total GRE-V plus GRE-Q) than in many other PhD programs. Another possible explanation is that faculty members give good grades to students who write well and appear to think analytically about the major topics covered in our courses.

Students who write well and think analytically, however, do not necessarily hit home runs when it comes to research. Look at the rightmost column in Table 1.1, which shows correlations between the six predictors available at the time of admission and which 56 of the 90 students made it all the way to a PhD. Not one of the six variables had a significant relationship with getting the PhD. If anyone tries to tell you that graduate admissions committees know at the time of admission who will get a PhD and who will not, tell them you have a few ballparks you would like to sell them.

The reason you cannot predict who is going to get the PhD is that my institution's graduate program, like most PhD graduate programs, changes the rules once new students arrive. We do not award doctoral degrees to students who do nothing more than get good grades. Instead, we award doctoral degrees to students who demonstrate research competence and publish in the professional literature. I asked three faculty members to rate the demonstrated research competence of these 90 graduate students and to estimate how many publications each student had at the time that he or she left the program. The three faculty members displayed high agreement on who was good at research and how often students had published. As you might expect, faculty ratings of research competence were also highly correlated with how many publications the student produced during his or her stay in the program. At the bottom of the rightmost column of Table 1.1, you can see how well these ratings of research competence and publication predicted getting the PhD. Clearly, students who were good at research finished the program, whereas students who were not as good at research, *even many of the students who excelled in graduate course work*, tended to strike out.

Experienced faculty members know that it does not take a genius to get a PhD. I do not ever recall meeting a new graduate student and thinking that the student was too dumb to succeed in graduate school. All 90 of the students on whom I have data were more than smart enough to succeed. The only factor that separated them seemed to be motivation. I had one student who came to us with straight A grades and 1450 GRE V + Q. He got the top grade in every course in his first semester and then *dropped out of the program*! Once he saw what my colleagues and I did for a living, he knew that he could not force himself to spend the rest of his life doing it as well. He could not see himself sitting in an office all day asking and answering questions about abstract theoretical processes. Most of the 34 students who left our program without a PhD were very similar to him. They had the verbal ability. They had the analytical ability. They could get outstanding grades. When it came to research, though, it soon became apparent to them and to the faculty that they had no interest and were just going through the motions. If you find yourself resenting the time you spend on research, do yourself a favor. Get out! You are in the wrong PhD program. Either go to a different PhD program or reconsider your decision to become an academic.

If you find yourself not loving research and less than thrilled about designing, conducting, and writing up research studies, one of the saddest decisions you could make is to go through the motions just to get a PhD. You might grudgingly continue in a PhD program just to get those magic letters after your name, but you have also boxed yourself into one of life's least pleasant corners. You have spent valuable years establishing credentials that qualify you to do one thing—a thing you do not enjoy. Also, without a reasonable publications record and enthusiastic faculty letters of recommendation, your job prospects will be slim. It would be much wiser to take a master's degree and find a job, perhaps in industry, that better suits your interests.

Not everyone has a genuine *passion* for doing research. I have a colleague who was once warned by his chair, at a school that emphasized teaching, that he had better stop spending so much time on research if he wanted to get tenure. He continued anyway! I have had students who entered the program without funding (because their undergraduate grades and GRE scores were abysmal), put themselves into many thousand of dollars of debt because they loved doing research, and are now distinguished faculty members at other institutions. People who find doing research boring (or even annoying) do not make it in PhD programs. People who love doing research get rewarded. As much as we would like to, we cannot predict which is which from the admissions materials, because we have no way of knowing who will be turned on by doing the type of research that we do.

Entering graduate students should make it their mission in a PhD program, therefore, to discover a type of research that they love doing. Look for journal articles that you think make more fascinating reading than the best novels. Look for articles and research presentations that have you shaking your head and saying, "Wow! I wish I had run those studies!" Look for research programs that get you so exited you cannot stop thinking about related concepts and cannot wait to get in the lab to test the latest ideas. If you have the type of interests that lead to a successful academic career, you will succeed in your mission to identify the research agenda that will become the love of your life.

WHAT THE FACULTY WANT FROM YOU

When you enter a graduate PhD program, you need to alter your self-concept. From grade school until graduate school, teachers rewarded you for sitting in class, taking meticulous notes, spending a lot of time studying the texts and your lecture notes, and taking exams on what you had learned. When you did well at these activities, you earned praise, respect, and other rewards from parents, teachers, and (sometimes) peers. You took pride in being very good at taking exams and standardized tests. If you are like most of us, you derived a large part of your self-concept from these skills, at which you excelled.

Suppose you entered a PhD graduate program and kept doing exactly what you had done all through your education. You read all the assigned texts, arrived at each class punctually, took thorough notes, went home to memorize the study materials, and aced all the exams. When your adviser mentioned getting involved in research, you promised yourself that you would do so as soon as you had finished impressing the faculty with how smart you were in their courses. You would probably be shocked to be warned that the faculty had put you on probation and that they suspected you would not make it all the way to a PhD.

The warning might arise because you misunderstood what faculty members wanted from you as a student in their PhD program. Most faculty members want to show you how to do research and scholarship. The want to prepare you for an academic or other research-oriented career. They know that no one is ever going to pay you to sit in a classroom, take notes, and score well on exams. They expect you to alter your self-concept—to draw your self-esteem not from being a student but from being a researcher and scholar.

Admittedly, the messages you receive from faculty members are usually mixed. They would be appalled if you were to pay no attention to courses. They want you to demonstrate a grasp of the basic concepts in their (and your) academic discipline. They want you to pass all your required courses and excel in at least some of them. Never forget, though, that the way to a faculty member's heart is through genuine enthusiasm for research.

To illustrate my point with a success story, when I moved from one university to another I was not ready to begin research immediately at the new place. I was staying up half the night, surrounded by unpacked boxes both at work and at home, to write lectures for courses I had never taught before. Within a day of getting the key to my new office, though, there came a knock at the door. A new first-year graduate student entered and told me that she wanted to do research with me. I put her off with talk of being swamped and subtly suggested that she try again during the following semester. The next day, she was back talking about an idea that I had suggested under "future directions" in a recent article. I got rid of her as politely as possible. The following day, she was back asking about whether I thought the best way for *us* to do the study might be with a 2×3 or a 2×4 design, and which control groups *we* needed. She would not take no for an answer!

I regaled my new faculty colleagues with stories about this pest who would not go away, and how she kept insisting that she and I start a research project immediately. From that moment I knew, and so did all my colleagues, that we had a winner! She understood right from the start that her self-esteem, not to mention her future academic career, depended not on grades but on research and scholarship. She had made the transition from what I call an "undergraduate mentality," in which grades are all-important, to a more professional perspective based on learning *how* to do what would be required in later academic employment. She went on to earn the PhD, land an academic position, gain tenure, and win awards for her teaching excellence. She is currently chair of a university psychology department.

Successful graduate students do their homework before applying to PhD programs. They use the Internet, professional journals, and other sources to identify the exact line of research in which each faculty member is currently interested. They choose a department in which one of more faculty members are recognized experts in knowing how to conduct a specific type of research. When they arrive, they take the initiative. They beat down the faculty member's door. They insist that he or she teach them how to do it right. They become passionate about participating in and extending the faculty member's ongoing program of research. They understand that faculty members value them as research apprentices who will evolve into research collaborators.

Successful graduate students also understand the time constraints of publishing research. In many disciplines, the typical study takes a full academic year to design, conduct, analyze, interpret the results, and write a report of just one study. Many of the prestigious peer-reviewed journals look for three or more such studies to support a connected narrative in one submitted manuscript. Then the manuscript might have to undergo several revisions. It might easily take three years from conceptualizing the idea for the research project to final approval from an editor. And all that time is spent putting just one line on your vita! You can easily see from this typical time table why graduate students need to begin to build publications from day one and not wait until the third or fourth year of a PhD program to set out on the publication trail. When faculty members turn to writing those all-important letters of recommendation for you, which comes sooner than one would wish, you will find that they evaluate graduate students the same way they evaluate candidates for a faculty position in their department: on their academic vita.

KEEPING SCORE: YOU *ARE* YOUR VITA

Since I have been in my department, we have hired more than half the current faculty. I have been intensely involved in all of these searches, both during the time I was department chair and later. Would it surprise you to know that I have *never* seen the graduate transcript of any of my colleagues? We do not request a transcript of graduate grades because my colleagues and I would regard that information as useless. We are trying to hire the best scholars, not people who got the best grades in their graduate courses.

The information that we need to arrive at a short list of applicants is contained in the letters of recommendation and, primarily, in the academic vita. Wise graduate students, therefore, will start at day one of their first year in a PhD program to develop a strong vita. My advice to new graduate students is to put your vita on your computer immediately. Alter your perspective so that you derive your professional self-respect entirely from what is on that document. From the start of graduate school on, throughout what we hope will be a long and productive career, you *are* your vita.

At first, you might find it depressing to construct an academic vita, because many of the headings will be followed by blank lines. Do not worry about it. Everyone starts that way. One reason for constructing an academic vita is to remind you that it is empty. Write in your appointment book a time once a month when you will print your vita and think about how you could improve it. Being reminded that you have an empty vita, like the prospect of being hanged in the morning, is a wonderful way to concentrate your attention on what matters.

Everything you do in graduate school should have as its ultimate goal developing your academic vita. Let us start at day one of the PhD program and imagine that you have only headings, with no entries in any of the categories. One of the categories on an academic vita is "Professional Memberships." Every discipline has professional organizations to which faculty members belong. Most of these organizations have student memberships that are relatively inexpensive. Some of the student memberships even include free subscriptions to one or two of the organization's publications. Ask which of these organizations your faculty members belong to and respect, find out about student memberships on the Internet or elsewhere, and *join*. Overnight you will have filled in some blank places on your vita and established that you are a serious, professional, motivated person.

Now consider those graduate courses that you are required to take. Some of them may be in areas of your discipline that do not interest you. If you balk at putting time and effort into courses that are not in your own area of specialization, however, you will establish a poor reputation in the eyes of faculty members. Always remember that faculty members talk to each other frequently about graduate students. Most faculty members do not look favorably on students who pick and choose when they are going to work hard, any more than they would want a new faculty colleague who had that trait. Instead of blaming the faculty for making you take courses in an area other than your own, you should welcome the opportunity, because it exposes you to ideas that might be useful in building your academic vita.

Many of the best research ideas in any academic discipline come from thinking about connections between seemingly disparate areas of research. I remember my mentor telling me in the first year of graduate school that he had an advantage over me in coming up with good research ideas. His advantage was that he did not read the current journals in his own area! He was not kidding. If you read only the ideas in the most recent journals in your own area, you might think about ways to refine the ideas in those articles, but they are still someone else's concepts. Ideas derived from a journal article's concepts will most likely have far less impact on the field than nonderivative ideas. It is much more profitable to read the latest ideas in an area (or discipline) different from your own and think about parallels to the central questions that you and your adviser are studying.

We may not know how to teach graduate students to formulate creative hypotheses (although see McGuire, 1997, for helpful hints), but we do know that generating important new questions is more valued in academia than mechanically answering questions that have been generated by others. We also know that nonobvious ideas, which usually make the greatest contribution, frequently arise from thinking in depth about areas of scholarship other than our own. You should view those "required" courses as opportunities to develop nonobvious ideas about your own area of research. If you do, you will be on your way to adding important lines to the section of your vita where you list your publications.

No matter what anyone tells you, no matter the academic position you seek, to be competitive you need to place lines on your academic vita under "Publications." I've participated in many academic job searches. Busy faculty members are typically confronted with several boxes bulging with applicants' folders. In each folder they find the applicant's cover letter, lengthy letters of recommendation, reprints of published work, various other materials the applicant thought would help his or her cause, and an academic vita. Most committee members head straight for the vita. They often turn immediately to the "Publications" section. At this point, many of them do not know (or care) about your name, your gender, or any of the other background information usually included on the front page. They want to see what you have contributed to the published literature in your discipline.

Be warned. Do not attempt to fool faculty committees by including in the "Publications" section articles that are only under review, abstracts of conference publications, your unpublished master's thesis, or anything other than articles that have passed peer review and are either already printed or granted final acceptance and in press. Do include all of these that you can, and send reprints of the strongest contributions.

Except for very unusual academic positions, the typical committee member spends approximately 10 seconds examining the folder of an applicant who has no genuine academic publications before coding that application as an automatic "REJECT!" Knowing the fate of such applications at day one of graduate school should tell you where to place your efforts. Yes, you have to do well at your courses. Yes, you have to take your teaching assistant and other assigned duties seriously if you are going to learn the tools of the trade and get good letters of recommendation. But when you are under crushing time pressures, as you will be, print your vita and spend a few moments contemplating those blank lines under "Publications." Remember that you *are* your vita. If the "Publications" section stays blank, that is just what you will be to most faculty search committees—a blank, a nothing, not worthy of more than 10 seconds consideration.

Even if you discover during graduate school that you find research boring but love teaching, you will eventually need publications. You might be able to find an academic position that emphasizes teaching over all else and will hire you based primarily on your teaching record. If you do, however, you will likely discover six years down the road that most of the small colleges want to see some publications during those six years to support a positive tenure recommendation. They might not provide much in the way of facilities for conducting research, but having a few publication lines on your vita helps and a lack of publication lines hurts your tenure chances. At the very least, you are going to have to produce some published reviews of other people's research, which are almost impossible to accomplish if you have no love for the research topic.

Exhibit 1.1 shows a sample vita. It is only a sample, but it includes the most typical categories. You can probably find better examples of an academic vita on the Internet and elsewhere. Your faculty mentor will be happy to comment on which additional headings you should include. As long as I was going to invent a fictitious vita, though, I felt that I might as well give you a lofty target. During graduate school, try to make your vita look as much as possible like that of Sally O. Superstar. It is unlikely

---

EXHIBIT 1.1
Sample Academic Vita

Sally O. Superstar
Curriculum Vitae

Office Address
Department of XXX
University of YYY
YYY, ZZZ 99999-9999
Phone: (555) 555-5555
e-mail: SOS@YYY.edu

Biographical Data
Birthdate: February 30, 1985
Place of Birth: YYY, ZZZ
Citizenship: USA
Social Sec. #: 333-33-3333

Education
PhD   University of YYY   June 2011 (Expected)
MS   University of YYY   June 2009
BS   University of ABC   June 2007

Honors and Awards
2011   Elected to National Academy of Sciences
2007–2011   National Science Foundation Graduate Fellowship
2003–2007   ABC University Scholarship

Professional Memberships
American XXX Association
American XXX Society
Regional XXX Association

Publications
Superstar, S. O. (in press). The meaning of everything. *Science*.
Superstar, S. O., & Faculty, F. O. (2011). The meaning of the universe. *Science, xxx*, xxx–xxx.
Faculty, F. O., & Superstar, S. O. (2010). The meaning of life. *Science, xxx*, xxx–xxx.

Manuscripts Under Review
Superstar, S. O. The meaning of meaning. *Science*.

continued

EXHIBIT 1.1
Continued

Manuscripts in Preparation
Superstar, S. O. Meta-meaning. *Science.*

Conference Presentations
Superstar, S. O. (2010, Aug.). *A general theory of life's place in the universe.* Invited address presented at the American XXX Association Convention, Sea of Tranquility, the Moon.
Superstar, S. O. (2009, Aug.). *Life.* Invited address presented at the American XXX Society Convention, New York.

Teaching Experience

Lecturer	Seminar on Life	Spring 2011	University of YYY
Lecturer	Mechanisms of Life	Fall 2010	University of YYY
Lecturer	Principles of Life	Spring 2010	University of YYY

Professional References
Dr. Frank O. Faculty, Chair
Department of XXX
University of YYY
YYY, ZZZ 99999-9999
Phone: (555) 777-7777
e-mail: FOF@YYY.edu

Dr. Margaret O. Member
Department of XXX
University of YYY
YYY, ZZZ 99999-9999
Phone: (555) 777-7777
e-mail: MOM@YYY.edu

Dr. Paul O. Prof
Department of XXX
University of YYY
YYY, ZZZ 99999-9999
Phone: (555) 777-7777
e-mail: POP@YYY.edu

that you will be elected to the National Academy of Sciences as a graduate student, but you can at least join a few professional associations.

You can also do what the fictitious Sally has done. Start by publishing once or several times as a junior author with Frank O. Faculty, or whoever your mentor happens to be. Go on to publish as first author with your mentor. Then show that you can extend your mentor's work into brilliant new directions, possibly publishing your PhD dissertation on your own. Include any manuscripts you have under active editorial review and in preparation, just to show that you have new work in the pipeline. List all your conference presentations, but beware compiling the type of vita that has page after page of presentations and only one or two publications in refereed journals. Most departments do not want faculty members who merely present data at conferences and do not bring the work to completion by publishing it for the wider academic audience. List your teaching experience. For some types of academic positions, attach to the vita a teaching portfolio that explains your teaching philosophy, experience, and practices. Finally, list the people who will write letters of recommendation for you, so that interested departments can contact them directly.

Always remember, though, that the most important lines on your vita are found under the "Publications" heading. During my last year of graduate school, my mentor gave me the best advice I have ever heard for aspiring academics, whether in graduate school or later in their careers. I urge you to make a sign with these 10 golden words and tape it to the wall directly behind your desk so that you cannot help but see it every day. Do not settle for good grades in graduate courses. Do not settle for conference presentations. Do not settle for papers that are endlessly in preparation. Instead, *"Get it out the door with your name on it!"*

CONCLUSION

The transition from undergraduate to graduate study involves a transition from student to scholar and researcher. Many of the skills that guarantee success as an undergraduate (e.g., strong test-taking skills and good grades) can be unrelated to success as a graduate student, where the ability to conduct research—both effectively and prolifically—is the strongest measure of success. For some students, this transition is difficult, and successful graduate students are those who are able to discover research areas they truly enjoy and who are able to translate this interest into publications, the holy grail of graduate work. This chapter has sought to point out some of the basic keys to accomplishing this goal, such as researching programs before entering graduate school, starting research immediately on entering graduate school, and pressing faculty for training and guidance. Although the formula is not a guarantee for success, the strategies outlined can increase students' chances of having successful graduate careers and thus improve their prospects of achieving their ultimate aim, faculty positions.

REFERENCES

McGuire, W. J. (1997). Creative hypothesis generating in psychology: Some useful heuristics. *Annual Review of Psychology, 48,* 1–30.

Sternberg, R. J., & Williams, W. M. (1997). Does the Graduate Record Examination predict meaningful success in the graduate training of psychologists? A case study. *American Psychologist, 52,* 630–641.

2

AFTER GRADUATE SCHOOL: A FACULTY POSITION OR A POSTDOCTORAL FELLOWSHIP?

KATHLEEN B. McDERMOTT AND TODD S. BRAVER

As you begin to consider options for your dissertation, it is probably time to start thinking seriously about the next step in your academic career. One big question with regard to this next step is whether you will pursue a postdoctoral fellowship (sometimes referred to as a postdoc) or go straight into a faculty position. This chapter considers some of the factors that may aid you in tackling this decision.

Twenty or so years ago, postdoctoral fellowships were fairly rare in psychology and often taken by those who could not secure tenure-track jobs directly following graduate school (although there were certainly exceptions to this generalization). The situation has now changed, and postdoctoral fellowships are now being increasingly pursued by even the most marketable of graduates.

There are several reasons why postdoctoral fellowships are becoming increasingly common in psychology. First, interdisciplinary work is gaining esteem. Postdoctoral fellowships offer the chance to obtain expertise in a discipline different from (but complementary to) the one in which the graduate work was done. The ideal postdoctoral fellowship will not constitute

The authors are grateful to the following people for providing helpful comments on earlier versions of this chapter: Deanna Barch, John Bulevich, Edith Chen, Jason Chan, Lisa Geraci, Cindy Lustig, Beth Marsh, Greg Miller, Roddy Roediger, Jason Watson, and Jeff Zacks.

three more years of doing the same line of work that was carried out in graduate school but instead involve branching out into new territory. Second, in some subfields of psychology, skills are desired beyond those reasonably acquired during graduate training. A postdoctoral fellowship provides an opportunity to expose oneself to new disciplines and literatures and to add technical or methodological skills to one's repertoire. For example, a graduate student in a cognitive psychology program might decide to spend the first few postgraduate years learning neuroimaging techniques or other neuroscientific approaches to the study of cognition. With the increasing methodological sophistication of psychology as a whole, this pattern may begin to permeate other areas of psychology. Third, the changing nature of the social landscape has brought increasing acceptance of the need to achieve balance in one's career and personal life. Dual-career families are increasingly common, as are shared responsibilities for child rearing. Postdoctoral fellowships are sometimes pursued to accommodate these personal goals.

Certain reasons for pursuing a postdoctoral fellowship will be relevant for certain people and not others, and the decision of whether to pursue a postdoc will be made for different reasons. There is no universal checklist or flowchart to suggest whether a postdoc is right for you; rather, the decision will entail the weighing of a number of factors, some of which may be unique to your individual life situation. We want to suggest that accepting a tenure-track position immediately after graduate school is not always more desirable than a postdoc and that it is worth considering all your options before launching straight into your first faculty position.

In this chapter we lay out some of the pros and cons involved in both faculty positions and postdocs. We focus more on postdoctoral fellowships because faculty positions have traditionally been considered the default "next step" for people coming out of graduate school, and the advantages of these positions are widely known. We consider first some of the advantages of postdoctoral fellowships; we then consider some disadvantages to going this route. We also note that there are often constraints on making the decision; in other words, it is not always a case of determining what is the best professional decision but instead of determining what decision best satisfies the constraints of your personal life.

We then touch on the process of finding a postdoc and end with a brief discussion of the importance of making the most of your postdoctoral fellowship should you choose to go that route.

ATTRACTIONS OF A POSTDOCTORAL FELLOWSHIP

The attractions of a postdoctoral fellowship include an array of interwoven advantages, which converge on two general themes: A postdoc allows the expansion of your scientific background, skills, interests, and research experience, and it enhances the likelihood of obtaining and succeeding in your first faculty position.

Enhanced Marketability

One of the most obvious advantages of a postdoctoral fellowship is that it offers the opportunity to expand and strengthen your vita so that when you enter the job market a few years later, you will be a much more attractive candidate. You will also have another person who is familiar with your work who can write a well-informed reference letter for you.

A postdoctoral fellowship gives you the opportunity to demonstrate your strengths. This may be especially important for people whose research projects take a bit longer than normal to come to fruition or for late bloomers who may need a few extra years to really shine. For those who excelled in graduate school and were able to complete a series of projects, the postdoctoral fellowship offers the chance to show the world that it is you—not just your graduate advisor—who is capable of impressive work. A person who has flourished in graduate school may or may not be ready for a faculty position, depending on the role the advisor played in ensuring success in graduate school. A person who has succeeded while working in multiple labs and in multiple research subfields during his or her graduate and postdoctoral years probably has the skills and experience to also be able to succeed on his or her own.

In short, search committees seek junior candidates who have a high likelihood of making a smooth transition to being a productive faculty member; a postdoctoral fellowship can enhance this likelihood in their eyes. In addition to the factors mentioned, your marketability and—perhaps more important—your ability to handle a faculty position will likely be enhanced at least in part because of the advantages enumerated below that you can gain from a postdoc.

Broadening Your Research Domain

As mentioned at the beginning of the chapter, one of the primary reasons that people pursue postdocs is that they offer the opportunity to broaden one's knowledge base. It is becoming increasingly common for departments to seek prospective faculty who can bridge multiple traditional psychology subfields or who have an interdisciplinary perspective. Through a postdoctoral position it is possible to become such a researcher by combining your graduate training with expertise in new areas. This new expertise can come in multiple forms—learning a different discipline, working with a new approach or technique, or studying a different subject population.

Relevant examples include the cognitive psychology PhD who broadens into cognitive neuroscience by doing a postdoc in an animal neurophysiology lab; the social psychology PhD who gains statistical expertise by doing a postdoc in a lab that uses advanced statistical techniques, such as structural equation modeling; the clinical psychologist who desires greater research focus than was permitted by the clinical service demands of graduate school; and the personality psychology PhD who incorporates a developmental approach by doing a postdoc in a lab that works primarily with children.

The particular area you may choose for your fellowship will depend on your particular research focus and your interests. However, we wish to stress that postdoctoral fellowships are probably the most valuable if the goal is to broaden one's research into an area that is complementary to rather than fully redundant with the research approach studied in graduate school. The more angles from which you can approach your primary research question, the better.

Facilitating the Transition From Dependence to Independence

One of the most important (and perhaps underappreciated) benefits that a postdoc offers is that it is a chance for you to begin to function as an independent researcher without all the demands that tend to accompany one's first faculty position. The transition straight from graduate school to a faculty position can be extremely abrupt. All at once, one loses the continual guidance and deadline structure imposed by most graduate programs and is faced with committee work, teaching, graduate students (in some cases), undergraduate advisees, and the prospect of setting up one's own laboratory and launching a new program of research. Many universities will expect their new faculty to submit grants shortly after arrival. You may be asked to begin reviewing manuscripts for journal editors. In addition, you will need to produce quality manuscripts and to get them published. Furthermore, the expectations for your level of productivity will often exceed the level that you were accustomed to in graduate school. The sudden change can be overwhelming.

A postdoctoral fellowship greatly aids in that transition; as a postdoctoral fellow, you will typically be sheltered from teaching, supervision, and other service-related responsibilities. You will no longer, however, be given the level of guidance you may be accustomed to as a student. There will be no committee checking on your progress, assigning readings to you, or helping you set deadlines and goals. Many advisors take less of a protective, nurturing approach with their postdocs than with their graduate students; the view is often that once a person has an advanced graduate degree, it is up to him or her to succeed or fail. The postdoctoral advisor typically sees his or her role as providing financial support, a working atmosphere conducive to productivity, and some amount of guidance. They are unlikely, however, to coddle you. Therefore, this is a chance for you to begin to function independently, and to do so without the multitude of stressors inherent in faculty positions. You can gain confidence and expertise in your research and writing ability in the relative comfort of a secure (if only temporary) job.

Developing Scientific Skills

Many researchers do not emerge from graduate school completely prepared to be fully independent researchers. We suspect that this is probably the norm.

The *ideal* incoming faculty member will possess many skills and abilities. He or she will be able to write empirical papers, to initiate and lead large research projects, to develop collaborations, to build an integrated and programmatic line of research, to generate ideas regarding the appropriate next step in extending such a research program, to write successful grants, to give effective oral presentations, to motivate and supervise students, to manage the daily affairs of a lab, to effectively select and purchase equipment, to keep account of a research operating budget, to appropriately navigate the internal review board (IRB), and last, but definitely not least, to be an effective teacher (see chapter 5). The probability that you will emerge from graduate school with all (or even most) of these skills may be unlikely. There is no guarantee that a postdoctoral fellowship will teach you these skills; nor is it absolutely necessary to possess all these skills when you take your first job. But to the extent that a postdoctoral fellowship will allow you to become comfortable with performing most of these duties, it will greatly aid in your transition to your first faculty position.

In addition, it is sometimes the case that the graduate school years are not long enough for one to determine whether they are truly suited for a job at a research-oriented institution or whether a more teaching-oriented job is a better fit. The postdoctoral fellowship can allow you to buy time to exclusively focus on research, and thereby better figure out your research niche or reevaluate the type of career you might want. Note that your potential postdoctoral advisor will probably want to advise someone with research career plans, so it is important to at least go into the position with the desire to succeed in finding a niche in research. Moreover, if you are confident that you would prefer a faculty position that primarily values teaching, a postdoctoral fellowship will probably not be an advisable career choice because it is primarily a chance to beef up one's research abilities and experience and to form a research plan for the future.

Training/Experience

Everyone has strengths and weaknesses, and we believe that it is worthwhile to periodically evaluate them. Even within your research area, you probably have weaknesses. If your advisor is particularly rigorous methodologically, you may emerge from graduate school with a weakness in theoretical understanding. Conversely, if your advisor is a broad thinker with a penchant for grand theories, you may not pick up all the nuances of rigorous empiricism during your graduate career. To the extent possible, we suggest trying to find a postdoctoral position in a lab that has strengths in your areas of weakness. You will likely be able to offer your new laboratory a set of skills or a theoretical position that will enhance the existing environment. In turn, you will benefit from your new environment. In many cases, the bigger the leap from your existing area to your new area, the more you will learn from your experience.

Balancing Personal and Professional Goals

Along with the development in professional abilities during the postdoctoral years will come confidence in your ability to handle the challenges of a successful academic career. We believe that postdoctoral fellowships can be immensely helpful in building confidence in the ability to juggle a near-impossible workload while still finding time to enjoy life. Such confidence comes with the perspective that only additional experience can provide. Anything you can do to diminish the anxiety that is often present in beginning your first tenure-track position will benefit you. The step from postdoctoral fellow to faculty member is simply not as great as that from graduate student to faculty. We do not wish to imply that postdoctoral fellowships are primarily for the insecure; instead, we are suggesting that regardless of a person's confidence in his or her ability, he or she will likely develop skills and perspective in a postdoc that will allow him or her to tackle the first job with greater skill and grace than might otherwise have been possible.

We are consistently amazed at the importance of managerial–people skills in the everyday running of a laboratory. In the academic environment you will be surrounded by people with a range of different motivations, backgrounds, and working styles. It is simply not ideal to try to manage everyone in a similar fashion or to adopt a dictatorial approach. Some people prefer direction, interpersonal contact, and advisor-imposed deadlines, whereas others work best when left alone. Some like to work through the night, whereas others want to leave in time to pick up their children from school. The bottom line is that your job as the head of a lab will be to foster creativity and productivity in everyone who works with you. The more experience you have with viewing the inner workings of laboratories, the more equipped you will be to handle these issues in your own lab. Our advice is to watch how particularly effective mentors interact with their students, postdocs, and staff; also, you might watch the junior faculty (or even the senior faculty) and try to learn from their mistakes. They will inevitably make them! (We have certainly made our share.)

Research Utopia

A postdoctoral fellowship offers the benefits of a research career without the burdens. You can take advantage of your advisor's resources to do research that you might not otherwise be able to afford in the beginning of your career. You retain some of the advantages of being a graduate student (guidance and support) without the costs of training-related obligations (classes, theses); in addition, you will obtain some of the advantages of being a faculty member (well, maybe not the parking privileges!) without the costs typically associated with faculty positions (i.e., teaching, committee work, advising). This is your chance to focus solely on research for several uninterrupted years. You can think of it as a several-years sabbatical. If used wisely, a postdoctoral fellowship can be a powerful way to jump-start your research career.

Depending on the job you will eventually take, your postdoctoral years may be the last time for awhile (at least until your own lab group is built) that you have local colleagues who do research similar to your own. Often junior faculty are hired to fill in an area in which a department is lacking. For example, you may be the only developmental psychologist in your department. If so, you will likely miss the intellectual company of being surrounded on an ongoing basis by colleagues who can readily offer insight into your work.

One appealing aspect of postdoctoral fellowships is that, in most cases, not a lot of structure is imposed on you. However, we should note that some postdoctoral environments are highly structured. Typically, you can find out beforehand the general lab atmosphere by talking to graduate students or other postdocs in your prospective laboratory or by talking to your prospective postdoctoral advisor (or your graduate advisor). The funding source will likely play a role in the extent to which there is consistent pressure on you to perform in the postdoctoral position. If you bring your own funding, your time will likely be much more your own than if you are being paid off of a grant to accomplish specific work that your advisor has committed to doing. Your personality and professional goals will help determine whether you desire or shun a structured environment.

The bulk of this chapter has covered the reasons to consider seriously a postdoc, even when a faculty position is an option. As noted, the reason for emphasizing the advantages of postdocs is that this line of thinking has only recently emerged in the field of psychology. As you have probably surmised, we are strong believers in the potential advantages of a postdoctoral fellowship.[1]

Nonetheless, there are certainly reasons that one might take a job immediately on graduation from graduate school. Most of these reasons are probably familiar to you. Nonetheless, we outline a few of these reasons next.

Some people's personalities are such that they value independence greatly. There are no doubt times in everyone's graduate career in which they become tired of working for someone else and eagerly anticipate the day in which they have no one to answer to directly. An additional issue is that people get more credit for their own work if they are independent faculty members than if they are working in someone else's lab. The head of a laboratory is almost always seen as the principal investigator (PI) on research projects. This desire to be one's own boss is probably one of the biggest attractions of academia. The prototypical academic personality might be said to be the independent, strong-willed person. Such people might be ready to be on their own very quickly, and may shun the idea of working under another's direction for any longer than is necessary. This may be especially true for those individuals who were granted a great deal of independence in graduate school and thrived under those conditions. In this case it may be difficult to move on to a structured postdoctoral fellowship in which there is little freedom to develop one's own ideas.

The people most likely to decline the option of a postdoc are those who want a fast-track career. For such individuals, it is likely that a postdoc will seem like a detour in the way of what they really want—a job that can take them quickly to tenure. It is worth considering, however, that a successful postdoctoral career can lead to going up early for tenure; it is not necessarily the case that these years will be lost time in terms of years to tenure. (Of course, the importance that the goal of quick tenure should play in one's career plans can also be debated.)

---

[1] You may be wondering about the career choices made by the authors of this chapter. The two of us chose different approaches. One of us (KM) turned down the option of a tenure-track faculty position and took a postdoctoral position out of graduate school. At the time many colleagues argued that this was a risky choice. (As noted, we think the view on this has changed quite a bit recently.) The other of us (TB) accepted a tenure-track job at a research-oriented university before finishing his PhD, primarily for personal (not professional) reasons. Although he is happy with his decision, he sees enormous value in pursuing a postdoctoral fellowship and would have done so had his personal situation allowed it. In sum, although the authors took different routes, we agree that a postdoctoral fellowship offers a unique opportunity, which may sometimes be overlooked.

There may be family considerations in choosing the next step to your academic career. Having a spouse or children often causes people to want to settle down and to minimize the number of moves made. A faculty position will probably be a longer term position than a postdoctoral fellowship. A faculty position will typically pay more than a postdoctoral fellowship, although to the extent that a postdoc enables you to obtain a higher tier job (or to enhance the number of months of summer salary you can later cover off grants), this short-term financial difference may be compensated for quickly.

Of course, family considerations can also lead one to desire a postdoctoral fellowship; if your spouse has a stable job in the city in which you did your graduate work, you may want to stay put for awhile. We strongly suggest that in this case you pursue work in another laboratory and that you still try to use the fellowship as a chance to learn a new area and not just as a continuation of graduate school.

OTHER CONSTRAINTS INVOLVED IN THE CHOICE

As discussed in chapter 1, toward the end of your graduate career you will need to make an objective evaluation of your accomplishments and abilities. You will need to answer the difficult question: How well would you likely do if you were to enter the tenure-track job market? For this you will want to talk to your mentors and trusted senior faculty, who should be able to give you guidance and an honest opinion regarding how your vita might compare to those of other job candidates. If your department is hiring, it might be good to ask if you could see the vitae of the candidates being interviewed. (Although the complete files on job applicants are considered privileged information, vitae are typically treated as public information.) If it appears that your chances on the job market will be poor, you may want to concentrate your efforts on finding a strong postdoctoral position. It may also be the case that your chances on the job market are very strong and you still decide that a postdoc offers advantages that you want to pursue.

As discussed previously, this decision may interact with some personal decisions. Some people may decide to pursue a job even if the chances look slim because they may feel they need this security because of their family situation. Perhaps they need the stability or greater salary offered by jobs (relative to postdocs). Perhaps they have children who need a more stable environment than offered by a postdoc, which is transient. In dual-career families, many job choices are constrained by geographical or personal considerations (e.g., the spouse's career). What might otherwise be your first choice might have to be adjusted by these personal factors. What is best for your career may be somewhat different than what is best for you when considering the whole spectrum of your life. The result may be a willingness to accept a position that you might not otherwise have chosen.

It is our observation that if you are willing to make concessions, you will likely be able to find either a faculty position or a postdoctoral fellowship. The more attractive your vita, the fewer concessions you will have to make.

FINDING A POSTDOC

Chapter 1 explains the hiring process in the field of psychology. Finding a postdoctoral fellowship involves a similar process but is a much less structured endeavor; we highlight just a few of the differences.

Postdoctoral fellowships can arise from candidate-initiated awards. In this case, a senior graduate student will apply to an agency or a foundation for postdoctoral funding. A prominent approach in the United States is through the National Research Service Award (NRSA) program through the National Institutes of Health. For this application, one needs a willing sponsor (i.e., the application is to work with a specific person to carry out a specific line of research, not just to receive money to go to some unspecified school). Foundations also sponsor postdoctoral fellows and have similar procedures, which can be determined by tracking down an application from the foundation. For minority students, there are special programs (e.g., through the National Science Foundation).

Another approach is to identify a willing sponsor who has an existing grant from which he or she could fund you. This might be an individual investigator with a grant or a training grant or center grant, which is given to a larger body of investigators. This initially might seem like a more attractive option; after all, it is a lot less work in that the burden is on the sponsor and not the potential postdoctoral fellow to secure the money. An important consideration, though, is that in all such cases, these positions would require you to conduct a line of research that has been funded. The good news is that there would likely be plenty of money to perform work that you might not otherwise have the resources to perform until you receive your own grant. The downside is that there would be less room for creativity and independence in that the principal investigator would be hiring you essentially to carry out work they have committed to do. You will want to be sure that you are willing and eager to carry out the work they have planned before committing to such a fellowship.

Our primary piece of advice with respect to the application process is to begin early. Asking a potential mentor to sponsor an application that is due in one month is not the way to impress him or her. Rather, it would be a good idea to begin to explore postdoctoral options about a year before one would be ready to begin. The best-fit postdoctoral positions tend to be those that are lined up early. A number of postdoctoral positions are advertised in the same manner as faculty positions, such as through trade newspapers (the American Psychological Association *Monitor*, the American Psychological Society's *Observer*, and the *Chronicle of Higher Education*), departmental mailings (usually posted in some central location or office) or electronic distribution (bulletin boards, mailing lists, newsletters). However, one critical difference between faculty and postdoctoral positions is that often potential postdoc positions are not advertised widely or at all. In many of these cases, the investigator may have funding available, but is not actively seeking applicants. In such cases, as in those where outside funding is going to be obtained, it is necessary for you to make the first move in determining whether a potential postdoctoral advisor has interest in having you join his or her lab.

Making a first approach to a potential postdoctoral advisor can be daunting. If possible, it is nice to have an introduction (e.g., by an advisor or colleague at a conference). Ask your mentor for suggestions about good fits for a postdoctoral position and see if he or she would be willing to introduce you to these people (and perhaps even be willing to broach the subject beforehand with the potential postdoctoral sponsor).

If this approach is not an option (and often it is not), we suggest crafting a short letter (to be sent either by standard mail or e-mail) to your potential sponsor. It would be a good idea to include your vita, too. Tell them a little about your research interests and ask if they might be willing to discuss with you the possibility of your joining their lab (either through an existing, funded position or by sponsoring a postdoctoral application by you). Do not expect an immediate, positive response. Your sponsor will likely want to see some reprints, a statement of research interests, to talk to your references, and to hear from you about what you would expect out of the arrangement. If possible, your sponsor will probably want to do an informal interview at a conference or at least talk to you on the telephone. In some instances, the sponsor may fly you out for a formal interview and may even ask you to give a talk to the lab group or even to the department. We suggest treating this stage as seriously as you would an application for a faculty position: Prepare your application materials carefully; dress professionally for the interview; and give a well-prepared, organized talk. One of your major hurdles will be to capture the interest of your potential sponsor.

MAKING THE MOST OF YOUR POSTDOC

The advice that a postdoctoral fellowship offers significant benefits assumes, of course, that you make the most of your postdoctoral experience. Simply "having done" a postdoc—even in a very high-profile laboratory or at a prestigious university—will be of little use if you have not seized the opportunity to broaden your research and show evidence of productivity. Having an impressive "pedigree" becomes less critical the more advanced you get in your career; what matters more over time is one's own accomplishments. You will want to enter the job market after your postdoctoral fellowship with concrete accomplishments (ideally in the form of refereed journal articles) and a well-formed plan for the future. In this section, we briefly describe some of our thoughts on how to maximize the success of your postdoctoral fellowship if you choose to pursue one. This topic was recently discussed in length as a special feature in *Science* (1999; see also Feibelman, 1993), and we highly recommend reading these materials for additional advice.

One of the most important potential pitfalls to be aware of is the tendency to lose focus as a result of the lack of structure in postdoctoral positions. There are generally no milestones or specific accomplishments required of a postdoctoral fellow. Nevertheless, you do not want to let up just because no one is keeping close tabs on your progress; you will want to do that for yourself. We believe that the most successful postdocs (and faculty, for that matter) are those who learn quickly to impose some structure in their research lives. This typically means creating internal deadlines for yourself. In general, it is a good idea to know specifically (and realistically) what you want to accomplish in the next day, month, and year. Have a plan. In the best scenario, you may even have a friend or colleague with whom you discuss your plans for the near future; we like to swap a list of goals for the next six (or so) months with another person; you can then help evaluate each other's progress periodically.

In addition, a postdoctoral fellowship is a great time to form a long-range plan for research. Taking a faculty position right out of graduate school may entail a difficult transition as one tries to make the leap from one's dissertation (and small extensions of that dissertation) to novel, independent lines of work. Even if your postdoc involves focused work on a particular grant or project, it offers a chance to think and develop a solid plan for pursuing your own research program on beginning your career as an assistant professor.

In the event that you do not yet have a strong vita, a postdoc can offer you the chance to "catch fire." The chances to perform the following activities will vary from situation to situation. Certainly you will want to spend a great deal of time writing papers and leading projects during your fellowship. If possible, it would also be good to begin to supervise other students (usually undergraduate students). Forging collaborations with people other than your postdoctoral sponsor is a good idea if it is possible, although if you are funded by a grant to your sponsor (and do not have your own money through an NRSA or another mechanism), this may not be an option. Even if formal collaborations are not possible, however, you can always talk to other people in your department, learn about their interests, and generally try to soak up the culture of the department. One useful way to begin such discussions might be to volunteer to give a talk at a departmental seminar series; in addition to giving you speaking experience and the chance to obtain feedback on ideas, it opens the door for interested colleagues to talk to you about your work. Another good idea is to join, or better yet, start up a journal club as a way of beginning discussions with others in the department who share your research interests. Similarly, attending departmental talks will give you the opportunity to learn about work being done around you and might lead to interesting discussions (and possibly collaborations) with colleagues.

You may also want to talk to your advisor about potential opportunities to begin reviewing manuscripts for journals. He or she can suggest ways in which you might do this. Included in these might be your advisor requesting permission from journal editors to pass on manuscripts to you that they do not have time to review or encouraging you to write journal editors to portray your willingness to review for the journal (including a very brief, two- to three-sentence summary of your research interests and areas of expertise). If possible, you might ask your advisor to read your first few reviews before submitting them; they may be able to suggest changes in tone or approach that might enhance the effectiveness of your review.

Similarly, you may want to begin learning about the grant writing process during your postdoctoral years. If your mentor is working on a grant, it may be possible to assist in the process. Simply learning the structure and organization of grants may prove invaluable experience. In some cases (e.g., people who are considering future appointments in medical schools or people doing research requiring great expense), learning to write grants will be one of the most important achievements of the postdoctoral years.

One tendency we have noticed is that postdoctoral fellows can sometimes become a bit isolated from the rest of the department, especially in departments in which there are only a few postdocs. Postdocs are sometimes left out of faculty and graduate student events simply because they do not fall into either category. We think this oversight can be overcome, but it might be something to consider working on if you do decide to take a postdoc. One suggestion is to talk to people, try to make contacts among various groups of people, and get on e-mail lists (of talks, departmental events, etc.), and generally make yourself known (in an appropriate way). In addition, it is worthwhile to network and link up with other postdocs, so that you become more visible as a departmental group. The more people see you at events to which you are invited, the more they will think of you as part of the departmental community and remember to include you. That said, it is also the case that given your limited time in a postdoctoral position, it does not make sense to pour yourself into making countless social contacts at the expense of work, only to find yourself moving again in a couple of years. After all, the primary goal is typically to accomplish as much work as possible within a short period of time and then move on.

CONCLUSION

Choosing the ideal next step after graduate school can be difficult. No single answer applies to everyone. In addition, there is probably no right or wrong answer for most individuals; productive, ambitious, bright people will succeed in the field regardless of where they begin their postgraduate career. We have tried to outline some of the factors that may enter into your decision with a focus on some of the advantages and disadvantages of postdoctoral fellowships. Regardless of how you spend your first few postgraduate years, we encourage you to make the most of whatever situation you enter.

REFERENCES

Feibelman, P. J. (1993). *A Ph.D. is not enough! A guide to survival in science*. Reading, MA: Addison Wesley.

Postdocs working for respect. (1999). *Science, 285*, 1513–1535.

3

THE HIRING PROCESS IN ACADEMIA

JOHN M. DARLEY AND MARK P. ZANNA

As faculty members whose university careers have spanned more years and more colleges than we care to remember, we have frequently been involved in the process of hiring new faculty members. One overwhelming discrepancy about the process strikes us: University and college departments of psychology have a set of procedures and rules by which new faculty members are hired, but these rules are rarely known or understood by the job applicants. As a result, we have seen excellent graduate students present themselves poorly and fail to get good jobs. Your task during the hiring process is to put yourself forward as an autonomous, self-organized, and self-starting individual; we hope this chapter will help you to do so.

We wish to thank numerous individuals who read and commented on previous drafts of the chapter, including Jo-Anne McDowell, Thane Pittman and Shelagh Towson. Special thanks go to Phil Zimbardo, whose graduate seminar on professional issues helped us frame many of the issues covered in this chapter. Earlier versions of this chapter appeared in Zanna and Darley (1979) and Darley and Zanna (1980).

THE BEGINNING: IDENTIFYING AND
APPLYING FOR POSSIBLE JOBS

Since writing the version of this chapter that appeared in the first edition, we have noticed that in the intervening years it has become more common for a postdoctoral position to intervene between the PhD and taking the first job. Postdoctoral positions were originally common in the physical sciences and seem to us to have entered psychology first in the more physiologically oriented fields, then moving into cognition, and are now also common in social and personality psychology.

Where You Are Coming From

Increasingly, graduate students are taking a postdoctoral position before taking their first academic research and teaching position (see chapter 2, this volume). In much of what follows, we will use the generic phrase "student" or "graduate student" to refer to the job seeker. But we will often mark some considerations that are unique to the job seeker who is a postdoctoral fellow. For instance, we suggest a conversation that a job-seeking graduate student needs to have with his or her faculty advisor. Postdoctoral fellows need to have a similar conversation with their advisors, one that may have one more complexity to navigate. Postdoctoral positions often have a variable duration. That is, the position is funded and available for one, two, three, or even more years. The length of time that a person stays in the position needs to be carefully handled. The considerations are these: For the faculty member supervising the position, it is most useful if the postdoctoral fellow remains in the position for more than one year. Getting up to speed to function well in a new setting generally takes more than a year. Putting this another way, the postdoc, to leave in a year, would arrive in the new work setting just about the time it is necessary to apply for academic jobs for the next year! Certainly, the postdoctoral supervisor could not write an informed letter of reference, and no new lines of research would be anywhere near completion. For these reasons, we think that the minimum time to spend in a postdoctoral position is two years.

All of this, of course, should be a subject of conversation between the graduate student and the potential postdoctoral supervisor before their joint decision to work together to offer–take the position. One frequent arrangement involves two-year (three-year) postdocs applying for a few jobs that would be particularly desirable in the fall of their first (or second) year as a postdoctoral fellow, and applying for all relevant jobs in the fall of the second (third) year.

Your Faculty References

If you are a graduate student, in the summer of your last year of graduate school, decide which three or four faculty know you the best. In addition to your research advisor, consider faculty with whom you have done research or taught, or from whom you have taken sufficient course work so that they can give a confident estimate of the range of your skills and talents. If you have read chapter 1 in this volume and followed its advice, you will be in a good position to do this, because you have planfully had significant contact with those faculty members.

Next comes an extremely important step: Discuss with your advisor (and other faculty) the kind of job for which you are looking. What sort of balance of teaching, research, and practice are you seeking? Is your research likely to be basic or applied? Do you seek a college, university, or applied setting? Remind the faculty of those experiences that qualify you for various jobs so that they can comment on these experiences in their letters. Also, find out the faculty's perception of your skills and talents; their verbal and written recommendations will be critical in determining your job possibilities. Out of this discussion will emerge some kind of definition of the appropriate job for you to seek.

If you are a postdoctoral fellow, then you have the more complex task of arranging for reference letters that document both your graduate career and your postdoctoral career. Some mix of letter writers from both institutions is expected by the letter readers, and it would be odd if the mix did not include both your graduate thesis advisor and your postdoctoral supervisor. In addition, it is useful if your thesis advisor can comment with some knowledge about your progress since leaving your graduate institution. Therefore, do keep your thesis advisor posted about your postdoctoral progress. While we are on the topic, we ought to mention that occasionally, given the pressing demands of the postdoctoral experience, the postdoc may not have been able to write up one or more research reports that are "owed" to the graduate advisor. Asking the graduate advisor for a reference, after a silence of some years, will not be a pleasant task, and the letter that the graduate advisor now drafts may refer to this failure. Do not put yourself in this position.

Finding Possible Jobs

It used to be that you would earnestly scan the *APA Monitor*, the *APS Observer*, the *Chronicle of Higher Education*, and the newsletters and publications of various American Psychological Association (APA) and Canadian Psychological Association (CPA) divisions and interest groups. This is still a good idea, but almost always now, the job listings are posted on e-mail listservs that faculty and graduate students can receive. Ask your faculty to indicate the listservs on which your sorts of jobs will appear, and arrange for faculty to forward these to you or sign up for them yourself. These lists generally have the postings well in advance of their formal appearance in the publications noted.

Current job seekers perceive the job market as tight. As a consequence, you are not likely to find or get the Platonic perfect job that you have fantasized about in your more optimistic moments. This fact will affect your job search in various ways. First, although this chapter is mainly about getting an academic job in psychology, because that is what we know about, you should definitely explore nonacademic job possibilities. If you are clinically trained in a science–practitioner program, look carefully at the Bootzin chapter in this volume. Industry, the federal and state–provincial governments, and school systems all use psychologists. Talk to faculty members about these other job possibilities (and see chapter 4, this volume), but remember that they may not have as complete a network of contacts outside the academic community as they have within it. If any recent graduates from your PhD program have taken industrial or government jobs, learn what you can from them. (In fact, invite at least one PhD from your program who has taken a nonacademic job to the appropriate visiting speakers' series for your department. If there is a business or medical school at your institution, talk to any psychologists working there and find out what they do and how they got their jobs. Increasingly, psychology PhDs are finding their way into business and management schools.

Another job possibility is the postdoctoral position. It gives you a chance to do research relatively free from the teaching pressures of a normal beginning faculty member (although getting some teaching experience while on a post-doctoral fellowship is advisable) and for that research, perhaps, even to be published. Primarily for this reason, postdoctoral fellowships are an increasingly desirable alternative in all fields of psychology. Sources of support for postdoctoral work in Canada are available from the Social Sciences and Humanities Research Council and the Natural Sciences and Engineering Research Council and in the United States from the National Institutes of Health and the National Science Foundation. We have shared our thoughts on the length of the postdoctoral position already. For more detailed information concerning the postdoctoral option, see chapter 2, this volume.

HOW WIDELY AND HOW DEEPLY SHOULD YOU APPLY FOR POSITIONS

Our advice would be that when exploring any or all of these alternatives, do not let geographic or lifestyle preferences rule out otherwise excellent jobs. Some about-to-be PhDs decide they have always wanted to live in a warm and benign climate and wish to limit their job search to California or British Columbia. Others feel that it would be impossible to live outside large urban environments. Still others feel they could not survive within those confines. It is perfectly reasonable to hope that you will get a good job in one of your favorite places, but it is totally unreasonable to refuse to look at jobs that do not match these preferences. Your lifestyle is important to you, but so is your career. Let us be explicit. Both authors of this chapter grew up in Minneapolis, a wonderful city that is often cold and always midwestern. When graduate students announce that they will only consider job prospects in some idiosyncratically desirable climate or setting, we have a silent but powerful reaction—they are not completely serious about their commitment to psychology, and we probably adjust our reference letters accordingly.

Of course, there are some real and valid reasons for geographic limitations on one's search. One very real limit to job-search flexibility is imposed by the career commitments of one's partner. Many married couples deal with this problem, at least for a year or so, by living geographically separated, but we also know a lot of divorces that have resulted from this sort of situation. If this is an issue for you, articles in the *American Psychologist* (e.g., Bryson, Bryson, Licht, & Licht, 1976; Madell & Madell, 1979; Matthews & Matthews, 1978) have presented several points of view on the problems of professional pairs that might be of interest (see chapter 17, this volume).

If your search is geographically restricted, consider writing a blanket letter to all the institutions that are geographically possible for you, even if they have not advertised a vacancy. They may discover one when the fall teaching term begins. Also, put a system in place to track the e-mails that departments circulate as the fall semester approaches and they discover that circumstances require adding faculty to cover teaching needs.

Another potential job-search restriction is imposed by the American–Canadian border. On the basis of his experience, Iacono (1981) has argued that it is easier for Americans to obtain jobs at Canadian universities than vice versa, because American universities will only bother with immigration procedure hassles for outstanding foreign candidates. Although following the passage of North American Free Trade Agreement, the border is less of a problem (in both directions), but we still have the feeling that the situation varies considerably depending on both the candidate and the institution. On balance, we would suggest that you apply for every job in which you are interested regardless of which side of the border it is on.

One final note: In this day of word processing and mail merging, it is easy to set up a system that seems efficient and that maximally distributes your letters. (And, as this implies, you can bring joy to the lives of both the departmental secretaries and your advisor if you do, in fact, supply addresses and search committee titles in a form suitable for mail merging.) But pause for a minute. First, do not apply for a job that, when you stop to consider it, you know you would not accept. It is insulting to the institution that offers you the job, creates ill will for your advisor (and, possibly, future students in your program), and blocks offering the job to candidates who really want it. Second, it is useful for you to have marked for your advisor those jobs for which you are a perfect (or, at least, a close) fit, given the institution's actual description of the position. It will sometimes be the case that your advisor will add specific comments designed to demonstrate that fit to the general letter he or she writes for you. But if you have appeared with a list of 50 institutions to which you wish to apply (and we have seen students do this), it is going to be difficult for your advisor to add these specific comments. Here is a possible compromise. Target a few institutions that excite you and that have job descriptions that you fit. Draft your cover letter to those institutions in a way that makes it clear that your interests do, indeed, fit their job descriptions. Give you advisor the paragraphs that contain your ideas about your fit to these institutions. With this assistance, your advisor may be able to individuate the reference letter to those institutions.

What to do about other institutions that are attractive to you but have job descriptions that do not exactly fit what you do? Yes, it is possible that once they see what it is you do, and your productivity and documented teaching skills, they might be sufficiently dazzled to ask you to come for an interview. But let us face it: That is not likely. So your advisor's general letter and your individual letter is about all that is possible to expect these institutions will hear about you.

THE VITA

Your vita is an important document. With your reference letters, it determines the jobs for which you will be considered. There is no single, set format for the vita; start by listing everything you have done and then review your vita to make sure that it displays all your relevant skills (e.g., if you have been a teaching assistant, remember to include a summary of your teacher evaluations), interests, and talents. If some of these skills are not obviously documented, include paragraphs describing them. Also include paragraphs indicating your work "in progress," especially your thesis proposal, and your future research directions. Read chapter 1 in this volume and look at the vitas prepared by graduate students senior to you. This is important: Treat your vita as you would any other manuscript. Present your first draft to several faculty members, including your advisor, for comments and then revise.

You might also include a list of courses you could teach. Be neither parochial nor grandiose; do not suggest five courses that on examination prove to be variants on your thesis, but, on the other hand, do not claim to be able to teach every conceivable course in the university catalogue. Psychology departments are frequently looking for faculty to teach introductory psychology and various statistics courses. If you are capable of teaching such courses, and are interested in doing so, say so on your vita. However, this claim is to be regarded as a commitment. Do not make it lightly.

Your papers and publications will be a major element of your vita, and a frequent question is whether to send them. We think you should. Reprints are not bulky and are useful to committees making decisions about whom to invite. Also send preprints of papers in press. Do not send papers in preparation or under editorial review unless you are convinced that the write up adequately presents the research. First drafts rarely do so.

GETTING THE COMPLETE RECORD TO
THE HIRING INSTITUTION

When hiring institutions are ready to make their decisions, they will choose from among those candidates with complete files. Make sure that you are one of them. Job advertisements often include application deadlines implying that you have several months to complete your file. Do not wait! Do not allow yourself to be seduced by fantasies about how much more impressive your vita will be tomorrow when you write up that old data, or when your three convention presentations are accepted, or when that journal editor finally gets around to accepting your manuscript. Some institutions will begin narrowing the field and issuing invitations long before the advertised deadline, so get your materials in early. (You can always send an "addendum" to your vita at a later point in time.)

A complete job application typically consists of your vita, whatever (p)reprints you think are appropriate, a letter from your advisor and two other faculty members, and a cover letter from you. More and more frequently, we now see a one- or two-page statement of research directions sketching the applicant's thoughts about a five-year research program and often a page about teaching philosophy.

Give your letter writers the necessary addresses and tactfully check back with them after a decent interval to see that they have actually mailed the letters. Faculty members recognize that these letters are critical to your career, but they are busy people and this kind of letter is difficult to write. Therefore, they need a good deal of lead time, especially for the first letter requested.

The Hiring System (Such As It Is)

Having sent off all your materials, you must now endure the discomfort of waiting for a reply. The wait may be a long one and the response, when it comes, may not be what you were expecting, so be prepared! The academic hiring system is not a model of efficiency. The people making the hiring decisions are faculty members who have backed into taking that responsibility. They are overloaded, they are not professionals at hiring, and they tend not to be completely organized. They are also probably somewhat embarrassed at having such great decision-making power over other people's lives. As a result, the communications you do receive may be somewhat unclear or even, if coming from several sources, apparently contradictory.

Obviously, the high ambiguity of the hiring situation will make you anxious or depressed. If you are not invited for an interview, you will feel anger at those who did not invite you and be suspicious that your faculty reference writers may not be pushing you hard enough. Simultaneously, you will feel despair about your own skills, abilities, and self-worth. Expect all this; it is easier if you are prepared for it.

BEFORE YOUR VISIT

Let us assume that the happy event has occurred and you have been invited for a job visit. Congratulations! You have already achieved a great deal. Universities receive hundreds of applications for every position they advertise, and typically do not invite more than three or four people for an interview. Jobs are scarce and to be considered for one is no mean feat. Let us now tell you some things that will increase your chances of getting the job.

1. Set up your travel plans in advance. Before you respond to the invitation, check your schedule and travel arrangements. When could you visit? How can you get there? The university or college website will often present this information. Do not fail to look it up. The only items of travel information you should expect your contact person to provide are local transportation details and accommodation arrangements. This is your first chance to present yourself as an organized and effective individual. Do not miss it.

2. Research the institution before you visit it. Read the catalogues on file at your university for background information. Check the institution's website. Is it rural or urban? What is its history? What are its strengths and sources of pride? Seek out the faculty members in your psychology department who know something about the institution and learn about it from them.

3. Research the department you will be visiting. When invited to give a talk, you might ask your contact person to send you the brochure(s) the department has prepared for prospective graduate students or simply get the faculty list from the department's website. (However, do not assume that all departments have actively updated websites.) For the people in your own immediate field, review what they have published. Look for some of their work by author searches in the *PsychInfo*. Read several abstracts and some articles. Faculty websites will often give you a sense of the person's general interests and current research directions, and may allow the downloading of in-press articles. Here is the point: If there are some individuals whose work is close to your own, know it well. And you should also have a sense of what faculty in areas adjacent to your own have done, particularly if they are distinguished scholars. An eminent colleague of ours, one with quite a good sense of humor, found nothing humorous about a job candidate who asked, "What exactly is your area of research?"

4. Find out before (or during the visit) as much as you can about the search process. Although we know of only two case studies of this process (Quereshi, 1980, 1983), you should be able to find informants who can answer questions about the search procedure of the institution you are visiting. Are several candidates usually interviewed or only a few? Do all faculty members get to vote on job candidates or are hiring decisions made solely by the search committee or the chair of the department? Regarding the job for which you are applying, is the department looking for an excellent general candidate or are skills specific to a particular area more important?

5. Find out about the talk. Most hiring institutions expect a candidate to give a talk, but *not* all hiring institutions convey these expectations clearly; some use quaint code words such as "say a few words to a few of us about your research." When you respond to the invitation, find out *exactly* what sort of talk is expected. At this time, you could also mention the kind of equipment you will need for your talk as well as your talk's title.

THE TALK THAT (POSSIBLY) GETS OR LOSES THE JOB

For better or worse, your talk may be the single most important determinant of whether you get the job offer. The way in which you present your material is thought to tell a great deal about your research and teaching abilities, your ability to think on your feet, and your overall personal style. For many of the faculty, your talk is the only contact they will have with you, and so their impressions will be formed considerably by it. When preparing and practicing the talk, think of it as a performance, and remember that a performance works best when it has been carefully scripted and when the performer has total control of the material.

It is of course true that a job talk, like many brief samples of behavior, is not highly predictive of job performance, a finding from organizational psychology with which many social scientists are familiar. Knowing this, even if you do not give a great talk, those who think you would be a good person to hire will seek to make the case that you should be hired. But why give them that burden and require them to expend the social capital that arguing your case will require?

What to Talk About

Rather to our surprise, our comments on job talks in the first edition of this book created some controversy. This was so because we assumed that "the talk" was always going to be a talk on the candidate's research. Of course, and increasingly so, this is not always the case. Sometimes, often at an institution with a primary emphasis on teaching, the talk might be a simulation of a lecture that might be given in an introductory course. One of the most brilliant lectures we ever heard was given by Roger Brown on the question of what it would mean to say that primates comprehended speech. He reviewed research, but not his own research. However, he was a distinguished scientist with an international reputation when he did so. The target for this book is the beginning scientist, and we continue to think that the prototypical job talk that is expected is a presentation of the candidate's research. But it is well to get very clear—in advance—what sort of talk the institution that has invited you expects.

Assume that you are expected to give a talk about your research. Such a talk makes better narrative sense if it is on completed research; a feeling of anticlimax is inevitable if hypotheses are proposed, a method is described, but no data are presented. On the other hand, if you propose to follow your thesis up in future research, then you should talk about it, even if you do not have data. Because your thesis presumably reflects more of your own thinking than other research you may have done with your advisor, the presentation of your thesis may help to establish the independence of your work from that of your advisor. Ideally, you have at least some data and can tell a story in progress, bringing people along with you through the chapters. This approach can make for an extraordinarily exciting colloquium.

Who Will Be in the Audience?

You better begin by finding the answer to this question and think through what the composition of the audience implies about the composition of your talk. The key audience is likely to be faculty members and perhaps advanced graduate students. If the institution does not have a graduate program, undergraduate students will be an important segment of the audience. Psychologists from every area are often involved in the decision-making progress and are likely to attend your talk. The mixed nature of your audience means that although you can assume that everybody is familiar with general psychological language, you should explain more specialized terms. You also need to explain the context of your research in enough detail so that audience members outside your own research field can understand it. An all-too-frequent after-colloquium comment is, "It was technically OK, but *why* did he (or she) want to do it in the first place?"

Length and Structure of the Talk

Your talk should be approximately 45 minutes long, fitting into a normal class hour and somewhat shorter than a regular colloquium. Present your ideas in a less complex way than you would in a written paper; remember, oral comprehension is significantly poorer than reading comprehension.

Begin with an introduction that puts the work in a context understandable to psychologists in general and by implication makes clear the importance of the research. Refer to the historical background of your work and describe recent developments in the area, but do so succinctly. (Be sure to cite the individual who began the general research area and any researcher in that area who is likely to be in the audience!) After 10 minutes you should have finished the introduction and be talking about your own work.

After 10 minutes you should have finished the introduction and be talking about your own work. We have seen this advice quoted with some scorn, so we had better clarify it. The advice is not that in any kind of talk you are giving, you should be talking about yourself within 10 minutes! Instead the advice is that, if you are giving the standard research talk that needs to be completed within 45 minutes, about 10 or 15 minutes is all the time you can allocate to positioning your research into a scholarly context, although this is a topic that you can revisit at the conclusion of your talk. In any event, in our experience those job talks in which the candidate leaves only 15 to 20 minutes to talk about his or her own research have tended to be disasters!

Unless your most important research innovation is procedural, present just enough procedural detail in your method section so that the audience is clear about what happened to your participants. Mingle results and discussion sections; present a relatively small block of data, comment on its meaning, and then move on to the next block. For instance, you might first present the results that make clear that your manipulations worked and come to that conclusion; then go on to the results that speak to your hypotheses.

Near the end of your talk make very clear that you know the limits to what you have shown. All research has limits. People will be more impressed if you show a mature awareness that such limitations exist. At the very end of your talk make a brief but explicit statement regarding future research directions and then conclude with a summary (or take home message) of what you have shown.

Mechanizing Your Talk

We may well call the 21st century the Century of PowerPoint. But we may not. We have heard about organizations that have now banned PowerPoint presentations because they are confining and brain deadening. Probably the best advice is to have some PowerPoint-like material, but to use it imaginatively. For instance, you could present pictures of apparatus, stimulus materials, and typical participants in action. When presenting the research, you can lay out your design on a first slide, fill in control group results on a second slide, and then move to a third slide that adds the data from the experimental groups bearing on your hypothesis. With this approach, you can build your own suspense.

It surprises us to have to say this, but make sure that whatever you present will be readable from the back of a good-sized room. (This is an advantage of PowerPoint; its standard font sizes are readable from a distance.)

Alternatives to computer-driven presentations are using overhead transparencies as you talk or handouts of the data that are passed out beforehand. We advise against handouts because people are likely to read a handout at inappropriate times. (We once saw a faculty member, who figured out the results while the speaker was still thrashing around in the introduction, cut in with a question about the interpretation of the results.) With overhead transparencies, you can control the rate at which it is presented, but it may be difficult for people to read and may give a slightly amateurish tone to your presentation.

We will say more about this later, but as you prepare your talk, remember that it may need to be given under rather different conditions than prevail at your home institution. Think ahead with defensive pessimism. What if, because of some mysterious computer glitch, your PowerPoint slides will not project on the host institution's system? (This happened to one of us while giving a rather major talk. Luckily, the speaker had thought to bring his own projector as well as his own computer, and the situation was salvaged. This is what we mean by defensive pessimism and its utility.) Most experienced speakers we know who use PowerPoint also take along overhead transparencies just in case, and we have often seen them use these transparencies while other speakers, who placed their unconditional trust in the more sophisticated projection technologies, were seriously disrupted.

Of course, these and similar disasters have happened to many of us. So we should not be judgmental when they happen to a job candidate, right? Not quite. Although the audience may try to be nonjudgmental, the candidate has lost a chance to make a good impression, and this certainly will harm the candidate's case—even for psychologists, who ought to know about the fundamental attribution error!

While we are at it, here is a multiple-choice test. Which is better, option a or option b? (a) giving a good job talk in day-old clothes or (b) giving a slideless, halting job talk in fresh clothes? The answer is a, which means that everything necessary for your talk goes with you on the plane and not in the luggage compartment to be sent ahead to some exotic location that is not the destination of your interview. (We have seen the "lost-luggage colloquium," and it is a painful sight.) One change of clothes, toiletries, and the talk manuscript will all fit into a carry-on bag!

We are being more than a little obsessive about this, and we know it (because all of our friends tell us so). What we are trying to do is model a state of mind that will get you to the job interview in a prepared state, with all that you need with you. We hope that if you achieve this state of mind, you can relax—a bit.

Practicing the Talk

Practice your talk not once but several times. You might even videotape one version, but probably not your first attempt, because that may depress you. Try it out on fellow graduate students, and then on faculty members, particularly those in other areas. Note what questions people ask, and begin to build some of the answers into the talk. You may not deal explicitly with all the questions that arise, but having heard them during a rehearsal, you will be ready to answer them at the actual performance. From rehearsals, you may get a version of your talk that goes well but that is 14 minutes too long. This is not solved by talking faster when you get to the real talk! Instead, decide which sections can be cut or omitted.

To Read or Not to Read the Talk

Knowing that they will be anxious initially and that it is important to set the context of the talk correctly, many speakers have the first few paragraphs of their talk written out in full. They also may have the last few paragraphs of the talk written so that they can state their conclusions precisely. In between, they rely on an outline or a series of slides–overheads to cue them. Other speakers are able to give a successful talk from a series of notes written on one sheet of paper or even with no notes at all. Past experience suggests to us that job candidates are not among those speakers.

WHAT YOU WANT TO KNOW ABOUT THE PLACE WHERE YOU MIGHT LIVE AND WORK

Certainly, the department that is considering hiring you wants to know a good many things about you. However, it is wise not to forget that you want to know a good many things about them also. But what it is all too easy to forget is that, under the assumption that you will spend at least a few hours every once in a while doing what is called "having a life," there is a good deal you want to know about the town that surrounds the academic institution and the sorts of lives that people in that town enjoy. Let us examine each of these questions in turn.

Information About the Department

Although you need the answers to quite a few questions, do not ask every question explicitly. During your visit, answers will frequently come unobtrusively, and much of the necessary information will be volunteered. At some point, get off in a corner by yourself and look over your list of questions to see what answers you have. Determine what else you need to know and then tactfully ask about it.

1. What is the teaching load? How is it distributed between graduate and undergraduate courses? Are you needed for specific courses? Can you teach a new course? What are the typical class sizes? Is there a reduced teaching load for first-year faculty members? At American universities, can one obtain a "summer salary" by teaching in the summer term?
2. What sorts of supports for teaching are available? Is there a well-stocked library with an organized reserve system? Is there a budget for photocopying? For films? Are there graduate student teaching assistants? What norms govern teaching at the institution?
3. What are the department's expectations for faculty research? Does the department expect you to obtain a research grant and, if so, when? Some departments are structured so that

departmental members rarely publish. Others expect a continuing stream of research output. What are the department's norms for research productivity?

4. What space is available for your research? Would the space be yours alone or shared with other faculty? What are the sharing rules? Is space relatively plentiful or in short supply?

5. What sorts of support and equipment are available for your research? What about shop and computer facilities—what are they like and how are they billed? Does the institution allot starter money to beginning faculty members for their research? Is money available for space modifications? Are travel funds available and, if so, what are the requirements for obtaining these funds? Is there a secretarial pool? Is it free or is it billed? What is its quality? (This is one area in which you can get faculty to talk freely and endlessly.)

6. How are research participants obtained? Is there a research participant pool associated with the Introductory Psychology courses? Has contact been made with various school settings? How are infrahuman animals obtained? What are the animal care facilities? Are animal caretakers available or do you need to build up this sort of staff? Who pays?

7. What are the odds on getting tenure? What criteria do the department use for tenure and promotion? How are these decisions made? When? Historically, what has been the promotion rate? Is the job, in fact, a tenure-track position? If not, what is the probability that it could become one? (Find out whether budget or enrollment projections exist for the institution as a whole and the psychology department in particular and check them out. Such figures may provide some indication of the tenure situation.) How does the situation "feel" to junior faculty? Are they anxious and concerned about tenure and promotion? Is the possibility of collaboration reduced because they regard themselves as being in competition with one another? Is there a sharp division between the junior and senior faculty?

8. What is the consulting policy within the university? What is the pattern of consulting within the department?

9. What is the quality of the undergraduate students? (Of course, this question is especially important at a solely undergraduate institution.) In at least the advanced undergraduate courses, are students bright and well-motivated? What is the reputation of psychology as a major? What sort of expectations do

the undergraduates have for contact with faculty members? Is there such a thing as an honors thesis? Who does it? Have any theses been published lately?

10. If the hiring institution has a graduate program, much of your research life will be spent with graduate students. Are they intelligent and motivated to do research? Do they help and support each other? Is there an active graduate student culture? What are their career aspirations? What sorts of placements have they received in the past few years? In what ways do they get involved in research? How are they supported? Do they have to spend unproductive time earning money to continue their graduate training? Are they full-time or part-time students? At some institutions, new faculty cannot immediately supervise PhD theses. If this is the case, ask junior faculty if it is difficult to supervise graduate students at any level.

Information About the University

Because much of this information is standard, universities frequently have booklets that include it, particularly the less controversial elements.

1. What is the beginning salary? What has been the pattern of increases over the past few years? How were the increases determined?

2. What is the standard initial contract period? What is the standard renewal contract period?

3. Does the university provide moving expenses?

4. What is the sabbatical leave policy? What is the maternity–paternity leave policy?

5. What are the university's retirement policies and what other benefits does it offer its faculty? Some universities have group health or life insurance plans, faculty medical and dental clinics, day care centers, and the like.

6. Every university has dimensions along which departmental contributions to the university are assessed. Determine the reward contingencies at this university. Is the department "paid off" for high national visibility of its faculty? Is teaching efficiency important to the university administration? If so, how is teaching efficiency measured?

In learning about a new department and university, keep an open mind. We have often encountered candidates whom we would label "almamater"-

centric. That is, they tend to assume that our university operates just like theirs and, worse, they are offended to discover that this is not always true, even when the differences involve rather trivial bureaucratic details. Our simple advice is do not assume every university is exactly alike!

Information About the Community

Although as a junior faculty member, you will undoubtedly be spending most of your time at the university, you will need somewhere to live. Find out the living circumstances of the other junior faculty. Does the university offer any assistance in finding or financing housing? Stop in at a local real estate agent and get some feel for area rents and costs. Pick up a local newspaper and check on houses for sale and apartments for rent.

Find out what employment opportunities exist for your spouse. The department you are visiting may not be set up to answer these questions, but someone should be able to refer you to appropriate resource people. You should also check the general availability of day care centers and the quality of the schools your children would be attending.

Finally, find out as much as you can about the physical, cultural, and recreational climate of the community. Will you have to buy an entirely new wardrobe or develop a taste for country music? What are the shopping facilities and restaurants like? These issues may not be critical in determining whether you take the job, but they are important.

THINGS PEOPLE WILL WANT TO KNOW ABOUT YOU

We have already discussed what people seek to learn from your job talk, but there are other things that various people want to know about your professional self-definition, and we will consider a few of these topics next.

Your "Classification"

Faculty members, particularly those outside your own research area, will attempt to determine the general context of your psychological thinking. Within what research tradition are you working? Have you been affected by recent developments in psycholinguistics? Within social psychology, are you a cognitive social psychologist? You can describe yourself in a detailed way with faculty members in your own research area. But when questioned by other faculty members, you should be prepared to place yourself reasonably accurately within psychology in one or two well-chosen sentences.

The Five-Minute Drill

It is useful to be able to give one other sort of presentation. We have labeled it the five-minute drill. Perhaps one faculty member missed your job talk; perhaps for another you want to describe a line (or future line) of research you did not cover in your colloquium. We suggest that you be prepared to relate the theoretical context of your research, the specific hypotheses you are testing, the general procedures you are using to test them, and the outlines of the results you are getting (or would hope to get)—all in five minutes! Your major task is to convey the importance and excitement of this research succinctly so that you can, then, discuss your work with the person rather than lecture him or her during your time together.

To convey what you are up to without going into excessive detail is a surprisingly difficult task, and, at first, requires considerable thought and discipline. We suggest that you explicitly think through what you would say and practice it. When practicing, keep in mind that you may be relating your research to a colleague in another area who may need to know a bit more about some aspect (e.g., methods) of the research. Our advice is think through, in advance, modifications of your presentation as a function of a variety of possible audiences.

Although we believe the ability to present your research in capsule form will be useful on job interviews, we also want to point out that this form of presentation is, in fact, the way experienced psychologists communicate with one another about their research at conventions, conferences, or on colloquium visits. To be able to do this well indicates not only that you can communicate effectively about your research but also that you fit the prototype of the experienced psychologist.

Teaching

Think about what you want to teach. For those courses you want to teach and for those you will be expected to teach, have some ideas about what texts you will use and the general nature of the topics you would cover. Evidence that you have investigated the department's teaching needs and patterns shows your organization and your interest in the institution and suggests that you will be a good teacher.

Hidden Agendas

Inevitably, there will be some reservations concerning the merits of your candidacy. Typically, these reservations originate from two sources. First, concerns arise from a department's multiple needs, or from faculty members' various perceptions of the needs of the department. For example, the undergraduate advisor may have been counting on you to teach introductory psychology. Someone else may have been planning on getting someone to help out with the undergraduate or graduate courses in statistics. Still others may have hoped that you would be able to teach and to do research that enriched their own graduate training program, and so on.

Second, many faculty members' most vivid impression of you will come from the job talk, and, of course, it is impossible to deal with everything that is on each individual's mind in that context. For instance, if you did not talk in detail about your statistical procedures, someone may be concerned about your sophistication in this area. If you did cover your statistics in great depth, someone else may wonder about your ability to teach the more theatrical, introductory lecture courses.

Given these possibilities, it makes sense to ask your host about possible reservations about your candidacy so that you can deal with them during your visit. Because this is a delicate matter, we suggest you frame your inquiry by asking your host to identify possible concerns that have been raised with respect to your candidacy as a result of the multiple needs of the department. Raising this question, of course, requires tact. Your task is to make clear that it is perfectly reasonable that there will be those concerns, and they are not to be taken personally. And as you will see in the section that follows about "Your Host and Your Schedule," there may be a person who will be willing to respond to a carefully worded question of this sort.

THE VISIT AND AFTER

Although departmental tribal customs for the visit vary widely, some similarities exist. Usually the visit will last at least one full day, perhaps a day and a half or two days. Try to arrive the night before your visit, get a map, and orient yourself to the campus and the town. This simple act of independence impresses faculty out of all proportion to its difficulty.

Your Host and Your Schedule

One faculty member, usually in a research area similar to your own, probably will be responsible for coordinating your visit. Your host will have your schedule, but do not be surprised if it is not yet complete. If free time has been left on the schedule so that you can have some input, take the initiative and ask to see people or facilities of particular interest to you.

This person may have a second and more important function to fulfill. This is to communicate to you how the department works from his or her own perspective. Particularly if this person is a junior faculty member, or if you can find a person who is, then you have what anthropologists call an "informant." This person is often licensed to give you a reasonably candid picture of the way things really work. A department is wise to get this information to the candidate. It is not so much that the more senior faculty want to keep this information from you, but that it is just that they have trouble recreating the perspective of a younger faculty member.

Individual Meetings

There probably will be four or five individual meetings scheduled with those faculty members who have identified themselves as being nearest your interest areas, hopefully those you researched before your visit. Double-check on them; find out what they are likely to be talking to you about and whether they have any stylistic idiosyncrasies. Do any of them believe in high-stress interviewing, for instance? You know a great deal about most of the faculty members; do not be embarrassed to ask about any new names. In the actual visits you can expect to talk about faculty members' research and some aspects of your own research.

The Chair (And Perhaps the Dean)

At this meeting, you will probably be told about the more straightforward aspects of the job—starting salary, formal fringe benefits, and so on. Here, you might also ask about the time frame of the hiring decision—that is, how soon they will be able to make up their minds.

Talk Preparation

As soon after you arrive as possible, ask to see the room in which you are to give your talk. Do not be shocked. Frequently the room is a "temporary" one, without permanent projection equipment (but with a promise that portable equipment will arrive in time for your talk). There may not be a projection screen or shades for all the windows. There may not be a podium or pointer. Do not panic, but do test the actual equipment you will use in the actual room in which you will use it. Remember that if your talk is somehow botched by the apparatus, people will "understand." However, they will not have heard you give your best talk, and you are unlikely to have a second chance to do so.

Before your talk, arrange to be off by yourself for perhaps half an hour so you can think yourself into what you want to say. Some departments have a tradition of a coffee hour before the talk; in that case, do your preparation just before the coffee hour.

Find out about certain micro details and local customs. Will somebody introduce you? At the end of the talk, does someone call for questions or close the talk at a particular time or are you expected to do so? Do people interrupt the talk with questions, or do they hold them until the end? If you have a relatively organized presentation, you could suggest that people hold questions until the end, unless they are unclear about some detail that would decrease their comprehension of the rest of the talk. Find out, perhaps from your host, the kind of comments to expect. Does this department have a tradition of general politeness, or do they believe in "grilling" the speaker? Be prepared to be grilled, and do not take it personally. Different traditions prevail at different institutions. Do not be surprised by them.

As an aside to our colleagues: We have found, through trial and error, that the entire job interview goes somewhat more smoothly when candidates give their talks in the morning rather than in the usual afternoon colloquium time slot. Not only are the individual meetings facilitated by having something concrete to talk about, but the candidates themselves are less fatigued. This is especially true when candidates have flown west through several time zones the night before.

"Social" Events

There may be a social hour after your talk or dinner with faculty members or a party after dinner. Do not be confused by the "social" nature of these events; you are still being evaluated. The faculty members are trying to discover what kind of human being you are on a wide variety of dimensions. But they are also giving you the chance to determine whether you would want to be their colleague. These are people with whom you are proposing to spend a lot of time. What would it feel like? Do graduate students come to these parties? What barriers seem to exist between graduate students and faculty and between junior and senior faculty? Do they seem comfortable with each other?

Drinking goes on at these events. If you drink, go ahead and join in. *But pace yourself.* Others may be able to go home early but you are the "birthday person," the guest of honor. Do know your limits, and leave in time to get enough sleep so that you are alert for the next day's activities.

After the Visit

You survived the visit and even enjoyed parts of it. Do not fall apart yet; there are still important details with which to deal.

1. Send a list of your expenses with attached receipts to the chair unless someone else was specifically mentioned. If at all possible, and even if it means taking out a short-term loan, try not to be importunate about money. You will took better

if you cope with this problem yourself, rather than asking for special treatment. Everybody knows that graduate students are not rich. They will process the request for reimbursement as quickly as they can.

2. If you promised material to any faculty members during your visit, send it promptly.

3. Settle down to wait. Either the chair or your host might have told you when the university would probably reach a decision. In our experience, they are almost always too optimistic. If they say two weeks, do not be surprised to wait a month or more.

A Final Note on Practice Effects

In our experience whatever stress and anxiety that is experienced by job candidates is greatly reduced after their first job interview. In fact, after one or two interviews candidates are often as (if not more) calm and organized about the interviewing process than the departmental hiring committee!

NOT GETTING THE JOB OFFER: HEARING NO AND HEARING NOTHING

After your wait, one of three outcomes may occur. You may get the job, fail to get it, or not hear anything about it.

Hearing No

You may get a polite letter saying that the institution you visited is not going to offer you the job. Try not to be too depressed. In our experience it is rare that a candidate who has been interviewed does not get an offer because the hiring committee has a low opinion of the candidate. More likely the committee discovered some mismatch between the candidate's talents and interests and the job, which became apparent only at the interview. Take our word for it; we are generally impressed by the job candidates we invite, even those to whom we do not offer the job.

Hearing Nothing

As you must know by now, academic decision making always takes a long time. But you should face another possibility. Because you were invited for an interview, it is clear that you are one of the best candidates for the job. However, you are certainly not the *only* good candidate. So the university may already have offered the job to another candidate. But that does not mean you are out of the running. If that person declines the job, it may be offered to you next—but the university did not want to explain that you are their second choice and resolved their dilemma by not communicating with you at all. Eventually, you will probably hear from them.

GETTING THE JOB OFFER: TAKING THE JOB

Although you may find this difficult to believe, for most students, after a certain number of cycles through the search and interview process, a job offer does materialize. Then what?

It Is a Job You Really Want

Let us assume you are generally enthusiastic about the institution and want to accept the job offer. Telephone them and say so. But before you finally commit yourself, resolve any questions that are important to you. Perhaps you and your spouse should make a second visit to the institution, so that you both can see where you may be spending the next few years. Determine whether the institution can cover this expense or not.

What about your contract? It will probably consist of a letter from the dean or chair offering you a job as an assistant professor at a certain salary. Respond with a letter accepting the job, and include a paragraph or two about issues important to you. You do this not to "sue the bastards" if they fail to live up to the contract but simply to remind them of your expectations so that they can facilitate your development. (See Bernstein, 1978, for a more complete discussion of items for contractual consideration.)

You may be able to negotiate some points with the institution, but as a person being offered your first position, you are in a poor bargaining position. Do state your needs clearly and strongly, but unless you really mean it, do not make your acceptance of the job conditional on these points. Because the department presumably wants you to be happy and productive, it may be flexible about those elements of the job that are under its control, although some aspects of the job offer, such as starting salary, tend to be set at a university-wide level. (There is one exception to this prototypical situation: If you have a second job offer in hand, you will have considerably more power with which to bargain.)

Juggling: Being Offered the Job You Might Want

Assume a slightly more complicated set of circumstances. You have received a job offer, but not one from your first-choice institution. You will probably be asked to reply within two weeks, so you had better move fast.

If you have already visited your preferred institution, you or your advisor can ask fairly directly if they want to make you a job offer. But be prepared for ambiguous responses, such as "yes, if the university approves this year's budget request" or "yes, if Candidate X turns the job down." Neither of these answers is helpful, given the time pressure, but you can ask the institution making the offer to give you a few extra days to resolve your conflict. They may be able to do so.

If you sent your vita to an institution in which you are terribly interested and have not been invited for a visit, your job chances are slim. But we know about closure; you may need to play this through until you find out this institution is not a realistic possibility. You or your advisor can call the institution and find out as much as possible about where you stand in their decision-making process. Again, the likeliest outcome is vagueness.

Given all this vagueness, it is our experience that people frequently take the first job they are offered. After pursuing all these possibilities, the bird in the hand proves considerably better than beating about bushes that may contain no birds at all.

Finishing

Congratulations! You have a job: Now retrieve your head and return to graduate school. Notice that pile of materials gathering dust in a corner? That is your thesis. *Finish it!* This may be the single most important piece of advice in this chapter. Our experience has clearly shown that the anguish associated with completing a thesis increases astronomically when students attempt to complete it in absentia. During your first teaching year, you will have little (and, perhaps, no) time to work on your thesis. Also, the role of faculty member is not well-matched with the essentially graduate student obligation of finishing a thesis. For these reasons, many students who leave with all but their degree never do get the degree. And not completing the thesis can cost you considerably. At some universities, your job will pay less and have a lesser title and you may actually lose the job if you go too long with your thesis uncompleted. At all institutions people notice. Failure to complete the degree is a real handicap.

In certain ways, we envy those starting out their careers in psychology in the 21st century. When we wrote the first edition of *The Compleat Academic*, there were only a few books giving career advice to people in psychology. Now, and we do hope that this is a trend that we had something to do with starting, there are a good many such books that give excellent advice on many aspects of one's career, from getting mentored in graduate school (Johnson & Howe, 2002), to careers in psychology (Sternberg, 1997), to elegant displays of data during your talks (Nicol & Pexman, 1999), to grant getting (Illes, 1999), and of course to teaching (Perlman, McCann,

& McFadden, 1997; Sternberg, 2000). You would be wise to find your way to the American Psychological Association's website and scan the list of books they publish, to the American Psychological Society's website and examine publications, and also to Lawrence Erlbaum Associates academic resource book list and see what you need to read at various stages of your career.

CONCLUSION

We have described the hiring process as we see it, but other people have other perspectives and you need to know about them. We hope you can use this chapter as a starting point for initiating more extensive discussions about the hiring process with your advisor and other relevant faculty members.

REFERENCES

Bernstein, B. E. (1978). Points to ponder when seeking a new professional position. *Professional Psychology, 9,* 341–349.

Bryson, R. B., Bryson, J. B., Licht, M. H., & Licht, B. G. (1976). The professional pair: Husband and wife psychologists. *American Psychologist, 31,* 10–17.

Darley, J. M., & Zanna, M. (1980). An introduction to the hiring process in academic psychology. *Canadian Psychologist, 22,* 228–237.

Iacono, W. G. (1981). The academic job interview: The experiences of a new Ph.D. in the job market. *Canadian Psychology, 22,* 217–227.

Illes, J. (1999). *The strategic grant seeker.* Mahwah, NJ: Erlbaum.

Johnson, W. B., & Huwe, J. M. (2002). *Getting mentored in graduate school.* Washington, DC: American Psychological Association.

Madell, T. O., & Madell, C. M. (1979). A professional pair at the job market: A reply. *American Psychologist, 34,* 275–276.

Matthews, J. R., & Matthews, L. H. (1978). A professional pair at the job market. *American Psychologist, 33,* 780–782.

Nicol, A., & Pexman, P. M. (1999). *Presenting your findings: A practical guide for creating tables.* Washington, DC: American Psychological Association.

Perlman, B., McCann, L. I., & McFadden, S. H. (Eds.). (1997). *Lessons learned: Practical advice for the teaching of psychology.* Washington, DC: American Psychological Society.

Quereshi, M. Y. (1980). *Correlates of the employability of college/university teachers of psychology.* Paper presented at the 88th Annual Convention of the American Psychological Association, Montreal, Quebec, Canada.

Quereshi, M. Y. (1983). *Correlates of the employability of psychologists in academia: A cross-validation.* Paper presented at the 91st Annual Convention of the American Psychological Association, Anaheim, CA.

Sternberg, R. J. (1997). *Career paths in psychology: Where your degree can take you.* Washington, DC: American Psychological Association.

Sternberg, R. J. (2000). *Teaching introductory psychology: Survival tips from the experts.* Washington, DC: American Psychological Association.

Zanna, M. P., & Darley, J. M. (1979). On getting your first job in academic psychology. APA *Journal Supplement Abstract Service, 9,* 45–46.

4

BROADENING THE JOB SEARCH:
JOBS OUTSIDE OF ACADEMIA

PATRICK C. KYLLONEN

Other than the fact that he works in a nonacademic job, it is difficult to imagine a more prototypical academic than Jack. He was born into a family of successful academic psychologists, is a recipient of an Ivy League PhD, works at being a playwright in his spare time, and is a coauthor of a book on baseball. In contrast, Ann was the person nominated by all the members of her department to be the one most likely to pursue a nonacademic job. Before graduate school, she had worked for a couple of years in a clinical setting. On entering graduate school, she knew she was headed for an applied setting. Or take me. By the time I was in my second year in graduate school, like all my colleagues, I was convinced that I would be teaching at a research university in a couple of years. When my advisor's research grant unexpectedly ran out, the announcement of a nonacademic job in a military laboratory suddenly appeared quite attractive.

Preparation of this manuscript was supported in part by funding from the Research and Development Division of Educational Testing Service. I thank Phuong Huynh, Dan Eignor, Irv Katz, James Kaufman, and Nikki Hawkins for comments on earlier drafts of this article.

Our stories are more typical than the average psychology graduate student might assume. Approximately half of all *research* psychologists work in nonacademic settings (APA, 2000). Surprised? As graduate students, our world is populated by academics. We are taught by them and advised by them. Our advisors are most familiar with the research of other academics, and so we read their writings, we see them at conferences. As if that were not enough, we marry them in astonishingly high numbers (Wilson, 2001). Is it surprising that we are scarcely aware of the huge and thriving world of nonacademic psychologists that resides outside the halls of academia?

The purpose of this chapter is to consider what jobs are available outside academia, what it is like to work in one of them, their advantages and disadvantages, preparation for such jobs, and where to find them. The jobs nonacademic psychologists perform and the settings in which they work are quite diverse. But there are common themes and distinctions separating such jobs from the more typical academic positions. And there may be more reason than ever to be aware of such jobs. As psychology matures, demands from nonacademic sectors for the talents of PhD-trained psychologists are increasing. At the same time, as teaching vacancies created by the retirement of full-time tenured professors are being replaced with graduate students and adjuncts (Leslie, 1998), there may be a stagnation or even decline in the availability of traditional tenure-track academic positions. This need not be cause for despair. Although every graduate student has been told that there is no better job in the world than being a tenured professor, nonacademic jobs often enjoy some distinct advantages over their academic counterparts.

WHAT JOBS ARE THERE OUTSIDE OF ACADEMIA?

According to the American Psychological Association's (APA; 2000) nonacademic jobs website, about half of the nonacademic jobs are in private companies, either for profit (37%; e.g., Microsoft, Psychological Corporation) or nonprofit [13%; e.g., Educational Testing Service (ETS), the Ball Foundation]. About 20% are in government (e.g., the Department of Defense, Veteran's Administration, the National Science Foundation, National Aeronautics and Space Administration, Center for Disease Control), and the remaining 28% are self-employed (e.g., private consultant, test developer). I have worked in two of these setting categories—for the government (the Department of Defense), and for ETS, a nonprofit. In my jobs I have interacted with numerous individuals in the other sectors as well. These include large contractors (e.g., Price-Waterhouse Coopers, Hughes, IBM), small contractors (Galaxy Scientific Incorporated, Research Development Corporation, Essex), consulting firms, Internet companies (e.g., Knowledge planet.com; embark.com), computer companies (e.g., Microsoft, Control Data Corporation), and freelancers (e.g., computer programmers, consultants, test developers). Another significant group, in which I have not worked, is the medical sector.

According to projections from the Bureau of Labor Statistics's *Occupational Outlook Handbook* (http://stats.bls.gov/ocohome.htm), sector percentages will not change dramatically over the next decade or so, although there is likely to be some declines in the government sector and some growth in the profit and self-employed areas. It is likely that jobs in the health and computer sectors will increase. This is not to say that a particular job in the health or computer field will be in a growth setting or that a government job will be a sinking ship. These are just trends. But from personal experiences in both growing and declining organizations (thankfully, my current setting is in the growing category), I can say it makes a dramatic difference in all the things that matter about a job—hiring, firing, research support, morale, and quality of life.

Psychologists perform a wide variety of jobs in these settings. These include research, policy, training, design, and evaluation, and they involve work in cognitive, social, personality, human factors, and other substantive domains. For example, cognitive and human-factors psychologists work in usability labs, testing new information technology products. Educational psychologists conduct evaluation studies of school programs for state and federal agencies. Industrial–organizational psychologists can be found throughout industry in a wide variety of roles, such as heading a training department in an insurance company or writing surveys for companies interested in evaluating or improving their organizational climate. One comes across many PhD social psychologists who retool for industry, by joining the Society for Industrial and Organizational Psychology or the Human Factors Society, perhaps even getting licensed (as an industrial–organizational psychologist), then working as a human resources manager in a large company; I know of one who was recruited by the CIA. A mathematical psychologist I worked with is now a chief scientist in a small consulting company that performs a variety of jobs—evaluation, comparable-worth studies, setting cut scores for hiring and promotion tests. Another mathematical psychologist is testing products for Motorola. My observation has been that psychologists working in the government and nonprofit sectors often work in jobs similar to those in academia. But psychologists working outside those sectors, either as freelancers, consultants, or as employees in private for-profit companies, tend to do much more varied work and to stray in quite interesting and creative ways from their graduate training.

DIFFERENCES WITH ACADEMIC JOBS

Besides having a number of friends and colleagues in academic positions, I actually worked in one, for an extremely enjoyable, stimulating, and enriching three years at the University of Georgia. I only left because while at Georgia, I was doing a considerable amount of research with the Air Force Research Laboratory. When the laboratory manager of the project on which I was working resigned, I was given the opportunity to replace him. I decided that I would regret it if someone else took the job and took the project in a direction I did not think would be as productive. So I took the plunge, causing one academic colleague to remark that I was making a fatal move and that she had never heard of anyone voluntarily leaving academia before (working on the other side of the fence, I can now say that many voluntarily leave academia at varying times in their career; and, for that matter, many return, also at varying times in their career). Nevertheless, the experience provided me with some basis on which to compare academic with nonacademic jobs.

Although there is variety within both worlds, and exceptions to all these rules, some of the features I believe most reliably separate the two spheres are discussed next. Which is better? That, of course, depends. It depends on the particular job, and it depends on the criterion. Different people value different criteria.

Autonomy

Autonomy typically ranks high on surveys of factors associated with job satisfaction, and there are few jobs that provide more autonomy than an academic one. The academic chooses what research to pursue, and over time often even chooses what courses to teach. There really is not the concept of a boss telling you what to do. Despite the trappings (large office, personal secretary, access to the budget), a department chair is not really a boss. It is different in nonacademic settings. Typically, someone else is making the decision about what research you do. As a junior researcher, that someone else is often your boss who assigns you a project. As a senior researcher, the someone else is often a client or funding agency. Now in practice, this distinction is not as severe as it sounds. Academic researchers, particularly ones at prestigious research universities, often feel pressured to land large research grants and contracts, which makes them care more about what the funding agencies are supporting than about following their muse. And nonacademic researchers can be working under such a broad project umbrella that they can pursue research projects largely of their own choosing, within bounds. Still, this is a rather basic difference between academic and nonacademic jobs.

Time Is Money

The accounting systems of nonacademic jobs vary, but for the most part, workers are aware that they are accountable for their time. There is a sense of having to "cover" one's time with projects. For example, at ETS, every hour is billable, and we complete time sheets at the end of each day by entering project accounting codes and the amount of time (rounded to the half hour) charged to each project on which we work. In contrast, rarely do you encounter an academic who has even a vague sense of the relationship between time and money (other than for on-the-side consulting jobs). Even academics who are working on a grant or two, for which they have submitted a budget listing the percentage of time they will devote to that grant, often seem rather oblivious to the specific number of hours they are expected to and actually put toward a particular project.

There are some interesting implications of this arrangement. An obvious problem with such time accounting in nonacademic jobs is a shortage of time to think, write, and engage in what are sometimes called professional activities. Typically, there are no projects in nonacademic jobs covering such "superfluous" activities. Enlightened employers, of course, such as my own, appreciate the value of allowing or encouraging their employees to engage in these activities. Still, this is a fairly important distinction between academic and nonacademic jobs.

Pressure, Deadlines, and the 80–20 Rule

Another implication of time accounting is the importance of the 80–20 rule ("Pareto's principle," Koch, 1998). The 80–20 rule says that 80% of the output is caused by 20% of the input, so that 80% of the value is produced in the first 20% of the time spent on a project. This means that the optimal stopping point from a cost–benefit perspective is long before you might think the work is finished or ready. Unlike in academia, where subtle, picayune distinctions can be the basis for a lively three-year debate argued in the pages of a prestigious journal, in the nonacademic world, one does not have the luxury of checking out every last lead suggested by the data or pursuing that one final analysis that might finally unlock the mystery of your results. Rather, there is more typically the flavor of an assembly line: You get your one shot, you write it up as you proceed, and when it is over, you turn to the next project. The assumption is that you are fooling yourself in thinking that perseverating in reinterpretations or additional analyses will yield much of worth, or at least compared to what you might get working on something else during that time. And there may be something to this idea. This attitude might seem troubling to a graduate student on the heels of completing a labor of love dissertation, who might think it is important to "do it right or not at all." Or a graduate student might see projects as opportunities not just to solve the immediate problem at hand but to think, learn, and grow, to say nothing of writing it up and publishing it in a prestigious scientific journal to communicate to graduate school friends that one is still around. However, there are always evenings and weekends.

Harder to Become World's Expert

Related to this notion of deadlines and 80–20 rules, the pace and variety of projects that confront a nonacademic researcher make it difficult to develop truly specialized expertise in any given area. Not impossible— there are many world-class experts from nonacademia—just, on average, more difficult. The academic researcher is rewarded for going where no one has gone before on a topic and for patience and perseverance in pursuing a narrow question. In contrast, nonacademic researchers are often forced into being generalists, flitting from topic to topic, picking up a bit here and a bit there, specializing in gender bias this month, age discrimination the next, and intelligent tutoring systems next year. Not that this is a bad feature. Many people seem to like the variety and change of pace and the opportunity to learn about new fields. After all, 80% of what you learn in an area is accomplished during the first 20% of time studying that area.

Team Mentality

A major difference between academic and nonacademic jobs is the team concept. There are teams in academia, consisting of a professor and graduate students (with the occasional postdoc), but roles are predefined. Although graduate students can be quite self-directed and technically proficient, they are still aware of their role as apprentices, and it is the professor who gets the grants, makes the major decisions, and hands out assignments. It is typically quite different in nonacademic jobs in several ways. First, roles change constantly. One might be a team leader on one project and a role-player on another. And teams are commonly rearranged for every project—which can be every month or two. Also, the academic-style team of one expert and many students or apprentices is rare in nonacademic jobs. More typical is the team of experts, with every expert contributing a different kind of expertise. For example, there can be a team with experts in functional areas—research, development, marketing, strategy. Or teams with several kinds of subject-matter expertise—cognitive psychology, social psychology, computer science, linguistics. Most common, of course, are combinations, of a cognitive and social psychologist from research, a computer scientist from the technical support group, a marketing person (who might have majored in psychology), and an MBA from the product group, for example.

Individual Glory Versus Distributed Credit

Related to the team mentality is the concept of credit for successes. I remember an academic colleague from a major research university commenting on how refreshing it was to go to a meeting where participants generously tossed out good, productive ideas without worrying about who would claim those ideas as their own. I too have found myself frustrated sometimes in dealing with academics who seem protective about certain ideas, worrying that discussing them will result in losing control of them (especially with someone who is in a position to apply them). One of my favorite lines, spoken by a colleague addressing a senior researcher who was complaining about someone trying to run with her ideas, is, "At your stage, you shouldn't be complaining, you should be jumping for joy that someone is actually reading your stuff, let alone wanting to actually use your ideas." I think credit-sharing is generally much freer in nonacademic jobs than in academic ones, probably at least partly because in nonacademia, the bottom line is what your project produces, not so much what you independently produce. In academia, there really is no concept like that—you are evaluated on your individual scholarly production; individually authored articles are evaluated more favorably than coauthored ones; and the position of one's name on a coauthored article is important. This of course happens in nonacademic settings, but because you are evaluated on a broader range of output, it happens less.

Collaborators

In academia, one's primary collaborators are students. Occasionally another academic is a collaborator, but that seems to be fairly rare (wife–husband teams may be an exception). Part of this is because of the fiefdomlike structure of academia—dukes may cooperate, at a safe distance, but joint rule is out of the question. Part of this is because in a department, one often finds oneself to be the sole expert in a particular research area. Occasionally a colleague in one's discipline area visits for a few days or a sabbatical, and occasionally such a visit results in a collaboration, but this is rare. In contrast, outside academia one's collaborators are typically equal-status colleagues. There is often a certain critical mass of people working together on the same or similar areas or providing complimentary perspectives on a particular area (see the section on team mentality earlier in the chapter). Indeed I always thought that one of the attractions of some nonacademic settings is that they recreated the idyllic graduate school experience of my youth, with many people sharing a common research and knowledge interest.

Cooperation Versus Competition or Build It Up Versus Tear It Down

Criticism and differentiation are key concepts in an academic job in psychology. Much of what one learns in graduate school is a certain skepticism, as manifested for example in practice on how to critique an idea or a theory, or in socialization on going against the grain of prevailing opinion or common wisdom. This skeptical attitude carries over to the academic research enterprise as well, and many important papers have been written that essentially are critiques of someone else's work. In nonacademic jobs there seems to be considerably less emphasis on the critiquing side of the job and much more on the constructing side. That is, the employer generally does not care as much about a detailed critique on the flaws in some approach to solving a problem as he or she is in the fact that you have an approach to solve the problem, wherever or from whomever it may have come. If it does not work perfectly, fine; the point is it is something! That is, there is a general, pragmatic build-it-up flavor to what an employer wants and expects from you, in contrast to the skeptical attitude that allows you to pinpoint subtle flaws in a complex line of reasoning that gives you points in an academic setting.

Working With People

Nonacademic jobs seem much more likely to involve working with others for a greater proportion of one's day. Certainly academics regularly teach, meet students, meet with their research groups, and occasionally talk with colleagues, their chair, and committee members. Still, much of the day, at least according to the stereotypical image, is one spent in solitude, reading or writing, with the door closed. This contrasts with most nonacademic jobs, where one is in constant contact and communication with others, by phone, electronically, or face-to-face.

Meetings

In fact, I spend about a third of my day in meetings, on average, with supervisors, supervisees, project coworkers, clients, and visitors. Topics vary. With my supervisor we discuss accomplishments, plans, new directions, budget, and personnel issues. With those I supervise it is research strategies (ideas and clients), consulting (e.g., statistics or design), counseling sessions (e.g., personnel problems, desires), and occasionally kudos (e.g., completed proposal) or reprimands (e.g., falling behind on a schedule). There are also formal end-of-the-year appraisals or beginning or midyear objective-setting meetings. Although there are annual appraisals in academia, my experience has been that nonacademia seems to take the formal appraisal process more seriously. This may be because there are greater implications (more variance in outcomes). In addition, once a month we hold a get-together for the whole center, where we go around the table letting everyone know in 5 or 10 minutes what we are working on, what troubles we are having, where we might need help, and so on. We also have once a month "brown bags" where one of us or a guest talks in more depth about a project. Let us not forget the increasingly popular conference call meeting with clients and project team members. Speakerphones and 1-800 conference call numbers are invaluable for these. We occasionally conduct video–teleconference meetings, but these do not seem typically to add much to what can be done by speakerphone.

"Importance" of Research

When I was in graduate school, a cynical colleague commented on the process of conducting research and getting it published in good journals, concluding that "none of this really matters, but it's the game." The game refers to the process of choosing a research topic, collecting, analyzing, then reanalyzing the data when the first batch of hypotheses do not work out, adjusting the framing and the hypotheses while "beating the data into submission," and finally, writing it up so that it will be attractive to the most prestigious journal possible, given the constraints of the data. One completes this process, stuffs and stamps the envelope, then waits six months to see if one has "won" the game (the additional game of responding to editors' negative feedback letters will be ignored for the sake of brevity). This may be somewhat of an exaggeration, but it captures something about the publish-or-perish culture. In contrast, research conducted in nonacademic settings is typically taken quite seriously, with someone other than a reviewer and editor actually using the findings—and it happens fairly quickly. There is often severe time pressure on getting the research results, and a potential user is often not at all interested in whether the findings are disseminated in a scientific journal. To the user, the research is often considered finished when the researcher has a finding to report. This is why the presentation is often the endpoint of research in a nonacademic setting, with a more formal write-up put off beyond some distant time horizon.

Some like the idea of their research being applied to solve a real-world problem and like the challenge, pace, and constant flow of new problems. Others seem to believe that the compromises that inevitably have to be made in application attempts, such as stopping a project before it is really finished or collecting data in the field rather than in the laboratory, detract from the progress possible in conducting basic research. And preferences may vary over time. Personally, for example, I am much more enamored with applications now than when I was in, or freshly out of graduate school. In its introductory letter to me, after I accepted employment, the ETS discussed the gratitude I would feel for "working with our clients." A decade ago I would have been puzzled, but when I read that four years ago I understood.

There are basic research jobs in nonacademic settings. But accountability issues always lurk in the background. One interested in conducting basic research with an employer willing to support it in nonacademia must be prepared to understand the big-picture context of the basic research. This may include a mental plan sketched out about the connections between the basic research and the killer application it will make possible down the road. Research conducted for its own sake is possible and even encouraged at the top universities, but is generally tolerated at best and prohibited at worst in nonacademic settings. The idea of multiyear projects is rare, and when it does happen, it is because the principal investigator has been creative in clearly showing how Year 2's activities are quite distinguishable from Year 1's.

Publishing, Presenting

This raises the question of why nonacademic researchers ever publish anything for general scientific consumption. For example, in a recent project several colleagues and I developed a problem-solving assessment for a strategic consulting company, which was interested in using it for screening applicants. Once we developed the assessment, collected data on it, and provided score interpretations, the client had no additional interest in the dissemination of the research. This, in spite of the fact that during the course of the project we solved some intriguing problems and made some interesting advances, ones surely worthy of a scientific article. But, in fact, not only was the client not interested in pursuing such a write-up, we were asked to sign a confidentiality agreement *not* to disclose much about the assessment at all. My management was happy that we completed the project and the client was happy with what we delivered. No additional action was necessary. This is not completely atypical in nonacademic research, and in some industries (e.g., computer) and organizations (e.g., the CIA), confidentiality and secrecy are the rule rather than the exception (yes, the CIA employs PhD psychologists; http://www.cia.gov/cia/employment/jobpost ings/psychologist.htm).

At the same time, there are reasons for employers to allow and even encourage publishing and presenting. For one, many employers recognize that it is important for their employees to be members of the "hidden college" to stay on top of the latest research, months or even years before it appears in print, to be connected to the movers and shakers of a field, to be in the loop, to know where things are going. For another, like rock musicians and professional bodybuilders, PhDs do not want to spend their careers cloaked in anonymity but want to put the results of years of toil and determination in full view, to say nothing of being able to keep in touch with colleagues from graduate school. This means to see and be seen in the journals and at the conferences. To satisfy this need, employers might have to allow and even encourage publication and conference presentations to attract the top talent. (Incidentally, on the project described in the previous paragraph, we are in the process of writing it up, although we are changing details and suppressing identities to comply with the confidentiality agreement.)

Loyalty to the Company Versus to the Profession

An academic is a free agent, building her resume to increase her market worth, acquiring research assistant and teaching assistant experiences and perhaps a coauthorship or two during graduate school; journal articles and book chapters as an assistant professor; and committees, fellowships, awards, editorial boards, and editorships along the way. A sense of loyalty to the field ("social psychology" or "neuroscience") is commonly stronger than loyalty to one's employing institution. This is reflected in the concept of the "academic gypsy" flitting from institution to institution, jockeying for a better deal, more research support, less teaching, a nicer office, or better graduate students, but always remaining loyal to one's field. In this context, fulfilling professional responsibilities—serving on an APA or National Research Council committee, or an editorial board, or being appointed an editor or an officer in a scientific society—increase one's reputation and hence market worth. These are plums academics seek, and the fact that they are mostly voluntary (i.e., unpaid) activities does not diminish their value. In contrast, the reward structure for participating in these kinds of activities is not as great in the context of a nonacademic job. For one thing, an employee's worth to an employer is related to what that employee produces for that employer. In nonacademic jobs, this often means what research one produces, not how prestigious a committee one is able to serve on. It is important for a university's prestige (and consequent marketing) to show that its employees serve on important national committees and are in charge of prestigious scientific journals. It is not often very important for nonacademic employers to tout such accomplishments from their staff. By the same token, an employee in a nonacademic setting is not rewarded much for participating in such activities. As long as it is done on one's own time, an employer is unlikely to complain, but on the other hand, the employer is not likely to allow an employee to spend 30% of her time on professional activities. Again, the caveat to this general rule, which is that an employer can attract better talent by permitting such activities, still holds (see the earlier section on publishing, presenting).

No Teaching, No Students

The most obvious difference between an academic and nonacademic job is teaching. In nonacademic jobs, there is none. Some people like this, some people do not. Teaching can be stimulating and challenging, and the opportunity to watch eager, enthusiastic students learn and grow can be quite rewarding. On the other hand, teaching is a lot of work, particularly when one starts out. Teaching detracts from research, both in time spent before class, with the endless preparation, and after class, with the nonproductive hours spent descending from the lecture high. Not only that, but one can be tempted to fit one's research not to the pursuit of important topics but to address issues that come up in teaching per se or topics that interest one's students. In other words, teaching can drive the research rather than the other way around.

Compensation

Compensation is an important (for many, the most important) feature of a job, and many people, particularly in nonacademic fields, seem to believe that compensation is an attractive advantage of nonacademic jobs. One hears, for example, that nonacademic jobs start out paying 20% more or even higher than academic jobs and that the advantage stays with nonacademic jobs. Salary surveys, such as ones conducted by the APA (Williams, Wicherski, & Kohout, 2000) and the Society for Industrial–Organizational Psychology (Katkowski & Medsker, 2000) do suggest an average advantage in nonacademic salaries, but there are many factors that complicate the issue. Nonacademic jobs themselves vary quite dramatically by industry (e.g., consulting firms pay more than the government does) and job (management pays higher than research). Academic salaries vary by doctoral versus nondoctoral granting—and public versus private institutions and by department (e.g., business and medical schools pay psychologists more than psychology departments do). And experience is a powerful moderator in both academic and nonacademic jobs: In both, pay tends to increase with experience, up to 20 to 25 years experience or so, then flatten out or even decrease after that. So there may be a slight compensation edge for nonacademic jobs, but only on average, with lots of circumstantial variability in both settings. The idea that you cannot make very good money in academia is false, as is the idea that industry always pays more.

The Tenure Pressure Cooker and Security

The good news about academic jobs is that in exchange for participating in a grueling and challenging pressure cooker for six years, you may be rewarded with the most secure job on earth: the tenured professorship. The pressure cooker consists of working incredibly hard, long, and stressful hours and having no time for anything else. During those hours you teach large introductory classes outside your area of interest to sleepy undergraduates, carve a niche by conducting sustained research in a narrow research area, secure funding, present and publish frequently, and demonstrate good citizenship by serving on university faculty committees. With tenure, you transition from that to teaching the classes you want, having the grant agencies contact you, thumbing your nose at requests to participate on committees in which you are not interested, and reveling in past accomplishments. Of course, this is a result of the momentousness of the tenure decision. It is a little bit like taking a six-year-long Faculty Aptitude Test. There is nothing comparable in nonacademic jobs, because eternal job security is never achieved (tenure is only found in academia). If anything, there is a reverse pressure cooker phenomenon, in which the stakes are low for the new hire, who can easily find another job but who is quite valuable to an employer because his or her knowledge and energy levels are high relative to introductory wage levels. With experience, the nonacademic employee's pay, and correspondingly, pressure to produce, increases. The edge then goes to both kinds of jobs, but at different times. Security (and perhaps job satisfaction) may very well be higher in the nonacademic job for the first six years or so, but after that, the edge in security definitely goes to the academic job. Informally, one of the most highly cited reasons that I have heard for choosing a nonacademic over an academic job is the desire to avoid the tenure pressure cooker.

Resources

I have heard countless complaints from assistant professors who find that they have to battle their employer to secure basic office supplies and get a telephone installed, to say nothing of a desktop computer, notebook, palm device, email account, or web access. Consistent with the free agent theme, academic departments often view the securing of resources and support to be the responsibility of the individual faculty member, and the new, incoming faculty member has the most difficult time of all. And with a chair who is not really a boss, there is no one to whom the new faculty member may go to ask for help. This can be quite frustrating and seen as another challenge thrown up as an obstacle to be overcome in the battle for tenure. In contrast, the employer in the nonacademic setting typically showers copious support on new arrivals, so that no time is wasted, and the new researcher hits the ground running. For example, at the ETS, we survey new employees before they begin work to find out what support they need. We get their e-mail accounts in order and ensure their web access and software is working. Support staff are even evaluated on the degree to which this support is provided before new employees arrive. Once here, employees find themselves with plenty of supporting secretarial and research assistant staff, who help the effort in any way they can. This is common in nonacademic jobs. There are certainly exceptions—nonacademic jobs that do not provide this kind of support (e.g., smaller companies) and academic jobs that do (e.g., when support is treated as a recruiting lure). But on average, support is better in nonacademic jobs.

Travel

The overall amount of traveling probably does not differ much in academic and nonacademic settings. There certainly is individual variability—in either job, there are those who travel a lot and those who travel a little or not at all. The main difference seems to be that academics tend to squeeze all their traveling into the nonteaching summer months and plan it far in advance. Traveling in nonacademic jobs tends to be spread more evenly throughout the year and occurs more spontaneously (with less planning). Whereas academic travel tends to be meetings and especially conferences, nonacademics tend to travel to more meetings and fewer conferences, and meetings are often with clients and potential funding sources. The advantage to traveling in nonacademic settings is that the school calendar does not interfere with (and make difficult) traveling plans. If one needs to meet with someone, the meeting is scheduled. Delay tolerance is on the order of days or weeks, whereas with academics, it may take many months to find and schedule a meeting involving traveling.

Job Expectations

There are several additional differences between academic and nonacademic not covered elsewhere, which are summarized next.

Do Not Take It Home With You

You do not punch a clock or even have fixed work hours in academia, but you never leave your work behind, either. It follows you like a determined shadow wherever you go. Evenings and weekends are great times to get caught up on reading, preparing lectures, and marking students' papers and quizzes. No matter how much you have done, there is always more reading, writing, marking, and preparation to do, requiring discipline to leave it behind, get it out of your mind, and relax. Nonacademic jobs are much more 9 to 5. The hours tend to be more rigid. After all, given the role of teams and support staff—much more so than in academia—you depend on others and they depend on you to be available during the day. At the same time, when the workday is over, one can more easily leave it all behind with a clear conscience when one goes home at night.

Obviously these are ideals. Many in nonacademic settings work at least occasional nights and weekends, particularly when projects, reports, or grant applications are due, and many academics work hard on trying to establish normal hours. But there definitely is a tendency difference, and I have heard many nonacademic workers cite the advantage of leaving it behind as a key factor in their selecting a nonacademic job.

Variety of Projects

It is common in nonacademic settings to be working simultaneously on four to eight projects in various stages and in varying intensities. Some may be in write-up, some in analysis, some in conceptualization, some in preproposal stages. One project may occupy 80% of one's time this week, with the remaining projects splitting the remainder; or they may be equally divided. Juggling responsibilities, making sure that no balls drop, and keeping track of progress, status, and deadlines are important parts of the job. This is true in academic settings as well, of course, but in academia the different projects tend to be clearly separable—teach, grade essays, meet with students, do research—and typically only a research project or two is at an active stage at any one time.

Pushed Into Administrative Track

A career path for an academic begins at postdoc, lecturer, or assistant professor, progressing through the ranks of associate, then full professor, perhaps detouring through stints as department chair or even dean on occasion. But these administrative stints are always voluntary, and often temporary, and deans and chairs typically step down at some point to get back to what they love to do best, full-time teaching and research. In nonacademic positions, the career trajectory is often much more one way, without the detours, beginning at bench scientist, then proceeding through project manager, supervisor, department or branch head, division head, vice president, and so forth. With each promotion, the advancing careerist accumulates more management and supervisory responsibility and is compensated accordingly. But at the same time, he or she becomes increasingly removed from the data collection, analysis, and problem-solving activities that might have drawn him or her into psychology in the first place. One hears talk about dual-track opportunities in nonacademic jobs, meaning that it is possible to advance in an organization by becoming increasingly knowledgeable and proficient in a technical specialty, in addition to accumulating more supervision and management responsibility. However, in practice, a true dual-track situation in nonacademic jobs is often hard to find.

PREPARATION FOR CAREERS OUTSIDE OF ACADEMIA

The skills that make psychology PhDs attractive to employers are the ones that make graduate students attractive to their advisors. These include the ability to conceptualize a problem, to design an approach to study it, to know how to collect and analyze data, and to communicate what you did, in both written and oral form, in reports, memos, PowerPoint presentations, and one-on-one face-to-face meetings. Analysis and communication abilities are typically strong suits for the psychology graduate. Much of this comes naturally to those who out of both interest and training have spent many years acquiring the behavioral science approach to understanding and dissecting the world of people.

As far as what has been most useful from formal study in graduate school, I have found that research methodology and analysis and quantitative skills tend to be the most marketable. Essentially all quantitative and methodology courses I took in graduate school have repaid themselves many times over in their value and in the opportunities I have received as a result of taking them (not that learning stops at graduate school).

There are also skills I found to be valuable after graduate school that graduate school did not really prepare me for. In this category, I would rank near the top the ability to explain research designs, findings, theories, or models to nonpsychologists, both technical (e.g., engineers, physicists) and nontechnical (e.g., marketing staff, managers). A particularly interesting flavor of this skill is to add a persuasive component to the didactic slant of such an explanation. Particularly challenging and important is to develop the ability to convince a nonpsychologist who might hold a strong contrary opinion regarding what it is you are trying to express. Ranked close to this is the ability to summarize technical ideas in either 10 seconds, 1 minute, 5 minutes, or at any other interval of time one is permitted.

In addition to these technical skills, social skills play an extremely important role in nonacademic settings, probably more so than in academic settings. It is possible to be quite a successful academic with poor or terrible social skills, where social eccentricities and idiosyncrasies are not only tolerated but expected and even interpreted by adoring students as charming. These same behaviors do not give one points in nonacademic settings and can impair one's career progression. But in addition, just simply the ability to work with teams, to be flexible in both giving and taking directions, to be able to persuade, cajole, or inspire others, and at the same time not to resent having to follow someone else's orders from time to time are important skills and attitudes in nonacademic settings. Another important social skill is the ability to network, to listen to others' discussions of what they do and to inform others of what you are doing, to draw connections, and to see opportunities to partner or collaborate, to move things forward. This occurs at meetings, in the lunch room, at welcome celebrations ("meet and greets"), at birthday lunches, at awards ceremonies, cocktail parties, coffee breaks, everywhere.

Having a positive can-do attitude is enormously important in nonacademic settings. This requires some attitude adjustment from graduate school, where one is taught to be skeptical. Healthy skepticism is always important, of course, but in general, one is much more positively rewarded for constantly pushing things forward, trying things out, and expressing optimism. Flexibility is another attitude valued in nonacademic settings. This means flexibility to drop what you are doing on a moment's notice, to set aside a project to return an e-mail from one's boss, to be willing to take on a project on a topic you do not see as falling into your area of expertise (but one that needs to be done and you know as much about as anyone else around).

There are many other skills that are important for success in a nonacademic setting, such as budgeting, managing, and supervising, but I believe that these are relatively easy to learn and that the most important determinant is one's willingness to treat them as important parts of the job.

SEARCHING FOR JOBS OUTSIDE OF ACADEMIA

Everyone knows where to find academic jobs. One will find hundreds of jobs listed each month in the back pages of the APA *Monitor*, *Chronicle of Higher Education*, and American Psychological Society's *Observer's Employment Bulletin*. The specialty societies produce additional listings, and may even be a better source. Examples are the Society for Personality and Social Psychology (SPSP)'s listserv, the American Educational Research Association's (AERA) AERA.net job postings, the Society for Industrial–Organizational Psychology's JobNet, and specialty journals, such as *Cognitive Science*, all of which have websites. And everyone knows the season: The first wave of ads hits in November, peaks in January, and starts tailing off through the spring, all timed for the academic position that begins the following fall semester.

Finding a nonacademic position is much less formal and predictable, and there is no season driven by an academic calendar. There are many nonacademic positions listed in the sources mentioned, but there are additional sources as well, such as general Internet job ad sites (e.g., monster.com; jobsmart.org, jobbankusa.com, cweb.com, nationjob.com), newspapers, such as the *New York Times*, the *Los Angeles Times*, and other large city dailies. (The *New York Times* and the *Los Angeles Times* also have excellent job-search engines available through their websites.) Working through some of these sources can be a bit like searching for shiny gold coins in the Daytona Beach sand, duty for which not everyone is fit.

Informal job searches are much more common in nonacademic settings than they are in academic ones. Formal job searches involve posting an announcement, usually for several months, having a fixed application deadline (e.g., February 1), conducting formal job talks and formal interviews (e.g., from February 15–28), with a short list of candidates, then making a decision (e.g., on March 1) and sending notices to all those involved. Informal job searches often occur by word of mouth, may or may not be widely posted, may happen quickly or not at all, and are not on a fixed schedule. If the person or unit doing the hiring knows about someone "really good" this person might ask him or her to visit, perhaps ask him or her to give a talk, casually discuss employment possibilities with him or her during the visit, and then in the next several weeks, perhaps call back with an employment offer. The challenge for the prospective applicant is being known by the ones doing the hiring. How does that happen? One way is by making oneself known by attending conferences, job fairs, talks, meetings, and engaging in other general networking behavior. The other is through internships, summer programs, postdoctoral fellowship programs, sabbaticals, visiting scholar programs, and the like. Many large employers of psychologists have such programs. For example, the National Research Council has a visiting scholar and postdoctoral fellowship programs. My employer, the ETS, has all these programs. There is the Inroads program, a support, intern, and job placement program for talented minority applicants. And many others too numerous to mention. Someone who has worked in these programs for an employer has a huge edge over applicants who are not personally known by hiring staff.

CONCLUSION

There are many reasons to be cognizant of the world outside academia, not the least of which is that you might want to work in it. It is certainly true that there is no job like a tenured professor's, as other chapters in this volume will attest. Still, interests, opportunities, or circumstances lead half of the research PhDs in psychology to nonacademic positions. There is such a wide variety of nonacademic jobs and settings that it is difficult to make sweeping generalizations about what they are like. Nevertheless, it is fair to say that there are many and varied opportunities outside of academia and many satisfied and productive psychologists working in nonacademic jobs today.

SOURCES AND ADDITIONAL READINGS

The APA's Science Directorate (2000) hosts an excellent, must-visit website on nonacademic careers for scientific psychologists (www.apa.org/ science/nonacad.html). In addition to a breakdown on settings and types of jobs, the site reviews preparation and job searching strategies and provides links to related sites. It also includes an archive of the popular "An Interesting Career in Psychology" columns that regularly appear in APA's *Monitor on Psychology* publication. The site and the brief autobiographies in particular make for fascinating reading, even if you are not in the job market.

The American Psychological Society also runs a fascinating series in the *APS Observer*, called "Psychological Scientists in the Private Sector," which also is must reading (also available on the web, at http://www.psycho logicalscience.org/observer/private_sector/). A personal favorite is Pirolli's (2000) inspiring "More Time for Research."

The previous edition of this book contains an excellent chapter on nontraditional jobs (DeJong & Saxe, 1987), which is complementary to the material given in this chapter. Other useful reading for those interested in finding out about or pursuing nonacademic careers includes Keller's (1994) *Academic Paths* and Sternberg's (1997) *Career Paths in Psychology*. These both cover primarily academic career paths but also include valuable nonacademic stories and information as well. Nonacademic careers are the topic of a lovely book by Princeton University doctorates Susan Basalla and Maggie Debelius (2001), *So, What Are You Going to Do With That?* Although the authors received their PhDs in English, their experiences and insights seem equally well-suited to behavioral science PhDs, and their comparisons of academic with what they call "postacademic" life make for enjoyable reading. Not only that but their book is filled with good, practical advice, including sample cover letters, excellent resume writing tips, interviewing advice, and many additional resources and websites. There seems to have been a recent spurt of interest in nonacademic careers, and news articles are popping up with increased frequency. Articles by Murray (2000) in *The Monitor on Psychology* and by Smallwood (2001) in the *Chronicle of Higher Education* make for quick, enjoyable reads.

REFERENCES

American Psychological Association. (2000). *Non-academic careers for scientific psychologists*. Retrieved on March 5, 2003, from http://www.apa.org/science/nonacad.html

American Psychological Society. (2000, Nov.–Dec.). Psychological scientists in the private sector. *APS Observer, 13*(9–10), 4–15; 8–24.

Basalla, S., & Debelius, M. (2001). *So, what are you going to do with that? A guide to career changing for M.A.'s and Ph.D.'s*. New York: Farrar, Straus, and Giroux.

DeJong, W., & Saxe, L. (1987). An incompleat guide to working as a nonacademic researcher. In M. P. Zanna & J. M. Darley (Eds.), *The compleat academic: A practical guide for the beginning social scientist* (pp. 205–224). Mahwah, NJ: Erlbaum.

Katkowski, D. A., & Medsker, G. J. (2000). *Income and employment of SIOP members in 2000*. Retrieved October 19, 2001, from http://siop.org/tip/backissues/tipjul01/websalarysurvey.pdf

Keller, P. A. (1994). *Academic paths: Career decisions and experiences of psychologists*. Hillsdale, NJ: Erlbaum.

Koch, R. (1998). *The 80/20 principle: The secret of achieving more with less*. New York: Bantam Doubleday Dell.

Leslie, D. (Ed.). (1998). *Part-time, adjunct, and temporary faculty: The new majority? Report of the Sloan Conference on Part-Time and Adjunct Faculty*. New York: Alfred P. Sloan Foundation.

Murray, B. (2000). The growth of the new PhD. *Monitor on Psychology, 31*(10), 24–27.

Pirolli, P. (2000). More time for research. *American Psychological Society Observer, 13*. [on-line version] http://www.psychologicalscience.org/observer/private_sector/pirolli.html

Smallwood, S. (2001, Jan.). Psychology Ph.D.'s pass on academe: Star graduates turn down faculty jobs, finding better pay and less stress in industry. *Chronicle of Higher Education, XLVII*(18), A10–A12.

Sternberg, R. J. (Ed.). (1997). *Career paths in psychology: Where your degree can take you*. Washington, DC: American Psychological Association.

Williams, S., Wicherski, M., & Kohout, J. L. (2000). *Salaries in psychology 1999. Report of the 1999 APA salary survey*. Washington, DC: American Psychological Association.

Wilson, R. (2001, April). The backlash against hiring couples. *Chronicle of Higher Education, XLVII*(18), A16.

II

TEACHING AND MENTORING

5

TIPS FOR EFFECTIVE TEACHING

DOUGLAS A. BERNSTEIN AND SANDRA GOSS LUCAS

We know a senior professor whose sole preparation for college teaching came during his third year in graduate school—in the form of a one-sentence letter assigning him to teach an undergraduate introductory course the following term. Quite a few important items were left out of this "teacher preparation" letter. It said nothing about (a) what topics to cover, (b) how to create a syllabus, (c) how to select textbooks, (d) how to prepare lectures and class activities, (e) how to evaluate students' performance, or (f) how to handle student-related problems such as grading complaints, classroom disruptiveness, make-up exam requests, and referrals to the counseling center. He had to learn these things—and everything else that college teachers should know about teaching—through trial and error in the classroom. It is no wonder that facing that first class was one of the most frightening experiences of his life (Bernstein, 1983).

This story is not unusual. Many new professors enter their first classrooms after having spent years as apprentices to expert mentors in research and scholarship but with little or no formal preparation for their role as a teacher (Golde & Dore, 2001; Mervis, 2001). They are forced to rely on their wits and their guts, along with informal advice, the examples set by their own teachers, and readings on how to survive in the classroom (e.g., Boice, 1996; Brown & Atkins, 1988; Buskist, 2000; Cannon & Newble,

2000; Curzan & Damour, 2000; Cyrs, 1994; Davis, 1993; Flood & Moll, 1990; Johnson, 1995; Lambert, Tice, & Featherstone, 1996; Magnan, 1990; Markie, 1994; McKeachie, 1999; Meagher & Devine, 1993; Royce, 2000; Sawyer, Prichard, & Hostetler, 2001; Weimer, 1993).

YOUR ROLE AS A TEACHER

If you are like many new academics, it was interest in your chosen field of study, not the prospect of teaching it, that led you to pursue a graduate degree and an academic career. In fact, the realization that teaching is a major part of academic life may have dawned on you only slowly over your years of graduate study and may have come into focus only as you were discussing teaching assignments with prospective employers.

What Is the Task?

The teaching task you face as a new professor depends mainly on the level, type, traditions, and orientation of the academic department you have joined. If you are at a major research university, you might be asked to teach only two courses per term, and perhaps only one of these will be at the undergraduate level. If you are especially lucky, you might at first be assigned only one course (perhaps a graduate seminar) so that you can get your bearings, establish your lab or scholarly work, and the like. If you are at a large community college, you are far more likely to be thrown into the deep end of the teaching pool, because you were probably hired primarily, or exclusively, as a teacher. If you are not expected to engage in research or scholarship, your teaching assignment might include two or more sections of two or more courses, for a total of four to six classes per term. Obviously, the heavier your teaching assignment, the more courses you have to prepare, the less experience you have in teaching them, and the less support there is to ease the burden, the more daunting and stressful the teaching task is likely to be. The difficulty of that task is also influenced by the characteristics of the students.

Who Is the Audience?

In the 1960s, the typical college student was a White, middle-class male who was enrolled for full-time study and whose expenses were paid primarily by his parents. He did not hold a job during the academic year, and he entered college with a B average. He expected to perform at an average level, and his main goals probably included developing a meaningful philosophy of life (Astin, Parrott, Korn, & Sax, 1997). The profile of the average college student has changed dramatically since then (Astin, 1990; Astin et al., 1997; Dey, Astin, & Korn, 1991; Erickson & Strommer, 1991; Menges & Weimer, 1996; National Center for Education Statistics, 1999, 2001; Sax, Astin, Korn, & Mahoney, 1998, 1999, 2000).

For one thing, more students than ever are taking courses on a part-time basis, usually because financial need forces them to hold a full- or part-time job. Today's college students also tend to be older than those of the past, and since 1980, females have outnumbered males, currently making up 55 percent of all undergraduates. The percentage of college students representing various ethnic minority groups has increased, and by 2025 minority students will collectively constitute the majority of all college students. There are now more college students with less than adequate academic preparation and more students with special needs stemming from physical or cognitive disabilities. There is also more academic disengagement. Today's college students report more in-class boredom and absenteeism than students did in the 1960s. They say they work hard for teachers they like but are more likely to slack off, and even cheat, in the courses of teachers they do not like. In addition, first-year college students who experienced "grade inflation" in high school tend to be surprised and resentful when the level of effort that once led to As or Bs now earns only Cs or Ds. Finally, today's college students are more likely to seek the goal of being well-off financially than of developing a meaningful philosophy of life.

In short, you will encounter students who represent a wide range of ethnic backgrounds, abilities and disabilities, interests, motivations, and expectations. Some will be diffident and frightened; others will be overconfident and unrealistically optimistic. Whether they are full- or part-time students, many will be trying to fulfill academic obligations while dealing with a job, financial pressures, family responsibilities, relationship problems, and other stressors. Preparing to deal with the diversity of today's students is one dimension of the task you will face as a new college professor. In the remainder of this chapter, we address many others, beginning with what may be your first question: How do I start?

PREPARING YOUR COURSES

Careful planning and preparation of your courses is vital if you are to minimize your teaching anxiety and maximize your teaching effectiveness.

Goal Setting

Establish your course goals in light of your goals as a teacher (see Angelo & Cross, 1993, for a useful list) and what purpose each course is designed to serve. Is it a prerequisite for other courses and, if so, what are they? What courses, if any, are prerequisites for yours? Is your course part of a specialized sequence? In other words, where does your course fit into the departmental curriculum? Knowing what your students are likely to know already will help you to establish a starting point, and the appropriate level, for your lectures and reading assignments. Knowing what your students are to take away from your course will help you decide what to cover and how to cover it. Are they to leave the course with a detailed knowledge of a relatively narrow area, with a general appreciation of the major themes of your discipline, with improved skill at problem-solving, critical thinking, writing, studying, or what? Your lectures and other class activities would probably touch only on the basics of your discipline if you are offering a general survey course but would focus on the more subtle nuances in an upper level course for senior honors students. Answering these goal-related questions will help you to make numerous other decisions as you organize your course. The first of these might be which textbook to choose.

Choosing a Textbook

If you are expected to choose your own textbook, start by examining the ones that have been used by others in your department who taught the course recently. Unless you are pressed for time, check out what faculty at other institutions are using. You can do this by visiting the websites of other departments in your discipline and identifying the books listed in the online syllabi for courses similar to yours. Use e-mail to solicit comments on these books from the instructors. Once you have a short list of possibilities, contact the publishers' sales representatives (all publishers have websites to help you do this; just type in the company name at google.com) and ask for an examination copy of each book, along with any ancillary materials that might be available to accompany it. These ancillaries may include an instructor's resource manual, test item bank, transparencies, PowerPoint presentation slides, student study guide, problem sets, case examples, or supplementary readings.

Use a 5-point scale (from "excellent" through "acceptable" to "unacceptable") to rate each textbook on whatever criteria you see as most important in meeting the goals for your course. We tend to focus on criteria such as readability; interest to students; accuracy of content; coverage of content; scholarship; level of presentation; and quality of the ancillary package. More detailed textbook rating systems are available elsewhere (e.g. Hemmings & Battersby, 1990).

Creating a Syllabus

Your syllabus or course outline is one of the most important documents you will give to your students. A properly constructed syllabus serves not only as a preview and road map of the course, it is also a guide to what your students can expect from you and what you will be expecting of them. At most colleges, a course syllabus is a binding contract that allows penalties to be imposed on students who fail to meet their responsibilities and also allows students to file complaints against professors who do not follow announced grading procedures or who otherwise depart substantially from what they promised to do. Accordingly, consider carefully what you say in your syllabus, say it clearly, and then stick to it. (If you must make changes after the course begins, do not just announce them in class. Distribute a written notification to all students.)

The first step in creating your syllabus is to look at a calendar. Mark, and count, the number of class meetings you will have available for lectures or other teaching activities, not forgetting to subtract standard vacation days such as Thanksgiving or spring break. Note, too, any class meetings that coincide with Kwanza, Yom Kippur, Ramadan, or other religious holidays that may not be official vacation days. Campus rules or common sense may dictate that you not schedule quizzes, exams, or other graded assignments on those days. And do not forget to mark any days on which your own commitments will require a guest lecturer to stand in for you. Marking the calendar gives you an overview of your course and makes it easier to see the optimal placement, and spacing, of quizzes and exams. It will also help you see whether the submission deadlines for term papers or other projects you might be planning to assign will allow you enough time to grade those assignments before the end of the term.

In deciding what to put in your syllabus, err on the side of including too much rather than too little. The more information about the course you provide, the fewer questions you will have to answer in class—or, at least, the easier it will be to refer questioners to their syllabus. At minimum, your syllabus should provide the following information:

1. The name, number, and title of your course (e.g. Biology 101, Introduction to Biology);
2. The days, time, and location of class meetings (e.g. MWF, 10 AM, 101 Chem Annex);

TABLE 5.1
Sample Schedule of Class Sessions

Date	Class lecture and topic	Assigned readings
8/28/02	Introduction	
8/30/02	Subfields and careers in psychology	Chapter 1
9/4/02	NO CLASS (Labor Day Holiday)	
9/6/02	Research methods in psychology	Chapter 2
9/11/02	Research methods in psychology	Chapter 2
9/13/02	Human development	Chapter 12
9/18/02	Human development	Chapter 12
9/20/02	EXAMINATION 1 (Covers Chapters 1, 2, & 12. Bring pencils and your student ID.)	
9/25/02	Return and discuss exam	
9/27/02	Learning	Chapter 6

3. Your name, office address, office phone, and e-mail address. (If you decide to include your home phone number, indicate the hours during which calls are to be made.);

4. The schedule for your office hours;

5. A list of all required and recommended readings and other materials, along with information about whether, and where, any of these materials can be found on reserve in the library;

6. A list of what will occur at each class meeting, along with the readings or other assignments that are to be completed before each meeting (see Table 5.1);

7. A description of *exactly* how student performance will be evaluated and how final grades will be determined; list the number of exams and quizzes, whether they will be essay, multiple-choice, or short-answer, how many items will be included on each, and how much each will count toward the final grade. (We discuss various grading systems below.);

8. A brief summary of the course and your goals in teaching it. Here is an example:

This course offers an introduction to the more applied areas of psychology, including research methods, developmental psychology, learning and memory, thinking and intelligence testing, health psychology, personality, psychological disorders and their treatment, and social psychology. Throughout the course, you will be encouraged to develop your ability to think critically about psychology and about topics outside of psychology. You will get much more out of the lectures and discussions if you read the assigned book chapters before you come to class.

9. A comprehensive list of your course policies, pet peeves, and rules of etiquette. These can include statements such as "All

students in this course will be treated with respect"; "Attendance is important to me"; "Late papers will be assessed a 2-point daily penalty"; "Please enter quietly if you come to class late"; "No eating or drinking in class, please"; "I hope each of you will visit me at least once during my office hours"; and the like. In short, spell out everything you do and do not want to happen in class, and the consequences of rule violations. Some of these policies will be unfamiliar to your students, so do not leave them guessing or finding out about them the hard way.

Your syllabus helps to establish the way your students perceive you as a teacher (Erikson & Strommer, 1991), so it should convey a firm but friendly tone. It should also show that you care about your teaching—an attribute consistently associated with good teacher evaluations at the end of the term. So construct your syllabus with care, ask for advice on it from experienced colleagues, and before you distribute it, be sure to eliminate misspellings or other errors that might inadvertently convey a lackadaisical attitude.

Evaluating Student Performance

You will quickly discover that most students are at least as interested in how their performance will be evaluated—and how grades will be determined—as they are in what the course has to offer them. We discuss grading systems in the next section; in this section we present some alternatives for evaluating student performance and some ideas for evaluation procedures that can enhance learning. Try to match your evaluation tools to your goals for the course. If one of your goals is to promote critical thinking, for example, assigning "thought papers," analytical essay exams, or comprehension-oriented multiple-choice tests would be better than giving tests focused on defining key terms. On the other hand, if teaching definitions or vocabulary is a major goal, key-term tests might be ideal.

Tests and Quizzes

The most commonly used option for evaluating student performance is, of course, the written test, and its briefer cousin, the written quiz. These can be constructed in essay, short-answer, or multiple-choice format.

Essay and short-answer tests can be constructed relatively quickly, they provide an assessment of students' writing ability, and they can set tasks that require high-level analysis of course material (Jacobs & Chase, 1992). Essay tests can be scored using analytical or global quality methods (Ory

& Ryan, 1993). The analytical method is usually easier to defend when students raise challenges. It requires you to write an "ideal answer" containing specified elements with predetermined point values. You then compare each student's essay to the ideal answer and award points according to which, and how many, specified elements are present. The grade assigned to the test as a whole is based on the total number of points earned (Ory & Ryan, 1993). In the global quality scoring scheme, you assign a score to each student based on either the total quality of the response relative to other student responses or in relation to your own general criteria (Ory & Ryan, 1993).

The main disadvantage of essay and short-answer tests is that they require an enormous amount of instructor time if they are to be read carefully and graded systematically. Before deciding on the essay or short-answer format, therefore, estimate how much time it will take to grade each question, increase that estimate to be on the safe side, and multiply the result by the number of students in your class. Then multiply that figure by the number of tests to be given during the course, and decide whether the resulting time commitment is realistic in light of your other academic responsibilities.

If the time required for grading essay or short-answer tests is likely to be unmanageable, consider using a multiple-choice format for some or all student performance evaluations. Multiple-choice tests have the advantage of being quickly scored by an optical scanner, and, with the proper computer networking facilities, the results can be electronically downloaded into an instructor's computer-based grading roster. Among the disadvantages of multiple-choice tests are that they take a long time to write and an even longer time to write well (Jacobs & Chase, 1992; Ory & Ryan, 1993). In addition, no matter how careful you are, some items may be misunderstood, interpreted in unexpected ways, or vulnerable to double meanings, all of which can confuse students and lead them to make inquiries during the test and raise challenges afterward.

Regardless of the format you choose, we suggest that you analyze your tests and quizzes using a table of specifications (Jacobs & Chase, 1992; Ory & Ryan, 1993). Each row of this table should represent one concept, phenomenon, principle, theory, or other content element to be tested. Each column should represent a cognitive skill to be demonstrated, such as defining terms, comparing concepts, applying principles, analyzing information, and the like. Each of the table's cells thus represents the intersection of a particular bit of course content and the level of skill being tested (see Table 5.2 for an example). You can use this table to plan the content and level of the items you are about to write or choose from a test-item bank. If you have already written or chosen a set of items, enter a digit representing each item into the cell that best represents its content and level. Looking

TABLE 5.2
A Sample Table of Specifications

Content	Cognitive skills		
	Knowledge	Comprehension	Application
Classical conditioning	1	1	2
Shaping			1
Reinforcement	1	1	
Observational learning		1	
Latent learning			1
Cognitive processes	1		

Note. This small table of specifications was created to plan a 10-item quiz on learning principles in an introductory psychology course. Tests and quizzes need not assess every possible concept at every possible cognitive level. Notice that, here, three items test basic knowledge (definitions), three more test deeper understanding, and four test students' ability to apply what they know about the concepts tested. Jacobs and Chase (1992) offer ideas on creating such tables for courses in any discipline using Benjamin Bloom's taxonomy of cognitive skills: knowledge, comprehension, application, analysis, synthesis, and evaluation (Bloom et al., 1956).

at the resulting pattern of entries will tell you how well the test or quiz covers the lectures and assigned readings, and at what level.

We also recommend that you consult references on item-writing (e.g. Jacobs & Chase, 1992; Ory & Ryan, 1993) before drafting your items. And before duplicating any test or quiz for distribution, have it reviewed for typographical errors, double-meanings, and other problems by an experienced colleague and also by a trusted friend or family member who can read it from the perspective of a student.

Writing Assignments

Making writing assignments will help your students to improve their writing and will help you to better evaluate their knowledge of course material. In small classes, these might include a 10-page term paper, whereas larger enrollments might only permit one-page assignments that can be graded relatively quickly using the analytical approach mentioned earlier. You might assign several of these mini-papers to cover a broad spectrum of course material. As an alternative to mini-papers, consider asking students to keep course-related journals, to write letters to friends or relatives in which they explain course material, or to summarize what they find during a course-related search of the World Wide Web (Davis, 1993; Erickson & Strommer, 1991).

In other words, in making writing assignments, think beyond the usual term paper. The results are likely to be more interesting and challenging for your students and less burdensome for you. Other references contain more specific ideas for such assignments and how to grade them (Davis, 1993).

Applying the Psychology of Learning to Student Evaluation

In the persona of Father Guido Sarducci, comedian Don Novello touted the advantages of the "Five Minute University," in which students could spend five minutes learning all the information they would have remembered five years after completing a standard college degree. This hilarious notion is based on the not-so-funny fact that, no matter how you evaluate your students, the results all too often reflect their ability to store information until it is no longer needed to earn a good grade. The fact that most students forget most of what they hear or read in a course within a few weeks or months (e.g. Rickard, Rogers, Ellis, & Beidleman, 1988) is consistent with the results of laboratory research on human learning and memory in general (Anderson, 2000). In short, students' *performance* on course evaluations does not necessarily reflect long-term *retention*, which is what most teachers think of as *learning*. There is probably no way to prevent this forgetting process, but research in cognitive psychology suggests that certain evaluation procedures might help students to retain course information longer (e.g., Bjork, 1979, 1999).

First, long-term retention is improved when students engage in numerous study sessions (distributed practice) rather than when they "cram" during a single session on the night before a quiz or exam (massed practice). Consider giving enough exams and quizzes so that students will be reading and studying more or less continuously. You can also promote distributed practice by including a few unannounced, or pop, quizzes, or by allowing students to earn a point at each class session by answering a single "quick-quiz" question based on the reading assigned for that session.

Second, students assume that if a term or concept or phenomenon looks or sounds familiar as they study for a test, they will be able to retrieve information about it on the test. This is not necessarily the case. To help students correct this mistaken idea before it is too late, consider giving one or two noncredit quizzes to help them more realistically assess the state of their knowledge as they study. This is easy to do if your course has a website on which practice quizzes can be posted. You can accomplish the same goal by giving more quizzes than you plan to include in final grade calculations and allow students to drop their lowest quiz scores.

Third, long-term retention can be improved by creating "desirable difficulties" (Bjork, 1999). For example, learning is aided by opportunities to repeatedly retrieve, restore, and again retrieve the same information, especially when the student is asked to do so randomly, not in the same order in which material was originally presented (e.g., Bjork, 1999). Consider giving "cumulative" exams and quizzes that require students to retrieve information about past as well as current course material, and present the items in random order.

Setting Up a Grading System

Students want letter grades and, at all but a few colleges, teachers are required to give them. Assigning grades in a satisfactory way takes some doing, and, as always, some planning (Ory & Ryan, 1993; Walvoord & Anderson, 1998). There is no "best" grading system, but in this section we describe a few golden rules for assigning grades (Davis, 1993; Ory & Ryan, 1993).

First, grading must be *accurate*, meaning that course grades must reflect each student's level of competency. Accuracy is best achieved through the development of thoughtful assignments and relevant grading criteria.

Second, grading must be *fair*, and just as important, it must be *perceived* as fair by students. Set up a system under which students can be confident that those who turn in equivalent performances will receive equivalent grades. Your system should make it clear that students whose total scores, or percentage of available points, fall within certain ranges will receive certain grades.

Third, grades must be dispensed *consistently*, meaning that the grading system described at the beginning of the term is not subject to unannounced, unpredictable, or repeated changes. Your syllabus should list each and every category in which points can be earned (tests, quizzes, papers, class projects, class participation, extra credit options, and the like), and how many points can be earned in each category. Assign points only on the basis of these categories, and do not make special deals with individual students. Do not base grades on how much you like particular students, how hard they are trying, or other factors that cannot be quantified and announced in advance. Similarly, do not base grades on students' improvement during the course; doing so can create a disadvantageous ceiling effect for those who do well to begin with. Avoid basing final grades on just two or three assignments. The more graded components you can include—within the limits dictated by class time and grading time—the more representative of student performance those grades are likely to be (Ory & Ryan, 1993).

Following these golden rules will make it easier to follow a final one: namely that grades must be *defensible*. Your grading system should allow you to explain and justify—to students or anyone else who has a right to ask—how and why each student's grade was determined. If you heed these basic rules, you will find teaching less stressful, not only because your students will know what to expect and thus will be less likely to argue about grades, but also because you will be far less vulnerable to charges of capricious grading.

The first step in setting up your grading system is to decide whether to use a norm-referenced system (also referred to as "grading on a curve"), a criterion-referenced system (also called "absolute" or "standards of excellence" grading), or some combination of the two. Norm-referenced grades can be assigned using a planned distribution (e.g., students who place in the top 10% of points earned get As; the next 20% get Bs, the next 40% get Cs, the next 20% get Ds, and the bottom 10% get Fs). Notice that, in this system, all possible grades will be assigned, but the actual number of points associated with each grade will vary from class to class, depending on how well the best students do. Criterion-referenced grades are assigned individually, regardless of the performance of any other student or the class as a whole. The simplest form of criterion-referenced grading gives an A to anyone who earns, say, 90% of the points available in the course or on a particular assignment, a B to those earning, say, 80 to 89%, and so on.

The advantages of criterion-referenced grading are that (a) students are evaluated on an absolute scale determined by the instructor's definition of what constitutes mastery of course material; (b) final grades indicate the degree to which students achieved that mastery; and (c) because students are not competing against each other, they tend to be more cooperative with each other (Ory & Ryan, 1993). Potential disadvantages of criterion-referenced grading include the fact that it can be difficult to determine what criteria are valid in a given course, especially when it is taught for the first time. For example, is it reasonable to expect students to achieve at the 90% level, given the difficulty of the material? If no one reaches that level, will you be comfortable assigning no As? Answering these questions is easier after you have taught the same course more than once, which is why criterion-referenced grading might not be the best system for new teachers (Ory & Ryan, 1993).

Norm-referenced grading has the advantage of rewarding students whose academic performance is outstanding relative to the class (Ory & Ryan, 1993). It can also prevent grade distortions when, for example, even the best students perform poorly because a test or other assignment was flawed in some way. In such cases, the best of the poor performances would still earn As; under a criterion-based system, everyone might receive an F. Norm-referenced grading can, however, lead to some unfortunate consequences, especially when there is little variability in the performance of a given class. Under such a system, even if all your students earned at least, say, 80% of the points available, some of them would still receive Cs, Ds, and Fs. And even if none of your students scored above 50% on any graded assignment, some of them would still get As, Bs, and Cs. In these (thankfully rare) cases, anyone unfamiliar with the characteristics of the class in question could easily be misled about the meaning of norm-referenced grades (Ory & Ryan, 1993).

To exploit the strengths of both norm-referenced and criterion-referenced systems, consider a hybrid approach. For example, you might try a less restrictive norm-referenced system, which compares each student in a particular class to the performance of the best students in that class. Thus,

EXHIBIT 5.1
A Hybrid Grading System

Your grade will be based on the total of your scores on four examinations, plus any extra-credit points you earn. If a standard grading system were used for this course, you would have to correctly answer 90% of the 280 exam items (or 252 points) to get an A, 80% (or 224 points) to get a B, and so on. However, the grade cutoffs will be a bit less demanding than that. Instead of comparing your total score to a perfect score of 280, we will compare it only to the average of the top 10% of the students in this class. So grades for the course will assigned as follows:

A = at least 95% of the average of the top 10%;
B = at least 85% of the average of the top 10%;
C = at least 75% of the average of the top 10%;
D = at least 65% of the average of the top 10%;
F = less than 65% of the average of the top 10%.

For example, if the average score of the top 10% of students turns out to be 260 points, you would need 247 points for an A, 221 points for a B, and so on. This system makes it a little easier to get a good grade. The only problem is that you will not know what the exact grade cutoffs are until the end of the semester, when the average score earned by students in the top 10% of the class can be calculated. To help you get a rough estimate of how you are doing, I will announce the average score of the top 10% of students on each exam. By October 27, 2002, which is the last day on which you can drop a course without penalty, you will have had two examinations and should have a reasonably good idea of your standing in the course.

Note. This section from a course syllabus explains the hybrid grading system that we have found useful in an introductory course over the past 20 years.

you could assign an A to anyone who earns at least 90% of the points earned by the top five students; those earning 80% of those points would get a B, and so on. Under such a system, there is no predetermined grade distribution. It is theoretically possible for every student to earn an A, assuming they all do very well in the course. Our own favorite hybrid system was described by Barbara Davis (1993) and developed by Frank Costin for a large, multisection introductory course. In this system, you first compute the mean (average) score of the top 10% of all students—on anything from a quiz to an end-of-course point total. You then use this mean as a benchmark for establishing letter grades. For example, to earn an A, students would have to earn at least 95% of the benchmark; earning a B would require 85% of the benchmark; a C would require 75% of the benchmark, and so on (see Exhibit 5.1). Notice that this hybrid incorporates many of the advantages of both norm-referenced and criterion-referenced grading systems. It allows all students to earn an A if they do well enough; it does not penalize students for poorly designed evaluation instruments; and, because most courses enroll at least a few outstanding students, it typically requires a high absolute level of achievement, not just a high relative standing within the classroom, to earn a high grade. Though this grading system is unfamiliar to many students, we have found that they like it better than either strictly criterion-referenced or strictly norm-referenced systems.

Establishing Student Communication Channels

Publicizing your grading system is just one way of establishing the clear communication with you that students will find valuable and reassuring. You should also allow students to ask questions and raise issues before, during, and after class—and outside of class, too. The traditional format for out-of-class communication is the office visit.

Office Hours

Many instructors follow a rule of thumb that says that they should be available for in-person meetings with students for at least two hours per week per course. This is a reasonable plan, and here are some tips for implementing it:

1. Set up your office hours so they do not match the likely scheduling of your students' other classes. Office hours at 9 a.m. on Monday, Wednesday, and Friday, or Tuesday and Thursday, will make visits impossible for students who have a class at those times. Be aware, too, that office hours in early morning or late afternoon (especially on Friday) will probably not attract many visitors. Indeed, no matter when you schedule them, office hours may not be busy times (except just before and after tests) unless you promote them a bit.
2. Encourage students to visit you in your office. Remind them that they do not have to have a problem to meet with you, and that, unlike in high school, talking to an instructor is not "brown-nosing." Give them an agenda, suggesting, perhaps, that office hours would be a good time to discuss questions they have about lectures, prospects for careers in your field, and the like. If your class is small enough, give a writing assignment early in the course and require students to meet with you to discuss topics. Invite students who performed below average on the first graded assignment to stop by to discuss ways of improving.
3. Be in your office during office hours. If you must be gone for a few minutes, leave a note on your door telling a visitor when you expect to be back. Failure to appear at scheduled office hours is often mentioned among students' pet peeves about faculty, and can lead to negative teaching evaluations.

4. Leave your office door at least partly open during student conferences unless the student requests that you close it before discussing a private matter.

E-Mail

Electronic office hours are becoming increasingly popular supplements to face-to-face office meetings. Using e-mail, students can contact you at their convenience from wherever they have access to the Internet. Using the same access, you can offer virtual consultation from wherever you are. E-mail also gives you the luxury of responding at your convenience, and after you have had time to formulate thoughtful replies. Students like knowing that you are available online, and they are more likely to ask a quick question about a homework problem or a writing assignment than if they had to wait for a scheduled office hour. In addition, some of your more reticent students will feel freer to ask questions and to present ideas via e-mail in a way they would not have done in class or during an office visit (McKeage, 2001).

E-mail is not a panacea, however. When students are experiencing an academic problem, or if they need information about where to turn for a personal problem, they may want to talk to you in person. Also, because e-mail does not allow students and teachers to see or hear each other, e-mail communication can result in misunderstandings. Finally, the apparent remoteness of e-mail sometimes leads people to make ill-advised comments that would not have occurred in person. So although students are receptive to virtual office hours (McKeage, 2001), a mixture of electronic and face-to-face communication is probably ideal.

The fact that most students check their e-mail several times a day (P. Askew, personal communication, Jan. 23, 1998) makes it feasible to set up a class mailgroup through which you can communicate with all your students at once and through which your students can communicate with each other. An active mailgroup offers a good way to remind students of upcoming deadlines (these should also be listed in the syllabus and repeated in class, as well!), answer a question that came up after a class, or steer students to websites or other sources of information you have recently discovered. One instructor we know e-mails "virtual lectures" to her students following class sessions at which she ran out of time to present important material.

THE FIRST DAY OF CLASS

The anxiety that you may feel on the first day of class stems partly from the fact that you are meeting a group of strangers. Once you and your

Save e-mails for as long as students can appeal grades

students get to know one another and begin to form a working relationship, class sessions typically become much less stressful and a lot more enjoyable and productive. There are some things you can do both before and during the first class meeting to hasten this process.

Exploring Your Classroom

At least a week before the new term begins, visit each classroom in which you will be teaching and familiarize yourself with its layout and systems. If the room is normally locked, be sure you have a key. Locate the switches for lighting, projection screens, temperature, and other aspects of the classroom environment that you will need to control during class. Does everything work properly? Is there a podium or table for your notes and other teaching materials and equipment? If not, contact the appropriate campus office to report malfunctions or request items you will need.

If the room is equipped with an overhead projector, slide projector, audio- or videocassette player, or computer-based teaching station, be sure you know how these items operate, where spare projector bulbs are located, and how to replace bulbs if they burn out during class. If you are not sure about any of these things, contact the campus office that services instructional equipment. That office can probably also provide information on how to get keys or combinations for any equipment that is in locked storage in your classroom. If you will be bringing your own projector, laptop computer, or other equipment, locate electrical outlets for plugging it in and any connections you will need to gain access to a campus computer network. If you will need to use window shades to darken the room during audiovisual presentations, be sure they work properly; if they do not, ask the appropriate campus office to correct the problem before classes begin.

If you plan to use a chalkboard, dry-erase board, or flip chart, confirm that there is chalk or felt-tipped pens, and just in case, plan to bring your own supply. Finally, be sure that there is enough seating in the room to accommodate the number of students enrolled in your class.

Establishing Yourself as a Teacher

The first day of class will be your first opportunity to shape students' perceptions of you as a teacher, to establish your rules for the course, and to illustrate the kind of classroom environment you want to create. Even if you simply distribute your syllabus, go over the grading system, make a reading assignment, and let the students leave early, you will be sending a message about yourself, your course, and your approach to teaching. In this example, students could easily get the message that class time is not particularly valuable, that you may not care much about teaching (or them), that they can expect you to do most of the talking, and that they should sit passively and listen. Once such perceptions and expectations have coalesced over the first three weeks of class, they are unlikely to change much (Emmer, Everston, & Anderson, 1979). Following are some tips for establishing a more desirable set of student expectations on the first day. Arrive early, with all of the materials that you will need, including sample copies of the reading materials you will be assigning. Be prepared to tell students where they can get these materials and whether they are on reserve in the library (Davis, 1993). Put your name and the name and number of your course on the chalkboard, overhead projector, or computer screen. While waiting for class to begin, greet and make small talk with students as they enter the room. These simple things suggest that you care enough about your teaching to show up on time, fully prepared.

When class begins, introduce yourself, and perhaps say a few words about your background, your academic and scholarly activities, maybe even your hobbies and other outside interests. This information helps to establish you as a person as well as a teacher. You might also let your students know how to address you—as Dr., Mr., Miss, Mrs., Ms., Professor, Doug, Sandy, or whatever.

Next, distribute your syllabus and go over its most important elements, including the number and types of graded assignments and how final grades will be determined. Once you have covered the course basics, *be sure to ask for questions*. Do so by saying something like "OK, what questions do you have for me?" rather than "Any questions?" The former conveys more interest in being helpful than the latter. After you invite questions, scan the classroom. This, too, demonstrates that you really want students to respond. Be sure to wait long enough for students to work up the nerve to raise their hands (believe it or not, some students will be as nervous in addressing you as you are in addressing them!). If no questions are raised, have a few in mind to get the ball rolling. You could say, for example, "You might be wondering if the exams are cumulative (or whether attendance is mandatory, or what to do if you have to leave class early, or how to choose a paper topic, or where the lab is)." Then give the answers in a friendly way. In short, if you want your students to feel free to ask questions throughout the course, offer them genuine opportunities to do so on the first day, and then reward them when they respond.

After discussing the course, you might want to get some information about your students. The simplest way to do this is to distribute index cards on which students can list their name, academic major, e-mail address, courses they have taken in your discipline, and topics they are especially interested in studying in your class. Reading these cards can give you a better idea of who your students are, how well they are prepared, and the range of their interests. Spending a few minutes during the second class session discussing some of the interests expressed (or some of the inevitable funny responses) is another way to show your commitment to teaching and your interest in students. In relatively small classes, you might ask students to tape a picture of themselves to the back of these cards, so you can more easily learn their names.

Finally, if you want to encourage your students to participate actively in your course, plan something for the first day that requires them to do so. Many of the activities listed later, for example, can supplement, or substitute for, the index card method for gathering information about students.

In a small class, ask students to say a few words about themselves and their interests, perhaps including something about themselves that is unique or about why they are glad to be in class. In larger classes, ask students to form groups of four in which they can introduce themselves and their interests, and possibly exchange contact information that could help establish study groups.

To stimulate syllabus-related questions, ask the class to form groups of four or five and give each group an index card on which they are to list their questions about the course and its requirements (Erickson & Strommer, 1991). After a few minutes, collect the cards and answer the questions.

To assess what students are interested in learning, simply ask them to call out their high-interest topics. Write each one on the board or an overhead transparency and say a few words about whether, and when, the topics will be covered in the course (McKeachie, 1986).

To provide a preview of the challenges you will be posing in your class, present a case study, problem, or controversy and ask the students to analyze, solve, or discuss it (Erickson & Strommer, 1991).

If you have a few minutes left at the end of the first class, ask your students to jot down and turn in their reactions. This little exercise not only shows that you care what your students think, it also provides you with immediate feedback on how the first day went (McKeachie, 1986).

DEVELOPING YOUR TEACHING STYLE

Just as no two personalities are exactly alike, no two teachers have exactly the same teaching style. In developing yours, you might at first find yourself imitating some of your favorite teachers. That strategy might help to some extent, but in the long run it is best to simply be yourself. If you have a humorous streak, let it show while you are teaching, but if you do not normally tell jokes or make puns, do not try out a comedy act in class. If you are enthusiastic about life and your discipline, do not suppress your feelings, but if you tend to be low-key, do not try to create false energy. Students like teachers who display almost any style, as long as it is authentic and as long as the teacher cares about teaching. They tend to dislike even the flashiest or most scholarly style if it is perceived as mere posturing.

Being genuine is a good first step in developing your teaching style, but you will also need other skills to do a good job in the classroom. These skills include giving lectures, asking and answering questions, generating class discussion, and conducting classroom demonstrations and activities.

Effective Lecturing

Lectures are not the only way to teach, but they are the heart of most courses. Becoming a good lecturer takes some work, and though we have no guaranteed prescription for achieving this goal, there are a few guidelines for preparing and delivering useful lectures (Diamond, Sharp, & Ory, 1983; Office of Instructional Resources, 1999).

First, decide what content you want to cover in a particular lecture and then prepare more material than you will need. Overpreparation will ensure that you have plenty to talk about if nervousness causes you to proceed too quickly or if something is not working and you decide to skip ahead. Although you should *prepare* a lot of material, do not try to *cover* too much of it in any single class (Zakrajsek, 1998). Remember that students learn—and are responsible for learning—by reading, by talking to teachers and fellow students, and by doing lab work, class projects, papers, and other activities, not just by listening to lectures. So do not rush your lectures to cover "everything" in detail. If you do, you will be exhausted, and your students will be overwhelmed. There is evidence that most students can only comprehend three to five major points in a one-hour lecture, and four to five major points in a 90-minute lecture (Lowman, 1995). The best lecturers tend to concentrate on those few important points (Tozer, 1992) and to present them in several ways to ensure that everyone understands.

Second, as you prepare your notes, keep in mind that students' attention is usually highest during the first 10 minutes, and then tends to wane (McKeachie, 1999). Think of the class period in four to five segments of 10 to 15 minutes each, then try to plan something in each segment that is likely to recapture attention. At the beginning of each lecture, and at various points along the way, introduce topics or subtopics in a way that will catch the listener's interest, perhaps by posing a problem, a dilemma, a mystery, or question, or by assigning a class activity. Students also find it easier to pay attention when they can see how each topic fits into a big picture, so put a brief overview of the lecture's content on the board, an overhead transparency, or in a handout. Audiovisual stimuli help hold attention, too. If you are describing a historical event, an economic principle, or the symptoms of schizophrenia, for example, do not depend on your words alone to keep students riveted. Add a compelling photo of the event, a practical example of the principle, or a video of a patient. Also, do not risk losing students' interest simply because you mention unfamiliar terms without defining them and showing how they are spelled. Remember to sprinkle your lecture notes with examples of, or analogies to, the concept or phenomenon or principle that you are describing. These do more than attract attention; many students have told us that it was our examples or analogies (not necessarily our brilliant presentations) that helped them to understand and remember important material. If possible, use examples and analogies that are vivid, offbeat, or funny, and certainly ones that relate to your students' life experiences (Office of Instructional Resources, 1999; Tozer 1992; Zakrajsek, 1998). You can also retain attention by showing how each new topic is related to those already covered or to those that will be covered later. Using linking transitions helps students to perceive your lecture as a coherent whole, not a laundry list of unrelated topics.

Third, as you lecture, be sure that all your students can hear you. In larger classes, or if you have a soft voice, you may need a microphone. Be sure students can see you, too. Do not sit or stand where you will be invisible from certain seats. Moving around the room a bit as you lecture can help you to hold attention and to make eye contact with everyone—though many students find frantic pacing to be distracting.

It is ideal to present each lecture as a fascinating, spontaneous story, without depending heavily on notes or appearing to give a canned speech. Reaching this level of comfort and smoothness takes time and practice, however, and some people are just better at it than others. To help reach your own full potential, present some or all of your lectures to a video camera, a tape recorder, a friend or family member, or even a pet! You will be amazed at how much easier it is to give a lecture in class when it is not the first time you tried it.

In the classroom, keep checking on your students' reactions. Do they appear to understand you or are they confused? Are they "with you" or are they thinking of other things? Students' facial expressions and posture will tell you a lot about their level of interest and involvement, but you can also ask them for more explicit feedback. Rather than posing the perfunctory "Are there any questions?" question, show your students you care how the lecture is going by asking if the information is making sense, if it is hanging together, if you are going too fast or too slow, and the like. Or ask a specific question about something you have just presented to assess how clearly you presented it. Remember that even the best teachers have some students who become bored, fall asleep, or leave class early, so do not be too hard on yourself when these things happen.

Finally, bring each lecture to an organized close by summarizing its key points or asking the students to do so. Do not hesitate to generate some curiosity about your next lecture by offering a "tease" about something it will contain.

Answering and Asking Questions

If your lecturing style lets students know that you truly want them to understand the course material, they will inevitably ask questions. The way you handle these questions can solidify or undermine your relationship with the class. First, listen carefully to each question—without interrupting—to be sure you understand it. Second, reward students for asking questions by looking at them in a friendly way as they speak, and perhaps tell them that this is a good question. Third, if you can answer the question, do so. If not, do not be afraid to say that you are not sure of the answer. Above all, do not demean the questioner or make up an answer. Instead, promise to provide an answer at the next class or via e-mail to the group. Then keep your promise! Students do not actually expect you to know everything about your discipline, and they will appreciate your openness and willingness to find answers for them. (You can also encourage the class to do their own research on particularly interesting questions, but do not make it mandatory or students will perceive the assignment as punishment for asking questions.)

Some new teachers hesitate to ask questions of their students in class for fear that no one will respond. You can minimize this problem by making sure that your question is stated clearly and then waiting long enough for students to come up with the answer and work up the nerve to raise their hands. Unfortunately, most teachers tend to wait only one to three seconds after asking a question before answering it themselves. If your wait time is that brief, your students will not only find it hard to answer your questions, but may get the message that you do not really want them to try. In one study, teachers trained to increase their wait time to three to five seconds found that more students answered questions, and they gave longer answers (Tobin, 1987). If you give your students just a few extra seconds to think, you will probably find them more responsive to your questions.

Promoting Class Discussion

Like other classroom skills, learning how to generate discussion of course material takes some practice. A few guidelines follow (for more details, see Brookfield & Preskill, 1999; Davis, 1993).

First, if discussions of particular topics are planned for certain class sessions, tell your students what reading or other preparation is required. Some teachers not only assign prediscussion reading but also hand out a list of questions on which discussion will focus. Others ask students to complete a "one-minute paper" about the discussion topic immediately beforehand to ensure that the students have given it at least a minimal amount of thought.

Second, let your students know if there are to be discussion rules—such as raising hands before speaking. If highly charged topics are to be discussed, you will also want to explain that there is no place in class for racist, sexist, homophobic, or other *ad hominem* remarks. These rules make it less likely that your class discussions will degenerate into chaos or a hostile exchange.

Third, begin each discussion with a clear focus. For example, you might start by asking students to comment on or analyze a reading assignment, a newspaper story, a controversial idea, or a case study. You could also pose a specific question, or ask students to react to a videotaped or role-played situation (Davis, 1993). As students begin to speak, encourage their participation by nodding your head, making eye contact with the speakers, and, if others do not join in, by asking the class to react to what has been said. As the discussion develops, do not feel obligated to respond to every comment—or at least leave plenty of wait time before doing so. If you do not dominate the situation, your students will eventually begin to respond to each other. If you fill brief silences with a mini-lecture, discussion will probably dry up (Brookfield & Preskill, 1999).

Fourth, remember that some discussions start more easily in small groups (Erickson & Strommer, 1991). You can divide larger classes into groups of three to six, have them discuss a topic for a while, and then ask a representative from each group to report on the results and invite reactions from other groups.

Fifth, terminate the discussion a few minutes before the end of the class period so that you will have time to clear up any misconceptions or misinformation that might have been created, to summarize the most important points raised, and to suggest additional reading or web-based research that will help students follow up on what they have learned.

Classroom Activities and Demonstrations

Classroom discussions are just one way to promote *active learning*, the process in which students do something other than passively watching and listening as classroom events unfold. A wide variety of other active learning methods are available as well (Bonwell & Eison, 1991; Silberman, 1996). Here are just two of them.

Group Work

In an active learning method called "jigsaw" (Aronson, 1978; Smith, 2000), a class is divided into groups, and each member is given (or is responsible for getting) one component of the information the group will need to perform a task or solve a problem. For a group to succeed, each member must spend some time as an expert who tells the others what he or she knows or has discovered. In a jigsaw activity, every member of the group—even those who would normally remain passive in class—has an important and active role to play if the group is to succeed.

Demonstrations

Telling students about course material is important, but it can be more memorable when you offer a demonstration that allows them to experience it for themselves. To take just one example, after lecturing about the existence of a blind spot where the optic nerve exits the human eye, a teacher could move on to the next topic or, instead, take a minute to allow each student to find his or her own blind spot. The instructor's manuals that accompany textbooks in many disciplines are filled with ideas for such active learning demonstrations, and they can also be found in journals devoted to the teaching of particular disciplines and on a vast number of discipline-specific teaching-oriented websites. Discipline-neutral journals such as *College Teaching, The Teaching Professor*, and *The National Teaching & Learning Forum* also provide tips for active learning demonstrations. Finally, do not forget to ask your more experienced colleagues to tell you about active learning demonstrations that they have found useful. We urge you to use all of these sources to create a set of demonstrations that can spice up and reinforce the content of virtually every lecture. Before trying them in class, however, always rehearse them with friends or colleagues. Procedures that seem simple on paper can be complex and tricky in practice.

Teaching Style and Class Size

The teaching style you develop will serve you well in any classroom, but you may have to make some adjustments for certain classes. The conversational tone and the small-font transparencies that worked well with 12 senior students seated around a seminar table may not hold the attention of 300 introductory students listening to you speak from the stage of an auditorium. In that auditorium, you will probably need a podium, a laser pointer, a microphone, large diameter chalk, and large-font overheads or PowerPoint slides. You may also have to make changes in how you structure your class, including how much time you spend lecturing versus conducting classroom demonstrations and activities. It is not impossible to set up group work in a class of 300, but it is more challenging. Using the "think-pair-share" technique, for example, you can pause after each 15-minute lecture segment and use the overhead or computer display to pose a lecture-related problem or multiple-choice question. Ask the students to choose the answer they think is correct and then to compare their answer—and the reasoning behind it—with the person next to them. This consultation process will help more students understand why the correct answer is correct when you reveal it. It is also likely to help students in a large lecture hall remain more attentive.

If you will be teaching large classes, we suggest that you do further reading on ways to adjust your teaching style to accommodate them (e.g. Davis, 1993; MacGregor, 2000).

FACULTY–STUDENT RELATIONSHIPS

Most students will enter your courses with positive expectations about you and with high hopes of enjoying themselves and doing well. These expectations provide the foundation for a good learning experience and a good teaching experience. The suggestions we have made so far should help you build on that foundation by offering a well-organized course in a consistent, planful, and caring manner. Let us now consider some additional suggestions for establishing productive and mutually respectful student–faculty relations.

The Ethical Use of Teacher Power

Even if you have never taught before, your students will (correctly) perceive you as having power and authority, if for no other reason than that you will be assigning grades. Unless you tell them otherwise, they will probably address you as "Professor," or "Doctor," and they will look to you to establish the rules and the interactional style for the course. The power differential that pervades all aspects of your relationship with students is valuable. It allows you to conduct your class according to your plan. Students do not want you to abdicate your authority, but it is important that you do not abuse your power (Keith-Spiegel, Wittig, Perkins, Balogh, & Whitley, 1993).

For example, it should go without saying that you should not date your students. Even when initiated with the best of intentions on both sides, such relationships contain inherently coercive elements that can be harmful to students. You must also be careful not to inadvertently impose your political, moral, or religious beliefs on students. It is all too easy to err in this regard, because the views you express in a lecture or discussion will carry the weight of authority, and if you push those views too hard, students may feel coerced to accept them or even adopt them—on papers and exams, at least. Remember, too, that casual remarks that appear to condone excessive drinking, illegal drug use, or the like can legitimize these activities in students' minds, even though you might have meant them as a joke or to show that you are "hip."

Think carefully about the messages you send to your students through other means, as well. You are probably not sexist, but you might give the wrong impression if your syllabus contains only male or only female pronouns. Sexism can be inadvertently communicated through your classroom behavior, too. Research on (male and female) college teachers' questioning style suggests that many of them more often call on males than females and that they tend to spend more time helping males discern correct answers (Hall & Sandler, 1982; Sadker & Sadker, 1994). Ideas for avoiding these biased questioning patterns are available (Sandler & Hoffman, 1992).

In short, we recommend that you do all you can to make all your students feel themselves to be accepted and included as individuals. This means, for example, not asking a minority group student to tell the class how people in that group "feel" about the topic under discussion. Use classroom examples that are diverse enough to let your students know that you do not presume they are all Americans, heterosexuals, Christians, males, Whites, Blacks, females, or representatives of any other particular group. Scan the entire classroom as you lecture or lead discussions so that you can see all students who raise a hand or show a quizzical expression. Take care to avoid even well-intentioned remarks or jokes that are likely to be offensive to any subgroup of students. For example, current laws bar same-sex marriage, so suggesting that all your students will someday marry would not include those who are gay and lesbian. If you plan small group discussions in class, *assign* students to groups rather than letting them self-select in a way that might be too homogeneous or that excludes certain individuals based on gender, ethnicity, disability, or whatever. On quiz and exam questions, use ethnically diverse names for hypothetical people and make sure that the examples and terms used will be familiar to all your students. To take a blatant example, certain international students and those who are not Jewish might be clueless about an item that involves a Seder.

Dealing With Student Requests, Complaints, and Problems

Inevitably, some of your students will come to you with requests, excuses, and problems. How well you are prepared for them and how you handle them is another aspect of your teaching style.

Excuses

Some students will offer excuses for their failure to show up for a class, a quiz, or an exam or to turn in a term paper or other assignment. When this happens, take a firm, rational, but caring approach by accepting the

EXHIBIT 5.2
Dealing With Student Excuses

APPLICATION FOR A PSYCHOLOGY 2012 CONFLICT EXAMINATION
FALL SEMESTER, 2002
Dr. Douglas A. Bernstein

After completing the information requested below and obtaining the necessary signature, please give or fax (XXX-XXXX) this form to your instructor by the deadline listed below. Once we have verified the accuracy of the information you have provided and confirmed that your reason for requesting a conflict exam is acceptable, an alternate exam date, time, and place will be arranged. All conflict exams will take place after the regular exam.

Important note: Unless you are requesting a conflict exam because of a last-minute illness or emergency, this form must be turned in at least 14 days before the date of the regularly scheduled exam. If you miss this deadline you will not be eligible for a conflict exam. The submission deadlines for each exam are as follows:

Deadline for submitting Exam 1 conflict form: September 6, 2002
Deadline for submitting Exam 2 conflict form: October 4, 2002
Deadline for submitting Exam 3 conflict form: November 1, 2002
Deadline for submitting Final Exam conflict form: November 29, 2002

Please provide the following information:
I, _____ certify that I am unable to take the Psychology 2012 exam scheduled for _____, 2002 because (Please be clear and specific when describing your reason and be sure to obtain a confirming signature):

_____
_____
_____
_____

Your name: _____ Your signature: _____
Your SS# _____ Your phone number: _____
Your e-mail address: _____

Confirmed by (please print name): _____
Signature: _____
Position or relationship to student: _____
Telephone number: _____
E-mail address, if available: _____

Note. Here is a form we have used to help students establish the legitimacy of their excuse for missing an exam. You can create versions of this form for dealing with excuses relating to any academic situation.

excuse but asking for verification (see Exhibit 5.2 for examples). This authoritative solution tends to reduce the number of students who present gratuitous excuses and also eliminates the need to engage in *ad hoc* policy making or rule-changing (Bernstein, 1993).

Returning and Dealing With Complaints About Test Items

When you return tests or quizzes in class, some students who are unhappy with their scores may shout out questions about items they missed

EXHIBIT 5.3
Item Review Form

Request to Review an Exam Question

Name _____ Student ID # _____

Instructor's Name _____ Section _____

Question # _____ Form _____

I believe that answer _____ should also be considered correct because:

_____

_____

_____

_____

I found supporting evidence on page(s) _____ in the textbook

Note. This particular form is designed for multiple-choice exams, but it can be adjusted to deal with essay, short-answer, and other testing formats. In looking for evidence to support their views, many students discover why their chosen answer was wrong; so although they may not turn in the form, it may still help them learn.

and argue with you about correct answers. This process can create chaos in the classroom and tension in the teacher. To minimize the conflict and maximize student learning, we recommend a system that uses your authority firmly, but fairly. After you have graded a quiz or exam, but before you return it, rank the items from most-missed to least-missed. Then, after returning the results, tell the class that you will now review the items, beginning with the most-missed. To make this task easier, copy items in large font onto transparencies or PowerPoint slides, display them one at a time, then explain why each correct answer is correct. For short quizzes, review all the items. For longer exams, review the 10 to 20 most difficult items—or whatever number you have time to cover; this will address the vast majority of questions, and you can invite students to discuss the rest during office hours.

If students have easy-to-answer questions about the items, answer them. If they raise more involved objections, ask them to pick up an item review form after class, fill it out and return it within, say, a week (see Exhibit 5.3). Tell them that you will review all submitted forms and announce your final decisions in class. This simple system not only eases emotional distress in class, but lets students know that you will seriously consider their views. In our experience, only students with well thought-out complaints take the time to complete the forms. If you decide that a complaint is valid, announce that you will give credit to everyone whose response deserves it. If you reject an appeal, announce that, too, and if you have time, jot a brief response on all review request forms before returning them to the students.

Dealing With Individual Student Needs and Behavior Problems

As noted earlier, more college students than ever have special needs related to physical–cognitive disabilities or other characteristics. Accommodating these students typically involves allowing them extra time or providing a special location for quizzes or exams. Your department administrators and the campus rehabilitation center can provide advice and guidelines about how best to respond to requests from these students.

Sometimes, students require individual attention because of annoying, disruptive, irresponsible, or otherwise inappropriate behavior. You can deal with some of these students simply by following our guidelines for setting up, publicizing, and sticking to course rules. For example, if your syllabus describes a two-point per day penalty for late assignments, you will not have to discuss the consequences of tardiness with individual students (though you might allow them to submit an appeal form similar to the one in Exhibit 5.2).

The most common "problem" behaviors students exhibit involve minor classroom disruptions, such as talking during lectures. There are many strategies for coping with these behaviors. For example, you can ask the offending student if something you said was unclear, you can stroll over near the offender while lecturing, you can ask for quiet, and you can discuss the situation after class on an individual basis. Other sources (e.g., Goss, 1995; Mann et al. 1970) offer a more detailed list of potential classroom problems and how to deal with them. We merely point out that the way you deal with one student's problematic behavior can have a ripple effect on other students' perceptions of you (Kounin, 1977). If your style is reasonable and measured, it will solidify your standing as an authoritative but fair teacher. If it is excessive, capricious, or abusive, you run the risk of alienating the entire class. It is a fine line teachers walk in this regard, so we recommend that, when in doubt about how to handle classroom behavior problems, underreact the first time, and seek advice about what to do next. If you encounter students whose behavior suggests a mental disorder or other serious problem, seek advice from the student counseling center.

ASSESSING AND IMPROVING YOUR TEACHING

Your teaching skills will improve with practice, especially if you collect and pay attention to evaluative feedback on how you are doing. This feedback can be summative (e.g., end-of-term evaluations designed to "grade" your teaching) or formative (e.g., comments from students or others designed to guide your teaching during the term). You will probably be required to obtain summative feedback, usually in the form of computer-scored course evaluation questionnaires filled out by your students. Though you may worry most about summative evaluations because of their role in guiding administrators' decisions about your salary, promotion, and tenure, do not fail to gather some formative evaluations, too. They can help you to improve your teaching in time to affect the summative evaluations.

Evaluations by Students

In Medieval times, formative evaluations were quantified by the amount of money university students dropped into their professor's mortarboard at the end of class (Weimer, 1993). Your students will not do this—even if you wear a mortarboard—so you will have to ask for their formative evaluations. Do this at a point far enough into the term that they are familiar with you and your course but early enough to be useful in shaping your behavior before the course is over. The third or fourth week of classes is an ideal time, particularly if you have administered and returned a quiz or some other graded assignment. The evaluation need not be elaborate or time-consuming. You could simply ask students to list three things they like about the class so far, three things they do not like, and three suggestions for change. Another option is to create a short survey about aspects of the course that are of greatest interest to you. It might ask students to complete sentences such as: "The textbook _____". "The teacher's ability to explain concepts is _____", The organization of the course _____."

To promote honest and thoughtful responses, be sure to explain that the evaluations are anonymous and that you will use the feedback to improve *this* course as well as your teaching skills in general. You will not want to, or be able to, follow every student recommendation and correct every perceived fault, but after you have read and considered these formative evaluations, take a few minutes in class to thank your students for their comments, discuss their feedback, and explain any changes you will (or will not) be making.

Reading student evaluations can be a bit depressing because even the best teachers leave some students dissatisfied, and because new teachers, especially, tend to underemphasize positive comments and brood about the negative ones. To view formative comments in a more rational way, create a two-by-two table, and label its four cells as follows: positive comments, negative comments, suggestions for improvement, and factors beyond my control. A comment that "lectures are interesting" would go in the positive comments cell. "The quizzes are difficult" could go in either the negative comments or positive comments column, depending on your goals. If you deliberately give difficult quizzes to better prepare students for your tests, this would be a positive comment, but it should prompt you to tell the class why the quiz questions are difficult. "I hate having class at 8:00 AM" goes into factors beyond my control, but let the students know that you are aware of how they feel and perhaps plan to include a few more active learning events to keep everyone involved. "Put an outline on the board" would go in the suggestions for improvement cell.

Before deciding what to change, count the number of students making each statement. If only one person claims the class pace is too slow, the problem probably lies with that student's needs and interests. During your class discussion of feedback, you might want to ask whoever made that comment to visit you during office hours. If *all* but one student find the class boring, you would want to consider ways to address the problem. When in doubt about how to respond to student feedback, discuss it with an experienced colleague or someone at your campus instructional development office.

Other, quicker, means of getting continuous feedback on your teaching can take the form of one-minute papers, mentioned previously (Angelo & Cross, 1993). For example, if you are wondering how clear your lecture is at any particular moment, you can stop and ask your students to jot down the things that confused them during the last few minutes. Reading these papers later can tell you what you need to clarify at the next class session and may also guide the pace of your lectures or the number of examples you give. This simple exercise sends a clear signal to students that you care about your teaching, which can have a profound impact on their summative evaluations.

Evaluations by Colleagues

Like formative feedback from students, constructive feedback from an experienced colleague can be of enormous benefit in improving your teaching. So, scary as it might be, consider asking a colleague to visit a couple of your classes and ask for his or her observations about your teaching. Some colleges formalize this kind of evaluation by arranging for pairs of faculty—usually from different departments—to sit in on each other's classes. At other institutions, the department executive officer or someone from the campus instructional development office makes these visits.

Whatever the case may be, try to focus on what you can learn from the experience rather than worrying about its possible negative results. Meet with the visitor beforehand to describe your goals for the class to be observed, outline and explain the methods you will be using, and identify the aspects of your teaching that you are most interested in improving. After the visit, arrange another meeting to discuss the visitor's observations. In this meeting, be open and willing to accept criticism as well as praise, and thank the visitor for helping you to strengthen your teaching skills.

Self-Evaluation

Watching ourselves teach can be at least as valuable as getting evalua-tive comments from students, colleagues, administrators, or faculty develop-ment experts (Centra, 1993). Therefore, in addition to practicing lectures for a video camera, you might want to arrange for periodic videotaping of your classes. Watch each tape in private, then again in the company of a friend, a colleague, or someone from the campus instructional development office. The process may be stressful at first (during the first minute of watching his first tape, one of our teaching assistants exclaimed, "I will never wear those pants again!"), but we think you will also find it extremely useful in developing your teaching style and improving your teaching skills.

To conduct a longer term evaluation of your teaching, consider creating a teaching portfolio or dossier containing all your syllabi, exams, quizzes, student evaluations, and the like (see Davis, 1993; Seldin, 1991; Shore et al. 1986; for details on how to do this).

Faculty Development Activities

There are many other resources available to help you improve your teaching. Do some reading about the teaching enterprise. Several publishers specialize in books and journals for college instructors; adding your name to their mailing list will keep you up to date on scholarly books on college teaching. Several journals and newsletters also contain information about college teaching. Some are discipline-specific; others mentioned earlier, such as *College Teaching, The Teaching Professor,* and *The National Teaching and Learning Forum,* focus on college teaching in general.

Participate in local workshops and seminars for new teachers and teaching assistants that might be offered by your department or by your campus instructional development office. Also consider attending conven-tions that focus on the teaching of courses in your discipline, and remember that regional, national, and international conventions in your discipline may include sessions aimed at teaching as well as research and scholarship.

USING TEACHING TECHNOLOGY

No matter how hard you work at improving your lecturing, it is unlikely that you (or any other teacher) will consistently hold the attention of a class by lecturing alone. As noted earlier, most teachers need at least some audiovisual material to provide the variety and details necessary to make their presentations clear and interesting. One study found that virtually all of the material college teachers put on a blackboard or overhead transparency appeared in their students' lecture notes. Just 27% of "important" information that was only presented orally made it into students' notes. In addition, students with lesser academic abilities benefited most from the instructors' use of audiovisual aids (Baker & Lombardi, 1985).

Today, the array of teaching technology goes far beyond blackboards and overhead projectors. And although ever-more sophisticated teaching technology has made teaching easier in some ways, it is also making it more complicated. Using PowerPoint or visiting live Internet web pages during class can make course material more immediate and memorable, but you will have to devote some time and effort to ensure that these presentations blend smoothly into the class session. If you do not prepare well, practice with the equipment, and double-check that everything is working properly before you begin each class, you may have nothing to show when the time comes or become so distracted by the technical aspects of your presentation that its overall quality suffers. Remember that each element in the available spectrum of educational tools can have value. So before deciding to log on to the Internet to show students a set of paintings, a rare manuscript, a personality test, or a celestial constellation, ask yourself whether you can get the same educational value from simpler alternatives such as slides, videos, or transparencies. If not, the high-tech methods will justify the extra effort required to use them. However, do not simply assume that a higher tech method is always better. Choose your educational tools on the basis of their ability to add value, not just because they are the next new thing.

CONCLUSION

Has this chapter left you wondering how you will find the time to deal with all that teaching entails while still meeting the other academic obligations your new job requires? If so, welcome to the club. The truth is that no matter how much time you plan to devote to teaching responsibilities, it will be less than you need. Especially at the beginning of your teaching career, it always takes longer than you think to plan class sessions, meet with students (or answer their e-mail), grade exams or papers, set up and administer record-keeping systems, accommodate students with special needs, and the like. But do not despair. Your first term of teaching will probably take more time than any subsequent one, given equivalent course loads. This is because, as you gain experience and build your arsenal of teaching materials, methods, and systems, teaching will become progressively easier and less time-consuming—though never effortless or quick.

We think that teaching can best be integrated into your academic life by following a few basic rules. First, save everything. Do not delete or discard grade rosters, exams, quizzes, papers, student correspondence, the results of student evaluations, or anything else related to a course for at least two years, and perhaps longer. Having these materials handy may save a lot of time and trouble when a student asks to see a hand-scored paper from last term or claims that there was an arithmetical error on a final grade.

Second, keep good records about how each class went, not only in terms of what worked and what did not but also whether you are ahead of or behind the schedule listed in the syllabus. Spend a few minutes after each class marking up your class notes to remind you what to do, and what not to do, the next time you present that material, run that activity, or the like. And mark your notes to indicate how much material you actually covered during each class, so you can compare it to what you had planned to cover. These few minutes of *post mortem* reflection can help you to reshape your plans, avoid mistakes, fix problems, and thus save time when you start planning the next version of the course. To help in this regard, create a folder for each class session and use it to store the notes, overhead transparencies, and other materials that you used, or plan to use, for that session. (If you prefer to gather this material by course rather than by session, we suggest using a large three-ring binder for each one.) If you are as obsessive–compulsive as we are, you might even use each folder's inside cover to create a reminder list of all the handouts, videos, books, demonstration equipment, computer disks, and other things you will need for that session. These folders can also be used to file newspaper articles, notes on good examples or interesting applications of concepts, and any other information you might encounter that will help you to update and freshen each class session the next time it comes around.

Third, create your own versions of the teaching forms we have suggested for dealing with student excuses, complaints about test items, and the like. Developing form-driven routines for handling these matters will not only save you time but also reduce the number of *ad hoc* decisions that you have to make each time you teach.

Fourth, build a directory of useful phone numbers, e-mail addresses, and websites that will help you to refer students to various kinds of help, to campus services and facilities, and to sources of additional course-related information. Having these handy—and keeping copies at home as well as at the office—can make discussions and e-mail exchanges with students more efficient and more valuable.

Fifth, do not try to reinvent the wheel. Whatever you encounter in your courses—whether it is students calling you at midnight or dogs mating in your classroom—has probably already happened to other teachers. So find a senior mentor in your department and take advantage of his or her knowledge and expertise. By doing so, and by taking to heart the other advice offered in this chapter, your teaching experience can be one of the most rewarding aspects of your academic life. And if it is, remember to do what you can to pass on what you have learned to those new teachers who, with sweaty palms and hopeful hearts, will follow in your footsteps. We wish you all the best, professor.

REFERENCES

Anderson, J. R. (2000). *Learning and memory: An integrated approach*. New York: John Wiley & Sons.

Angelo, T., & Cross, K. P. (1993). *Classroom assessment techniques: A handbook for college teachers* (2nd ed.). San Francisco: Jossey-Bass.

Aronson, E. (1978). *The jigsaw classroom*. Thousand Oaks, CA: Sage.

Astin, A. (1990). *The Black undergraduate: Current status and trends in the characteristics of freshmen*. Los Angeles: Higher Education Research Institute, Graduate School of Education, University of California.

Astin, A., Parrott, S., Korn, W., & Sax, L. (1997). *The American freshmen: Thirty-year trend*. Los Angeles: Higher Education Research Institute, Graduate School of Education and Information Studies, University of California.

Baker, L., & Lombardi, B. (1985). Students' lecture notes and their relation to test performance. *Teaching of Psychology, 12*, 28–32.

Bernstein, D. A. (1983). Dealing with teaching anxiety. *Journal of the National Association of Colleges and Teachers of Agriculture, 27*, 4–7.

Bernstein, D. A. (1993). Excuses, excuses. *APS Observer, 6* , 4.

Bjork, R. A. (1979). An information-processing analysis of college teaching. *Educational Psychologist, 14*, 15–23.

Bjork, R. A. (1999). Assessing our own competence: Heuristics and illusions. In D. Gopher & A. Koriat (Eds.), *Attention and performance XVII. Cognitive regulation of performance: Interaction of theory and application* (pp. 435–459). Cambridge, MA: MIT Press.

Bloom, B. S., Englehart, M. D., Furst, E. J., Hill, W. H., & Krathwohl, D. R. (1956). *Taxonomy of educational objectives: The classification of educational goals*. New York: David Mckay.

Boice, R. (1996). *First-order principles for college teachers: Ten basic ways to improve the teaching process*. Boston: Anker.

Bonwell, C., & Eison, J. (1991). *Active learning: Creating excitement in the classroom. ASHE-ERIC Higher Education Report No. 1*. Washington, DC: George Washington University School of Education and Human Development.

Brookfield, S., & Preskill, S. (1999). *Discussion as a way of teaching: Tools and techniques for democratic classrooms*. San Francisco: Jossey-Bass.

Brown, G., & Atkins, M. (1988). *Effective teaching in higher education*. New York: Methuen.

Buskist, W. (2000). Common mistakes made by graduate teaching assistants and suggestions for correcting them. *Teaching of Psychology, 27*, 280–282.

Cannon, R., & Newble, D. (2000). *A handbook for teachers in universities and college: A guide to improving teaching methods*. Sterling, VA: Stylus.

Centra, J. (1993). *Reflective faculty evaluation: Enhancing teaching and determining faculty effectiveness*. San Francisco: Jossey-Bass.

Curzan, A., & Damour, L. (2000). *First day to final grade: A graduate student's guide to teaching*. Ann Arbor: University of Michigan Press.

Cyrs, T. E. (1994). *Essential skills for college teaching. An instructional systems approach.* (3rd ed.). Las Cruces: Center for Educational Development–New Mexico State University.

Davis, B. G. (1993). *Tools for teaching*. San Francisco: Jossey-Bass.

Dey, E., Astin, A., & Korn, W. (1991). *The American freshmen: Twenty-five year trends, 1966–1990*. Los Angeles: Higher Education Research Institute, Graduate School of Education, University of California.

Diamond, N., Sharp, G., & Ory, J. (1983). *Improving your lecturing*. Urbana–Champaign: Office of Instructional Resources, University of Illinois at Urbana–Champaign.

Emmer, E., Everston, C., & Anderson, T. (1979, April). *The first week of class . . . and the rest of the year*. Paper presented at the American Educational Research Association meeting, San Francisco. (ERIC Document Reproduction Service No, ED 175 861)

Erickson, B., & Strommer, D. (1991). *Teaching college freshmen*. San Francisco: Jossey-Bass.

Flood, B. J., & Moll, B. J. (1990). *The professor business: A teaching primer for faculty*. Medford, NJ: Learned Information.

Golde, C. M., & Dore, T. M. (2001). *At cross purposes: What the experiences of today's doctoral students reveal about doctoral education*. Retrieved on September 1, 2001, at http://www.wcer.wisc.edu/phd-survey/report%20final.pdf

Goss, S. (1995). Dealing with problem students in the classroom. *APS Observer, 8*, 26–27, 29.

Hall, R., & Sandler, B. (1982). *The classroom climate: A chilly one for women?* Washington, DC: Project on the Status and Education of Women, Association of American Colleges.

Hemmings, B., & Battersby, D. (1990). In M. Weimer & R. A. Neff (Eds.), *Teaching college: Collected readings for the new instructor* (pp. 47–48). Madison, WI: Magna.

Jacobs, L., & Chase, C. (1992). *Developing and using tests effectively*. San Francisco: Jossey-Bass.

Johnson, G. R. (1995). *First steps to excellence in college teaching* (3rd ed.). Madison, WI: Magna.

Keith-Spiegel, P., Wittig, A., Perkins, D., Balogh, D., & Whitley, B. (1993). *The ethics of teaching: A casebook*. Muncie, IN: Ball State University.

Kounin, J. (1977). *Discipline and group management in classrooms*. Huntington, NY: Robert E. Krieger.

Lambert, L. M., Tice, S. L., & Featherstone, P. H. (Eds.). (1996). *University teaching: A guide for graduate students*. Syracuse, NY: Syracuse University Press.

Lowman, J. (1995). *Mastering the techniques of teaching* (2nd ed.). San Francisco: Jossey-Bass.

MacGregor, J. (2000). Restructuring large classes to create communities of learners. In J. MacGregor, J. Cooper, K. Smith, & P. Robinson (Eds.), *Strategies for energizing large classes: From small groups to learning communities. New Directions for Teaching and Learning, 81*, 47–61.

Magnan, B. (1990). *147 practical tips for teaching professors*. Madison, WI: Magna.

Mann, R. D., Arnold, S., Binder J., Cytrynbaum, S., Newman, B., Ringwald, B., et al. (1970). *The college classroom: Conflict, change, and learning*. New York: Wiley.

Markie, P. J. (1994). *A professor's duties: Ethical issues in college teaching*. Lanham, MD: Rowman & Littlefield.

McKeachie, W. J. (1986). *Teaching tips: Strategies, research, and theory for college and university teachers* (8th ed.). Boston: Houghton-Mifflin.

McKeachie, W. J. (1999). *Teaching tips: Strategies, research, and theory for college and university teachers* (10th ed.). Boston: Houghton-Mifflin.

McKeage, K. (2001). Office hours as you like them: Integrating real-time chats into the course media mix. *College Teaching, 49*, 32–37.

Meagher, L. D., & Devine, T. G. (1993). *Handbook on college teaching*. Durango, CO: Hollowbrook.

Menges, R. J., & Weimer, M. (Eds.). (1996). *Teaching on solid ground: Using scholarship to improve practice*. San Francisco: Jossey-Bass.

Mervis, J. (2001). Student survey highlights mismatch of training, goals. *Science, 291*, 408–409.

National Center for Education Statistics. (1999). *Statistical Analysis Report, August 1999. An institutional perspective on students with disabilities in postsecondary education*. Washington, DC: U.S. Department of Education, Office of Educational Research and Improvement (NCES 1999-046).

National Center for Education Statistics. (2001). *Digest of Education Statistics, 2000*. Washington, DC: U.S. Department of Education, Office of Educational Research and Improvement (NCES 2001-034).

Office of Instructional Resources. (1999). *Handbook for teaching assistants at the University of Illinois at Urbana-Champaign*. Available online at www.oir.uiuc.edu/did/index/html

Ory, J., & Ryan, K. (1993). *Tips for improving testing and grading*. Newbury Park, CA: Sage.

Rickard, H. C., Rogers, R., Ellis, N. R., & Beidleman, W. B. (1988). Some retention, but not enough. *Teaching of Psychology, 15*, 151–152.

Royce, D. D. (2000). *Teaching tips for college and university instructors: A practical guide*. Saddle River, NJ: Prentice-Hall.

Sadker, M., & Sadker, D. (1994). *Failing at fairness: How America's schools cheat girls*. New York: Macmillan.

Sandler, B., & Hoffman, E. (1992). *Teaching faculty members to be better teachers: A guide to equitable and effective classroom techniques*. Washington, DC: Project on the Status and Education of Women, Association of American Colleges.

Sawyer, R. M., Prichard, K. W., & Hostetler, K. D. (2001). *The art and politics of college teaching: A practical guide for the beginning professor* (2nd ed.). New York: Peter Lang.

Sax, L., Astin, A., Korn, W., & Mahoney, K. (1998). *The American Freshman: National Norms for Fall 1998*. Los Angeles: Higher Education Research Institute, Graduate School of Education and Information Studies, University of California.

Sax, L., Astin, A., Korn, W., & Mahoney, K. (1999). *The American freshman: National norms for fall 1999*. Los Angeles: Higher Education Research Institute, Graduate School of Education and Information Studies, University of California.

Sax, L., Astin, A., Korn, W., & Mahoney, K. (2000). *The American freshman: National norms for fall 2000*. Los Angeles: Higher Education Research Institute, Graduate School of Education and Information Studies, University of California.

Seldin, P. (1991). *The teaching portfolio: A practical guide to improved performance and promotion/tenure decisions*. Bolton, MA: Anker.

Shore, B., Foster, S., Knapper, C., Nadeau, G., Neill, N., & Sim, V. (1986). *The teaching dossier: A guide to its preparation and use*. Ottawa: Canadian Association of University Teachers.

Silberman, M. (1996). *Active learning: 101 strategies to teach any subject*. Boston: Allyn & Bacon.

Smith, K. (2000). Going deeper: Formal small-group learning in large classes. In J. MacGregor, J. Cooper, K. Smith, & P. Robinson (Eds.), *Strategies for energizing large classes: From small groups to learning communities* (pp. 25–46). New York: Jossey-Bass.

Tobin, K. (1987). The role of wait time in higher cognitive level learning. *Review of Educational Research, 57*, 69–95.

Tozer, S. (1992, August). *Personal communication at the University of Illinois, Urbana-Champaign*. Talk presented at the Teaching Assistants Orientation, Champaign, Illinois.

Walvoord, B., & Anderson, V. J. (1998). *Effective grading: A tool for learning and assessment*. San Francisco: Jossey-Bass.

Weimer, M. (1993). *Improving your classroom teaching*. Newbury Park, CA: Sage. (Volume 1 of a ten-volume series collectively titled *Survival Skills for Scholars*.)

Zakrajsek, T. (1998). Developing effective lectures. *APS Observer, 11*, 24–26.

6

MENTORING: MANAGING THE FACULTY–GRADUATE STUDENT RELATIONSHIP

MARK P. ZANNA AND JOHN M. DARLEY

Because supervising graduate student research is such a significant component of a faculty member's responsibilities, it is important to discuss, both explicitly and in more general terms, how to structure and manage the faculty–graduate student research relationship. In this chapter we suggest a model for advising graduate student research and describe some of the pitfalls, particularly for new faculty, in establishing a meaningful and productive research relationship.

Doing research with graduate students, and the professional and personal relationships that are formed in the process, is one of the most exciting and rewarding aspects of being an academic psychologist. The knowledge that you will interact with bright, creative, and eager-to-learn students throughout your teaching career will do a great deal to keep you fresh, motivated, and stimulated with new insights. Training graduate students is,

---

We wish to thank Shelley Hymel, Louise Kidder, Arie Kruglanski, Ken Rubin, Nicole Shelton, and Betsy Zanna, who read and commented on previous drafts of the chapter.

perhaps, the one aspect of academia that makes a professor's career sharply different from almost all others.

Having said this, it must seem that we are consigning our colleagues who teach at undergraduate colleges to a second-class existence. This is not so. In these colleges honors majors often take on many aspects of the graduate student role. They do research studies for their theses, and often there are college funds to pay undergraduates to serve as research assistants on faculty research projects. Committed senior undergraduates often function at the same level as many, particularly master's-level, graduate students. They may know less, on the average, about statistics and experimental design, but they may well know more about the theories near and dear to their professor's heart. Faculty working in colleges will need to make some adjustments to the recommendations that follow but will find that many of them are relevant in their research work with undergraduates.

THE "MODIFIED APPRENTICESHIP" MODEL

We begin by describing a (perhaps idealized) model of advising graduate student research.

Sources of Research Ideas in Faculty–Student Collaborations

The central issue to be dealt with initially by faculty members is how to identify a research project on which their graduate students will work. On the one hand, the faculty member might wait until the graduate student brings forward a research proposal of his or her own. Alternatively, the faculty member might assign the graduate student to work on the next experiment in the faculty member's research grant. We would suggest that neither of these options is sensible. The first is too unrealistic; the second is too authoritarian. Instead, we suggest a model for advising graduate students that we call the modified apprenticeship model, which lies somewhere between these two extreme alternatives.

When a graduate student begins graduate school, he or she is either explicitly matched with a faculty advisor or asked to seek one out. When we are paired with or approached by a graduate student, we certainly attempt to discover that graduate student's interests, but we also are quite firm in giving that student an initial project that derives primarily from our own research interests. We do this to ensure that the student gets the benefit of our time and expertise in an area that we know well and begins early in his or her graduate career to learn the multiple tasks of doing research.

Does this mean we "hand" our graduate students a project? Not exactly. Graduate students are *not* research assistants. Instead, we give our students an idea with, perhaps, some thoughts about how that idea might be turned into a study. The student, then, does some background reading, develops some ideas of his or her own, and together we design the study. Although we may have thought (perhaps a lot) about a design and a procedure beforehand, our students are genuinely engaged in working with us on the design and procedure, and, in fact, their participation at this stage of the project almost invariably improves the study. Graduate students have often thought of ingenious solutions to the inevitable, unforeseen problems that arise in designing a study. Also, because they will eventually play the role of experimenter, it is useful for them to structure the experimenter–participant interactions. In doing so, they will create an experimenter's "personality" with which they are comfortable.

The Number of Research Directions Possible

It is our goal to have a first-year graduate student begin collecting (most probably pilot) data by the end of the first term or the beginning of the second term. However, during this time, or as soon as possible, we also begin to discuss research that derives from the graduate student's own interests. We find it very important for graduate students to be working simultaneously on, at least, two lines of research. If one line of research bogs down, the other may be productive and students may be shielded from feeling anxious or depressed about their progress on research and, more important, their research abilities. If one line of research gets held up while waiting for the availability of participants, ethics committee clearance, or for a number of other reasons, the second line of research provides something else on which to work. As we have indicated, the first line of research usually stems from our interests, and we think it ought to be started quite quickly. The second line of research stems more from the interests of the graduate student, and the graduate student can be doing the reading and developing the research ideas while working on the first line of research. Typically, the graduate student's master's thesis comes from the first line of research. In fact, the master's thesis often reports the first study completed. If all goes well, the doctoral thesis comes from the second, more independent line of research developed by the graduate student. Incidentally, this latter line may change several times in the course of the graduate student's career. Students need not stick with initial ideas that prove experimentally or theoretically intractable. What this means is the relationship between a graduate student and a faculty member begins, as it must, unequally, but shifts toward a more equal-status relationship, that of research colleague, by the end of the graduate student's career.

When we suggest that a graduate student should have an independent line of research, we do not mean that the research line must necessarily be divorced entirely from the research interests of the faculty advisor. In fact, particularly in the beginning of the faculty member's career, advising will probably go better if that line is related to one or more of the faculty member's interests. The simple point is that it should be a line of research, a set of studies, that the graduate student takes the lead in developing. When we say the first line of research should stem from the faculty member's interests, we do not mean to deny the possibility of what often happens: The graduate student sees the need for and designs a second research study (or set of studies) that might not have been conceived of by the graduate advisor. If we are playing our advising role properly, the graduate student can move that line of research forward in interesting and, possibly, unforeseen directions.

Later in this chapter, we will discuss the problems that arise when authorship credit and authorship order questions arise. But one element of good advice about it is to have discussions with graduate student collaborators early in the process of doing a study rather than leaving the discussion to the end stages of the process and discovering that different people have been operating under different assumptions. If we tie this into the present discussion about having two projects going simultaneously, because the faculty member is the major source of ideas and designs on the first project, it would be natural for the faculty member to be the first author. If the faculty member thinks that the tasks the graduate student will do on this project do not warrant an authorship, this needs to be clear in advance. In our experience, most advisors would include the student who does a good job on various aspects of the research as an author. On the second project, for which the graduate student has a more originating role, it would seem reasonable that the student emerges as first author, if the student's contributions are sustained throughout the course of the project.

Working With Other Faculty

We encourage our students to work with at least one other faculty member. In fact, the graduate training programs that seem to us to work best are those in which the faculty take collective responsibility for each and every graduate student in the program. In such programs collaboration often develops between faculty members and graduate students, such that various teams of faculty and graduate students collaborate on various research projects. When possible, we sometimes try to facilitate this collaboration by having another faculty member designated as a second, or backup, advisor for each graduate student. The backup advisor can play various useful roles, ranging from friendly critic (or devil's advocate) to full-fledged collaborator.

For this system to work best, faculty members ought to be willing to play this role for each other's students. Thus, all faculty gain the benefits of having another advisor for their students, but must, in turn, be willing to serve as backup advisor for other faculty as well. This role proves particularly valuable when a faculty member goes away on leave; the backup advisor, who is well aware of the graduate student's research progress, can quite easily step in as the main advisor.

There is another important reason for our recommendation of a system in which students have a chance to work with one or more advisors. A graduate student who works only with a young, relatively unknown faculty member and does not seek the opportunity to work with a more senior, more internationally known faculty member, may be acquiring a severe handicap on the job market. Therefore, a system in which graduate students know that they have a chance to rotate advisors is, in fact, a system that makes it possible for them to choose to *begin* working with a younger faculty member. Otherwise, they, most likely, would have to choose against working with the beginning faculty member.

How Many Students to Advise?

The modified apprenticeship system we have described has an important limit. We have found it works best when a faculty member has three or, at most, four graduate students to advise. In fact, we would be able to cope with three or four students only if the graduate students were at different stages of their graduate careers. In this way the more senior graduate students can "show the ropes" to the more junior graduate students and pass on some of their skills to those graduate students. This not only helps the faculty member and the junior graduate students, it also helps the senior graduate students learn some of the skills involved in training students to do research. In universities in which undergraduates do honors theses, many faculty members may also involve their graduate students in supervising undergraduate theses. The graduate student benefits from this opportunity to teach senior-level undergraduates as well. This can be overdone, however. Although it is perfectly appropriate for a graduate student to help supervise an independent honors thesis, especially if it is in an area of his or her own research expertise, the undergraduate may, rightfully, resent being advised primarily, or even solely, by a graduate student.

We might clarify for beginning faculty the implications of what we are saying. In spite of the irrepressible desire to begin rapidly and to get a great deal of research completed, we would advise the beginning faculty member not to take on three first-year graduate students. Far better to take on graduate students at the rate of one a year; some of the training done with the senior graduate students can subsequently be passed along by them to the younger students. Put simply, do not overload yourself.

DIFFICULTIES OF ADVISING GRADUATE STUDENTS

We now turn to some of the pitfalls in establishing a meaningful and production research relationship.

The Mentor's Dilemma

One central aspect of the task of a faculty member who is training a graduate student is to turn that student into a researcher capable of designing incisive, conceptually clean experiments that help to reveal the underlying processes that are operating to produce the phenomenon of interest. (Earlier in this chapter we noted that it is precisely the task of designing and doing these sorts of experiments with graduate students that has given us so much joy during our careers.) To do this successfully, we often use pedagogical techniques. One prominent technique involves framing a problem in such a way that the student is led to discover on his or her own just how the experiment should be designed and operationalized. A variant of this ploy is to present competing hypotheses in such a way that leads the student to have an insight that pits the two hypotheses against each other in a fruitful way. There is a bit of licensed pedagogical deception practiced in this instance: The faculty member leads the student to an insight (or set of insights) that the faculty member already has had by framing the problem in a way (or, more generally, providing the background information) that led the faculty member to the insight in the first place. The faculty member then gasps in wonder at the student's brilliance! The rationale behind this sort of technique is that the student makes the resulting experiment his or her own, and carries it out with the dedication and tenacity that this identification has produced—and that is often necessary for the successful completion of a research project.

There is a wonderful description of this kind of benign deception in the obituary Charles Harris (2001) wrote about Hans Wallach. Harris was explaining why Wallach had been the source of so many students who went on to successful research careers.

> With students, Wallach often conveyed the impression that he was simply thinking aloud, engaging with them in a spontaneous search for insights. He not only encouraged them to think incisively, he also made them feel that they were doing it on his level, collaborating with him in his analysis of a problem. A former student offered this description: "He would become utterly involved in whatever question we were

focusing on. . . . If any of us were ever able to contribute some glimmer of possible understanding, his face became radiant with delight—even when what we had thought of went directly against his favorite theory."

Harris continued, "In retrospect, I surmise that he put considerable effort and planning—and even some play acting—into his teaching." For example, on one occasion, at least, Wallach left the room, paced the hall, and returned to say, "I've been struggling to solve a problem. I know it's not our topic for today, but I hope you can help me."

Harris, a distinguished perceptual researcher in his own right, goes on: "Some years later I told him I was perplexed about that incident because I had since learned that he had solved the puzzle in an article he had published a year earlier. With a broad grin he replied, 'Yes, I know.' "

In that charming case, the issue of publication credit did not arise. But suppose the faculty member had led a student to an insight on which he or she actually went on to do research? Who ought to be the first author on the resulting brilliant paper? We already know (cf. Ross & Sicoly, 1979) that each participant in a joint enterprise, even a student and a faculty advisor collaborating on research, has a tendency to overestimate the degree, or the value, of his or her individual contribution. So this background tendency creates an authorship dilemma in any case. But the interesting irony is that the mentor, as good pedagogue, has greatly exacerbated the dilemma of authorship allocation by making the student believe that he or she has contributed the original idea, in addition to all the hard work that the student actually contributed to the execution of the project. So the student, benignly tricked at the beginning of the experiment, will carry it out with the induced hope that he or she will be the lead author. As Keith-Spiegel and Koocher (1985, p. 352) have noted, one of the most frequent sources of conflict, and of accusations of violations of ethics codes, arises from the authorship dilemma between student and faculty member. We suspect that many of these acrimonious disputes have their origins in the unintended consequences of the initial adoption of the mentoring stance by the faculty member. Irony indeed!

What to do about this dilemma is not easy to say. For senior faculty members, for whom the question of evaluation based on authorship is in the past, the situation is often resolved by giving the student first authorship. This is not so easy to do, however, for a younger faculty member struggling to establish an academic reputation—and to gain tenure. Our suggestion for younger faculty is to have a conversation very early in the faculty–student relationship that generally alludes to the faculty member's lead role in the general area, perhaps one that has been staked out by the faculty member's grant proposal. This conversation can be reinstated after the student's "discovery" of the proper design or procedure of a specific experiment. As the data collection is completed, the faculty member might also take on some of the paper drafting tasks, such as writing the introduction, to demonstrate a continuing involvement in the project.

One thing emerges clearly. Collaborations in which participants of unequal power are involved are fraught with this problem. They will be best avoided by early and clear understandings of the division of labor and the division of authorship credit for the project, and these understandings can and should be revisited if the division of labor shifts during the conduct of the project. Letting each participant form egocentric and unspoken "understandings" virtually guarantees corrosive misunderstandings. We all know this. What the concept of the mentor's dilemma introduces into the discussion is an understanding of how it is that the faculty member, originally functioning in the mentor role, induced the student to regard him- or herself as the conceptual origin of the study, a fact that the mentor now forgets.

Having realized the force of the mentor's dilemma, we do not think that our advice provides a complete solution about how it ought to be handled. We only can hope that by articulating the dilemma both student and faculty member are more likely to recognize the complexities of what is, in fact, a highly complex and emotion-laden issue.

The Psychological Situation of the New Faculty Member

This is our vision of how the graduate student–faculty advising relationship would work in an ideal situation. But, of course, there are many ways in which the relationship could go wrong. Because many of the difficulties are likely to arise from the complexities of the personal relationship that develops between the new faculty member and the graduate student, we need to analyze the particularly difficult transition that is being made by the new faculty member. In our view, this transition is likely the source of a number of these complexities.

As new faculty members move to their new teaching setting, they are likely to experience a great deal of situationally induced loneliness as well as a good deal of ambiguity about the demands being made on them. That ambiguity produces a lot of additional anxiety. Because of their age and lifestyle similarities, new faculty members are often drawn to graduate students as potential friends. Yet, because of the recently acquired status of the faculty member, a gap has been created that is not only difficult, but also inadvisable, to bridge.

Many of the problems encountered by new faculty in establishing a professional research relationship with graduate students stem from this tendency to look to graduate students for friendships. The necessary but sad truth that the new faculty must recognize is that they have taken a place on the opposite side of the desk from graduate students. This is enormously hard to appreciate because a mere two or three months earlier the new faculty member was him- or herself a graduate student. Nonetheless, the beginning faculty member must recognize that the essence of his or her job is to teach and train graduate students and, in so doing, they must advise, direct, and *evaluate* graduate students. The responsibility to sanction a student—for example, to place a student on probation—is one responsibility that we all hope will occur rarely. Nonetheless, evaluation, both positive and negative, is one of the essential components of the relationship between faculty and students, and it is one that almost always is underestimated by beginning faculty. The following is a classic manifestation of the problem.

A faculty member may become involved in a hand-holding relationship with a graduate student, giving advice on his or her personal life. More than giving advice, the faculty member may be drawn into giving sympathy, even therapy. Not only does this take an emotional toll on the new faculty member, it can also consume an inordinate amount of time. Time spent providing therapy is time not spent in providing graduate education. More to the point, time spent in this way implicitly, but in fact absolutely, undermines the essential evaluative nature of the relationship between faculty and student. (Although we cannot expand on it, it is important to point out an obvious fact: This trap may be harder to avoid for female or minority faculty members, if only because such faculty are often in "shorter supply.")

It is interesting (and, perhaps, ironic) to note that if a new faculty member is perceived by other faculty members as not having an appropriately role-limited relationship with graduate students, then that faculty member is limiting his or her effectiveness as an advocate for graduate students. Every faculty member will, at some time, want to be an advocate for a particular graduate student; will want to convince other faculty that this student has talents and skills and potential that other faculty may not have glimpsed. In addition, most faculty will be drawn, at some time, into mediating a conflict between another faculty member and a graduate student (perhaps even at the request of a graduate student). Neither task is effectively accomplished by any faculty member who is seen by faculty colleagues as having an inappropriately personal relationship with the graduate student in question. The faculty member's ties to the graduate student provide an all-too-ready alternative explanation for the advocacy. Thus, exactly because the junior faculty member will want to act as an advocate and, possibly, a mediator, it is advisable to establish appropriately structured relationships with graduate students from the beginning.

Finally, it is difficult for the beginning faculty member who identifies closely with a graduate student to do academic advising. For example, sometimes it is necessary for a faculty member to explain to a graduate student that although he or she has been struggling under vast and real personal problems, nonetheless, as a consequence of the lack of academic progress, he or she must be put on academic probation or leave graduate school. As well, sometimes it is necessary to advise a graduate student that, notwithstanding his or her conflict with a particular faculty member, the graduate student has been assigned a teaching assistantship with that faculty member or that the faculty member will (or ought to) be a member of the student's thesis committee. A relationship with a graduate student that makes it difficult to carry out any of these communications or, worse, makes the faculty member appear to have betrayed the student, is symptomatic of role confusion on the part of the graduate student and, most certainly, the new faculty member.

Prototypical Examples

We will illustrate several possible beginnings of disaster. Shortly after arriving at his or her first teaching institution, the faculty member is likely to be subject to a flattering approach from one or more mid-career graduate students, all of whom seek to have the faculty member work with them in various ways. Many acute problems lie herein. If the graduate student has not successfully met the demands of the faculty, he or she may have no one with whom to work. Facing the necessity to work out some sort of thesis project, such a student is often somewhat desperate to find a faculty advisor and is willing, often unconsciously, to be very seductive to do so.

A related case is one we might label the rescue mission. A graduate student who has many talents and a well-developed interest pattern may be a "misfit" in the particular graduate program that the new faculty member has just joined. That is, although in a perfect world, there ought to be a faculty member willing to work with the graduate student on the problem that interests the graduate student, no such faculty member, in fact, exists. This may be particularly poignant for the new faculty member who may recall a graduate student within his or her own graduate program who was similarly misfitted. Moreover, feeling a commitment to the success of this newly joined graduate program, the new faculty member may see this situation as a waste of the graduate student's talents. Given these factors, and given a belief that there is a general obligation of the system to help every graduate student, the new faculty member may feel that the obligation to help rests with him- or herself. Such an obligation or commitment, we might add, could last several years!

Such obligations are not unequivocal and it is frequently unwise for the new faculty member to take responsibility for advising graduate students in such circumstances. Let us add a personal note. Both of us, when we began teaching, took on graduate students because we were subject to the feelings we have just described. Many of our colleagues report to us that they also have done so. The simple fact of the matter is that it is very difficult to say "no," especially when one is a new faculty member. Nevertheless, and interestingly, most of us report that we acted very differently when we moved to our second teaching institution or grew more experienced in our first. Given a second chance, we tended to be very cautious about taking responsibility for students who had been admitted some years before we arrived or had bounced around among several other advisors.

We have suggested that there are highly idealistic reasons for supervising graduate students. Let us now suggest that there are some less idealistic ones as well. All of us have an image of how much work we could accomplish on our own research if we could simply have another pair of hands helping with the task. That, too, can be a motivation for taking on graduate students. Put simply, we think this is a rather poor motivation. Almost every experienced graduate advisor we know would suggest that advising graduate students is not an efficient way of getting one's own work done. Although this may be less true when a student is just beginning graduate school, it certainly becomes more and more true as the graduate student gets closer to doing his or her PhD thesis. This is as it should be, because it is appropriate that graduate students work on their own problems for their theses. For these reasons, both structural and personal, a number of difficulties lie in wait for the beginning faculty member in establishing relationships with graduate students, particularly graduate students who are already some distance through the graduate program.

These problems are exacerbated when a new faculty member is not merely friendly with, but, in fact, is a close friend of a graduate student. Not only will difficulties arise from the disproportionate amount of power possessed by the faculty member, but such friendships can generate additional problems among both other graduate students and faculty colleagues. Some graduate students, concerned about the distribution of resources and entitlements within the graduate student program, may feel that a faculty member's friendship gives one of their peers an unfair advantage. Faculty colleagues may fear that information confidential to the faculty community will be transmitted to the graduate student community. The ambiguous role of the junior faculty member may also confuse faculty colleagues about the junior faculty member's commitment to faculty member status. They also may not know how to treat, or interact with, the graduate student friend.

Partial Solutions to the Problem

Our first and, perhaps, best advice is straightforward: Maintain a professional distance from the graduate students. Although it is appropriate to discuss professional ambitions and personal matters insofar as they affect the graduate student's training and alternate job preferences, it is inappropriate to dwell on discussions of personal matters if they provide what may become an excuse for doing inadequate work in graduate school. Short of medical and life-threatening emergencies, it is most important for graduate students to keep their careers on track. Should a graduate student have serious personal or psychological problems, the best thing a faculty member can do is advise the student to seek professional help.

One other consideration that ought to be kept in mind that will naturally limit interactions with graduate students is the effective management and allocation of time. All of us are prone to make commitments to graduate students that are not completely warranted. At the very least, we should recognize that this ought to limit taking on other commitments. Although a commitment to an occasional rescue mission may be appropriate and even honorable, a sequence of such commitments signals an inappropriate orientation in a faculty member.

In any event, *before* agreeing to advise a graduate student it is wise to discuss the student's past performance with relevant faculty members, consult the student's records and files and, if you have any misgivings whatsoever, commit yourself only to a trial period, during which time the student knows he or she must demonstrate an ability and motivation to progress on some research project.

Testing a Student's Research Ideas

To help you decide whether to commit yourself to advising a graduate student, especially a mid-career student, you might ask the student the following six questions (developed by a colleague for just such an occasion):

1. "What are you interested in doing/finding out?" (i.e., "What's the big question?")
2. "Why are you interested in doing this?" (i.e., "What's so important about this topic/question?")
3. "How does what you are interested in doing relate to what's already known?" (i.e., "What does the literature tell us—or what's old?")
4. "How does this research differ from and/or extend previous research?" (i.e., "What new knowledge is likely to result—or what's new?")
5. "How are you going to do this?" (i.e., "What's the design and, possibly, the procedure?")
6. "What do you expect to find?" (i.e., "What are the hypothesized results?")

By posing these questions, one can assess the amount and, more important, the quality of thought that has gone into the research being proposed by the graduate student. A student who does not pass this test is not likely to convince our colleague to be his or her advisor (or even, for that matter, to serve as a member of his or her thesis committee).

Finally, before taking on a PhD student it makes sense to serve on a few MA and PhD thesis committees to gain a perspective on what is, and what is not, considered acceptable as a thesis; how much direction it is normative for the advisor and committee members to give; and so on. We strongly recommend that new faculty members do this as soon as possible.

Danger Signals

Let us try to mark certain danger signals for any new faculty member.

1. If you find you are consistently committing yourself to advising graduate students on PhD theses that are outside your own area of expertise, watch out! You do not have the time to learn these areas, and you are unrealistic if you think that you can successfully advise people without knowing the areas. You are saying "yes" too often and run the risk of spreading yourself too thin.

2. If, in your first year, you find yourself advising a host of students who were admitted before your arrival, beware! If these students are genuinely going to do work in your interest area, that is one thing. If, however, they are doing work in a scattered range of fields, that is a problem. You certainly run the risk of being perceived as the person on whom to "dump" problematic graduate students—and, if your time is taken up with senior students, you will not be able to admit students for whose entire graduate education you will be responsible.

3. If you find yourself advising a number of students and are disappointed by the rate at which those students are progressing toward their theses, you may need to examine what is going on! You may have committed yourself to a number of students who are highly competent excuse-givers but who are not equally competent graduate students.

4. Finally, if you find yourself, out of a sense of duty, advising a number of students from whom you are not getting any enjoyment, any intellectual stimulation, or any personal benefit, something is wrong. You may be overestimating your resources, overestimating your available time and, it is important to note, overestimating your skills and knowledge in the areas outside your own expertise. Advising students is a major responsibility that you should not take lightly; but it should also be a challenging and stimulating activity.

Avoiding Difficulties

We recognize that this advice may appear to be inordinately dispassionate. It is. However, there are many strategies that will allow junior faculty members to become less deeply embroiled in the lives of the graduate students in their departments or programs. First, we would suggest that junior faculty members consciously develop professional and personal relationships with individuals, other than graduate students, who share the faculty members' concerns. Beginning faculty members might recall their own graduate student peers. Although relationships with these individuals may have been competitive in the last year or two of graduate school, chances are that at least some of these individuals are experiencing many of the same feelings of isolation and uncertainty. These friends are but a phone call (or e-note) away.

Second, one can seek friendships with other assistant professors in your department as well as other departments within the university. This is sometimes quite difficult to do because assistant professors are busy, and members of academic departments frequently stay to themselves. Still, with a certain amount of effort one can turn up some very interesting people with whom one can talk about mutual anxieties and concerns and who may even become friends.

CONCLUSION

In the first half of this chapter we discussed a model of advising graduate student research. Doubtless there are other equally effective models. Because this is one of the central aspects of a faculty member's professional life, we urge beginning faculty members to develop their own model for graduate training and to strive to make it work. We hope that by discussing problems often encountered by beginning faculty in establishing research relationships with their graduate students, we will have helped beginning graduate advisors adapt to this critical new role.

Because the second half of this chapter is concerned with the pitfalls of being too close to graduate student advisees, if we have erred in our advice, we have probably erred on the side of suggesting that the faculty–graduate student relationship be too distant. But if our modified apprenticeship model, described in the first half of this chapter, works, this distant relationship will, in fact, evolve over time into a closer, more collegial relationship, especially by the time students complete their PhD theses. So, by the end of a student's graduate career the relationship between the faculty member and the (now former) graduate student ought to be no different from the relationships the faculty member has with his or her faculty colleagues.

Sometimes faculty colleagues become close friends; often not. But always there ought to be mutual trust and respect.

REFERENCES

Harris, C. (2001). Hans Wallach (1904–1998). *American Psychologist, 56*, 73–74.

Keith-Spiegel. P., & Koocher, G. (1985). *Ethics in psychology: Professional standards and cases.* New York: Random House.

Ross, M., & Sicoly, F. (1979). Egocentric biases in availability and attribution. *Journal of Personality and Social Psychology, 37*, 322–326.

III

RESEARCH AND WRITING

7

SETTING UP YOUR LAB AND BEGINNING A PROGRAM OF RESEARCH

JEFFREY M. ZACKS AND HENRY L. ROEDIGER III

A critical turning point in the life of any young researcher is striking out on her (or his) own. Let us talk about you, assuming you find yourself in this situation. You have completed five or more years of graduate school. Perhaps you also held a postdoctoral fellowship for two or three years after that. If you were lucky, you received good mentoring during your education. However, whether as graduate student or postdoc, someone else was basically in charge of the lab and was responsible for its operation. The transition from conducting research in a lab to being in charge of a lab, even a modest one, can be daunting. How do I begin a program of research? How do I recruit assistants? On what problems and issues should I work? Should I seek to collaborate or should I work independently? How will I gain resources? The aim of this chapter is to help consider various strategies for answering these questions and for making a successful transition from graduate student or postdoctoral fellow to independent researcher.

We would like to thank John Darley, Elizabeth Marsh, Julie Morrison, and Mark Zanna for their insightful comments on an earlier draft.

Parameters on the type of research career you can consider are set by the particular job you have taken. If you are at a high school or junior college, the formal research opportunities might be limited. However, they may not be as limited as you think. If you really want to do research and if you are creative, you should be able to design opportunities for yourself whatever your situation. Certain types of research (questionnaire research, some types of experimental research) can be done with paper-and-pencil materials in classroom-type settings with students, and today's inexpensive desktop computers make a large number of behavioral paradigms easily accessible. The Internet increasingly has become a viable source of participants for those without access to a large participant pool. In addition, you might be able to team up with researchers at larger institutions in the vicinity.

Let us briefly consider two scenarios for different types of jobs and some of the issues you might face in beginning a program of research.

The Teaching Environment: Is Research Possible?

Many PhDs just out of graduate school may find themselves in an institution with a low (or zero) budget for research. Besides high school and junior college jobs, some liberal arts colleges and universities see the role of their faculty as being teachers first and foremost. Psychologists in such institutions may have no laboratory space, no budget to buy equipment to support research, and also little or no money to travel to conferences. In addition, there may be no graduate students to help with research and no funds to pay research assistants. If you are a recent PhD in a situation with little support for research, you may simply look enviously at some of your graduate compatriots with large start-up packages, throw up your hands, and say "I will be a dedicated teacher and I will never do research."

There is absolutely nothing wrong with being a dedicated teacher, of course, but if you really have good ideas and want to do research, there is probably a way. Many psychologists have begun research with essentially no resources aside from their own ingenuity and a population of students in the vicinity. Students can serve as research participants and, once they have had some courses, can be research assistants and help conduct research as an independent study project or honors thesis. Teaching colleges with little support for research may be willing to fund work-study students to assist with research; this modest investment can often be extremely efficient. Some types of research require practically no money to start, just good ideas. This is true in nearly all areas of psychology (except most investigations in biological bases of behavior). Most fields include a wide variety of techniques, from simple methods to more complex (and equipment-driven) research strategies. Many famous psychologists got their start doing simple experiments, which often ask the most basic questions. Endel Tulving, a famous memory researcher, began his career at the University of Toronto. A recent biographical sketch noted that the Department of Psychology at the University of Toronto at that time (1956) lacked any kind of equipment. So his choice for a field of research had to be something that could be conducted without special tools. It was by default that he began his studies in verbal learning (APF Gold Medal Award, 1994). Even though Tulving had not been trained in the study of verbal learning and memory in graduate school (he had never even taken a course on the topic), he was able to make important contributions from the start, which escalated into a great career in the field. The ingenious mind finds interesting questions and devises appropriate tasks and experimental designs to address them. Many seminal experiments in psychology use quite straightforward techniques.

Another type of contribution one can make is the review article or book. Many fields are awash in empirical studies, but it may be hard to discern overall patterns or trends in the field. Major synthetic review papers and books can represent important contributions to scholarship that do not entail having access to research equipment or major financial resources. Indeed, with the power of the Internet, one need not even have a great library in the vicinity (although this helps). A person interested in research and scholarship can make a major contribution without having to leave the office if he or she produces a major review paper or book.

A third strategy, assuming you find yourself in a situation in which resources for research are not plentiful, is to find collaborators in situations where better research support is available. There may be a larger university nearby or a medical school with some researchers examining psychological topics with whom you can ally yourself. When pursuing this strategy it is wise to get an early start, establishing collaborative relationships if possible before you arrive at your new position.

The bottom line is that, if you are seriously interested in research, you should not despair if you find yourself in a situation in which there is not much support for research. By picking your types of problems carefully and making the most of whatever resources your own situation provides, you can make a contribution to your field.

Labs and Start-Up Packages: What to Do Next?

Suppose you have gone to a university that encourages research. You have been given some kind of lab, even if it is only a room or two, and you have been given start-up money to begin your research program. Are you home free? No, because you still have many important decisions to make. What questions will you investigate? What methods will you use? What equipment should you buy? Should you spend all your money early on, or save it and use it sparingly? There are no completely right or wrong answers to most of these questions and "it depends on the situation" may represent the correct (if unsatisfying) answer. The remainder of this chapter is essentially about analyzing your situation and thinking through what strategies you might use to get started.

No matter how much money you were allocated from your new university for start-up funds, you will soon come to believe it was not enough. Our advice is to buy what you absolutely need to begin your research program—do not hoard your money—but on the other hand, do not be profligate and buy everything in sight. Save some money for later, as new situations arise, if your university accounting procedures permit it. (Some universities require funds to be spent by the end of an accounting year, usually June 30.) Exactly how you invest your initial research funds will of course depend on what sort of research you do. However, some general suggestions can be made. Whatever else happens, spend the money required to keep your lab up and running. When undergraduate or graduate students become interested in working on a project, you want to be sure that the basic research infrastructure is in place to support them. This usually means computers, furniture, and may include specialized equipment or support staff. If you are at a research university and intend to maintain a medium or large laboratory, hiring a research assistant to have primary responsibility for paperwork and lab maintenance may be a wise investment.

The idea behind start-up money is just that—it is to get your research program started. So do not hoard your money unnecessarily. If you need more, you should write a grant seeking funds to the National Institutes of Health, the National Science Foundation, or other agencies or foundations. Your university probably has an office of sponsored research that can help explain the mechanics of the process to you, and you should also seek advice from one or more of your colleagues who have successfully attracted outside funding to support their research programs. (In addition, see chapters 8 and 9 in this book on seeking funds for research support from external agencies.)

Although you might think that your start-up funds are not sufficiently generous to sustain you very well, you should be appreciative of any funds at all. The whole concept of start-up funds is a relatively new one, especially in psychology. Even 30 years ago, in practically any university, scientists were not given lavish start-up packages such as are granted (at least to some people) today. The new researcher was expected to write a grant to fund his or her research, if funding was needed. However, because of competitive pressures among universities in attracting excellent researchers at the junior level and in coaxing senior researchers to move from one university to another, university administrators began giving start-up packages to new faculty. These vary widely depending on the scholar's discipline. Start-up money can range up to the hundreds of thousands or even higher in the physical sciences at major research universities, whereas a new computer and printer can satisfy someone engaged in humanistic research in a comparative literature or history department.

Start-up packages can vary considerably within psychology, depending both on the area of inquiry of the scholar and the type of university. Psychobiological research usually requires fairly sizable funding, and some areas of inquiry (such as neuroimaging) can require great resources by the standards of psychology. Researchers with highly technical research programs can in some ways be at a disadvantage despite the large start-up packages they are provided. The start-up permits them to acquire the lab and equipment, but the lab will represent a hungry mouth that needs continual large resources in the form of grants to remain functioning. Researchers with more modest needs may be freed from the continual writing of grant proposals and the attendant anxiety over attaining numerous grants. One modest grant might support their research quite handsomely.

WHAT SORT OF LABORATORY DO YOU WANT?

Laboratories can vary widely. In some scientific disciplines, the head of the lab may oversee teams of postdoctoral fellows, graduate students, paid research assistants, and undergraduate students. Often administrative assistants are hired to help manage the crew. However, such huge labs usually take years to develop. If you are just out of graduate school you will probably be looking at a more modest operation. Obviously, as discussed previously, the situation in which you find yourself (small college or large research university) will in part dictate the parameters of your lab. How much space do you have? Do you have access to graduate students? Can undergraduates aid in your research efforts? Do you have money to pay research assistants?

Our advice is to start small and make sure your lab works with the people you have before adding more. There is a real danger in allowing your lab to grow too fast. A new researcher in the department can become a magnet for graduate students. Before letting a, say, third- or fourth-year student come into your lab, you should think carefully. Yes, it is flattering to be approached, and yes, you need help. However, a relatively advanced graduate student suddenly looking to move to a new research mentor might not have been getting along with the previous mentor. Check out the history of the situation with other faculty. Often there can be quite good reasons for the switch, and the student may be excellent. But be careful. Often it is the chronically disgruntled student who wants to move on (or who has worn out his or her welcome with previous mentors). The situation may be mutually beneficial for you and the student, but go into it with your eyes open and consider carefully before making commitments (ones that may be difficult to undo later) on the spot.

The danger in adding too many people to a lab too fast is that each person will need considerable amounts of your time. All of us dream that just by adding another pair of hands, our research will go much faster. The trouble is that that those hands come with brains—and in fact a whole person—attached. You will need to explain the research to the brains, and make sure the person is provided with a supportive environment. Graduate students need much supervision; undergraduates may need somewhat less because their involvement in research is lighter, but still require your time. Research assistants who are paid must be given work to do. So, if you are not careful, you can spend huge amounts of time supervising graduate and undergraduate students and trying to generate work for paid research assistants. Because your new position will doubtless come with other heavy time requirements in the form of preparing new courses and serving on committees, having too many people suddenly dependent on you can absorb huge additional amounts of time and slow rather than facilitate the progress of your research program.

Think carefully about what research you want to do, trying to find the right balance between being too ambitious about what can be accomplished and yet not too cautious. Each person has to find his or her comfort zone with supervisees, the number of research projects ongoing at any one time, and the number of collaborations with other faculty.

There is a natural tendency for research projects to multiply over time. A project can be started during a conversation with a colleague or student very easily and naturally. Keep in mind that, to be successful, every project you start should be pursued with some vigor. Do not start so many projects that you know some will never be pursued to completion. Of course, you never know when a project begins if it will necessarily produce interesting results, but you can be sure that if you do not pursue the project it will not be successful. If you spend considerable time on the early stages of a project in which the data are never completely collected, you have wasted time that could have been spent more profitably. You need enough good assistants to get the job done, but not too many to leave you too scattered. Managing your personnel (and attending to their interpersonal relationships) takes time. Do not underestimate it.

SUPERVISING STUDENTS

Supervising students—especially graduate students—is a major responsibility, and is treated in detail in chapter 6, this volume. However, there are several issues of supervision that are particular to setting up one's lab, which we will address.

Most institutions provide the opportunity to involve undergraduate students in your research. At many colleges and universities this is considered an informal part of your teaching duties; rarely is it a formal requirement. There are two distinct roles an undergraduate can play in a research laboratory: that of student engaged in a supervised research (independent study) activity and that of employee paid by the researcher (sometimes with the support of the university or a federal work-study program). We believe that these two roles should be treated quite differently. Most student employees in a laboratory seek out these experiences because they are interested in the topic being studied, and they have the reasonable expectation that they will learn something about the techniques and theories being used in the lab. A professor, as employer, should support these interests in paid research assistants. However, students who come into the lab to undertake an independent study project have the right to expect much more. They should expect to be taught with the same professionalism as in any other university class. This is a substantial commitment on the faculty member's part, and should be considered carefully before taken on. Many professors, when working with an independent study student, develop a series of readings for that student and schedule regular meetings to discuss them. Some require written reports in addition to laboratory participation. The bottom line is that good undergraduates can be extremely valuable to a lab, but they often require considerable supervision, and undergraduates who are in the lab as students, rather than employees, deserve an experience as intellectually rewarding as any other class.

We would all like to flatter ourselves that as educators we are the dominant intellectual force in our students' lives. However, in most cases it is clear that students learn at least as much from other students as they do from their teachers and mentors. In a medium or large lab, there is ample opportunity for students who know more about something to teach those who know less. Postdoctoral fellows can work with and help train graduate students. Senior graduate students can teach techniques to new graduate students. Graduate students and postdoctoral fellows can supervise undergraduates. All of these relationships can be valuable to both the teacher and the student. They also benefit you by freeing you from teaching technical material repeatedly to each new person joining your lab. They can be encouraged by developing projects that pair graduate students with postdocs and undergraduates with graduate students or postdocs. However, it is important to remember that, at the end of the day, *you* are responsible for the training going on in your lab. In most cases, you will want to be sure you are having regular contact with everyone working in your lab, even if they are being supervised primarily by a graduate student or postdoctoral fellow. Some faculty prefer to schedule regular meetings with their undergraduate students, and many schedule regular graduate student meetings for this purpose.

If you hire a full-time or part-time nonstudent research assistant, a different set of issues come into play. A paid research staffer has a set of personal and professional goals that differ from those of the typical student. Often, paid research assistants are college graduates who are considering graduate study in the field in which they are working. Some of the brightest are recent graduates who plan to work in a lab for a year or two before applying to graduate school. When evaluating potential research assistants, there is sometimes a tradeoff between the enthusiasm and aptitude of the applicant on the one hand and the duration of his or her likely sojourn in the lab on the other. How this plays out depends on the time it takes you to train a new employee in the techniques used in your lab. In general, do not underestimate how long it will take for a research assistant to come up to speed—even a good one! It is to your advantage to hire employees whose professional development goals you endorse, and support those goals. Be sure you both have a clear understanding regarding how long the employee is committed to stay, how much time he or she will spend in the lab, and how his or her time will be structured. Depending on your research assistant's abilities and personal characteristics, you may need to provide substantial supervision to allow him or her to be productive and happy. A good paid research assistant can provide continuity as students move through the lab, and can be invaluable in supporting undergraduates in the day-to-day technical implementation of their research projects.

A full-time research assistant may not be the best choice when you are getting started. First, you may not feel comfortable expending the funds to support a full-time position. Second, as you yourself are getting settled in, you might have a hard time coming up with enough work to keep a full-time employee busy. Third, as a new faculty member you may have a harder time recruiting a top-notch research assistant than someone more established. One option to consider is "sharing" a research assistant with another colleague. The diversity of experience will be attractive to many applicants, and this strategy allows you to reduce the costs (in time and money) of getting a new person started.

Students' intellectual development, and the progress of research by students and paid staff, will benefit from regular contact with you. If your lab grows beyond a few people, handling this communication solely in one-on-one meetings can become hopelessly inefficient. Many researchers address this problem by holding regular lab meetings. Lab meetings also provide the opportunity for students and postdoctoral fellows to share ideas. Should you organize regular lab meetings, and what should they be like? The answer depends in part on the size of the lab. Large labs are more likely to have weekly meetings at which lab members present ongoing research, practice talks to be given at meetings, or present papers of interest to the group as a whole. Some faculty use lab meetings as a forum for visitors to address the group. For a medium lab, meetings may be scheduled less frequently and may spend more time discussing articles. Some faculty strongly encourage undergraduates to attend lab meetings, whereas others do not. For a researcher with two (or more) distinct lines of research, the question arises whether to have one large, combined lab meeting or multiple meetings. The answer again depends in part on size and also on the preference of the researcher and the specifics of the research programs. In any case, this is unlikely to be an immediate problem for a new researcher.

FEATURES OF A STRONG JUNIOR FACULTY RESEARCH PROGRAM

Research is a creative and personal activity—one size does *not* fit all. However, some features of successful early research programs cut across styles and areas of specialization. Successful junior faculty researchers generally achieve a substantial degree of independence from their PhD and/or postdoctoral advisor. This entails a bit of a balancing act, so our advice is mixed: Continue to develop this research relationship as your interests dictate, but not at the expense of other projects. With luck, you have had a good relationship with your mentor. Chances are, the two of you still have lots of research ideas and would be happy to pursue them collaboratively. Do so, by all means. A collaboration that works well for both partners is a catalyst for good research and a lot of fun. Moreover, maintaining ties with your mentor has practical advantages: He or she may be asked to evaluate you for years to come, and an active collaboration makes it easier to keep track of what you have been up to since finishing your degree. At the same time, however, you need to establish at least one prominent line of research that is primarily yours and that is independent of your mentor.

Why is it important to develop an independent line of research? First, multiple independent perspectives make for better solutions to scientific problems. Second, if you are to establish yourself as an independent agent within the scientific community, you will need to provide your colleagues with something to associate with you other than a line of research that is strongly identified with your advisor. Research funding and ultimately tenure decisions take independence from the advisor into account.

One way to help wean yourself from your PhD or postdoc advisor is to establish new collaborations. Your new university will probably present you with stimulating colleagues. Collaborative projects will help you integrate yourself into the life of the department, in addition to being scientifically rewarding. (We will say a bit more about collaboration in the penultimate section.) Presumably, the opportunities for collaboration were one of the positive features that attracted you to your current academic home. Now that you are there, take advantage of them!

As noted, you should certainly develop research that is primarily your own line of work, something with which you will be uniquely identified. Any collaborators on these projects should be students. Also, it is valuable practically to have one line of thinking for which you have a strong sense of sole ownership. This will be the work you can turn to when your collaborators are behind schedule or away on sabbatical, and it will generate the new ideas you can work through with a student.

Successful junior faculty researchers also tend to have continued at least one line of research that was well-established during graduate school or postdoctoral studies. Some new faculty feel a strong urge to strike out into something new and establish independence by abandoning their previous research interests. Others avoid this problem, but then never grow by learning new techniques. They continue to research themes that they already know well. Our advice is to take the best of both worlds. Continue with past research and past collaborations so long as these remain profitable, but also keep your eyes open for new problems, new issues, and new collaborators. It is important to preserve some continuity with the work you have done in the past. First, it is what you know best so you probably can be efficient in making additional progress. Second, in establishing a reputation for yourself you need to be identified with at least one consistent area or theoretical contribution. Third, building on what you have done before provides a safety net in case your first one or two new ideas do not pan out.

The suggestion to continue with a line of research may seem at odds with the suggestion to establish independence. One way to resolve this is to continue your dissertation or postdoctoral research in collaboration with your mentor, and also develop a new line of research on your own. Another is to push the work you did with your mentor in a different direction. You may now have resources available that allow you to ask questions you could not ask previously, such as those that require special participant populations or hardware.

Thus far, we have described old and new lines of research as if they were wholly separate entities. However, your research interests are likely to be related to each other, and work on disparate projects will draw on a common body of knowledge. Weaving common methodological and theoretical threads through multiple projects is a good thing. Successful junior faculty research programs are often described as *integrated*. Integration is valuable first because it maximizes your ability to leverage concepts and techniques from one project in the service of others. Integration also provides a more prosaic benefit, in that it allows your colleagues to easily keep track of who you are. A common concern expressed about some junior faculty is that they tend toward dabbling. When balancing multiple research projects, try to be clear in your own mind about how each relates to the other, and express that clearly when communicating to others about your research in a curriculum vita or website.

Integration is usually conceived of in terms of theoretical approach: Successful researchers tend to keep one eye on the "big picture," integrating across empirical results to draw conclusions about larger theoretical issues. When different research projects are not well-integrated, the amount of reading and thinking required to keep up with the relevant literature multiplies, and opportunities for cross-fertilization between research projects minimize. When different projects are well-integrated, synergies emerge that increase efficiency—and make broader understanding possible.

Integration can also derive from a common methodological approach. Some researchers succeed by seeing how new methods can be fruitfully applied to multiple problems. Important new empirical advances often come from the opportunistic application of clever methods, and productive research labs in general are characterized by a strong methods development component. (Some of our colleagues have expressed a certain degree of frustration with becoming known primarily as first-rate methodologists. It strikes us that this is a problem we might all hope to have, and one that is of minor long-term import.)

For these scientific and practical reasons, we suggest evaluating potential new research projects with an eye to how they fit into an integrated program of research. Does this great new idea have anything to do with the other things I am working on? Do I have the background to take on this proposed collaboration, or does it require extending myself into a new subfield? If questions such as these get "no" for an answer, think twice. Of course, research opportunities will come up that trump these concerns. Sometimes the problem is just too interesting to pass up or the collaboration seems like simply too much fun to miss. When you wind up with a project in your portfolio that does not seem to fit, think hard about the post facto connections it has to your other work. (For example, you may adapt your research program to accommodate the interests of an advanced graduate student.) Make these connections when you communicate about your work with others, and consider turning a project in a direction that forms a bridge between the apparent islands.

WRITING IT UP: THE FINAL STEP

A final characteristic of a successful junior faculty research program is that projects are followed through to completion. Most important, this means writing up your data and sending them out for publication. For some, this can be a major hurdle. Not every article comes easily to the fingers, particularly if the data are less clear than you had hoped. Moreover, by the time the data are in hand, chances are you have answered at least some of the questions that excited you to do the work in the first place. Taking the significant time required to communicate the answers can be easily put off, particularly when there are classes to be taught, students to be advised, administrative duties to attend to, and new questions and projects to go after. Everyone knows that the job is not done until the data are in print, but mustering the motivation to make it so can be a challenge.

The motivational challenge of writing can be dwarfed by that of revision. For some people, a tough set of reviews, particularly reviews that require new analyses or new data collection, can bury a manuscript in the back of the file cabinet. Although negative evaluations are always disappointing, abandoning a project when faced with disappointing reviews is rarely a smart choice. Talk about the reviews with a colleague or mentor. Some critical comments are simply off the mark; do not let these dishearten you unduly. Most tough reviews have valid points; addressing these is one of the most efficient ways to improve the quality of your research. Too often a project is abandoned or stagnates too long when it is actually quite close to completion because the researcher is reluctant to face up to negative reviews.

In any research career, some projects will go more smoothly than others. Some will bear out your predictions, some will reject them soundly, and some (many) will produce frustratingly ambiguous patterns of data. It is tempting to concentrate on whatever seems to be going best at the moment and let another line of research lag. This is a dangerous strategy because the project that is going great this week may be the one that stalls next week. (There are few safer bets!) Continuing to push forward on all active research projects helps ensure that at any given moment some worthwhile data are emerging. For many of us, this is as important to morale as it is to productivity.

Research projects have a lifespan, beginning with an idea and ending with a published report. Think of your laboratory as an ecosystem, and it becomes clear that it is desirable to have projects at various stages of development in the environment at any given time. Many of the adverse events we encounter in research selectively take out projects at a particular stage in the lifespan. If a "natural disaster" interferes temporarily with your ability to collect data, you can turn to writing up already-collected data. If teaching cuts heavily into your ability to write for a few weeks, you can continue supervising data collection. If all of your research is at the idea stage, the data collection stage, or in the process of being written up, these setbacks are more catastrophic. When you come up for tenure it will be important to demonstrate that your laboratory is a healthy ecosystem. It will be more important, though, to demonstrate that projects have made it successfully through their lifespan and emerged as published papers. The saying "publish or perish" holds true in some environments.

GENERAL PRINCIPLES

We have argued that choosing a style for your lab, supervising students and staff, and maintaining a strong research program are the keys to a successful junior faculty research career. A few general principles cut across these specific goals. We have cast these as four maxims. These revisit some of the issues we have discussed in previous sections with an eye to integration.

Make the Most of What You Have

Available resources vary widely across institutions and across departments within institutions. One of the keys to leading a successful research program is to identify and secure the critical resources you need to pursue your scientific objectives. For many research projects, the most important resources are equipment and personnel. For some projects, there may be substantial nonequipment expenses, such as participant payments, animal maintenance, biochemical laboratory analyses, supplies, or functional neuroimaging costs. Some projects may require significant collaborative arrangements to secure technical expertise, cell or animal lines, statistical expertise, custom equipment, or access to patient populations. Identify these needs early in the life of the project and make arrangements to meet them. For projects without expensive requirements it is often possible to dive in and start collecting data, cobbling together miscellaneous resources from internal sources. Other projects may require substantial negotiations or external funding to have a reasonable degree of success. If so, attend to these issues first rather than risk sinking your time and effort into a project that becomes blocked because of the absence of a key resource.

At the same time, keep a wide eye out for the resources that *are* available that allow you to answer your scientific questions. Be opportunistic in taking advantage of the facilities and people that distinguish your college or university. A colleague may have expertise that allows you to ask questions you would not otherwise be able to answer. You and your colleagues may benefit from sharing space, equipment, and even personnel (as noted previously). If your institution has a large participant pool, this facilitates noninvasive research that requires large sample sizes, which might be otherwise infeasible. If your institution has an established research center related to your line of inquiry, it may make available laboratory equipment, services, or even internal funding sources. If you are affiliated with or near a medical center, this may provide access to special populations.

Even more creative solutions are possible; a few follow:

security)

- Airports have been used as ready sources of large numbers of people with extra time to kill, who are often willing to participate in brief, noninvasive research for minimal compensation. One recent study of metaphors for time was conducted entirely at Chicago's O'Hare airport, in sessions lasting less than two minutes (Gentner, Imai, & Boroditsky, in press).
- The Ontario Science Center (MacLeod, 1989, 1991) and the San Francisco Exploratorium (Loftus, Levidow, & Duensing, 1992) are two museums that have played host to studies in which large numbers of visitors were recruited for brief studies of attention and memory.
- Zoos have provided numerous opportunities for observational and experimental studies of animal behavior.
- State and local governments sometimes have facilities that they are happy to make available for research. The Michigan Departments of Natural Resources and Transportation provided land, animals, and funding for a study of deer vision, in hope of learning something that would help keep deer off the roads (Zacks, 1986).
- The National Science Foundation (NSF) has for years made free supercomputer time available to holders of NSF graduate fellowships.
- A classic study of the effects of price changes on buying patterns was conducted by a research group that included a student whose family happened to own a chain of grocery stores (Doob, Carlsmith, Freedman, Landauer, & Tom, 1969).
- Existing data on automobile accident rates have been used to test the hypothesis that modern Americans are chronically sleep-deprived (Coren, 1996).

Invest Your Resources

A new position, particularly at a research university, may come with a commitment of startup funds to help you establish your research (see chapter 3, this volume). You may quickly secure an internal grant or an external pilot grant, or you may be lucky enough to arrive with substantial external funding. It can be hard to let go of this first infusion of research funding, and it can be hard to resist watching every penny. Resist! One concern we repeatedly hear from senior faculty about new faculty is that they slow their research careers by hoarding their resources. This strategy is penny wise and pound foolish. You may gamely stretch your initial research dollars, but if they are not invested in productive research projects, you will find it very difficult to secure more when those run out—and in the meantime, you will have impaired your ability to build a healthy research ecology.

We consider equipment, supplies, and travel costs for students and staff a wise investment of resources. One of the responsibilities of a principal investigator is to provide the environment in which students and staff can flourish. By doing so you increase their ability to focus on creative and productive research. Note, however, that we use the term "invest." The flip side of the impulse to hoard is the impulse to binge. With a little money in the bank and a pile of equipment catalogs, it is hard to resist the urge to order the 128-channel electroencepholography (EEG) setup or the huge disk drives that you never had access to in your mentor's lab. When ordering equipment, try to keep in mind what you need to do the work you have planned, and anticipate reasonably how the technology and your needs will develop over the next few years.

Invest Your Time Wisely

As a new assistant professor, the good news is that you are not likely to have the temptation to hoard your time. The bad news, of course, is that you will have little time to hoard! When it comes to your research, this means that you will need to make strategic choices about how to spend your time; you physically will not have the time to follow up on all (or even most) of the research ideas you come across. (See chapter 19, this volume, for more general issues about time management.) There are three questions one can ask when evaluating a potential research project. The answer to all three should be an emphatic yes if you are to proceed.

First, are you excited about the research question? If one plans to work on things that are not exciting, there are many more lucrative options than academic research. One of the great features of academia is the opportunity for each researcher to identify the questions that gets his or her blood pumping and work on those. It would truly be a shame to waste this opportunity. Moreover, if you are not excited, you are unlikely to produce high quality research in a timely fashion.

Second, is the research question related to the big issues you care about? (Recall the previous discussion of integration of the research program.) Many ideas are interesting, even exciting, but have the potential to sidetrack you from your primary interests. In general, successful young researchers tend to narrow their focus of interest, broadening later in their careers. One good reason for doing so is that you will be working with relatively limited resources in the short term, so what might be a minor sidetrack in a large laboratory could consume a substantial piece of your intellectual and monetary resources. More speculatively, it seems that many successful scientists often devote their early career to a deep understanding of a relatively narrow area. This allows them the opportunity to make truly original discoveries. One component of the later career, then, can be the generalization of these new discoveries to broader domains of application.

Third, is the research question you are considering *important?* Everyone defines importance differently, but there are a few things that importance is *not*. Importance is not simply interestingness. One may be very interested in the outcome of a good novel, but that does not mean the ending is important to the reader or to society at large. Importance is not simply originality. Research that is both important and original can have great impact on the field, but originality will not save a research project from triviality. Importance is not simply relevance to the existing literature. The 20th variant of an established paradigm is rarely an important exercise. At a minimum, for a research problem to be important it should address a theoretical issue that other researchers in your field care about. Even better is a research problem that has the potential to be of import to a broader community or address a significant societal problem. Avoid paradigm-bound research problems that address an outstanding debate within a small community but are unlikely to be of interest to those outside that community. A good test of importance (suggested to us by Mark Zanna) is this: Would you go out of your way to read about such a research project and be influenced by it if someone else did the work?

If the answers to all these questions are affirmative, you will need to work out exactly what sort of involvement you are going to have. Some projects will require primarily discussion and writing. Others will require hands on technical involvement. Others will require substantial supervising or commitment of fiscal resources. Once you decide a project is exciting, relevant to your larger research program, and important, you may need to make a tough decision about whether you can afford the commitment of your time and resources to carry it out.

Collaborate

Our final maxim is a single word: collaborate. Collaboration has come up already in the context of establishing independence from your PhD or postdoctoral mentor, where we pointed out that establishing new collaborations can help this process along. Collaboration has other virtues. It is efficient: Often, two heads really are better than one. Collaboration allows you to multiply your effectiveness, and some problems simply are not solvable without combining multiple sources of expertise. Collaboration stimulates new thinking: Two people thinking together often generate ideas that neither would come up with alone. Collaboration is fun: One of the pleasures of academia is its potential for collegial interactions, and rewarding research collaborations can be the most rewarding intellectual relationships one has. Finally, collaborating is strategic: Collaborating with other junior colleagues helps build a strong cohort. Collaborating with senior colleagues strengthens your ties to the department and makes it easier for the senior faculty to know how your research is going when it comes time for evaluations and an eventual tenure decision. Collaborating with colleagues at other universities integrates you into the broader research community and (as noted previously) may provide access to resources or expertise not available at your institution. (Traveling to conferences is an excellent way to establish such collaborations.)

However, collaboration can have its downsides. An unwieldy group of collaborators or a single unreliable or incompetent collaborator can lead a project into a quagmire. Taking on too many collaborations presents the possibility of becoming spread too thin. Most of us decrease in efficiency and quality of work once a certain level of task-switching is reached, and collaboration can impose additional shifts of attention. Some collaborations may not meet one of the three criteria presented previously: The project may not be exciting, it may be too far from the questions you are really interested in, or it may not be, in your judgment, important. If you build a reputation as an effective collaborator you are likely to find yourself beset by requests for collaboration. When considering a potential collaboration, watch for these red flags, and bow out gracefully if you see them.

CONCLUSION

If you are reading this chapter, chances are that the opportunity to conduct your own research was a big part of what pushed you through years of postgraduate study. You probably spent at least some time daydreaming about how *you* would do things when you were running the show. What did you like about other research operations you have seen? What did you hate? Now is your chance to take those likes and dislikes, build a comprehensive plan, and make it a reality. Each new PhD has his or her own image of an ideal research lab, and each junior professor confronts a unique set of resources and challenges. Think seriously about *your* ideal, reconcile this with the particular strengths of your job and academic community, and formulate a plan for a laboratory that will make you proud and happy. Then make it so.

REFERENCES

APF Gold Medal Award: Endel Tulving. (1994). *American Psychologist, 49,* 551–553.

Coren, S. (1996). Accidental death and the shift to daylight savings time. *Perceptual & Motor Skills, 83,* 921–922.

Doob, A. N., Carlsmith, J. M., Freedman, J. L., Landauer, T. K., & Tom, S., Jr. (1969). Effect of initial selling price on subsequent sales. *Journal of Personality and Social Psychology, 11,* 345–350.

Gentner, D., Imai, M., & Boroditsky, L. (in press). As time goes by: Understanding time as spatial metaphor. *Language and Cognitive Processes.*

Loftus, E. F., Levidow, B., & Duensing, S. (1992). Who remembers best? Individual differences in memory for events that occurred in a science museum. *Applied Cognitive Psychology, 6,* 93–107.

MacLeod, C. M. (1989). Word context during initial exposure influences degree of priming in word fragment completion. *Journal of Experimental Psychology: Learning, Memory, & Cognition, 15,* 398–406.

MacLeod, C. M. (1991). Half a century of research on the Stroop effect: An integrative review. *Psychological Bulletin, 109,* 163–203.

Zacks, J. L. (1986). *Do white-tailed deer avoid red? An evaluation of the premise underlying the design of Swareflex wildlife reflectors.* Washington, DC: National Research Council.

8

OBTAINING A RESEARCH GRANT: THE GRANTING AGENCY'S VIEW

JANE STEINBERG

There is only one guarantee in the world of grant hunting—the unsubmitted application will not be funded. Therefore, even though this chapter will explain targeting potential funders, writing irresistible applications, and planning your first award, the best advice is to take the plunge and enter the competition for grant money. But how do you begin? What do successful grant hunters know that you do not know? The advice offered is broadly generalizable across federal agencies, with examples drawn from the National Institutes of Health (NIH).

FINDING YOUR FUNDERS

Attracting potential funders is straightforward. You develop a research idea and then pitch it to potential funders. Select your idea carefully. You must be passionate about the idea because excitement sells. If a savvy new researcher (that would be you) has a thrilling idea, convincing others is

The information in this chapter is in the public domain and may be copied or reproduced without permission from the National Institute of Mental Health.

easy. Conversely, if you cannot muster enthusiasm for the idea, engaging others is difficult. Passion is also important because you just might win the grant. That requires another three to five years to conduct the proposed study. No one wants to be chained to a ho-hum project year after year. Perhaps you are not the passionate type, and your chair is prompting you to submit. Pick the next necessary chunk of work that will advance your field significantly.

Think broadly about the applications of your work so you can identify multiple potential funding sources. In psychology, researchers typically turn to the NIH or the National Science Foundation (NSF), but there are many others. Consider the Department of Defense for research in language training, listening comprehension, and computer-assisted learning. Consider the Department of Justice's Office of Juvenile Justice and Delinquency Prevention for research in preventing and controlling delinquency. There are many other pockets of money, all identified in the *Catalog of Federal Domestic Assistance* (http://aspe.os.dhhs.gov/cfda/index.htm). If your research idea fits with a federal program, check that program's website and get the name and telephone number of the professional in charge of the specific program. This person is called a program officer or staff contact. You will find links to program announcements describing the agency's activities in research, training, or service, as well as its particular submission and review process.

Be warned, the *Catalog* is huge. A clear idea of what you want to do winnows all of these funding sources down to the prime opportunities. In addition, understanding and articulating how your idea matches the funder's specific mission is essential for attracting funders. They want to support the best research to fill their programmatic goals.

The next step may feel awkward, but it is a smart move. You call the relevant program officers. Program officers help applicants compete for grants by pointing to unnoticed opportunities. For instance, in addition to program announcements and explaining the agencies' on-going efforts, there may be special announcements called Requests for Applications (RFA), which solicit applications in a particular area with a one-time receipt date. Program officers can also assist by describing the agency's review and award process and your chances of getting a grant. Here is how you can make the most of your call:

- Ask if the program officer prefers to work by telephone or e-mail and follow-up in this medium.
- Prepare a two- to three-sentence description of your project that conveys the research idea and its fit with the program.
- Be prepared when the program officer says that your idea does not fit with follow-up questions such as:

- How can I make it fit?
- Who does fund work in this area? Remember to ask about private foundations as well.
- Be prepared when the program officer says your idea is exactly what they fund with follow-up questions such as:
  - Will the program officer read and comment on a concept paper?
  - Are there any special announcements in this area that you missed on the website?
  - Is the program officer expecting to have money available for new grants in the next fiscal year? What is the estimated success rate for applications?
  - Where are the rules for applying and application materials?

Culling all of this information, especially the expected success rates for applications, should give you an idea about the most promising agencies.

MARKETING YOUR RESEARCH IDEA

Marketing may sound crass, but you want to target your effort to the funding sources that best relate to your research idea and have available money. There is no sense in competing for "dry" programs with no new money. There is great sense in finding the programs with plenty of available money that are tailored to you, your institution, or your idea. This section reviews four marketing tools for maximizing your chances of getting an award.

Get More Advice

If you find a program official who will analyze a concept paper, then send one! A concept paper is what you make it, but should include a description of what you plan to do and why. You may choose to include your analytical strategy or some budget figures. Program officers have good insight into what their reviewers like and what their funding portfolio needs. (More about reviewers and scientific review meetings appears later.) The program officer will provide a critique of your concept paper and some helpful suggestions regarding methods, other interested funders, and potential problems.

Sometimes program officers may not respond promptly. Do not take this personally. Give them a call to ask if your concept paper arrived safely and if so, schedule a telephone consultation. Take notes during the call, because you will want to reflect on all of the program officer's comments, not just the ones you selectively remember. If the program officer has written notes, ask if they can be sent to you.

Remember that program suggestions are advisory. If they make no scientific sense or turn your project into something you do not want to do, you need not follow the advice. The only exception to this rule-of-thumb is when the program officer is explaining *eligibility* to you. If a staff member says that you, your idea, or your institution is ineligible for a particular grant program, believe him or her. Do not waste your time seeking money for which you are ineligible. Take an example from the NIH. Among all of the NIH's research, training, and career awards (http://grants.nih.gov/grants/index.cfm), there is a special program called the Academic Research Enhancement Award (AREA), designed to stimulate research in schools that typically do not receive NIH grants (http://grants.nih.gov/grants/funding/area.htm). Institutions with considerable NIH grant support are ineligible to apply and are listed on the AREA grant website. No matter how narrowly your school missed the stated dollar threshold or how good your research idea is, if your school is on this list of ineligibles, you will not receive an award. You will not even receive a review.

As an aside, the AREA program also serves as an example of good marketing. If your institution is eligible for the AREA program, you have identified a source where the competition is limited and the funding rate of applications is quite good—from 28 to 39% for the past three fiscal years.

Make the Most of Rumors

Some years, the word is out that a particular agency has no money for new grants. Now it is true that some years at the NIH are better than others, but the NIH has always funded new grants. In fact, by the time "everyone" knows that a particular fiscal year is tight, the submission period for that year is probably finished and the next year's has begun. Say that in February of 2003, your entire department is buzzing with the news that the grant situation at the National Fiction Administration (NFA) is impossible. Even if this rumor is true, you may still want to apply immediately. If the imaginary NFA happens to be on the same cycle as the very real NIH, the next standing receipt date would be June 1, 2003, with a possible award made in April 2004. Sitting out the June submission actually means that you are now competing for NFA's 2004 money. This is unfortunate because Congress could have been very generous in the 2004 budget allocation to the NFA. Even more pragmatically, if you hear that everyone is sitting out a year, that is a fabulous time to submit! The available money is the same, but your competition is not even applying.

Then there is the rumor that submitting an application as a dry run is a shrewd strategy. Purportedly the reviewers analyze it and suggest changes, which is more exact than program officer feedback. In truth, anything but your best effort is counterproductive. I say this because in 20 years of working with applicants I have never had an applicant declare, "I'm so surprised I got a fundable score, I just slapped the application together." I have had many say they were surprised how demoralizing they found a poor score, even though the application was just a dry run. Not only are you discouraged, but a false start may tarnish you and your idea in the reviewer's eyes. Remember, the reviewers of the initial submission are likely to be asked to serve as reviewers on the revision as well. Finally, an NIH application can only be revised twice, so there are real costs to an application that is not ready for submission.

If you hear these or other rumblings about clever submission strategies, check them with the program officer.

Hedge Your Bets

You maximize the chances of getting an award by submitting the idea to all of the relevant agencies with available funds. Yes, each agency requires different applications, but revamping is typically a modest effort for the potential payoff. Here is a strategy that lets you compete for many different pools of money and protects you against any one agency having a bad year.

To be perfectly clear, it is wise to submit your idea to various agencies. It is *not acceptable* to take money for the same work from various agencies. Be sure to let your potential funders know about your multiple approaches and emerging offers, so they can help you make the most of them.

Road Less Traveled

Robert Frost was right, even though he was not talking about grants. When the grant-getting roads diverge, give full consideration to the one less traveled. We have reviewed the wisdom of seeking money from novel sources, as well as looking for programs with eligibility criteria tailored to you or your institution, such as AREA grant. There are other routes to explore. A grant is not the only way the government supports research, but it is typically the only source sought by academics. Few psychologists know about research contracts, and even fewer compete for them. In a contract, the government specifies exactly what it seeks in a Request for Proposals (RFP; e.g., a randomized clinical trial or a valid measure of depression in children). To compete, the researcher submits a written offer specifying how the requested research will be conducted along with a separate budget. These research contract proposals are reviewed by scientists, and those found technically adequate then enter into budget negotiations with the contracting officer. Note that all such RFPs are advertised in the *Commerce Business Daily* (http://cbdnet.access.gpo.gov/). The NIH also posts RFPs on its webpage (http://ocm.od.nih.gov/contracts/contract.htm). If the government happens to be contracting in your substantive area, you should consider competing.

Another road less traveled is submitting your research through a self-formed business. Congress has provided special funds for stimulating small businesses' entry into research. As you look through the *Catalog of Domestic Federal Assistance,* you will see that many agencies participate in various small business programs. The specifics for exploring this entrepreneurial approach and establishing a small business are summarized at the NIH's small business grants and contracts webpage http://grants.nih.gov/grants/funding/sbir.htm. The funding rates in the small business programs have been reliably good over the years.

PREPARING IRRESISTIBLE APPLICATIONS

Thrilling funders means sharing the excitement of your research idea in an application. Constructing such an application takes time, careful writing, and revisions. Remember that funders and their reviewers do not actually get to evaluate your idea. They can only assess its proxy: your application.

Begin by identifying your target date for submission. Give yourself the gift of time by calculating a comfortable game plan for preparing a competitive submission. Gage the necessary time by reading the materials in the funder's application kit and your institution's specific requirements. Get advice from your institution's office of sponsored research on the gauntlet of approvals it and the funders require. The office may also be able to give you some help with constructing a suitable budget. Then, calculate the time required to write a clear application and to make the most of your institution's resources.

Now you are ready to write. Use everything you know about the science of persuasion in developing your application. You want to make a few important points clearly and frequently, establish yourself as a credible source, and "inoculate" reviewers against any doubts others may present. These techniques are interwoven in the following suggestions.

State Your Aims

Specify your aims, state their originality and validity, and do this often. These aims should shine in each section of the application because they are the driving force for all of your decision-making—be it the design, analysis, staffing plan, or budget. Some successful applicants write their aims first, just to see if they can crisply express the value of their ideas and methods.

Remember, application writing is different from submitting a research article to a journal. In a grant application, you must justify your activities without the benefit of interesting results. That is, the aims of the project must be intellectually rich and have substantial promise. Promise is why reviewers adore applications with competing hypotheses. Such a design means that whichever way the results go, something is learned about opposing theories.

Background Literature

Application instructions typically encourage thorough background reviews, but such inclusiveness can rarely be achieved within the stated page limits. If thorough is not an option, be critical and provide a clear synthesis of the literature as it relates to your specific aims and hypotheses. In presenting this critical review, your insights should pique the reviewers curiosity yet maintain a tone of respect for another's work.

Preliminary Work, Supporting Tables, and Pilot Data

Preliminary work is a chance to present yourself as an expert. Describe what you have already accomplished and why it is intriguing. Explain how these results position you for successfully completing the proposed research.

Be sure to double-check this section carefully. In the rush to get preliminary work into an application, sometimes applicants accidentally document the wrong thing. For instance, an applicant presents the number of participants finishing the protocol in a given time because he or she is pleased to demonstrate that the duration is tolerable. The applicant does not see that the table simultaneously documents that only 1 in 10 participants completes the protocol. A low completion rate may trigger concerns about recruitment rates, time frame, selection bias, or floor effects for the reviewers. It may also trigger concerns for you and your proposed research design.

Research Design, Methods, and Analyses

A clear explanation of your procedures is essential but not sufficient. This section is your primary opportunity to convince the reviewers that you are ready to do important research. Rather than simply describing the design, engage the reviewers by walking them through your decision points and why your choice was preferable over other options. Reviewers must be assured you will provide a set of methods that will permit a rigorous testing of the hypotheses and valid interpretations of the data.

Reviewers also want to see that you can anticipate problems and understand the study's limitations. You should talk about the potential problems or limits of your study, without overwhelming the methods section. Such carefully titrated "inoculations" should convince the reviewers that you could deflect difficulties, not that the design is ill-conceived.

In the analytical section, focus on testing your primary hypotheses. Fully explain how you will test and interpret your findings and the limits of the data. Strive for simple tests of clear hypotheses. Do not feel obligated to recount every analytical method you know. A laundry list of fancy techniques that are irrelevant to your primary questions appears odd to reviewers. Tests of secondary hypotheses, subsequent analyses, or exploratory follow-up should be included as space permits.

Staffing

The roles of key personnel in an application can be confusing for new applicants. Funding agencies actually award the grant to an institution such as a university or hospital, not an individual. Technically, your institution is the applicant and, if an award is made, the grantee. On NIH research awards, the scientific leader is the principal investigator. This individual is designated by the grantee institution to direct the project supported by the grant. He or she is responsible to the grantee for the proper conduct of the project.

Few principal investigators are expert in all areas or have time to conduct all of their research by themselves. If you are proposing a study that involves areas or techniques that are new to you, be sure that your research team reflects the needed expertise. You can request support for an expert team member such as a co-investigator or a consultant. A co-investigator is involved with the principal investigator in the scientific development or execution of a project. A consultant provides professional advice or services on the basis of a written agreement for a fee. Consultants are not normally employees of the organization receiving the services. Be sure that any additional experts participate in conceptualizing the project, as well as in the writing and checking of the application. The reviewers will be looking to see if your team can collaborate successfully, and the application itself is an index of the team's ability. Staff additions enhance your capacity, demonstrate that you know what needs to be done, and can effectively diminish reviewers' concerns.

For many new researchers, their first application reflects their best guess on how they will delegate and supervise work. Talk to colleagues and see if they can give you insights into your work style. If you have to do everything yourself, budget for huge amounts of your time. If you can delegate and supervise, be sure to request staff with appropriate training and time in your personnel section. New applicants may find it helpful to develop a task analysis of what must be accomplished, by whom, and when.

Clarify, Clarify, Clarify

As you write, you will hear yourself saying, "The reviewers will know what I mean." I want you to know that they will not. If you are befuddled or frustrated in explaining your research idea, take a break and try again latter. Do not leave anything poorly described with the expectation that the reviewers will get your drift. Keep rewriting until you have a draft that is clear and within the page limits specified by the agency's application procedures.

With a respectable draft in hand, ask one or two trusted colleagues to read your draft. Even better, ask individuals who have served as scientific peer reviewers for a federal agency or who have successfully obtained grants. These readers should be interested in your general science, but not working in the exact area. You want someone who is outside of your lab's shared understanding of techniques, jargon, and assumptions. Do not include individuals who you hope to have serve as actual peer reviewers. Funders exclude individuals who have contributed to the development of the application, because such assistance is considered a conflict of interest.

When your readers are ready to comment, you must listen carefully to what they say. If you are lucky enough to find someone candid and constructive, brace yourself and take notes during the feedback. But do not expect candor from everyone. For some individuals, their best advice is hidden in self-effacing comments. When you hear, "I know that an expert in this area would understand page 22, so please do not change it just because I'm a dilettante," then rewrite page 22. A reader may use kind language to hint at underlying trouble. Gentle comments such as, "I would value your opinion on X's paper," may mean you need to take an extra look at this article before continuing. Glean what you can by thinking though all comments and their many meanings.

While your readers busily review your draft, read Strunk and White's *The Elements of Style* (e.g., revised, 2000). It does not matter which edition you have; this slim book contains evergreen advice on clear writing. The guidance in this book will help you structure an unbroken flow in telling your scientific story, an essential element in persuading a reviewer that your idea is important. Just my quick review before proofing this chapter prompted me to drop two pretentious foreign phrases (Rule V.20) and many needless words (Rule II.17). Practicing Rule II.20, keeping related words together, is an on-going battle.

Of course, scientific reviewers are not the grammar police. Nor is grammar a criterion in any agency's funding policies. You want clear and correct English because grammatical errors distract reviewers from the merit of your science. The readers should be focused on your research idea, not on deciphering what you might have meant. For instance, the repeated use of an undefined "this" may subtly scuttle an application. Although "this" is meant to refer to the entirety of the preceding sentence or clause, sometimes the preceding sentence or clause is complex—so complex that neither the reviewers nor the applicant understands the actual referent. Everyone makes a different assumption and continues down separate paths until the reviewers can no longer see how the methods test the hypotheses. Some reviewers start over to figure out what the applicant might have meant, but backtracking is aggravating and not always conclusive. Avoid misdirecting the reader by applying your renewed appreciation for grammar and simplicity in the next rewrite.

Irresistible applications are scientifically exciting, feasible, and easy to read. Allow yourself enough time to write a compelling version.

DIRECTING YOUR APPLICATION

One way or another, usually through overnight mail, applications wend their way to peer review. Each agency has many checks and balances to ensure the timely and correct processing of your application. This section offers some tips so that the correct treatment of your application never depends on an agency's self-righting tendencies.

Use Clear Language in Your Title and Abstract

Three times a year, large trucks deliver more than 10,000 applications to the NIH's receipt and referral office. NIH referral officers wade through these applications, reading the title and abstract, and pulling up submission and funding histories to provide the most expert review committee. Referral officers know a broad array of science, but the use of neologisms, terms borrowed from another area of science, or other idiosyncratic usage can jettison your application to the wrong reviewers. As an example, an application with a title of "The Role of Family Resemblances in Bilingual Children" can be sent to a genetics or cognitive review committee, depending on the clarity of the abstract. Such assignment errors are typically caught, but why take the risk?

Draft a Cover Letter

Do not leave anything to chance. Even with a clear title and abstract, tell the agency anything important about the handling of your application in a cover letter. Specifically state the announcement you are responding to and whether you have been in contact with any program official. If you prefer a particular review committee, state this and the reasons why (e.g., required expertise or conflicts of interest among the reviewers of another group). A letter may also contain names of individuals who should not serve as reviewers if they would be in conflict. These requests are typically honored, but NIH referral officers reserve the right to make the final assignment determination.

Check Your Mail

Many agencies, including the NIH, send receipt acknowledgments and notification about any assignments. These notices should be checked carefully. If you receive a notice indicating that your application has been sent to an improper review committee, please call the listed contact person immediately. If no such name appears, call your program officer. Do not wait until after the review to complain! In the unlikely event that this error goes unnoticed, you will be stuck with an inexpert review and a substantial delay while the re-review is arranged. Also, check that your name and your institution's name are correctly listed, asking for corrections as needed. These corrections can prevent a delay in the subsequent award process.

Be Eligible and Stay Eligible

Because you have read all the application materials, you know that you are eligible for this particular pot of money. Stay that way by following the application rules. For instance, the temptation to squeeze past the font-size or page limits can be excruciating. These arbitrary rules may feel bureaucratic compared to your need to capture all of your science; however, referral officers may return a noncompliant application without review. Even if you do slip by the referral officers, you want to be kind to the reviewers doing this volunteer work. Small fonts and extended applications can overwhelm reviewers considering 60 to 90 applications per round, three times a year.

PEER REVIEW: WILL IT HURT?

The thought of your application being raked over the coals in front of 20 leading scientists may be immobilizing, but this is a misconception. Discussions in review committees are typically collegial and respectful. After all, these reviewers are likely to be applicants and grantees, and they understand the effort that an application requires. Further, reviewers and the government staff usually try to give new investigators special consideration. That is why you can designate if you are a new investigator on the NIH application.

A large part of peer review actually takes place before the meeting. Peer review is directed by a program officer or by an individual devoted only to review activities. At the NIH, this review official is called the scientific review administrator (SRA). The SRA reads the applications to see the areas of science that must be considered and assigns two or more appropriate reviewers. Reviewers receive their assigned applications four to six weeks before the meeting and they prepare a written critique for each assigned application.

Reviews may be held by mail or telephone, but for the most part reviewers come to the Washington, DC, area for a two- to three-day meeting.[1] One by one, the strengths and weaknesses of the application are presented and debated. The critiques follow the agency's prescribed research review criteria. The NIH has five criteria for research grants:

1. _Significance_. Does this study address an important problem? If the aims of the application are achieved, how will scientific knowledge be advanced? What will be the effect of these studies on the concepts or methods that drive this field?
2. _Approach_. Are the conceptual framework, design (including composition of study population), methods, and analyses adequately developed, well-integrated, and appropriate to the aims of the project? Does the applicant acknowledge potential problem areas and consider alternative tactics?
3. _Innovation_. Does the project employ novel concepts, approaches, or methods? Are the aims original and innovative? Does the project challenge existing paradigms or develop new methodologies or technologies?
4. _Investigator_. Is the investigator appropriately trained and well-suited to carry out this work? Is the work proposed appropriate to the experience level of the principal investigator and other researchers (if any)?
5. _Environment_. Does the scientific environment in which the work will be done contribute to the probability of success? Do the proposed experiments take advantage of unique features of the scientific environment or employ useful collaborative arguments? Is there evidence of institutional support?

Reviewers move rapidly on clear-cut cases and devote more time to differences of opinion about the scientific or applied importance of an application. Reviewers justify their positions and respond to questions from

[1] Actual review procedures can vary greatly across and within an agency, so be sure to check the description of the specific program's review process.

any of the assigned or nonassigned reviewers. Once all information has been shared, some assessment of merit is taken. For those applications discussed at an NIH meeting, each reviewer assigns a priority score from 1.0 as the best to 5.0 as the worst. These scores are then averaged and multiplied by 100 for a priority score. Scores on the research applications are then percentiled, to provide some sort of comparison across the many review committees at the NIH.

A few days after the meeting, the scores are prepared and sent automatically to the applicant. A few weeks later, applicants receive their reviewers' critiques and a summary of any discussion. This confidential document is called the summary statement. It contains the score, any recommended time or budget changes, and any issues related to animal or human participants' use, as well as the name and telephone number of the assigned program officer. Typically, the program officer attends the review meeting and can help you interpret your score and the summary statement.

AFTERMATH

You either did well in review or not well enough. If you did well, your program officer will call or write with news of possible funding. Review your summary statement together so that you can address the reviewers' questions regarding budget and animal or human protection issues. Answer these questions to your program officer's satisfaction so these changes and additional information can be presented to the appropriate NIH advisory council. Council is the second step in the review process at the NIH, where public and scientific council members advise NIH staff on funding potential applications. With the council's approval, your application now may be considered for funding.

What if you do not receive a competitive score? Clearly, you will not get a grant with this application, but you need to decide if you should revise and resubmit. A revision can be well worth the effort. Even so, not all revisions are a good investment of your time. The summary statement and your program officer provide the best guidance in making the revision decision. Read over the comments and see if any strike you as valuable and addressable. If so, then you should revise and resubmit the application. Sometimes the comments are valuable, but you may not immediately think of a clever way to address them. Take some time and talk to your colleagues and program officer. If a strong approach arises, then revise and resubmit the application.

A summary statement may indicate that the ideas are not exciting. If the reviewers understood your application and complained about the lack of novel ideas or innovative techniques, then a revision is unlikely to improve their assessment. Sometimes the summary statement is not so direct. It may contain a comment about the general importance of studying the phenomenon or workman-like research plan, and then list many small questions or problems. Do not revise this application by addressing the minor questions. You have hit the intellectual doldrums and may need to drop the current research idea. Again, talk to the program officer to see why you and the reviewers differ so significantly on the merit of the research idea.

Other summary statements can be mystifying. Comments may seem off-base or poorly informed. Each subsequent reading brings waves of anger or disbelief. Should you revise or not? The answer is—it depends. Place some trust in your program officer and see what he or she has to say. If it appears that neither your program officer nor your reviewers understood your application, you must consider the possibility that the application was not clearly written. Rewriting so that the reviewers can assess your actual idea is a reasonable course, but do not consider this a minor effort. Clarity is not easily achieved.

If you find that the reviewers made an error, try to figure out its source and significance. Summary statements may contain errors that have little or no impact on your review or score. For instance, a reviewer states that there was no rationale for the sampling plan. The applicant knows that there was a rationale on page 33, so a complaint is lodged. It is likely that the reviewer should have been clearer and said there was no *convincing* rationale. This error probably did not affect your review or final score. In contrast, if all of the reviewers missed the applicant's convincing sampling rationale, then a significant error was made. In such a case, or where a lack of expertise or fairness is apparent, the NIH would offer a re-review of your application. For complete guidance on the NIH appeals process, please check http://grants.nih.gov/grants/guide/notice-files/not97-232.html.

A revision is simply part of the grant-getting game and a good use of your time if you can address the reviewers' concerns. A revision to the NIH must include a summary of your response to the previous review. Be grateful for the reviewers' helpful suggestions, humble in correcting the reviewers' misunderstandings, and convincing when explaining either your new approach or retention of the original plan.

PREPARING FOR THE FIRST GRANT AWARD

Whether through a first submission or a revision, congratulations are due on receiving your first competitive grant. You want to make the most of this grant because it will position you for the next award and a program of sustained support. You are now entering into the business of science, requiring areas of expertise that are rarely taught in graduate school. Here is a quick heads-up.

Count Your Electronic Pennies

These days the check does not arrive in the mail. The notice of grant award is sent electronically to your institution, which in turn notifies you when the spending can begin.

You should have a good understanding of your resources and how they may be used. Keep track of your expenditures and reconcile them with your institution's books. The exact language governing your award is contained in the terms and conditions of the notice of grant award sent to your institution, so be sure you have a copy. The notice will also contain the full array of references for all of the policies and regulations affecting how you may spend your grant funds.

Personnel

Grants lead to employees, which lead to supervision, which leads to difficult personnel situations. Managing staff and students will take increasing time and effort as your research program grows. Take some classes that teach essential skills such as interviewing techniques, strategies to get the best out of people, and how to handle conflict. Proper supervision motivates staff, ensures the work is done correctly the first time, and helps retain good staff.

Supervision is also the best prevention against breaches in procedures, which may mar your work or prompt an allegation of scientific misconduct. The allegation alone may bring your research to a standstill. To ensure fidelity to your procedures, let the staff know about the checks and balances you have put in place to confirm their work. Review their work products frequently. If anyone routinely runs more participants than all others, find out why. If the employee has a faster, valid method, then you may want to redesign the procedures.[2] If the employee's performance is too good to be true, then you will need to contact your institutional official for advice.

Paperwork

The government does run on paper. File all necessary reports and assurances on time to ensure the smooth flow of resources from one year

---

[2] Remember, any such changes may require a new review by the animal or human subjects protection committees at your institution. Employees should know to check with you before changing your procedures.

to another. Let your program officer know if you are running out of money too quickly or if you have not been able to spend the money as projected.

Change Happens

Nothing stays the same in research. Whatever you thought you would accomplish through your grant, three to five years can confound the best plans. You may find yourself ahead of schedule and hoping to use the grant money for some new activities. You may have a very sweet job offer and want to move your grant. Sometimes bad things happen. You may have a falling-out with a coinvestigator or fail to recruit all of the required participants. Be assured that the world of research grants is surprisingly flexible, as long as the scientific goals of the grant are met.

To find the answer to any possible question, you can read selected passages in the agency's grants policy statement (see the NIH's statement at http://grants.nih.gov/grants/policy/nihgps_2001/). To have that answer translated into plain English, simply call your program officer. Program officers can direct you through the sea of federal red tape. In addition, with their experience and substantial grant portfolios, they know how other researchers have resolved these same problems.

CONCLUSION

This chapter provides tips on successfully seeking grants. You now have a strong game plan for developing an application and know what to expect from the application submission and review process. For an even better understanding of the grant process, serve as a peer reviewer when asked. Your grant writing skills will improve dramatically. For a truly demystifying experience, you can spend a sabbatical year with the government. If Washington, DC, is not in your future, look for funding officials at professional meetings where they often talk about their programs and provide assistance in grant writing skills.

REFERENCE

Strunk, W., Jr., & White, E. B. (2000). *The elements of style* (4th ed.). New York: Longman.

9

OBTAINING A RESEARCH GRANT: THE APPLICANT'S VIEW

ROBERT J. STERNBERG

When I started my career—26 years ago—I had $5,000 in seed money from my university to get my research started, and no extramural (outside) funding. Today, my group (which calls itself the Center for the Psychology of Abilities, Competencies, and Expertise at Yale University) has more than $6 million in funding. Next year, who knows? My group may have a bit more, it may have a bit less, or it may have nothing. And that is the first lesson about obtaining research grants. It is an uncertain process: One never knows which grant proposals will get funded or how long one's funding will last. Even multiyear projects can disappear with the drop of a hat if Congress decides, for one reason or another, not to budget certain funds or if a foundation decides that its interests have changed.

Although funding is uncertain, there are things you can do to maximize your chances of getting and keeping your funding. This chapter discusses

Preparation of this article was supported by Grant REC 9979843 from the National Science Foundation and by a grant under the Javits Act Program (Grant No. R206R000001) as administered by the Office of Educational Research and Improvement. U.S. Department of Education. Grantees undertaking such projects are encouraged to express freely their professional judgment. This article, therefore, does not necessarily represent the positions or policies of these granting agencies.

the most important of these things. My comments are based on my own experiences in trying to get funded, experiences I have heard about from colleagues, and my experience working on a panel that funded research (sponsored by the Air Force Office of Scientific Research). But do not limit your learning to my experience! Talk to others in your department or unit who are experienced in getting grants, and ask them for tips. You might even ask to see their old grant proposals, just to get a concrete sense of what successful proposals look like. You might also want to consult some other sources on getting grants, such as Browning and Browning (2001) and Orlich (1996).

In this chapter I first explain why you should consider applying for a grant. Then I briefly describe the kinds of organizations that fund research. Then I describe the process of getting funded. Next I provide some techniques to maximize the chances of your getting funded. Finally, I discuss how proposals are evaluated. In the granting business, to some extent, you "make your own luck," and I should note that there are many kinds of grants. Some grants fund research, but others fund exclusively travel, teaching, or development of particular commercial products. My comments in this chapter focus on research grants.

WHY SHOULD YOU APPLY FOR A RESEARCH GRANT?

There are several reasons why you should consider applying for a research grant. First and most important, it will provide you with funds to do your research. Even relatively inexpensive research costs *something*, and having a research grant helps ensure that you can get done the research you would like to do. Second, research grants help support students. Many graduate students are supported partly or exclusively off research grants, and without such grants, some members of the next generation of researchers might never have the opportunity to be trained. Third, a research grant can free you from responsibilities you may wish to delegate to others. For example, you may use the research grant to pay someone other than yourself to test participants or to prepare stimulus materials under your direction. Fourth, research grants can provide you with summer salary if your institution pays you for less than 12 months. Many universities do, in fact, pay salaries for less than 12 months. For example, my own university pays nine-month salaries. A research grant can provide one, two, or sometimes even three months of summer support, thus supplementing the researcher's income. Of course, when you take summer salary, you are expected to work on the research during the time you are drawing the salary. Finally, obtaining a research grant marks you as a serious scholar and can help you when it comes time for promotion and tenure decisions. At a major research institution, getting a grant may be a sine qua non for promotion or tenure. Thus, it makes sense to apply for a research grant.

WHO FUNDS RESEARCH AND HOW DO THEY FUND IT?

There are many different kinds of funding organizations. Some of these organizations are very specific in the kinds of research they fund, whereas others are more general. The main types of organizations that fund university research are universities, governmental organizations, nongovernmental organizations, foundations, and corporations.

Universities often have limited funds to support the research of their own students and faculty members. These funds may be available to anyone who applies, or may only be available to certain individuals, such as new faculty members, junior faculty members, or faculty members who have not succeeded in gaining external support. The funds are typically awarded on a competitive basis. Universities are often willing and eager to provide first small seed grants to new faculty, so be sure to check on the availability of funding from your own institution.

Governmental organizations are sponsored by the United States, Canadian, or other national, state, and local governments. Examples of governmental organizations in the United States are the National Science Foundation (NSF), the National Institutes of Health (NIH), the U.S. Military (e.g., Army Research Institute [ARI], Office of Naval Research [ONR], and Air Force Office of Scientific Research [AFOSR]), and the U.S. Department of Education (e.g., the Office of Educational Research and Improvement [OERI]). National organizations such as these have regular grant competitions, and you can find out about these competitions either through your grants and contracts office or through the agencies' websites. State and local governmental organizations may have research funds but not have regular competitions for them.

Government grants are typically for three years, although they may be for less time (such as a year) or for more time (typically up to five years). It is important to realize that a commitment by the government to fund your research for a specified period of years does not guarantee you will actually get the funding you were promised. Many variables can intervene. The agency's budget may be cut by the government, resulting in your budget being reduced or sometimes even eliminated. The agency may be dissatisfied with your progress and terminate your funding (which is relatively rare but does happen). Or the agency may change its priorities and decide your project no longer fits its goals. You should thus be optimistic that commitments to you will be met, but you should by no means feel certain of it. Most grants require progress reports at least once a year, and it behooves you to do such reports with the utmost of care and to put your research in the most positive light possible. Some agencies also conduct site visits: Members of a team come to the site of the research to evaluate the quality of the work. These visits also should be taken very seriously.

Nongovernmental organizations are entities that are not tied to any one government or that are tied to multiple governments but that are run somewhat independently of these governments. Examples of nongovernmental organizations are the World Bank, North Atlantic Treaty Alliance (NATO), and World Health Organization (WHO). These organizations are less likely to have regular funding competitions, and you need to consult their websites or, if you have contacts, individuals within the organizations to find out about funding opportunities.

Foundations are privately owned and operated and typically are more targeted and mission-oriented than government in the particular kinds of research they will fund. Examples of foundations are the Spencer Foundation, the W. T. Grant Foundation, the John Templeton Foundation, the James McDonnell Foundation, and the MacArthur Foundation. There are hundreds of foundations that fund research, but the chances are that only a small number, if any, will fund the particular kind of research you want to do.

Corporations are private entities. They may be for-profit or nonprofit. Corporations tend to be the most selective in the kinds of research they fund. Typically they are interested in research that will improve sales of their products or services. You need to be especially careful in selecting corporations to which to apply for funding. Sometimes corporations have rules regarding publication of data that render problematical the receipt of funding from them. For example, they may insist on reviewing potential publications before they are submitted or they may have a nondisclosure policy that forbids publication at all. If the research does not go the way they hoped, they may lose interest in continuing funding of the research and may even hamper the research enterprise. It is therefore important to check carefully the terms to which you agree to make sure that the terms suit you as well as the corporation.

When we apply for research funding, we often investigate funding organizations that we think other researchers are *less* likely to apply to. Organizations such as the NSF and NIH receive huge numbers of proposals, because their funding priorities meet the needs of so many researchers and because these organizations are so visible. Ask yourself whether there might be organizations interested in your research that are not as widely sought after.

Also find out whether an organization requires a preproposal. A preproposal is a brief document, often of as little as three to five pages, that describes the concept of the proposed research, how the research would be executed, and the rough budget for the research. Preproposals are commonly required by foundations and corporations and by some governmental organizations as well (such as the military ones). Preproposals require a little extra work initially, but often can end up saving you a lot of time later on. If the organization does not accept your preproposal, at least you have saved yourself the bother of having to write a full proposal, a process that typically is quite time-consuming.

Even if an organization does not request a preproposal, often a program officer will be willing to chat with you or communicate by snail mail or e-mail regarding ideas you have. The program officer often can give you an idea of whether your idea sounds appropriate for the program he or she administers. Thus, it often makes sense to talk to the program officer, to make sure you are targeting your proposal to the right agency or group within that agency.

Most funding takes the form of either a grant or a contract, although there are hybrids as well. A grant is basically a sum of money that you are given with minimal restrictions to accomplish the research you have proposed. Although major changes in what you plan to do may require approval, generally granting agencies are somewhat flexible, realizing that plans change as time goes on. Contracts are agreements for prespecified and generally fixed deliverables—in other words, products that you agreed in advance to provide. You are expected to do pretty much what you said you would do and then turn over the products to the contracting agency. There is typically less flexibility in contracts than in grants. Nevertheless, there often can be some flexibility if you negotiate with whoever awarded the contract. Should you wish to change the terms of the contract, however, it is important that you get permission rather than doing so unilaterally without such permission from the funder.

THE PROCESS OF GETTING FUNDED IN A NUTSHELL

1. *Think up an idea.* The first step to getting funded is having an idea. The idea does not have to be the greatest one since sliced bread, and as I will say later, it is often better if it is not the "greatest" idea. You just need a good idea, or, at least one you can sell to a granting agency. People come up with ideas in different ways. Some do it on the basis of reading articles and deciding what needs to be done next; others do it by observing problems in the world around them; still others combine these and perhaps other techniques. Everyone has to find his or her own preferred ways of generating ideas. It usually helps you to get funded if the idea is theory-based—that is, it derives from some kind of existing theory or theory you are newly proposing. Innovative methodologies can also be of interest to many funding agencies.

In thinking about what to propose, keep in mind that many grant proposals represent collaborations. You might want to collaborate either with people in your own institution or in other institutions. Within your institution, you may choose to work with people in your own department or in another. Some of the best proposals are collaborate. And some programs even *require* that proposals be collaborative.

2. *Operationalize the idea*. Next you need to put the idea into terms that represent a program of research or development. In other words, you need to do something with the idea.

3. *Find out who might be interested in your idea*. There are thousands of sources of funding, although most psychologists stick to a much smaller number of sources. Find out what funding organizations might be interested in what you have to offer. You can get tips from colleagues, your department chair, the grants and contracts office of your college or university, or from books and the Internet. Electronic bulletin boards also can be helpful. You can list relevant keywords, and then when calls for proposals come out that use the keywords you provided, you will be notified of the funding opportunities.

4. *Write your proposal*. Next you write the proposal that presents your idea. Different organizations have different specific requirements about the format and content of a proposal. Typically you will need to state (a) what your "big" idea is, (b) why the idea is important, (c) what the theory is behind the idea, (d) what research previously has been done on the idea, (e) what research you propose to do, (f) how you plan to analyze the data from the research, (g) how much money you will need to do the research and how you will allocate the funds, (h) how you will handle human participant issues (such as informed consent and debriefing), (i) why you are the person (or team) to do the research (i.e., your qualifications), and (j) what resources are available that will enable you to get the research done (such as space, available equipment, the time you have available to do the research, and so on).

Be sure to proofread and check over your proposal. Reviewers typically donate their time to evaluating proposals. They do not want to see and may have little patience with typographical or word-processing errors in what they read.

5. *Solicit feedback on your proposal*. You may find, as I often have, that others readily can see flaws in your proposal that just are invisible to you. Therefore, ask colleagues for feedback before you finalize your proposal. Also read over your proposal from the standpoint of a reviewer. After I write a proposal, I always read it over as though I were a reviewer, and try to ask myself the questions I would ask were I reading the proposal for the purpose of reviewing it. Reading over your proposal with a critical eye can often resolve problems in advance so that reviewers do not have to bring them up.

6. *Get the proposal approved by your institution*. Almost all institutions have a formal approval process that a grant proposal needs to go through before the proposal can be submitted. This is so because the grant actually goes to the institution rather than to you. You may be the principal investigator (PI) or a co-investigator, but the actual allocation of funds goes to the institution, not to you.

Part of the approval process may be human participants approval, if, in fact, you are using human participants. Such approval can take time and so you should be sure to submit your human participant forms to your institutional review committee well in advance. Monitoring of rights of human participants has been tightening up over the years, and you may find that getting approval is nontrivial, even if the research seems to be benign. The NIH has started requiring potential PIs to get training in human participants protection, and at the time this chapter is being written, other governmental organizations are expected to follow suit.

7. *Send out the proposal on time*. Most funding agencies have deadlines. You therefore need to pay attention to the time frame in which you are allowed to send out your proposal. Deadlines tend to be strict. If you miss a deadline, you probably will have to wait until the next round of funding takes place.

It is usually a good idea to send the proposal to multiple sources of funding, but keep in mind that you typically will have to follow different formats for different agencies and you may need to "fine-tune" the proposal to make it match the requirements of each agency. Submissions to multiple funding sources are routine. By multiple submissions, you increase the chances of getting funding. Often, when you submit to multiple agencies, you will be required to declare on the proposal the full listing of agencies to which you sent the proposal. Also, if you are funded by more than one agency, you will, of course, be able to accept funding from only one of those agencies. Sometimes, when one is lucky enough to be multiply funded for the same proposal, the choice is easy, because not all of the agencies offer the same amounts of money or other resources. Thus, you may choose simply on the basis of which agency gives the better deal.

8. *Revise the proposal, if necessary; otherwise, abandon it for now*. Relatively few proposals are funded the first time around. Typically, they need to be revised. Therefore, expect to have to do a revision if your proposal is turned down. If you receive really awful reviews or simply cannot see how to revise the proposal into an acceptable form, stuff the proposal into a file drawer and wait. You may never see how to revise the proposal, but more likely, incubation will enable you to see things in a more positive light.

9. *Resubmit and explain what you have changed*. If you do resubmit, you typically will be expected to indicate how you have responded to the earlier reviews. You should follow all or most of the suggestions of the reviewers.

If you have chosen not to follow a suggestion of a reviewer or a panel of reviewers, explain why you have decided not to.

10. Get funded, or if not, start over. You may get funded, in which case, congratulations. Enjoy your funding. But whether or not you get funded, you soon will be back to writing proposals. For most of us, writing proposals is not a one-time thing. It is a regular part of a research career. Sometimes you will succeed, other times not. But whatever happens, soon you will be back to proposal writing again.

Those are the bare bones of the proposal-writing process. But of course, some proposals get funded, and others do not. What can you do to maximize the chances of your proposal's getting funded? One thing is to have the right frame of mind.

YOUR FRAME OF MIND

1. Believe in yourself. Proposal-writing is a time-consuming process. At times, you may draw a blank. Or you may become dissatisfied or even disgusted with what you have written. Moreover, when you get reviews back, you may feel even worse about yourself. It is easy to give up. Do not give up! Believe in your ability to get funded. Reverses are the rule, not the exception. The people who succeed in getting funded and staying funded are those who believe in themselves. They do not believe that every idea they ever have is a good idea. No one has only good ideas. Rather, they believe that, over the course of time, they will be able to produce research ideas that are worthy of funding, and that, ultimately, will get funded.

2. Go for it. For several years I thought that it was not worth applying for a grant to pursue my interests in the psychology of wisdom because granting agencies would find the topic just too flaky. In fact, my first proposal was rejected. We then wrote a different proposal, sent it to three foundations, and one foundation funded it for three years. I was shocked! Shocked! But the lesson is one I should have learned earlier. If you tell yourself you cannot get funded, you will not get funded, because you will never try. You have to *go for it.* You may or may not succeed, but the only way to know is to try.

3. Don't worry about having the greatest idea. What is the correlation between the quality of ideas in a proposal and its getting funded? If I had to venture a guess for my own career, it is probably about 0. Really bad ideas generally do not get funded. But sometimes, really good ideas do not get funded either. There are a number of reasons for this. Sometimes, really creative ideas do not fit into existing *Zeitgeists*, and reviewers may not understand them, know what to make of them, or see the value of them (Sternberg, 1999). Other times, really creative ideas threaten those who read about them. Reviewers may have a vested interest in another point of view, and may not be thrilled to read that what they have been thinking all along has been wrong. Still other times, really creative ideas just seem crazy. So if you have an idea that you think is pretty good but not world-shattering, do not worry about it. And if you think you have an idea that is world-shattering, be sure to express it in a way that makes as much contact as possible with the frames of mind of the reviewers. I have sometimes soft-pedaled ideas that I thought might antagonize reviewers in the hope that they then would react more positively. I do not "sell out" on the ideas, but I do soften the way I present them. Often, this technique has worked.

Sometimes ideas can be ahead of their time. Many of us have had the experience of applying for a grant, being turned down because the reviewers do not see the relevance of the problem or the research on the problem, and then reading some years later about funded research that does essentially what we proposed. If your ideas are particularly novel, then you have to go to special efforts to convince potential reviewers of the importance of the work.

4. _Persist!_ Because my group has been fairly successful in obtaining grant funding, some colleagues assume we must have a wonderful track record in getting grants. False! I can honestly say to colleagues that we have probably had more grant proposals turned down than any other individual or group of which I know. We just write more grant proposals. I have found that the rate at which my proposals have gotten funded has held more or less steady during my career, with minor fluctuations from time to time. The principal key to getting funded, therefore, is to write a lot of proposals and to send each proposal to several different funding sources.

Many people give up after being turned down once or twice. They conclude that their research—or they—are just never going to be funded. They are right. Their lack of persistence has guaranteed that they will not get funded because they have stopped writing proposals. When we get turned down, a frequent event, we just keep trying, and eventually something works out.

Some organizations may have a maximum number of resubmissions that they will allow. For example, the NIH currently allow up to two resubmissions of a rejected grant proposal. It is therefore important, when you revise, that you give the revision great attention and scrupulously take into account the comments of the reviewers.

5. _Thicken your skin._ One reason many grant-writers do not persist is that they are dismayed by the negativity and often even what seem like the personal insults contained in reviews. No one enjoys being flayed alive—metaphorically speaking—so it is easy to give up. A key lesson is never to take reviews personally and to ignore the tone if it is sarcastic or insulting. Simply concentrate on what is constructive in the reviews, and if you think you can respond to the reviews, do so without responding to their tone. Just take the substance of what is said and respond to that.

6. *Focus—do not be distracted*. There are almost always many things you would rather do than write a grant proposal. Few people delight in writing proposals; most proposal writers would rather be doing something else. Moreover, there are always many other things to do. Your course preparations need to get done. You may have scholarly articles begging you to write them up. Your committee work may be falling behind. Personal commitments may be on hold and need to be given more attention. Truly, anyone can find excuses not to write a proposal. But if you wish to do research, chances are good you will need at least some funding. So you need to focus on proposal-writing and find a way to make sure that your proposals get done, regardless of all the other things that genuinely need attention as well. You have to *make the time*.

7. *Find your right audience*. You can end up wasting a lot of time by submitting a proposal to a funding organization that simply does not fund the kind of work you are proposing. Before you write your proposal, make sure that the agency or agencies to which you are applying actually fund the kind of work you are proposing. Some funding agencies release the names of the individuals who serve on and head various grant panels, so that you can know in advance who is likely to evaluate your proposal. Even if you obtain such a list, though, you still will not know to what external referees the proposal will be sent for outside evaluation.

Now that you have gotten started, here are some things to attend to in writing the proposal itself.

YOUR PROPOSAL

1. *Tell a story*. You may think science is somehow the opposite of storytelling, but this is not the case. Good science tells a story. The story begins with a problem. It typically continues with people who, in the past, have tried to solve the problem (or who may not have correctly identified just what the problem is). And it continues with how you plan to solve the problem or at least contribute to its solution. So a good grant proposal has a narrative quality to it that holds the whole thing together. It has a big idea, like the plot of a story, and it develops the idea in a way that gives the whole proposal coherence, just like a story. If you cannot figure out the story behind your grant proposal, do not expect your reviewers to do so.

2. *Justify the scientific importance and interest of the research*. Because you have probably thought a lot about the research you are proposing, it may be totally obvious to you why the research is important. But do not expect it to be obvious to the reviewers of your proposal. You have to justify to them the importance of the research. Do not assume that others will see

this importance without your stating it. If you really do not know why the research is important, do not expect the reviewers to.

An ineffective argument for the importance of research is to point out that X, Y, and Z have been done, but A, B, and C have not yet been done, and your goal is to do A, B, and C. The fact that something has not been done does not, in itself, make that thing important. There are an infinite number of studies that could be done that have not been done and never will be done because no one will care about the results. You need to show why your particular set of studies is worth doing.

3. *Be clear, and then try to be clearer.* If you are writing a proposal about a specific area, chances are you have at least some expertise in that area. You therefore may assume that reviewers have the same kind and level of background you have. They may not. You must therefore be extremely clear in your presentation of ideas. Moreover, because you have thought about your ideas many times, it is easy, in writing, to leave gaps. After all, it should be obvious what you meant. But it rarely is obvious to anyone but yourself. Be as clear as you possibly can be, and after you have done that, try to be clearer yet. When you write, write for someone who is generally knowledgeable in your broad area of research (such as cognitive psychology, social psychology, developmental psychology, or whatever) but who is not necessarily specialized in the particular problem within the area or areas you are studying. (For tips on how to write clearly, you may wish to consult Sternberg [1993].)

4. *Organize your proposal carefully.* Actually, I think this is a statement made to me years ago by my graduate advisor, Gordon Bower. Proposals tend to be technical. They also tend to be complex. It is easy for a reviewer to get lost in the thicket. You therefore want to make sure your writing is as organized as possible.

Organize your proposal in a hierarchical way. Make sure the major points stand out, and that the minor points are properly subordinated. No reviewer possibly can remember everything you have written. By writing hierarchically, you ensure that the reviewer will remember the most important things—the things you really want him or her to remember.

5. *Sell your ideas.* After you have paid attention to how you present your ideas, you need to think about how you are going to sell your ideas. Good ideas typically do not sell themselves (Sternberg & Lubart, 1995). You have to sell them. No matter how good you may think your ideas are, do not expect it to be obvious to reviewers why your ideas are so great. You have to convince them. It therefore is important to write the proposal in a way that is not only descriptive but persuasive as well. You are not just saying what you want to do. You are telling the reader why anyone in his or her right mind will want to fund you to do it.

6. *Be comprehensive but selective in your literature review*. Usually, you are writing under the constraint of only being allowed a certain number of pages in your proposal. Thus, although it might be possible to devote the whole proposal to literature review, you need to be selective. Cite as much as possible of the research that is *directly* relevant to your proposal, but skip the stuff that, although peripherally relevant, does not bear directly on what you propose.

When people in my group write proposals, we try to keep in mind likely reviewers of these proposals. Most reviewers consider their work in the area to be important. After all, they may feel that they would not have been asked to review the proposal if their work were not important. So they will not be thrilled to see their classic book or article roundly ignored. The lesson is to try to cite likely reviewers, whenever possible.

Although you cannot be certain of who will review your proposal, you can make reasonable guesses. People who are central to the field, people who have reviewed your articles (should you know who any of them are), people you run into in professional meetings and symposia on topics of interest to you—these are among the likely reviewers. Write with them in mind, as you would wish they would do for you.

7. *Be respectful in your literature review*. Sometimes, the research one proposes is designed to set the record straight—perhaps to correct the errors the researcher sees in past work. But even if you believe past work has led to wrong conclusions, which you are going to correct, it is important to be respectful of this work. First, disagree though you may with those who came before you, these very scientists are the ones who created the methods or results that are serving as the basis for your work. Hence you owe them a debt, because you are building or rebuilding on their work. Second, it is unprofessional and, arguably, immature, to be disrespectful. Third, and pragmatically, the people who did this past work are those most likely to review your proposal, and if you are disrespectful toward them, you endanger the viability of your own proposal.

8. *Have a strong theoretical basis for your proposal*. One of the main reasons I have seen for rejections of proposals is that there is no theory, or the theory is only sketchily portrayed, or the theory is only marginally relevant to the research that is proposed. It is therefore important for you to pay close attention to the theory section of your proposal. Explain the theory clearly, and also the hypotheses that derive from it that are relevant to your research. Be sure you show how the hypotheses derive from the theory. Do not expect reviewers to see the derivation on their own. Then, when you are describing the research, make sure it is clear how the research tests the hypotheses that you generated from the underlying theory.

9. *Follow directions*. Funding agencies, especially governmental ones, have many rules to follow in the preparation of a proposal. Just following

all these rules and doing all of the required paperwork can become enormously time-consuming and, at times, can be frustrating. Yet it is imperative that you follow all of these nitty-gritty rules lest your proposal be returned or even rejected because you disobeyed the rules. I once had a proposal sent back and then had to wait for the next granting deadline because a few questions on a form inadvertently had not been answered. A colleague had a grant proposal sent back because he did not follow the requirements of the agency regarding margins.

Today, college and university grant and contract offices generally check for these mechanical kinds of errors, but ultimately it is your responsibility, not theirs, to make sure that the guidelines are followed. You do not want your proposal to be rejected because it did not follow the guidelines. If it must be rejected, it should be because of the science. Therefore, do not make yourself vulnerable by ignoring or flouting the rules. Be creative in your science, not in the mechanics of writing the proposal.

10. *Make sure your budget is reasonable and matches the proposed research.* Reviewers of grants are typically experienced and can recognize rather quickly when a project is underbudgeted or overbudgeted. If you underbudget, you are showing that you do not understand the full cost of the research, and your underbudgeting calls into question whether you really understand the resources your research requires. If you overbudget, you may give the impression of being more concerned about the money than about the research or even of being greedy. It therefore is important that your budget be reasonable. Some organizations state the evaluation of budgets is separate from evaluation of the merits of the work. My own experience, though, is that unrealistic budgeting can sour the way reviewers perceive the work you propose. You typically will be asked to provide a justification for your budget, and this justification should make totally explicit why you are requesting the level of funding and allocation of funds you have requested. Unfortunately, budgets are often cut before funding is awarded.

In budgeting, keep in mind that most institutions charge "overhead." Overhead is a portion of the grant or contract that the university takes out for its own use. In theory, overhead pays for things such as space, library usage, heating, electricity, costs to the university of administering the grant, and so forth. Rates of overhead vary widely among universities, and can reach 65% or more. The overhead may be computed on the whole grant or only on salaries and wages. For example, if the overhead rate is 50%, then the university will take 50 cents out of your grant for every dollar you spend. Rates of overhead are negotiated between the university and the funding organization.

Universities differ in their flexibility regarding overhead. Generally, though, they are willing to do some negotiation. For example, my own institution typically charges a fairly high rate of overhead but is willing to take less if the funding institution writes a letter saying it is their policy to pay less. You thus may have some leverage in negotiating rates, although probably not much.

Universities also may charge benefits on salaries and wages. This is money taken out of the grant to pay for employee benefits such as health care, retirement plans, life insurance, disability insurance, and so forth. Benefit rates vary widely across universities. From the researcher's standpoint, the important thing to realize is that you do not get to spend the entire amount of money that a funding agency allocates to you.

It is important also to realize that universities have policies regarding grant spending, and it is wise to check these policies. For example, when a grant is used to pay for a professional trip, the university may have a maximum daily amount that it will reimburse lodging or food expenses.

EVALUATION OF PROPOSALS

Each funding organization has its own criteria for evaluating proposals and its own timeline for doing evaluations. Evaluations may take just a few weeks, but typically require four to six months or even more.

Evaluations may be internal, external, or both. Internal evaluation means that employees of the funding organization evaluate the proposal. Such evaluations are common with foundations and corporations. External evaluation means that reviewers outside the funding organization—often people like you—evaluate the proposal and provide their evaluations to the funding organization. In writing your proposal, you need to keep in mind the reviewers who are likely to evaluate your proposal, and write with these potential evaluators in mind.

When proposals are sent out for review, they are sent out with the explicit understanding that the proposal is a privileged document. This means that a reviewer is not permitted to show or even discuss the proposal with others, and certainly is not permitted to use any of the ideas in the proposal for his or her own research. Usually, reviewers are asked to destroy the proposals after they are done reviewing them. In my experience, reviewers are basically honest in adhering to these guidelines. After all, they do not want people stealing their ideas! Of course, there can be a bad apple in any basket and there is no guarantee that things will go as they should. But in my experience, reviewers generally take their ethical responsibilities seriously.

Different organizations use different criteria in evaluating proposals, but certain criteria tend to be common across many different funding organizations. A first criterion most organizations use for evaluating a proposal is that of whether the proposal even fits the kinds of research the organization sees itself as funding. A second criterion is likely to be the scientific (or educational or commercial) value of the research. Organizations typically look for some degree of originality in a proposal, as well as quality of the way in which the research is designed and is to be executed. A third criterion is whether the data analysis is appropriate for the research that has been proposed. A fourth criterion often is the appropriateness of the budget. And a fifth criterion is the level of qualifications of the proposer and the facilities available to the proposer. This last criterion is important because it helps ensure that the research will get done—and get done well.

Now you are almost ready to write your grant proposal. All you need are some ideas and to set aside the time to put these ideas into the form of a proposal. Perhaps you would rather watch a football game, go for a picnic, or check out a new movie. But when these things are over, they are over. When you do a piece of research, it can have a lifelong impact on your career, and if it is really important, it can impact the field forever.

CONCLUSION

Would you like to get a grant? Chances are, you can and even will. Of course you need an idea, but chances are, you have that idea, or even more than one. So the main thing you need to do is organize yourself and your time to write a grant. You want to give it your best shot, but do not wait until you get every thought and every sentence perfect. Wait too long, and the time for doing the research may well be past! Find out the organizations that fund the kind of research you would like to do, and go for it. Most of all, remember the importance of persistence. Some lucky people are funded the first time around. Probably, many more are not. You may have to revise the proposal once or even twice. Or you may have to submit the proposal elsewhere. Or you may have to write a new proposal. But if there is one key to getting funded, it is persistence. Keep trying, and sooner or later, you will be funded. That is what we do. We know that not every grant we write will be funded. But we do not give up, and eventually, one proposal or another, some time or another, gets funded. And then, we are off and running.

REFERENCES

Browning, B. A., & Browning, B. (2001). *Grant writing (for dummies)*. New York: Hungry Minds.

Orlich, D. C. (1996). *Designing successful grant proposals*. Alexandria, VA: Association for Supervision and Curriculum Development.

Sternberg, R. J. (1993). *The psychologist's companion* (3rd ed.). New York: Cambridge University Press.

Sternberg, R. J. (1999). A propulsion model of types of creative contributions. *Review of General Psychology, 3,* 83–100.

Sternberg, R. J., & Lubart, T. I. (1995). *Defying the crowd: Cultivating creativity in a culture of conformity.* New York: Free Press.

10

WRITING THE EMPIRICAL JOURNAL ARTICLE

DARYL J. BEM

You have conducted a study and analyzed the data. Now it is time to write. To publish. To tell the world what you have learned. The purpose of this chapter is to enhance the chances that some journal editor will let you do so.

If you are new to this enterprise, you may find it helpful to consult two additional sources of information. For detailed information on the proper format of a journal article, see the *Publication Manual of the American Psychological Association* (APA, 2001) and recent articles in the journal to which you plan to submit your manuscript. For renewing your acquaintance with the formal and stylistic elements of English prose, you can read chapter 2 of the *Publication Manual* or any one of several style manuals. I recommend *The Elements of Style* by Strunk and White (2000). It is brief, witty, and inexpensive.

Because I write, review, and edit primarily for journals in personality and social psychology, I have drawn most of my examples from those areas. Colleagues assure me, however, that the guidelines set forth are also pertinent for articles in experimental psychology and biopsychology. Similarly, this chapter focuses on the report of an empirical study, but the general writing suggestions apply as well to the theoretical articles, literature reviews, and methodological contributions that also appear in psychology journals. (Specific guidance for preparing a literature review article for *Psychological Bulletin* can be found in Bem, 1995.)

WHICH ARTICLE SHOULD YOU WRITE?

There are two possible articles you can write: (a) the article you planned to write when you designed your study or (b) the article that makes the most sense now that you have seen the results. They are rarely the same, and the correct answer is (b).

The conventional view of the research process is that we first derive a set of hypotheses from a theory, design and conduct a study to test these hypotheses, analyze the data to see if they were confirmed or disconfirmed, and then chronicle this sequence of events in the journal article. If this is how our enterprise actually proceeded, we could write most of the article before we collected the data. We could write the introduction and method sections completely, prepare the results section in skeleton form, leaving spaces to be filled in by the specific numerical results, and have two possible discussion sections ready to go, one for positive results, the other for negative results.

But this is not how our enterprise actually proceeds. Psychology is more exciting than that, and the best journal articles are informed by the actual empirical findings from the opening sentence. Before writing your article, then, you need to analyze your data. Herewith, a sermonette on the topic.

Analyzing Data

Once upon a time, psychologists observed behavior directly, often for sustained periods of time. No longer. Now, the higher the investigator goes up the tenure ladder, the more remote he or she typically becomes from the grounding observations of our science. If you are already a successful research psychologist, then you probably have not seen a participant for some time. Your graduate assistant assigns the running of a study to a bright undergraduate who writes the computer program that collects the data automatically. And like the modern dentist, the modern psychologist rarely even sees the data until they have been cleaned by human or computer hygienists.

To compensate for this remoteness from our participants, let us at least become intimately familiar with the record of their behavior: the data. Examine them from every angle. Analyze the sexes separately. Make up new composite indexes. If a datum suggests a new hypothesis, try to find additional evidence for it elsewhere in the data. If you see dim traces of interesting patterns, try to reorganize the data to bring them into bolder relief. If there are participants you do not like, or trials, observers, or interviewers who gave you anomalous results, drop them (temporarily). Go on a fishing expedition for something—anything—interesting.

No, this is not immoral. The rules of scientific and statistical inference that we overlearn in graduate school apply to the "context of justification." They tell us what we can conclude in the articles we write for public consumption, and they give our readers criteria for deciding whether or not to believe us. But in the context of discovery, there are no formal rules, only heuristics or strategies. How does one discover a new phenomenon? Smell a good idea? Have a brilliant insight into behavior? Create a new theory? In the confining context of an empirical study, there is only one strategy for discovery: exploring the data.

Yes, there is a danger. Spurious findings can emerge by chance, and we need to be cautious about anything we discover in this way. In limited cases, there are statistical techniques that correct for this danger. But there are no statistical correctives for overlooking an important discovery because we were insufficiently attentive to the data. Let us err on the side of discovery.

Reporting the Findings

When you are through exploring, you may conclude that the data are not strong enough to justify your new insights formally, but at least you are now ready to design the "right" study. If you still plan to report the current data, you may wish to mention the new insights tentatively, stating honestly that they remain to be tested adequately. Alternatively, the data may be strong enough to justify recentering your article around the new findings and subordinating or even ignoring your original hypotheses.

This is not advice to suppress negative results. If your study was genuinely designed to test hypotheses that derive from a formal theory or are of wide general interest for some other reason, then they should remain the focus of your article. The integrity of the scientific enterprise requires the reporting of disconfirming results. *[handwritten: Then, why so rarely published?]*

But this requirement assumes that somebody out there cares about the hypotheses. Many respectable studies are explicitly exploratory or are launched from speculations of the "I-wonder-if . . . " variety. If your study is one of these, then nobody cares if you were wrong. Contrary to the conventional wisdom, science does not care how clever or clairvoyant you were at guessing your results ahead of time. Scientific integrity does not require you to lead your readers through all your wrongheaded hunches only to show—voila!—they were wrongheaded. A journal article should not be a personal history of your stillborn thoughts.

Your overriding purpose is to tell the world what you have learned from your study. If your results suggest a compelling framework for their presentation, adopt it and make the most instructive findings your centerpiece. Think of your dataset as a jewel. Your task is to cut and polish it, to select the facets to highlight, and to craft the best setting for it. Many experienced authors write the results section first.

But before writing anything, analyze your data!

End of sermonette.

HOW SHOULD YOU WRITE?

The primary criteria for good scientific writing are accuracy and clarity. If your article is interesting and written with style, fine. But these are subsidiary virtues. First strive for accuracy and clarity.

The first step toward clarity is good organization, and the standardized format of a journal article does much of the work for you. It not only permits readers to read the report from beginning to end, as they would any coherent narrative, but also to scan it for a quick overview of the study or to locate specific information easily by turning directly to the relevant section. Within that format, however, it is still helpful to work from an outline of your own. This enables you to examine the logic of the sequence, to spot important points that are omitted or misplaced, and to decide how best to divide the labor of presentation between the introduction and final discussion (about which, more later).

The second step toward clarity is to write simply and directly. A journal article tells a straightforward tale of a circumscribed problem in search of a solution. It is not a novel with subplots, flashbacks, and literary allusions but a short story with a single linear narrative line. Let this line stand out in bold relief. Do not make your voice struggle to be heard above the ambient noise of cluttered writing. You are justifiably proud of your 90th percentile verbal aptitude, but let it nourish your prose, not glut it. Write simply and directly.

FOR WHOM SHOULD YOU WRITE?

Scientific journals are published for specialized audiences who share a common background of substantive knowledge and methodological expertise. If you wish to write well, you should ignore this fact. Psychology encompasses a broader range of topics and methodologies than do most other disciplines, and its findings are frequently of interest to a wider public. The social psychologist should be able to read a *Psychometrika* article on logistical analysis; the personality theorist, a biopsychology article on hypothalamic function; and the congressional aide with a BA in history, a *Journal of Personality and Social Psychology* article on causal attribution.

Accordingly, good writing is good teaching. Direct your writing to the student in Psychology 101, your colleague in the Art History Department, and your grandmother. No matter how technical or abstruse your article is in its particulars, intelligent nonpsychologists with no expertise in statistics or experimental design should be able to comprehend the broad outlines of what you did and why. They should understand in general terms what was learned. And above all, they should appreciate why someone—anyone—should give a damn. The introduction and discussion sections in particular should be accessible to this wider audience.

The actual technical materials—those found primarily in the method and results sections—should be aimed at a reader one level of expertise less specialized than the audience for which the journal is primarily published. Assume that the reader of your article in *Psychometrika* knows about regression but needs some introduction to logistical analysis. Assume that the reader of the *Journal of Personality and Social Psychology* knows about person perception but needs some introduction to dispositional and situational attributions.

Many of the writing techniques suggested in this chapter are thus teaching techniques designed to make your article comprehensible to the widest possible audience. They are also designed to remain invisible or transparent to your readers, thereby infusing your prose with a "subliminal pedagogy." Good writing is good teaching.

THE SHAPE OF AN ARTICLE

An article is written in the shape of an hourglass. It begins with broad general statements, progressively narrows down to the specifics of your study, and then broadens out again to more general considerations. Thus:

The introduction begins broadly:	"Individuals differ radically from one another in the degree to which they are willing and able to express their emotions."
It becomes more specific:	"Indeed, the popular view is that such emotional expressiveness is a central difference between men and women. . . . But the research evidence is mixed. . . ."

And more so:	"There is even some evidence that men may actually. . . ."
Until you are ready to introduce your own study in conceptual terms:	"In this study, we recorded the emotional reactions of both men and women to filmed. . . ."
The method and results sections are the most specific, the "neck" of the hourglass:	"(Method) One hundred male and 100 female undergraduates were shown one of two movies. . . ."
	"(Results) Table 1 shows that men in the father-watching condition cried significantly more. . . ."
The discussion section begins with the implications of your study:	"These results imply that sex differences in emotional expressiveness are moderated by two kinds of variables. . . ."
It becomes broader:	"Not since Charles Darwin's first observations has psychology contributed as much new. . . . "
And more so:	"If emotions can incarcerate us by hiding our complexity, at least their expression can liberate us by displaying our authenticity."

This closing statement might be a bit grandiose for some journals—I am not even sure what it means—but if your study is carefully executed and conservatively interpreted, most editors will permit you to indulge yourself a bit at the two broad ends of the hourglass. Being dull only appears to be a prerequisite for publishing in the professional journals.

THE INTRODUCTION

The first task of the article is to introduce the background and nature of the problem being investigated. Here are four rules of thumb for your opening statements:

1. Write in English prose, not psychological jargon.
2. Do not plunge unprepared readers into the middle of your problem or theory. Take the time and space necessary to lead them up to the formal or theoretical statement of the problem step by step.
3. Use examples to illustrate theoretical points or to introduce unfamiliar conceptual or technical terms. The more abstract the material, the more important such examples become.

4. Whenever possible, try to open with a statement about people (or animals), not psychologists or their research (This rule is almost always violated. Do not use journals as a model here.)

Examples of opening statements:

> *Wrong*: Several years ago, Ekman (1972), Izard (1977), Tomkins (1980), and Zajonc (1980) pointed to psychology's neglect of the affects and their expression. [Okay for somewhere in the introduction, but not the opening statement.]
>
> *Right*: Individuals differ radically from one another in the degree to which they are willing and able to express their emotions.
>
> *Wrong*: Research in the forced-compliance paradigm has focused on the effects of predecisional alternatives and incentive magnitude.
>
> *Wrong*: Festinger's theory of cognitive dissonance received a great deal of attention during the latter part of the 20th century.
>
> *Right*: The individual who holds two beliefs that are inconsistent with one another may feel uncomfortable. For example, the person who knows that he or she enjoys smoking but believes it to be unhealthy may experience discomfort arising from the inconsistency or disharmony between these two thoughts or cognitions. This feeling of discomfort was called *cognitive dissonance* by social psychologist Leon Festinger (1957), who suggested that individuals will be motivated to remove this dissonance in whatever way they can.

Note how this last example leads the reader from familiar terms (*beliefs, inconsistency, discomfort, thoughts*) through transition terms (*disharmony, cognitions*) to the unfamiliar technical term *cognitive dissonance*, thereby providing an explicit, if nontechnical, definition of it. The following example illustrates how one might define a technical term (*ego control*) and identify its conceptual status (a personality variable) more implicitly:

> The need to delay gratification, control impulses, and modulate emotional expression is the earliest and most ubiquitous demand that society places on the developing child. And because success at so many of life's tasks depends critically on the individual's mastery of such ego control, evidence for life-course continuities in this central personality domain should be readily obtained.

Finally, an example in which the technical terms are defined only by the context follows. Note, however, that the technical abbreviation, MAO, is still identified explicitly when it is first introduced.

> In the continuing search for the biological correlates of psychiatric disorder, blood platelets are now a prime target of investigation. In particular, reduced monoamine oxidase (MAO) activity in the platelets is sometimes correlated with paranoid symptomatology, auditory hallucinations or delusions in chronic schizophrenia, and a tendency toward

psychopathology in nonclinical samples of men. Unfortunately, these observations have not always replicated, casting doubt on the hypothesis that MAO activity is, in fact, a biological marker in psychiatric disorder. Even the general utility of the platelet model as a key to central nervous system abnormalities in schizophrenia remains controversial. This study attempts to clarify the relation of MAO activity to symptomatology in chronic schizophrenia.

This kind of writing would not appear in *Newsweek*, and yet it is still comprehensible to an intelligent layperson who may know nothing about blood platelets, MAO activity, or biological markers. The structure of the writing itself adequately defines the relationships among these things and provides enough context to make the basic idea of the study and its rationale clear. At the same time, the introduction is not condescending nor will it bore the technically sophisticated reader. The pedagogy that makes this introduction accessible to the nonspecialist will not only be transparent to the specialist but will enhance the clarity of the article for both readers.

Examples of Examples

When developing complex conceptual arguments or introducing technical materials, it is important not only to provide your readers with illustrative examples but to select the examples with care. In particular, you should try to compose one or two examples that anticipate your actual findings and then use them recurrently to make several interrelated conceptual points. For example, in one of my own studies of trait consistency, some participants were consistently friendly but not consistently conscientious (Bem & Allen, 1974). Accordingly, we used examples of friendliness and conscientiousness throughout the introduction to clarify and illustrate our theoretical points about the subtleties of trait consistency. This pedagogical technique strengthens the thematic coherence of an article and silently prepares the reader for understanding the results. It also shortens the article by removing the need to explain the theory once in the introduction with hypothetical examples and then again in the context of the actual results.

This chapter you are now reading itself provides examples of recurring examples. Although you do not know it yet, the major example will be the fictitious study of sex differences in emotional expression introduced earlier to illustrate the hourglass shape of an article. I deliberately constructed the study and provided a sufficient overview of it at the beginning so that I could draw on it throughout the article. Watch for its elaboration as we proceed. I chose dissonance theory as a second example because most psychologists are already familiar with it; I can draw on this shared resource without having to expend a lot of space explaining it. But just in case you are not familiar with it, I introduced it first in the context of "examples of opening statements" where I could bring you in from the beginning—just as you should do with your own readers. And finally, the Bem–Allen article on trait consistency, mentioned in the previous paragraph, has some special attributes that will earn it additional cameo appearances as we continue.

The Literature Review

After making the opening statements, summarize the current state of knowledge in the area of investigation. What previous research has been done on the problem? What are the pertinent theories of the phenomenon? Although you will have familiarized yourself with the literature before you designed your own study, you may need to look up additional references if your results raise a new aspect of the problem or lead you to recast the study in a different framework. For example, if you discover an unanticipated sex difference in your data, you will want to determine if others have reported a similar sex difference or findings that might explain it. If you consider this finding important, discuss sex differences and the pertinent literature in the introduction. If you consider it to be only a peripheral finding, then postpone a discussion of sex differences until the discussion section.

The *Publication Manual* gives the following guidelines for the literature review:

> Discuss the literature but do not include an exhaustive historical review. Assume that the reader is knowledgeable about the field for which you are writing and does not require a complete digest. . . . Cite and reference only works pertinent to the specific issue and not works of only tangential or general significance. If you summarize earlier works, avoid non-essential details; instead, emphasize pertinent findings, relevant methodological issues, and major conclusions. Refer the reader to general surveys or reviews of the topic if they are available. (APA, 2001, p. 16)   *weaknesses*

The *Publication Manual* also urges authors not to let the goal of brevity mislead them into writing a statement intelligible only to the specialist. One technique for describing even an entire study succinctly without sacrificing clarity is to describe one variation of the procedure in chronological sequence, letting it convey the overview of the study at the same time. (You can use the same technique in your own method section.) Here, for example, is a possible summary of a complicated but classic experiment on cognitive dissonance theory (Festinger & Carlsmith, 1959):

> Sixty male undergraduates were randomly assigned to one of three conditions. In the $1 condition, the participant was first required to perform long repetitive laboratory tasks in an individual experimental session. He was then hired by the experimenter as an "assistant" and paid $1 to tell a waiting fellow student (a confederate) that the tasks

were fun and interesting. In the $20 condition, each participant was hired for $20 to do the same thing. In the control condition, participants simply engaged in the tasks. After the experiment, each participant indicated on a questionnaire how much he had enjoyed the tasks. The results showed that $1 participants rated the tasks as significantly more enjoyable than did the $20 participants, who, in turn, did not differ from the control participants.

This kind of condensed writing looks easy. It is not, and you will have to rewrite such summaries repeatedly before they are both clear and succinct. The preceding paragraph was my eighth draft.

Citations

The standard journal format permits you to cite authors in the text either by enclosing their last names and the year of publication in parentheses, as in A below, or by using their names in the sentence itself, as in B.

A. "MAO activity in some individuals with schizophrenia is actually higher than normal (Tse & Tung, 1949)."
B. "Tse and Tung (1949) report that MAO activity in some individuals with schizophrenia is actually higher than normal."

In general, you should use form A, consigning your colleagues to parentheses. Your narrative line should be about MAO activity in individuals with schizophrenia, not about Tse and Tung. Occasionally, however, you might want the focus specifically on the authors or researchers: "Theophrastus (280 b.c.) implies that persons are consistent across situations, but Montaigne (1580) insists that they are not. Only Mischel (1968), Peterson (1968), and Vernon (1964), however, have actually surveyed the evidence in detail." The point is that you have a deliberate choice to make. Do not just intermix the two formats randomly, paying no attention to the narrative structure.

Criticizing Previous Work

If you take a dim view of previous research or earlier articles in the domain you reviewed, feel free to criticize and complain as strongly as you feel is commensurate with the incompetence you have uncovered. But criticize the work, not the investigators or authors. Ad hominem attacks offend editors and reviewers; moreover, the person you attack is likely to be asked to serve as one of the reviewers of your article. As a consequence, your opportunity to address—let alone, offend—readers will be nipped in the bud. I could launch into a sermonette on communitarian values in science, but I shall assume that this pragmatic warning is sufficient.

Ending the Introduction

End the introduction with a brief overview of your own study. This provides a smooth transition into the method section, which follows immediately:

> Because this sex difference remains elusive, it seemed desirable to test Zanna's parental-role theory of emotional expression in a more realistic setting. Accordingly, in the study to be presented here, we exposed men and women to filmed scenes designed to evoke either negative or positive emotions and assessed their emotional reactions when they thought they were being observed by one or both of their parents. We also sought to examine the relation of emotional expression to self-esteem.

THE METHOD SECTION

The *Publication Manual* spells out in detail what needs to be included in the method section of an article. Here are some additional stylistic suggestions.

If you conducted a fairly complex experiment in which there was a sequence of procedures or events, it is helpful to lead the reader through the sequence as if he or she were a participant. First give the usual overview of the study, including the description of participants, setting, and variables assessed, but then describe the experiment from the participant's vantage point. Provide summaries or excerpts of what was actually said to the participant, including any rationale or "cover story" that was given. Describe the relevant aspects of the room. Show sample items from questionnaires, labels on attitude scales, copies of stimulus materials, or pictures of apparatus. If you administered a standard personality test or attitude scale, describe its general properties unless it is very familiar (e.g., the MMPI or the F scale). For example: "Participants then filled out the Marlowe–Crowne Social Desirability Scale, a true–false inventory that measures the degree to which persons describe themselves in socially desirable terms (e.g., 'I have never lied')."

The purpose of all this is to give your readers a feel for what it was like to be a participant. (This is true even if you used nonhuman participants. Thus it is more important to describe the schedule of reinforcement and the inner dimensions of the Skinner Box—what the animal actually experienced—then its outer dimensions and the voltage of the power supply.) Such information often bears importantly on the interpretation of the behavior observed, and readers should be in a position to arrive at their own judgments about their conclusions.

Name all groups, variables, and operations with easily recognized and remembered labels. Do not use abbreviations (the AMT5% group) or empty labels (Treatment 3). Instead, tell us about the success group and the failure group, the father-watching condition and the mother-watching condition, the teacher sample and the student sample, and so forth. It is also better to label groups or treatments in operational rather than theoretical terms. It is difficult to remember that it was the high dissonance group that was offered the small incentive and the low dissonance group that was offered the large incentive. So tell us instead about the $1 group and the $20 group. You can remind us of the theoretical interpretation of these variables later when you discuss the results.

The method and results sections share the responsibility for presenting certain kinds of data that support the reliability and validity of your substantive findings, and you must judge where this information fits most smoothly into the narrative and when the reader can most easily assimilate it. For example, if you constructed a new personality scale, you need to tell us about its internal homogeneity and other psychometric properties. If you employed observers, tell us about interjudge agreement. If you mailed survey questionnaires, give us the return rate and discuss the possibility that nonrespondents differed from respondents. If you discarded certain participants, tell us why and how many and discuss the possibility that this limits or qualifies the conclusions you can draw. In particular, assure us that they were not all concentrated in the same experimental condition. (Participants discarded during data analysis should be discussed in the results section.)

Discuss participant dropout problems and other difficulties encountered in executing the study only if they might affect the validity or the interpretation of your results. Otherwise spare us your tales of woe. Do tell us that some participants fled your high-stress treatment before you could assess their physiological response, but do not tell us that your dog ate your pigeon and you had to redo the experiment or that you could not run participants Tuesday night because the custodian inadvertently locked the building.

Manipulations and procedures that yielded no useful information should be mentioned if they were administered before you collected your main data; their presence could have affected your findings. Usually it will be sufficient to say that they yielded no information and will not be discussed further. You probably do not need to mention them at all if they were administered after you collected your main data unless you think that other investigators might try to pursue the same fruitless path. Sometimes, however, a "null" result is surprising or of interest in its own right. In this case, it should be treated as a regular datum in your results section.

After presenting the methods you used in your study, discuss any ethical issues they might raise. If the research design required you to keep participants uninformed or even misinformed about the procedures, how did you tell them about this afterward? How did you obtain their prior consent? Were they free to withdraw at any time? Were they subjected to any embarrassment or discomfort? What steps were followed to protect their anonymity? Were you observing people who were unaware of that fact?

If your study raises any of these issues, you should be prepared to justify your procedures. Moreover, you need to assure us that your participants were treated with dignity and that they left your study with their self-esteem intact and their respect for you and psychology enhanced rather than diminished. If you used nonhuman participants—especially dogs, cats, or primates—then you need to address analogous questions about their care and treatment.

End the method section with a brief summary of the procedure and its overall purpose. Your grandmother should be able to skim the method section without reading it; the final paragraph should bring her back "on line."

THE RESULTS SECTION

In short articles or reports of single empirical studies, the results and discussion are often combined. But if you need to integrate several different kinds of results or discuss several general matters, then prepare a separate discussion section. There is, however, no such thing as a pure results section without an accompanying narrative. You cannot just throw numbers at readers and expect them to retain them in memory until they reach the discussion. In other words, write the results section in English prose.

Setting the Stage

Before you can present your results, there are two preliminary matters that need to be handled. First, you should present evidence that your study successfully set up the conditions for testing your hypotheses or answering your questions. If your study required you to produce one group of participants in a happy mood and another in a depressed mood, show us in this section that mood ratings made by the two groups were significantly different. If you divided your participants into groups, assure us that these groups did not differ on some unintended variable that might bear on the interpretation of your results (e.g., social class, intelligence). If your study required you to misinform participants about the procedures, how do you know that they were not suspicious, that participants who participated earlier had not informed participants who participated later, and that your cover story produced the state of belief required for the test of your hypotheses?

Here is also where you can put some of the data discussed in the method section: reliabilities of testing instruments, judges, and observers; return rates on mail surveys; and participant dropout problems.

Not all of these matters need to be discussed at the beginning of the results section. In addition to data you think fit better in the method section, some of these other matters might better be postponed until the discussion section when you are considering alternative explanations of your results (e.g., the possibility that some participants became suspicious). Again, the decision of what to include is very much a matter of judgment. It is an important step, but do not overdo it. Get it out of the way as quickly as possible and get on with your story.

The second preliminary matter to deal with is the method of data analysis. First, describe any overall procedures you used to convert your raw observations into analyzable data. How were responses to your mail survey coded for analysis? How were observers' ratings combined? Were all measures first converted to standard scores? Some of these may also fit better into the method section and need not be repeated. Similarly, data-combining procedures that are highly specific can be postponed. If you combined three measures of anxiety into a single composite score for analysis, tell us about that later when you are about to present the anxiety data.

Next, tell us about the statistical analysis itself. If this is standard, describe it briefly (e.g., "All data were analyzed by two-way analyses of variance with sex of participant and mood induction as the independent variables"). If the analysis is unconventional or makes certain statistical assumptions your data might not satisfy, however, discuss the rationale for it, perhaps citing a reference for readers who wish to check into it further. If your method of analysis is new or likely to be unfamiliar to readers of the journal, you might need to provide a full explanation of it. Sometimes the quantitative treatment of data is a major part of an article's contribution. Variations of multidimensional scaling, causal modeling, and circumplex representations of personality data, for example, have been more important in some articles than the data to which they were applied. In these cases, the method of analysis and its rationale have the same epistemological status as a theory and should be presented in the introduction to the article.

And finally, if the results section is complicated or divided into several parts, you may wish to provide an overview of the section: "The results are presented in three parts. The first section presents the behavioral results for the men, followed by the parallel results for the women. The final section presents the attitudinal and physiological data for both sexes combined." But as I shall argue, this kind of metacommentary should be used sparingly. In most cases, the prose itself should make it unnecessary.

Presenting the Findings

The general rule in reporting your findings is to give the forest first and then the trees. This is true of the results section as a whole: Begin with the central findings, and then move to more peripheral ones. It is also true within subsections: State the basic finding first, and then elaborate or qualify it as necessary. Similarly, discuss an overall measure of aggression or whatever first, and then move to its individual components. Beginning with one of your most central results, proceed as follows:

1. Remind us of the conceptual hypothesis or the question you are asking: "It will be recalled that the men are expected to be more emotionally expressive than the women." Or, "We ask, first, whether the men or the women are more emotionally expressive?" Note that this is a conceptual statement of the hypothesis or question.

2. Remind us of the operations performed and behaviors measured: "In particular, the men should produce more tears during the showing of the film than the women." Or, "Do the men produce more tears during the showing of the film than the women?" Note that this is an operational statement of the hypothesis or question.

3. Tell us the answer immediately and in English: "The answer is yes." Or, "As Table 1 reveals, men do, in fact, cry more profusely than the women."

4. Now, and only now, speak to us in numbers. (Your grandmother can now skip to the next result in case she has forgotten her statistics or her reading glasses.): "Thus the men in all four conditions produced an average of 1.4 cc more tears than the women, $F(1,112) = 5.79, p < .025$."

5. Now you may elaborate or qualify the overall conclusion if necessary: "Only in the father-watching condition did the men fail to produce more tears than the women, but a specific test of this effect failed to reach significance, $t = 1.58, p < .12$."

6. End each section of the results with a summary of where things stand: "Thus, except for the father-watching condition, which will be discussed below, the hypothesis that men cry more than women in response to visually depicted grief appears to receive strong support."

7. Lead into the next section of the results with a smooth transition sentence: "Men may thus be more expressive than women in the domain of negative emotion, but are they more

expressive in the domain of positive emotion? Table 2 shows they are not. . . ." (Again, the "bottom line" is given immediately.) As the results section proceeds, continue to summarize and "update" the reader's store of information frequently. The reader should not have to keep looking back to retrieve the major points of your plot line.

By structuring the results section in this way, by moving from forest to trees, by announcing each result clearly in prose before wading into numbers and statistics, and by summarizing frequently, you permit a reader to decide just how much detail he or she wants to pursue at each juncture and to skip ahead to the next main point whenever that seems desirable.

Figures and Tables

Unless a set of findings can be stated in one or two numbers, results that are sufficiently important to be stressed should be accompanied by a figure or table summarizing the relevant data. The basic rule of presentation is that a reader be able to grasp your major findings either by reading the text or by looking at the figures and tables. Thus, figures and tables must be titled and labeled clearly and completely, even if that means constructing a lengthy title or heading ("Mean number of tears produced by two affective films as a function of affect valence, participant sex, parental observation, and self-esteem"). Within the text itself, lead the reader by the hand through a table to point out the results of interest: "As shown in the first column of Table 2, men produce more tears (2.33 cc) than women (1.89 cc). . . . Of particular interest is the number of tears produced when both father and mother watch (rows 3 and 4). . . ." Do not just wave in the general direction of the table and expect the reader to ferret out the information. For detailed information on figures and tables, see the *Publication Manual* (APA, 2001).

On Statistics

As you know, every comparison between groups or relationship between variables should be accompanied by its level of statistical significance. Otherwise, readers have no way of knowing whether the findings could have emerged by chance. But despite the importance of inferential statistics, they are not the heart of your narrative and should be subordinated to the descriptive results. Whenever possible, state a result first and then give its statistical significance, but in no case should you ever give the statistical test alone without interpreting it substantively. Do not tell us that the three-way interaction with sex, parent condition, and self-esteem was significant at the .05 level unless you tell us immediately and in English that men are less expressive than women in the negative conditions if father watches—but only for men with low self-esteem.

If your experiment used an analysis of variance design, your data analysis will automatically display the effects of several independent variables on a single dependent variable. If this organization is consonant with a smooth presentation of your results, lucky you. Go with it. But do not be a prisoner of ANOVA! If the narrative flows more smoothly by discussing the effects of a single independent variable on several conceptually related dependent variables, tear your ANOVA results apart and reorganize them. Statistical designs are all right in their place, but you—and your prose—are master; they are slave.

Just as your method section should give readers a feel for the procedures used, so too the results section should give them a feel for the behavior observed. Select descriptive indexes or statistics that convey the behavior of your participants as vividly as possible. Tell us the percent of children in your study who hit the Bobo doll or the mean number of times they did so. Remind us that a score of 3.41 on your 5-point rating scale of aggression lies between "slightly aggressive" and "moderately aggressive."

Do this even if the statistical analyses must be performed on some more indirect datum (e.g., the arcsin transform of the number of Bobo hits or the sum of three standardized aggression scores.) Display these indirect indexes, too, if you wish, but give the readers' intuitions first priority. For example, in our study of trait consistency, we analyzed a standard-score index of individual consistency, but we discussed the results in terms of the more familiar correlation coefficient—on which no legitimate statistical analysis could be performed (Bem & Allen, 1974).

After you have presented your quantitative results, it is often useful to become more informal and briefly to describe the behavior of particular individuals in your study. Again, the point is not to prove something but to add richness to your findings, to share with readers the feel of the behavior: "Indeed, two of the men used an entire box of Kleenex during the showing of the heart operation but would not pet the baby kitten owned by the secretary."

THE DISCUSSION SECTION

As noted earlier, the discussion section can either be combined with the results section or appear separately. In either case, it forms a cohesive narrative with the introduction, and you should expect to move materials back and forth between these two sections as you rewrite and reshape the report. Topics that are central to your story will appear in the introduction and probably again in the discussion. More peripheral topics may not be brought up at all until after the presentation of the results. The discussion is also the bottom of the hourglass-shaped format and thus proceeds from specific matters about your study to more general concerns (about methodological strategies, for example) to the broadest generalizations you wish to make. The sequence of topics is often the mirror image of the sequence in the introduction.

Begin the discussion by telling us what you have learned from the study. Open with a clear statement on the support or nonsupport of the hypotheses or the answers to the questions you first raised in the introduction. But do not simply reformulate and repeat points already summarized in the results section. Each new statement should contribute something new to the reader's understanding of the problem. What inferences can be drawn from the findings? These inferences may be at a level quite close to the data or may involve considerable abstraction, perhaps to the level of a larger theory regarding, say, emotion or sex differences. What are the theoretical, practical, or even the political implications of the results?

It is also appropriate at this point to compare your results with those reported by other investigators and to discuss possible shortcomings of your study, conditions that might limit the extent of legitimate generalization or otherwise qualify your inferences. Remind readers of the characteristics of your participant sample, the possibility that it might differ from other populations to which you might want to generalize; of specific characteristics of your methods that might have influenced the outcome; or of any other factors that might have operated to produce atypical results.

But do not dwell compulsively on every flaw! In particular, be willing to accept negative or unexpected results without a tortured attempt to explain them away. Do not make up long, involved, pretzel-shaped theories to account for every hiccup in the data. There is a $-.73$ correlation between the clarity of an investigator's results and the length of his or her discussion section. Do not contribute to this shameful statistic.

Ah, but suppose that, on the contrary, your results have led you to a grand new theory that injects startling clarity into your data and revolutionizes your view of the problem area. Does this justify a long discussion section? No. In this case, you should write the article so that you begin with your new theory. As noted, your task is to provide the most informative and compelling framework for your study from the opening sentence. If your new theory does that, do not wait until the discussion section to spring it on us. A journal article is not a chronology of your thought processes.

The discussion section also includes a consideration of questions that remain unanswered or that have been raised by the study itself, along with suggestions for the kinds of research that would help to answer them. In fact, suggesting additional research is probably the most common way of ending a research report.

Common, but dull. The hourglass shape of an article implies that your final words should be broad general statements of near-cosmic significance, not precious details of interest only to psychologists. Thus the statement, "Further research will be needed before it is clear whether the androgyny scale should be scored as a single continuous dimension or partitioned into a 4-way typology," might well be appropriate somewhere in a discussion section, but, please, not your final farewell. In my opinion, only Montaigne was clever enough to end an article with a statement about further research: "Because [the study of motivation] is a high and hazardous undertaking, I wish fewer people would meddle with it" (1580/1943).

You should probably settle for more modest injunctions: "If gender schema theory has a political message, it is . . . that . . . human behaviors and personality attributes should no longer be linked with gender, and society should stop projecting gender into situations irrelevant to genitalia. The feminist prescription, then, is not that the individual be androgynous, but that the society be gender-aschematic" (S. Bem, 1985).

In any case, end with a bang, not a whimper.

THE TITLE AND ABSTRACT

The title and abstract of your article permit potential readers to get a quick overview of your study and to decide if they wish to read the article itself. Titles and abstracts are also indexed and compiled in reference works and computerized databases. For this reason they should accurately reflect the content of the article and include key words that will ensure their retrieval from a database. You should compose the title and abstract after you have completed the article and have a firm view of its structure and content.

The recommended length for a title is 10 to 12 words. It should be fully explanatory when standing alone and identify the theoretical issues or the variables under investigation. Because you will not be able to mention all the features of your study in the title (or even in the abstract), you must decide which are most important. Once again, the data should guide you. For example, the most instructive findings from our fictitious study on emotional expression should determine which of the following is the most appropriate title: "Laughing Versus Crying: Sex Differences in the Public Display of Positive and Negative Emotions"; "Effects of Being Observed by Parents on the Emotional Responses of Men and Women to Visual Stimuli"; "Emotional Responses to Visual Stimuli as a Function of Sex and Self-Esteem"; "Sex Differences in the Public Display of Emotion as a Function of the Observing Audience"; "Public Versus Private Displays of Emotion in Men and Women."

The abstract of an empirical article should not exceed 120 words. It should contain the problem under investigation (in one sentence, if possible); the participants, specifying pertinent characteristics, such as number, type, age, sex, and species; the experimental method, including the apparatus, data-gathering procedures, and complete test names; the findings, including statistical significance levels; and the conclusion and the implications or applications.

Clearly the abstract must be compact, and this requirement leads many inexperienced writers to make it unintelligible. Remove unnecessary words and eliminate less important details of method and results. But then let it breathe. In particular, allow yourself the space to make the problem under investigation clear to a casually browsing reader. Often you can plagiarize and abbreviate key statements from the article itself. Here is an example:

When are men more emotionally expressive than women? One hundred male and 100 female undergraduates were individually shown a sad or a happy film, while being observed by one or both of their parents. Judges blind to condition rated participants' facial expressions, and a Lachrymeter measured their tear volume. Men cried more during the sad movie but laughed less during the happy movie than did the women (interaction, $p < .02$). However, men in the father-watching condition with low self-esteem (Darley Self-Concept Scale) cried less than all other participants ($p < .05$). It is suggested that sex differences in emotional expression are moderated by the valence of the emotion and—for men—by self-esteem and conditions of being observed.

If the conceptual contribution of your article is more important than the supporting study, this can be reflected in the abstract by omitting experimental details and giving more space to the theoretical material. Here is the title and abstract from our *Psychological Review* article on trait consistency (revised to conform to the new 100 word limit on abstracts of reviews and theoretical articles):

On Predicting Some of the People Some of the Time:
The Search for Cross-Situational Consistencies in Behavior

The recurring controversy over the existence of cross-situational consistencies in behavior is sustained by the discrepancy between our intuitions, which affirm their existence, and the research literature, which does not. It is argued that the nomothetic assumptions of the traditional research paradigm are incorrect and that higher validity coefficients would be obtained if the idiographic assumptions used by our intuitions were adopted. A study is reported which shows it is possible to predict who will be cross-situationally consistent and who will not. Personality assessment must not only attend to situations—as has been recently urged—but to persons as well (Bem & Allen, 1974).

REWRITING AND POLISHING YOUR ARTICLE

For many authors revising an article is unmitigated agony. Even proof-reading is painful. And so they don't. So relieved to get a draft done, they send it off to the journal thinking that they can clean up the writing after it has been accepted. Alas, that day rarely comes. Some may find solace in the belief that the manuscript probably would have been rejected even if it had been extensively revised and polished; after all, most psychology journals accept only 15 to 20% of all manuscripts submitted. But from my experience as an editor, I believe that the difference between the manuscripts accepted and the top 15 to 20% of those rejected is frequently the difference between good and less good writing. Moral: Do not expect journal reviewers to discern your brilliance through the smog of polluted writing. Revise your manuscript. Polish it. Proofread it. Then submit it.

Rewriting is difficult for several reasons. First, it is difficult to edit your own writing. You will not notice ambiguities and explanatory gaps because you know what you meant to say and you understand the omitted steps. One strategy for overcoming this difficulty is to lay your manuscript aside for awhile and then return to it later when it has become less familiar. Sometimes it helps to read it aloud. But there is no substitute for practicing the art of taking the role of the nonspecialist reader, for learning to role-play grandma. As you read, ask yourself, "Have I been told yet what this concept means?" "Has the logic of this step been demonstrated?" "Would I know what the independent variable is at this point?" This is precisely the skill of the good lecturer in Psychology 101, the ability to anticipate the audience's level of understanding at each point in the presentation. Good writing is good teaching.

But because this is not easy, you should probably give a fairly polished copy of the manuscript to a friend or colleague for a critical review. (If you get a critique from two colleagues you will have simulated a trial run of a journal's review process.) The best readers are those who have themselves published in the psychological journals but who are unfamiliar with the subject of your article. (A student from Psychology 101 would probably be too intimidated to give usefully critical feedback; grandma will be too kind.)

If your colleagues find something unclear, do not argue with them. They are right: By definition, the writing is unclear. Their suggestions for correcting the unclarities may be wrong, even dumb. But as unclarity detectors, readers are never wrong. Also resist the temptation simply to clarify their confusion verbally. Your colleagues do not want to offend you or appear stupid, and so they will simply mumble "oh yes, of course, of course" and apologize for not having read carefully enough. As a consequence, you will be pacified, and your next readers, the journal reviewers, will stumble over the same problem. They will not apologize; they will reject.

Rewriting is difficult for a second reason: It requires a high degree of compulsiveness and attention to detail. The probability of writing a sentence perfectly the first time is vanishingly small, and good writers rewrite nearly every sentence of an article in the course of polishing successive drafts. But even good writers differ from one another in their approach to the first draft. Some spend a long time carefully choosing each word and reshaping each sentence and paragraph as they go. Others pound out a rough draft quickly and then go back for extensive revision. Although I personally prefer the former method, I think it wastes time. For journal articles in particular, I think most authors should get the first draft done as quickly as possible without agonizing over stylistic niceties. But once it is done, compulsiveness and attention to detail become the required virtues.

Finally, rewriting is difficult because it usually means restructuring. Sometimes it is necessary to discard whole sections of an article, add new ones, go back and do more data analysis, and then totally reorganize the article just to iron out a bump in the logic of the argument. Do not get so attached to your first draft that you are unwilling to tear it apart and rebuild it. (This is why the technique of crafting each sentence of a first draft wastes time. That beautiful turn of phrase that took me 40 minutes to shape gets discarded when the article gets restructured. Worse, I get so attached to the phrase that I resist restructuring until I can find a new home for it.) A badly constructed building cannot be salvaged by brightening up the wallpaper. A badly constructed article cannot be salvaged by changing words, inverting sentences, and shuffling paragraphs.

Which brings me to the word processor. Its very virtuosity at making these cosmetic changes may tempt you to tinker endlessly, encouraging you in the illusion that you are restructuring right there in front of the monitor. Do not be fooled. You are not. A word processor—even in conjunction with a fancy "outline mode"—is not an adequate restructuring tool. Moreover, it can produce flawless, physically beautiful drafts of wretched writing, encouraging you in the illusion that they are finished manuscripts ready to be submitted. Do not be fooled. They are not. If you are blessed with an excellent memory (or a very large monitor) and are confident that you can get away with a purely electronic process of restructuring, fine, do it. But do not be ashamed to print out a complete draft of your manuscript, spread it out on table or floor, take pencil, scissors, and scotch tape in hand, and then, all by your low-tech self, have at it.

Omit Needless Words

Virtually all experienced writers agree that any written expression that deserves to be called *vigorous writing*, whether it is a short story, an article for a professional journal, or a complete book, *is* characterized by the attribute of being succinct, *concise*, and to the point. *A sentence*—no matter where in the writing it occurs—*should contain no unnecessary* or superfluous *words*, words that stand in the way of the writer's direct expression of his or her meaning and purpose. In a very similar fashion, *a paragraph*—the basic unit of organization in English prose—*should contain no unnecessary* or superfluous *sentences*, sentences that introduce peripheral content into the writing or stray from its basic narrative line. It is in this sense that a writer is like an artist executing a drawing, and it is in this sense that a writer is like an engineer designing a machine. Good writing should be economical *for the same reason that a drawing should have no unnecessary lines, and* good writing should be streamlined in the same way that *a machine* is designed to have *no unnecessary parts*, parts that contribute little or nothing to its intended function.

This prescription to be succinct and concise is often misunderstood and *requires* judicious application. It certainly does *not* imply *that the writer* must *make all* of his or her *sentences short* and choppy *or* leave out all adjectives, adverbs, and qualifiers. Nor does it mean that he or she must *avoid* or eliminate *all detail* from the writing *and treat* his or her *subjects only in* the barest skeleton or *outline* form. *But* the requirement does imply *that every word* committed to paper should *tell* something new to the reader and contribute in a significant and nonredundant way to the message that the writer is trying to convey.

You have just read a 303 word essay on brevity. It is not a terrible first draft, but a good writer or copyeditor would take its message to heart and, by crossing out all the nonitalicized words, cut it by 81%. Savor the result:

> Vigorous writing is concise. A sentence should contain no unnecessary words, a paragraph no unnecessary sentences, for the same reason that a drawing should have no unnecessary lines and a machine no unnecessary parts. This requires not that the writer make all sentences short or avoid all detail and treat subjects only in outline, but that every word tell. [59 words]

This essay on brevity was written by Strunk and White (2000, p. 23) under the heading: "Omit Needless Words." Obey their injunction, because it is the most important piece of advice in this chapter. Journal articles should also omit needless concepts, topics, anecdotes, asides, and footnotes. Clear any underbrush that clutters your narrative. If a point seems peripheral to your main theme, remove it. If you cannot bring yourself to do this, put it in a footnote. Then when you revise your manuscript, remove the footnote.

Copyediting other people's writing is good practice for improving your own. It is also less painful than editing your own and much easier than actually writing. Any piece of prose will do. Here was an exercise for my writing class; it was part of a letter Cornell sent out to potential graduate applicants. You may wish to try your hand at it.

> Psychology is a wide field of study, and we are not equally strong in all parts of it. At present, we regard our major strengths as lying in three broadly defined domains in which we have many faculty, and a couple of smaller areas in which also have appreciable resources. The three primary areas are Biopsychology, Experimental Psychology, and Personality and Social Psychology; the others are Mathematical/Differential Psychology and Experimental Psychopathology. The areas and the relevant faculty are listed below. Please note that this listing is informal; it does not imply that the listed faculty members have no other interests or can readily be fitted into predefined areas. The actual network of faculty interests and responsibilities is too subtle to be described in a letter such as this. The listing is just a rough and ready way to tell you what the Field of Psychology at Cornell is like. [149 words]

Here is a reasonable revision:

> Psychology is a wide field, and our major strengths are Biopsychology, Experimental Psychology, and Personality and Social Psychology. We also have resources in Mathematical/Differential Psychology and Experimental Psychopathology. The following list of faculty within areas provides a rough guide to the Field of Psychology at Cornell. Faculty interests are broader than this list implies, however, and do not always neatly fit the predefined areas. [65 words, a savings of 56%]

To maintain the vigor of your prose, try to spend at least 15 minutes each day omitting needless words. Your goal should be to reach at least 30% of all words encountered. (Copyedited versions of this chapter will be returned unopened.)

Avoid Metacomments on the Writing

Expository writing fails its mission if it diverts the reader's attention to itself and away from the topic; the process of writing should be transparent to the reader. In particular, the prose itself should direct the flow of the narrative without requiring you to play tour guide by commenting on it. Do not say, "Now that I have discussed the three theories of emotion, we can turn to the empirical work on each of them. I will begin with the psychoanalytic account of affect. . . ." Instead, move directly from your discussion of the theories into the literature review with a simple transition sentence such as, "Each of these three theories has been tested empirically. Thus, the psychoanalytic account of affect has received support in studies that. . . ." Do not say, "Now that we have seen the results for negative affect, we are in a position to examine men's and women's emotional expression in the realm of positive affect. The relevant data are presented in Table 2. . . ." Instead use a transition sentence that simultaneously summarizes and moves the story along: "Men may thus be more expressive than women in the domain of negative emotion, but are they also more expressive in the domain of positive emotion? Table 2 shows that they are not. . . ." Any other guideposts needed can be supplied by using informative headings and by following the advice on repetition and parallel construction given in the next section.

If you feel the need to make metacomments to keep the reader on the narrative path, then your plot line is probably already too cluttered, the writing insufficiently linear. Metacomments will only oppress the prose further. Instead, copyedit. Omit needless words; don't add them!

Use Repetition and Parallel Construction

Inexperienced writers often substitute synonyms for recurring words and vary their sentence structure in the mistaken belief that this is more creative, stylish, or interesting. Instead of using repetition and parallel construction, as in "Men may be more expressive than women in the domain of negative emotion, but they are not more expressive in the domain of positive emotion," they attempt to be more creative: "Men may be more expressive than women in the domain of negative emotion, but it is not true that they are more willing and able than the opposite sex to display the more cheerful affects."

Such creativity is hardly more interesting, but it is certainly more confusing. In scientific communication, it can be deadly. When an author uses different words to refer to the same concept in a technical article— where accuracy is paramount—readers will justifiably wonder if different meanings are implied. The example given is not disastrous, and most readers will be unaware that their understanding flickered momentarily when the prose hit a bump. But consider the cognitive burden carried by readers who must hack through this "creative" jungle:

> The high-dissonance participants were paid a small sum of money while being given a free choice of whether or not to participate, whereas the participants we randomly assigned to the large-incentive treatment (the low-dissonance condition) were not offered the opportunity to refuse.

This (fictitious) author should have written:

> High dissonance participants were paid a small sum of money and were not required to participate; low-dissonance participants were paid a large sum of money and were required to participate.

The wording and grammatical structure of the two clauses are held rigidly parallel; only the variables vary. Repetition and parallel construction are among the most effective servants of clarity. Don't be creative, be clear.

Repetition and parallel construction also serve clarity at a larger level of organization. By providing the reader with distinctive guideposts to the structure of the prose, they can diminish or eliminate the need for metacomments. Following, for example, are the opening sentences from three of the paragraphs in the earlier section on rewriting:

2nd paragraph: "Rewriting is difficult for several reasons. First. . . ."
5th paragraph: "Rewriting is difficult for a second reason:"
6th paragraph: "Finally, rewriting is difficult because it. . . ."

If I had substituted synonyms for the recurring words or varied the grammatical structure of these opening sentences, their guiding function would have been lost, the reader's sense of the section's organization blurred. (I try so hard to be helpful, and I bet you didn't even notice. That, of course, is the point.)

Finally, repetition and parallel construction can serve style and creativity as well as clarity. They can provide rhythm and punch: "A sentence should contain no unnecessary words, a paragraph no unnecessary sentences for the same reason that a drawing should have no unnecessary lines and a machine no unnecessary parts." They can establish metaphor: "A badly constructed building cannot be salvaged by brightening up the wallpaper. A badly constructed article cannot be salvaged by changing words, inverting sentences, and shuffling paragraphs." They can add humor: "The word processor encourages you in the illusion that you are restructuring. Do not be fooled. You are not. The word processor encourages you in the illusion that your drafts are finished manuscripts. Do not be fooled. They are not."

Jargon

Jargon is the specialized vocabulary of a discipline, and it serves a number of legitimate functions in scientific communication. A specialized term may be more general, more precise, or freer of surplus meaning than any natural language equivalent (e.g., the term *disposition* encompasses, and hence is more general than, *beliefs*, *attitudes*, *moods*, and *personality attributes*; *reinforcement* is more precise and freer of surplus meaning than *reward*). And the technical vocabulary often makes an important conceptual distinction not apprehended by the layperson's vocabulary (e.g., *genotype* versus *phenotype*).

But if a jargon term does not satisfy any of these criteria, opt for English. Much psychological jargon has become second-nature to us in the profession and serves only to muddy our prose for the general reader. (I once had to interrogate an author at length to learn that a prison program for "strengthening the executive functions of the ego" actually taught prisoners how to fill out job applications.) Unless the jargon term is extremely well-known (e.g., *reinforcement*), it should be defined—explicitly, implicitly, or by example—the first time it is introduced. (See the sample opening statements earlier in this article for ways to do this.)

Voice and Self-Reference

In the past, scientific writers used the passive voice almost exclusively and referred to themselves in the third person: "This experiment was designed by the authors to test. . . ." This practice produces lifeless prose and is no longer the norm. Use the active voice unless style or content dictates otherwise; and, in general, keep self-reference to a minimum. Remember that you are not the topic of your article. You should not refer to yourself as "the author" or "the investigator." (You may refer to "the experimenter" in the method section, however, even if that happens to be you; the experimenter *is* part of the topic under discussion there.) Do not refer to yourself as "we" unless there really are two or more authors. You may refer to yourself as "I," but do so sparingly. It tends to distract the reader from the topic, and it is better to remain in the background. Leave the reader in the background, too. Do not say, "The reader will find it hard to believe that. . . ." or "You will be surprised to learn. . . ." (This chapter violates the rule because you and your prose *are* the topic.) You may, however, refer to the reader indirectly in imperative, "you–understood" sentences: "Consider, first, the results for women." "Note particularly the difference between the means in Table 1."

Yeah! replaces my petpeeve

In some contexts, you can use "we" to refer collectively to yourself and your readers: "We can see in Table 1 that most of the tears. . . ." The *Publication Manual*, however, emphasizes that the referent of "we" must be unambiguous; for example, copyeditors will object to the sentence "In everyday life, of course, we tend to overestimate. . . ." because it is not clear just who is meant by "we." They will accept "In everyday life, of course, we humans tend to overestimate. . . ." or "In everyday life, of course, human decision makers often make errors; for example, we tend to overestimate. . . ."

Tense

Use the past or present perfect tense when reporting the previous research of others ("Bandura reported. . . ." or "Hardin has reported. . . ."), and past tense when reporting how you conducted your study ("Observers were posted behind. . . .") and specific past behaviors of your participants ("Two of the men talked. . . ."). Use the present tense for results currently in front of the reader ("As Table 2 shows, the negative film is more effective. . . .") and for conclusions that are more general than the specific results ("Positive emotions, then, are more easily expressed when. . . .").

Avoid Language Bias

Like most publishers, the APA now has extensive guidelines for language that refers to individuals or groups. If your article requires you to discuss any of the groups mentioned in this section, you should probably consult the detailed advice in the *Publication Manual* (APA, 2001, pp. 61– 76).

Research Participants

One distinctive group of people who appear in our journal articles are those whom we study. It is no longer considered appropriate to objectify them by calling them *subjects*. Instead use descriptive terms that either identify them more specifically or that acknowledge their roles as partners in the research process, such as *college students, children, individuals, participants, interviewees,* or *respondents*. You may still use the terms *subjects, subject variables,* and *subject sample* when discussing statistics or (at least for now) when referring to nonhuman participants.

Sex and Gender

The issue of language bias comes up most frequently with regard to sex or gender, and the most awkward problems arise from the use of masculine nouns and pronouns when the content refers to both sexes. The generic use of *man, he, his,* and *him* to refer to both sexes is not only misleading in many instances, but research shows that readers think of male persons when these forms are used (Martyna, 1978). Sometimes the results are not only sexist but humorous in their naive androcentrism: "Man's vital needs include food, water, and access to females" (Quoted in Martyna, 1978).

In most contexts, the simplest alternative is the use of the plural. Instead of writing, "The individual who displays prejudice in his personal relations . . . ," write "Individuals who display prejudice in their personal relations are. . . ." Sometimes the pronoun can simply be dropped or replaced by a sex-neutral article (*the, a,* or *an*). Instead of writing, "The researcher must avoid letting his preconceptions bias his interpretation of results," you can write, "The researcher must avoid letting preconceptions bias the interpretation of results."

If it is stylistically important to focus on the single individual, the use of "he or she," "him or her," and so forth is acceptable but clumsy if used often. Alternating *he* and *she* is both confusing and distracting. Similarly, alternatives like *he/she* or *s/he* are unpronounceable and grate on the eye. Do not use them.

You may find it instructive to review how I have dealt with the pronoun problem in this article. In particular, note the many references to the "reader" or "readers." Sometimes the plural worked fine (e.g., "Don't plunge readers into the middle of your problem. Take the time to lead them . . ."), but in other instances the imagery of the sentence required the stylistic use of the singular (e.g., "Lead the reader by the hand through a table . . ."). In these cases, I have tried to minimize using the awkward "he or she" construction.

Stylistic matters aside, however, you must be accurate in your use of pronouns when you describe your research or that of others. Readers must be explicitly told the sex of experimenters, observers, and participants. When referring to males, use male pronouns; when referring to females, use female pronouns. (See, for example, the earlier description of the Festinger–Carlsmith study, which used male participants.) Under no circumstances should you omit or hide sex identity in a misguided attempt to be unbiased.

The problems of gender reference become easier when we move away from pronouns. Words like *man* and *mankind* are easily replaced by terms like *people* and *humanity*. Instead of manning projects, we can staff them. The federal government has already desexed occupational titles so that we have letter carriers rather than mailmen; in private industry we have flight attendants rather than stewardesses. And in life, children need nurturing or parenting, not just mothering. In all these cases, you will find it easy to discover the appropriate sex-neutral term if you think of the activity rather than the person doing it.

Next, watch out for plain old stereotyping. The author who asserts that "research scientists often neglect their wives" fails to acknowledge that women as well as men are research scientists. If the author meant specifically male research scientists, he (she?) should have said so. Do not talk about ambitious men and aggressive women or cautious men and timid women if the use of different adjectives denotes not different behaviors on the part of men and women but your stereotyped interpretation of those behaviors. Do not make stereotyped assumptions about marital sex roles by saying that "The client's husband lets her teach part-time" if all you know is that the client teaches part-time. If the bias is not yours but someone else's, let the writing make that clear: "The client's husband 'lets' her teach part-time." "The husband says he 'lets' the client teach part-time." "The client says her husband lets her teach part-time." "The client says sarcastically that her husband 'lets' her teach part-time." The client and her husband are allowed to say such things. You are not.

Finally, select examples with care. Beware of your assumptions about the sex of doctors, homemakers, nurses, and so forth. Why not: "The athlete who believes in her ability to succeed . . ."? Let our writing promote the view that woman's vital needs are the same as man's: food, water, and access to equality.

Racial and Ethnic Identity

Preferences for names referring to racial and ethnic groups change over time. For example, *African American* and *Black* are currently acceptable terms, whereas *Negro* and *Afro-American* are now obsolete. Similarly, *Asian* and *Asian American* are currently acceptable designations, but *Oriental* is not. As these examples illustrate, hyphens should not be used in multiword designations, and terms such as *Black* and *White* are considered proper nouns and should be capitalized.

Depending on their historical countries of origin, individuals may prefer to be called *Hispanic*, *Latino*, or *Chicano* (*Latina* and *Chicana* for women). *American Indian* and *Native American* are both accepted terms for referring to indigenous people of North America; but, technically, only the latter category includes Hawaiians and Samoans. Native peoples of northern Canada, Alaska, eastern Siberia, and Greenland may prefer *Inuk* (plural, *Inuit*) to *Eskimo*. Alaska Natives include many groups in addition to Eskimos. It is often relevant to be more specific in describing your participants. For example, it may be pertinent to know that they were Cuban, not just Hispanic; Chinese, Vietnamese, or Korean, not just Asian.

If you are uncertain about how to describe your research participants, ask them how they prefer to be identified.

Sexual Orientation

Like terms referring to racial and ethnic identity, terms referring to sexual orientation also change over time. For example, the term *sexual orientation* itself is now preferred to the older *sexual preference*—which implies a temporary free choice rather than an enduring disposition. Although terms such as *homosexual* and *homosexuality* are still technically correct and may be used in phrases such as "a homosexual orientation" or "more Americans now accept homosexuality," they should be avoided when referring to individuals or groups. Instead of referring to *homosexuals* or *bisexuals*, use *lesbians*, *gay men*, or *bisexual men and women*. In some contexts, the word *gay* can be used to include both men and women (e.g., "the gay rights movement"), but when referring to individuals or groups, retain the distinction between gay men and lesbians.

Sexual orientation is not the same as sexual behavior. Not everyone who engages in a sexual act with a person of the same sex should be considered gay or lesbian, and hence you should not use the terms *homosexual behavior* or *heterosexual behavior*. Instead, describe specific instances of sexual behavior using terms such as *male–male, female–female, male–female,* or *same-gender sexual behavior.*

Note the use of the word *gender* in the previous sentence. Although there are differences in usage across and within disciplines, the term *sex* is usually considered to refer to biology; thus *male* and *female* are terms referring to sex. In contrast, *gender* usually refers to the cultural interpretation or elaboration of sex; thus *masculine* and *feminine* are terms referring to gender. This is not a hard and fast rule, however. For example, because the term *sex* can be confused with *sexual behavior*, the term *same-gender sexual behavior* was used in the previous paragraph even though it refers to a sexual interaction between two people of the same biological sex. The following example from the *Publication Manual* also illustrates the use of *gender* in a context where the term *sex* might be confusing: "In accounting for attitudes toward the bill, sexual orientation rather than gender accounted for most of the variance. Most gay men and lesbians were for the proposal; most heterosexual men and women were against it" (APA, 2001, p. 63).

Disabilities

When referring to individuals with disabilities, maintain their integrity as individuals and human beings by avoiding language that equates them with their conditions. Do not use nouns such as *neurotics, schizophrenics, manic-depressives, the mentally retarded,* or even *the disabled.* Also avoid terms that imply victimization (e.g., "suffers from schizophrenia," "AIDS victim") or that can be interpreted as a slur (e.g., *cripple*). In general, the preferred forms of description are "person with _____" or "person living with _____" or "person who has _____." *Challenged* and *special* are often considered euphemistic and should be used only if preferred by those who participate in your study.

There is one exception to these guidelines: the Deaf. (Note the capital "D.") Although some individuals with reduced hearing may find the term *hearing impaired* acceptable, many Deaf individuals do not. They regard themselves as members of a distinctive linguistic culture that communicates in a manual (sign) language. Accordingly, they take pride in referring to themselves as Deaf and do not regard themselves as impaired or disabled. Do not use the terms *hard of hearing* or *deaf mute* to describe them. If your study involved Deaf participants, ask them how they prefer to be described.

Common Errors of Grammar and Usage

The following errors seem to me to be the most frequent in journal writing (listed alphabetically):

Compared with versus *compared to.* Similar orders of things are compared *with* one another; different orders of things are compared *to* one another: "Let me not compare thee *with* previous lovers I have had; rather, let me compare thee *to* a summer's day." "Mischel's articles are often compared *with* Bandura's articles; Bem's articles are often compared *to* Mozart's sonatas."

Data. The word *data* is plural: "Analyze those data thoroughly."

Different from versus *different than.* The first is correct, the second, incorrect (although, alas for us purists, very common and gaining respectability). The confusion arises because *than* correctly follows comparative adjectives. Thus you are correct to suppose that life is more *than* psychology, that living a good life is harder in many respects *than* writing a good article, and that living well requires broader skills *than* does writing well. Just remember that life is different *from* psychology, that living a good life is different in many respects *from* writing a good article, and that living well requires skills different *from* those required for writing well.

Since versus *because.* *Since* means "after that." It should not be used as a substitute for *because* if there is any ambiguity of interpretation. *Wrong (but at least not ambiguous)*: "Since the study of motivation is a high and hazardous undertaking, I wish fewer people would meddle with it." *Better*: "Because the study of motivation is a high and hazardous undertaking, I wish fewer people would meddle with it." *Ambiguous*: "Since I read Montaigne, I have been tempted to abandon the study of motivation." This last case is correct if the writer is using *since* in the temporal sense: "Ever since reading Montaigne, I have been tempted. . . ." It is incorrect if the writer means *because*.

That versus *which.* *That* clauses (called restrictive) are essential to the meaning of the sentence; *which* clauses (called nonrestrictive) merely add additional information. The following example illustrates the correct use of both words: "Dissonance theory, *which* has received major attention, is one of the theories *that* postulates a motivational process. Thus, if a person holds two cognitions *that* are inconsistent. . . . " Most *whichs* in journal writing are incorrect. You should go on a *which* hunt in your own manuscripts and turn most of them into *thats*.

While versus *although, but, whereas.* *While* means "at the same time" and in most cases cannot substitute for these other words. *Wrong*: "*While* inferential statistics are important, descriptive statistics are the heart of your narrative." *Right*: "*Although* inferential statistics are important, descriptive statistics are the heart of your narrative." Or, "Inferential statistics are important, *but* descriptive statistics are the heart of your narrative." *Wrong*: "*While* I like personality traits, Mischel prefers a social learning approach." *Right*: "*Whereas* I like personality traits, Mischel prefers a social learning approach." On the other hand, the following usage is correct: "*While* I like personality traits, I find merit in Mischel's social learning approach." This can be seen by substituting "at the same time" for "while": "I like personality traits; at the same time, I find merit in Mischel's social learning approach."

PUBLISHING YOUR ARTICLE

Long ago and far away, a journal editor allegedly accepted a manuscript that required no revisions. I believe the author was William James. In other words, if your article is provisionally accepted for publication "pending revisions in accord with the reviewers' comments," you should be deliriously happy. Publication is now virtually under your control. If your article is rejected but you are invited to resubmit a revised version, you should still be happy—if not deliriously so—because you still have a reasonable shot at getting it published.

But this is the point at which many authors give up. As one former editor noted,

> in my experience as an associate editor, I thought a good deal of variance in predicting eventual publication came from this phase of the process. Authors are often discouraged by negative feedback and miss the essential positive fact that they have been asked to revise! They may never resubmit at all, or may let an inordinate amount of time pass before they do (during which editors and reviewers become unavailable, lose the thread of the project, and so forth). An opposite problem is that some authors become defensive and combative and refuse to make needed changes for no reason.

So do not give up at this point. Feel free to complain to your colleagues or rail at your poodle because the stupid reviewers failed to read your manuscript correctly. But then turn to the task of revising your manuscript with a dispassionate, problem-solving approach. First, pay special attention to criticisms or suggestions made by more than one reviewer or highlighted by the editor in the cover letter. These *must* be addressed in your revision— even if not in exactly the way the editor or reviewers suggest.

Second, look carefully at each of the reviewers' misreadings. I argued earlier that whenever readers of a manuscript find something unclear, they are right; by definition, the writing is unclear. The problem is that readers themselves do not always recognize or identify the unclarities explicitly. Instead, they misunderstand what you have written and then make a criticism or offer a suggestion that makes no sense. In other words, you should also interpret reviewers' misreadings as signals that your writing is unclear.

Think of your manuscript as a pilot experiment in which the pilot participants (reviewers) did not understand the instructions you gave them.

Analyze the reasons for their misunderstanding and then rewrite the problematic sections so that subsequent readers will not be similarly misled.
Compared with the average journal reader, reviewers are almost always more
knowledgeable about your topic, more experienced in writing manuscripts
themselves, and more conscientious about reading your article. If they did
not understand, neither will that average reader.

Third, when you send in your revised manuscript, tell the editor in a
cover letter how you have responded to each of the criticisms or suggestions
made by the reviewers. If you have decided not to adopt a particular suggestion, state your reasons, perhaps pointing out how you remedied the problem
in some alternative way.

Following are some fictitious examples of cover-letter responses that
also illustrate ways of responding to certain kinds of criticisms and suggestions
within the revision itself.

1. *Wrong:* "I have left the section on the animal studies un-
   changed. If Reviewers A and C can't even agree on whether
   the animal studies are relevant, I must be doing something
   right."
   Right: "You will recall that Reviewer A thought that the animal
   studies should be described more fully, whereas Reviewer C
   thought they should be omitted. A biopsychologist in my
   department agreed with Reviewer C that the animal studies
   are not really valid analogs of the human studies. So I have
   dropped them from the text but cited Snarkle's review of them
   in an explanatory footnote on page 26."

2. *Wrong:* "Reviewer A is obviously Deborah Hardin, who has
   never liked me or my work. If she really thinks that behavioral
   principles solve all the problems of obsessive–compulsive disorders, then let her write her own article. Mine is about the
   cognitive processes involved."
   Right: "As the critical remarks by Reviewer A indicate, this
   is a contentious area, with different theorists staking out strong
   positions. Apparently I did not make it clear that my article
   was intended only to cover the cognitive processes involved in
   obsessive–compulsive disorders and not to engage the debate
   between cognitive and behavioral approaches. To clarify this,
   I have now included the word 'cognitive' in both the title
   and abstract, taken note of the debate in my introduction,
   and stated explicitly that the article will not undertake a
   comparative review of the two approaches. I hope this is
   satisfactory."

3. *Right:* "You will recall that two of the reviewers questioned the validity of the analysis of variance, with Reviewer B suggesting that I use multiple regression instead. I agree with their reservations regarding the ANOVA but believe that a multiple regression analysis is equally problematic because it makes the same assumptions about the underlying distributions. So, I have retained the ANOVA but summarized the results of a nonparametric analysis, which yields the same conclusions. If you think it preferable, I could simply substitute this nonparametric analysis for the original ANOVA, although it will be less familiar to the journal's readers."

Above all, remember that the editor is your ally in trying to shape a manuscript that will be a credit both to you and the journal. So, cooperate in the effort to turn your sow's ear into a vinyl purse. Be civil and make nice. You may not live longer, but you will publish more.

REFERENCES

American Psychological Association. (2001). *Publication manual of the American Psychological Association* (5th ed.). Washington, DC: Author.

Bem, D. J. (1995). Writing a review article for *Psychological Bulletin. Psychological Bulletin, 118,* 172–177.

Bem, D. J., & Allen, A. (1974). Predicting some of the people some of the time: The search for cross-situational consistencies in behavior. *Psychological Review, 81,* 506–520.

Bem, S. L. (1985). Androgyny and gender schema theory: A conceptual and empirical integration. In T. B. Sonderegger (Ed.), *Nebraska symposium on motivation 1984: The psychology of gender* (pp. 179–226). Lincoln: University of Nebraska Press.

Festinger, L. A. (1957). *A theory of cognitive dissonance.* Stanford, CA: Stanford University Press.

Festinger, L., & Carlsmith, J. M. (1959). Cognitive consequences of forced compliance. *Journal of Personality and Social Psychology, 58,* 203–210.

Martyna, W. (1978). What does "he" mean? *Journal of Communication, 28,* 131–138.

de Montaigne, M. (1943). Of the inconsistency of our actions. In D. M. Frame (Trans.), *Selected essays, translated and with introduction and notes by Donald M. Frame* (pp. 119–126). Roslyn, NY: Walter J. Black. (Original work published 1580)

Strunk, W., Jr., & White, E. B. (2000). *The elements of style* (4th ed.). Boston: Allyn and Bacon.

11

INTELLECTUAL PROPERTY

JAMES L. HILTON AND JONATHAN R. ALGER

We know how dentists must feel. Tell someone that you spend your days thinking about copyright and intellectual property and you find yourself on the receiving end of countless strange looks. At best, people assume that you are benign. They expect you to tell them to obey the law and to seek permissions for the copies that they make—the copyright equivalent of daily flossing. At worst, they assume that you are more akin to Sir Laurence Olivier's character in *The Marathon Man*—your sole purpose in life is to instill great pain and trauma to no noble end.

So, at the risk of alienating potential readers of this chapter, we begin with a confession. We think copyright is both interesting and important. Indeed, if we were to nominate a single topic that does not get enough attention in academic circles, it is copyright. After all, information is the very lifeblood of any academic community. As scholars and teachers, we constantly create, transform, and transmit information to our students, colleagues, and the world at large.

Within our academic community, we typically see intellectual progress as requiring the free exchange of ideas. But we are surrounded by a world in which information is rapidly becoming a commodity—a piece of property with tangible value protected by copyright. In that world, legal, cultural, and technological changes seem to be rapidly moving toward a "pay per view" model in which each peek at information comes at a price and ideas are zealously guarded. How the academic community responds to these external pressures—in the ways that we decide what types and portions of works we will use in our classrooms, negotiate publishing contracts, establish authorship with students and colleagues, and dance with our academic institutions around the question of who owns teaching and research—is vital to our future as scholars.

In this chapter, we briefly review copyright law and then explore a series of case studies to examine some of the challenges copyright law and popular culture have for university policy, faculty life, and academic tradition. We believe the stakes in this area are high, and our goal throughout the chapter is less to provide answers than it is to provoke thoughtful reflection and discussion.

SETTING THE LEGAL STAGE

To understand the challenges and opportunities that copyright poses for the academy, it is necessary to understand the logic behind copyright law. Because this logic is often counterintuitive, we highlight key elements of copyright law through a series of "copyright surprises"—areas in which common intuition frequently leads to incorrect conclusions.

Surprise #1: Why Copyright Exists

Why does copyright exist? Most people think that the answer is both simple and obvious. Copyright exists to protect an author's intellectual property. Consider the evidence. Every movie comes with dire warnings from the FBI about the penalties that accompany unauthorized duplication. An entire generation of college students stands accused of using peer-to-peer networks and the high speed connections their institutions provide to steal millions of dollars worth of music from the recording industry. Even college professors begin to assert ownership over the content of their classes when commercial note-taking services come knocking. Surely, then, copyright is all about protecting property.

Except that it is not. The notion that copyright is primarily about protecting property is a fairly recent, and largely cultural, development. Instead, copyright is first and foremost about promoting learning. Protecting property is merely a means toward that noble end (Lessig, 2002).

How do we know that copyright is about learning? First, Article I of the U.S. Constitution tells us that it is. Article I is the part of the Constitution that enumerates the various powers of the Congress. Among these powers is the power to grant copyright protection to original works. It is intriguing that although the Congress is not told why it is given the power to tax, approve treaties, or declare war, Congress *is* told why it is given the power to grant copyright protection.

> The Congress shall have Power . . . To promote the Progress of Science and the useful Arts, by securing for limited times to Authors and Inventors the exclusive right to their respective Writings and Discoveries. (U.S. Constitution, art. I, § 8, cl. 8)

In other words, Congress is given the power to grant copyrights as a means to an end. From the beginning, the idea was that by granting authors control over their works, they would be stimulated to create new works and other people would be able to build on the ideas contained in those works.

Second, copyright gives authors and inventors a limited monopoly over their writings and inventions. Given that the Framers of the Constitution were generally skeptical of monopolies, what cause would be sufficiently important to warrant monopolistic control? As suggested by the language of Article I, the advancement of knowledge—not profit—is the purpose for this limited monopoly.

Third, the original requirements for gaining copyright protection included registering the work, announcing the work in one or more newspapers, publishing the work, and depositing a copy of the work with the secretary of state within six months of publication (Gorman & Ginsburg, 1993). If the sole goal of copyright was to protect the author's property, why include these hurdles? Perhaps because what they all have in common is that they promote access to the works and the ideas contained within them.

Surprise #2: What Copyright Does Not Protect

When the first author of this chapter was young and naive, he wrote a prospectus for a multimedia project that he was certain would make him rich. Before sending that prospectus to a host of publishers, he did two things. He registered the copyright and he mailed a copy of the prospectus to himself to have proof—via the postmark—of when he had committed the ideas to paper. When publishers began to indicate interest in the project, he hired an intellectual property attorney to guide him through the negotiations. The first question the attorney asked was, "What have you done so far?" As the story unfolded, the attorney began to giggle—never a good sign. He then called the author's actions "quaint." "Quaint" is not a word you want to hear from your attorney.

Where did the first author go wrong? Probably in many places, but most important, he failed to understand what copyright does and does not protect. Copyright protects virtually all forms of tangible *expression* including, but not limited to, poetry, prose, computer programs, artwork, movies, videos, written music, recorded music, plays, photographs, websites, letters, faxes, e-mails, and even PowerPoint presentations (Copyright Law, 17 U.S.C., 2001). The bottom line is that if the work involves a whit of creativity and is "fixed" in a tangible medium (e.g., written on a piece of paper, stored on a hard disk, recorded on a videotape, etc.) it is protected by copyright. But copyright does not protect *ideas*, mere *facts, titles,* or *short phrases.*

So when the first author sent out the prospectus, what did he want to protect? Not the expression. Prospectuses rarely make the *New York Times* bestseller list. He wanted to protect the ideas contained in the prospectus. But copyright law cannot protect ideas. Indeed, the whole rationale for creating copyright law was to give authors and inventors an economic incentive to share their ideas. Those ideas then become part of the public discourse and, in that way, further the progress of science and the arts.

The fact that copyright does not protect ideas comes as a surprise to many people and leads some to question its value. If copyright does not protect ideas, what does it protect?

It protects quite a lot. Copyright consists of a bundle of rights that include the rights to reproduce the work, distribute copies of the work, perform the work in public, display the work, and create derivatives of the work (Copyright Law, 17 U.S.C., 2001). In other words, in most instances, if you want to reproduce an expression, perform a work, or incorporate parts of a work in another work, you need the permission of the copyright owner. Why? Because copyright grants a monopoly over these uses to the author. Unless you can make a "fair use claim" (see discussion later in the chapter), you must seek the permission of the copyright owner to use part of the expression. What you do not need permission to do is to use the ideas contained in the work—a point made clear by the similarity of many of the plots that come out of Hollywood. If copyright protected ideas, the first boy-meets-girl love story would have had a lock on all subsequent variations on that theme.

Surprise #3: When Copyright Protection Begins

In sending the prospectus off to be registered, the first author made a second mistake. Copyright protection no longer requires registration. In fact, copyright protection is now automatic and begins at the moment of creation. All you have to do to protect a work is to create it. Even the © symbol is no longer required—although it is a good idea to display the © symbol, both to indicate to the world that you intend to claim and protect a work and in the event that you decide to avail yourself of redress through the courts.

Because copyright protection begins at the moment of creation and no longer requires registration, virtually every expression is protected by copyright. This means that virtually every note that you write, every memo that you type, every manuscript that you read, and every website that you visit is almost certainly protected by copyright. Even in those instances where the author does not wish to exercise his or her rights, the law still grants him or her *exclusive* control over those rights (Copyright Law, 17 U.S.C., 2001).

Surprise #4: The Incredible Shrinking Public Domain

Hold on a second. If memos, rough drafts, websites, and even faxes and e-mails are all protected from the moment of creation, what is left? Are there any works that are not protected by copyright? There are some unprotected works that fall into the public domain, but they are fewer than you might think. Essentially, works enter the public domain in one of a few ways. Either the work begins as a publication of the federal government, its copyright protection has expired, or the copyright owner deliberately chooses to place the work in the public domain. But keep in mind two cautions. First, although publications of the federal government are in the public domain, works commissioned by the federal government but published by someone else may not be in the public domain. Second, copyright protection extends for a very long time.

People often assume that copyright protection ends when a book goes out of print. In fact, whether a work is in print has nothing to do with its copyright protection. As a general rule, copyright protection currently extends for the life of the author plus 70 years. Moreover, every time Congress amends copyright law, they extend the term of protection. The bottom line is that if the work was created after 1923, it is very possibly protected by copyright. (Of course, the actual terms of protection are more complicated than that because they often vary as a function of media.) View an excellent summary of when different works pass into the public domain (Gasaway, 2001).

Surprise #5: Fair Use and Free Speech

Although copyright grants a monopoly to authors, it also carves out a limited number of exceptions for uses that contribute to the progress of science and the arts. The most important of these exceptions is the so-called fair use provision. Most people who have heard of fair use think that fair use is about making copies of works for educational purposes without the copyright owner's permission. Fair use is about multiple copies for educational purposes, but it is about much more than that.

Because copyright grants authors monopolistic control over their works, if it were left at that it would pose a significant threat to our First Amendment right to free speech. We could say anything we wanted in public, provided someone else did not already own the copyright to the words we wished to speak. Fair use deals with this threat by placing a limit on the monopolistic powers of the copyright owner:

> the fair use of a copyrighted work, including such use by reproduction in copies or phonorecords, or by any other means specified by that section (106), for purposes such as criticism, comment, news reporting, teaching (including multiple copies for classroom use), scholarship, or research, is not an infringement of copyright. (Copyright Act, 17 U.S.C. § 107, 1976)

In other words, it is fair use that allows you to quote someone while criticizing them. It is fair use that allows you to parody a work, even if the author does not want you to do so. And it is fair use that allows you to make multiple copies of a work for scholarly and educational purposes without first asking the copyright owner's permission.

That is the good news. The bad news is that this simple concept is difficult to implement because fair use decisions always involve a question of balance between the author's rights and the rights of the public. After establishing the principle of fair use, the statute goes on to enumerate four factors that must be considered in determining whether a particular use of a work is a fair use:

1. The purpose and character of the use, including whether such use is of a commercial nature or is for nonprofit educational purposes;
2. The nature of the copyrighted work;
3. The amount and substantiality of the portion used in relation to the copyrighted work as a whole; and
4. The effect of the use upon the potential market for or value of the copyrighted work (17 U.S.C. § 107).

Each factor can be viewed as a balancing act. Movement in one direction (e.g., nonprofit use of fact-based material incorporating relatively little of the original work with trivial effect on the market for the original work) tips the scales in favor of fair use. Movement in the other direction (e.g., for-profit use of a creative work taken in its entirety with demonstrable effects on the market for the original work) tips the scales in favor of requiring permission.

To complicate things further, although the statute identifies the four factors that must be considered, the courts have concluded that it is not necessary to "win" all four factors for a use to be considered a fair use (Crash Course in Copyright, 2003). It is possible, for example, to make fair use of someone else's material even in a for-profit venture. Newspapers do this all the time when they quote from copyrighted sources or include photographs of copyrighted works in reviews of public exhibitions. But change the situation slightly and suddenly permission is needed. For example, in a case in which a news magazine excerpted a key passage from Gerald Ford's memoirs, in which he disclosed for the first time his reasons for pardoning Richard Nixon, the Supreme Court held that even a relatively brief quotation from a book can constitute copyright infringement where the portion excerpted represents the heart of the work (*Harper & Row Publishers, Inc., v. Nation Enterprises*, 1985). In fact, the only way you can know *for sure* that your use of a work is a fair use is to go before a judge and have her rule that it is. So what should we do when confronted with this kind of ambiguity?

One possibility would be to follow the lead that publishers and other copyright holders have taken in proposing fair use guidelines. That is, in an attempt to reduce the ambiguity around fair use, publishers have proposed guidelines that outline their understanding of fair use (Agreement on Guidelines for Classroom Copying, 1976). There are, however, at least two problems with the publishers' approach. First, the limits they propose (e.g., allowing as fair use copies of either 1,000 words or 10% of a prose work, whichever is less) are too restrictive to be of much use in the classroom. Ten percent of an article does not provide much fodder for classroom discussion. Second, and more important, it would be easy to conclude from the mere existence of guidelines that they set the upper limits of what would be considered a fair use. In fact, they do not. What the guidelines establish is an unenforceable promise, on the part of publishers, to ignore uses that fall within their guidelines. But it is worth noting that, under the right conditions, the use of an entire work might be considered a fair use by the courts. Rigid adherence to the guidelines endorsed by the publishers provide the convenience of certainty at too steep a price.

A second possibility is to embrace the ambiguity built into the fair use statute. Fair use always involves a balance between the rights of the public and the rights of the copyright owner, and each case must be decided on its own merits. Recognizing that fact, and being able to articulate why you believe a particular use is a fair use, will provide protection should you find yourself dragged into court. Because, although it is true that a court is the only place to get a definitive answer on any particular fair use, there is a good faith educational fair use defense that provides shelter from the penalties associated with copyright infringement. Specifically, if you should find yourself in court charged with copyright infringement (and keep in mind that there have been relatively few educational cases that have gone to court), if you can convince the court that you honestly thought your use was a fair use, the court can waive all financial penalties (Remedies for Infringement, 17 U.S.C. § 504(c)(2), 2003). Although we recognize that the specter of being hauled into court terrifies most people, we nevertheless believe that the stakes are high. As publishers move increasingly to a pay-per-view model, we will surely lose fair use if we do not use it.

Surprise #6: Plagiarism Has Little to Do With Copyright Infringement

People assume that plagiarism is the same thing as copyright infringement. It is not. Nothing in copyright law requires you to cite a source, although the Digital Millennium Copyright Act (DMCA) does prohibit the removal of copyright information that the copyright owner has attached to a work (Digital Millennium Copyright Act, 1998). Citing sources for ideas and expressions is an academic tradition, not a legal requirement. Put another way, people often assume that if they cite the source, they will be protected from charges of copyright infringement. They will not. Imagine, for example, that someone scans an entire work, posts it to a website, and gives full credit to the author. The fact that the person gave credit to the author does not alter the fact that he or she violated the author's copyright. Giving credit where credit is due is an exemplary practice, it just does not mitigate copyright infringement.

COPYRIGHT IN ACADEMIC SETTINGS: CASE STUDIES

How should we approach the challenges that copyright law poses for the academic community? We think that two principles should serve as guides. First, we need to recognize that copyright does not have to be a zero-sum game. Many people assume that copyright is an all-or-nothing proposition in which the legal "owner" of a work inevitably has complete control of the work. In fact, the rights under copyright law can usually be divided among multiple parties in multiple ways to meet the needs and interests of all involved. The law simply sets default parameters; it does not prevent parties from reaching the most efficient and effective solutions with regard to use and dissemination of a work.

Second, we need to practice the golden rule of "do/due unto others." Academics find themselves in a unique position. At any given time, we occupy every role in the copyright equation. As authors, we produce a significant amount of copyrighted material and have a stake in making sure that authors' rights are preserved. As scholars and teachers, we depend on access to the copyrighted works of others and have a vested interest in preserving fair use. And with the power of the World Wide Web at our fingertips, we are increasingly taking on the role of publisher, which means that we are likely to care about how copyrighted information is disseminated. Keeping the competing demands of these roles at bay requires constant attention to the multifaceted nature of copyright. Put another way, every win that you have as an author could potentially translate to a loss you will have as a user of copyrighted works.

With these principles in mind, we now turn to a series of case studies to see how they might play out in a variety of settings.

Who "Owns" Courses and Course Materials?

Professor Wanda Profit

Assistant Professor Wanda Profit teaches an introductory sociology course for her department. She has put an enormous amount of effort into selecting materials, creating the syllabus and exams, and preparing her lectures. The course materials include a textbook, lecture outlines that she wrote, and photos and videos that she identified and digitized herself but for which she has not obtained permission.

The first question that comes to the minds of many faculty members is simply, "Who owns it?" Naturally, as always seems to be the case with the law, the answer is not simple. The short answer is that "it depends" on what the "it" is.

Certainly, colleges and universities have responsibility for their curricula and degrees or certifications, and principles of academic governance apply to the shaping of the content of the curriculum. The curriculum consists of various courses and, from that perspective, institutions "own" courses. Federal copyright law, however, applies only to "original works of authorship fixed in any tangible medium of expression" (Copyright Law, 17 U.S.C. § 102(a), 2001). A course as a whole is unlikely to meet this definition, unless it is an online course that has been entirely digitized. Oral lectures, for example, are not protected under federal copyright law unless they are fixed in some tangible medium—for example, they are tape-recorded or read from a written document. The facts and ideas discussed within a course are not, in and of themselves, protected either. Thus, much of the content of a traditional course is not "ownable" under copyright law. At most, the organization of the course materials might be entitled to thin copyright protection, as is any original compilation of materials.

Someone else probably owns other parts of the material. After all, although Professor Profit has developed some materials on her own—such as the syllabus and exams—she has also borrowed heavily from other sources. The textbook was probably written by someone else, and the photos and videos that she has included were almost certainly created by other individuals and are already owned by someone else. In face-to-face instruction, Profit can make a fairly compelling case for using the works without permission. Nothing about her use, however, grants her or her institution ownership of that material.

But clearly some of the course content is original and is protected by copyright. Who, for example, owns the syllabus, exams, or other original forms of expression created by Professor Profit? Under federal copyright law, an employer is considered to be the author of works prepared by an employee within the scope of her employment (Definitions, 17 U.S.C. § 101, 2003). This sounds simple enough, and it is easy to see how this standard applies to works specifically commissioned for use by the institution on its own behalf (such as an official committee report, for example). But what about scholarly works in which faculty members' expressions reflect their own individual theories and viewpoints within their fields of individual expertise? Although faculty members are paid to teach courses and conduct research, these general responsibilities do not usually include specific requirements instructing faculty members what to say in their scholarly works, where to publish them, and so forth.

In fact, the rights associated with copyright ownership include many rights that universities as employers normally do not exercise with regard to scholarly works, such as the right to edit such works or to decide whether and where to publish them. Long-standing principles of academic tradition and academic freedom protect faculty members' expression within their areas of professional expertise and are embedded in virtually all college and university faculty handbooks, collective bargaining agreements, or other university policies (AAUP, 2001).

As a point of law, however, the question of who owns scholarly works remains unclear. Before 1976, when federal copyright law was largely overhauled, an explicit "teacher's exception" existed in recognition of this academic tradition. The exception was not expressly mentioned in the subsequent codification of the law, however, and a debate has ensued ever since as to whether the long-standing academic tradition still has the force of law as an exception to the work-for-hire doctrine.

Fortunately, the law does not have to be the final word on this subject. Many institutions have promulgated intellectual property policies addressing questions of ownership and control of faculty members' scholarly works—often recognizing the rights and interests of faculty members as well as of the institutions themselves. View a useful collection of college and university intellectual property policies (Copyown Policies, 2003). In its recent *Statement on Copyright*, for example, the American Association of University Professors noted that "it has been the prevailing academic practice to treat the faculty member as the copyright owner of works that are created independently and at the faculty member's own initiative for traditional academic purposes (AAUP, 2001).

Thus, faculty members such as Professor Profit should start not by asking who owns a course but by thinking carefully about the individual components that make up the course and consulting their institutions' intellectual property policies.

> Now assume that Professor Profit's department asks her to retool the course for "distance learning" and gives her release time from one course and use of programmers from the university's media center to make the conversion. The course will be aimed at traditional degree-seeking students who are working toward an online degree. She makes the switch, and the course is now a regular part of the department's distance offerings. Unfortunately, Profit does not get tenure. She does, however, get an offer from another university that is interested in having her develop the same course for their distance learning program.

As noted, unlike traditional courses, online courses necessarily consist of copyrightable work(s). The form of communication guarantees that the creative expressions are fixed in a tangible medium and therefore subject to copyright protection. But to whom is the protection granted?

At first blush, it might appear that the course materials involved are merely another form of scholarly work in a new medium. The circumstances of their creation and fixation, however, may differ significantly from those involved in the development of traditional scholarly works such as articles, lectures, and textbooks. For starters, Professor Profit's department has specifically asked her to develop this particular material and has given her release time and technical support to do so. Unlike ordinary scholarly articles or classroom lectures, therefore, the university might be able to argue that it has specifically commissioned this particular work from Professor Profit and has given her support above and beyond normal use of university resources (such as libraries, secretarial support, ordinary computer use, and so forth) to accomplish this task. Furthermore, the university clearly seeks to use the material for its own purposes as part of its curriculum, and it has made its intentions known to Professor Profit from the outset. Given the expense involved on the front end in the development of online courses, it seems unlikely that the institution would choose to spend scarce resources on such a project with no expectation of continued use.

The questions of commissioning and resource allocation are not the only complications in this scenario. Online courses usually consist of more than lectures and other academic content that have been digitized. Technical support staff develop code to help deliver the course materials to students or to facilitate interaction among the students and instructor(s). This code itself may be protected by copyright, and the professor is unlikely to be able to lay claim to it as her own. If the technical staff are employed by the university to provide this sort of support in the creation of online courses, the work-for-hire doctrine will most likely apply to them—meaning that the university is considered the copyright owner of their work. (Take careful note: If independent contractors or outside consultants are used, a transfer of copyright should be obtained from those individuals.)

Finally, as discussed in the first scenario, the materials used in the course will likely be drawn from many different sources. We will talk a bit more about the use of other people's works shortly, but for now note that to the extent permissions are needed to make use of such works, those permissions should incorporate all of the uses that will be made of those materials.

So whether Professor Profit owns the course is a question that is ripe for a policy solution. A separate question is whether Profit can take the course with her to another institution once she has been denied tenure. After all, most faculty members would take their lecture notes, syllabi, and other course materials with them to a new institution—where they would normally be expected to build on their expertise and experience and to teach the same or similar courses. What about the university's interest in being able to make continued use of the course in which it has invested significant resources? By their very nature, many online courses are designed for possible asynchronous and repeated use—and such use might be necessary to recoup the costs involved in developing such courses.

This is precisely the type of situation where university policies on intellectual property should come into play and where it makes good sense to develop an agreement in writing early in the process to avoid misunderstandings when the project is completed. Professor Profit and her institution both have legitimate interests in this course, and the rights involved in copyright law may need to be unbundled to come up with a fair resolution that meets the needs of all concerned. Some of the relevant interests to consider in these situations when developing written agreements include the following:

From the faculty members' perspective:

- The ability to edit and control presentation of their work, and perhaps to exercise a right of first refusal in the preparation of subsequent versions;
- The ability to change and update materials over time, reflecting new research, evidence, or developments in their fields of expertise;
- The ability to create derivative or related works (for example, faculty members may want to retain the right to publish articles on subjects covered in online educational materials and courses);
- Professional recognition and credit (e.g., in tenure and promotion policies) both in and outside the institution with regard to their work;

- The extent to which they can take or make use of educational materials they create when they leave for another institution, for their own teaching and research purposes;
- The right to have a say in whether and how their works are commercialized and to share in the profits (if any) from such commercialization; and
- The right to share their work with peers in their disciplines (e.g., to check their work or to build on it).

From the institution's perspective:

- Use of such works for educational and administrative purposes (e.g., for teaching within the institution's programs, accreditation reviews, etc.);
- Timely revision and maintenance of course materials for continued use;
- Recovery of costs associated with the development of such works, and sharing of profits associated with the commercialization of such works; and
- Control and use of the university's name, seal, or marks in conjunction with such works.

As online education became more widespread, many people in and outside of academia speculated that huge profits were to be made by tapping into previously underserved markets and providing courses to millions of students in this country and overseas (Marchese, 1998). As the harsh realities of the Internet marketplace have gradually become apparent, however, these visions among faculty members, administrators, and others of becoming dot-com millionaires may be giving way to more realistic notions of how online education can be incorporated into the existing landscape of higher education as a whole. This scaling back of expectations may be a healthy development for academia, allowing institutions and individuals to focus once again first and foremost on the educational benefits and costs of online education.

Online education comes in many different variations in terms of formats, programmatic uses, and the nature and degree of faculty involvement. Thus, a one-size-fits-all approach will probably not work for most institutions. The interests of the faculty member, institution, and larger academic community all need to be considered in sorting out rights and responsibilities under copyright law.

Now imagine that Profit gets tenure and stays at the university. Her distance course has proven remarkably successful. Professor Profit goes on leave and one of her colleagues, Professor I. M. Leach, is asked to teach the course. When asked by the university for the online materials she developed, Professor Profit refuses to share them with her colleague because she considers them to be her intellectual property and because her colleague did not contribute to their development.

Should the university be able to use the material it helped support? This scenario once again points out the benefits of a written understanding covering the use of the course materials. Professor Profit may have legitimate concerns about how another faculty member might use or interpret her materials and about how or to what extent the content and delivery of the course will be attributed to her. A well-developed intellectual property policy or contract would contemplate this possibility and address the rights of both Professor Profit and the institution, while providing appropriate incentives to encourage creativity.

Leaving aside the intellectual property considerations for a moment, what about principles of academic freedom, university citizenship, or collegiality in this case? Both faculty members involved have academic freedom interests. Professor Profit will be concerned about how her materials are used and interpreted by another faculty member, and Professor Leach may want the freedom and flexibility to add his own perspectives and ideas throughout the course. After all, he might not agree with all of Professor Profit's ideas or theories—or he may simply have a different pedagogical approach to certain aspects of the course.

The institution has valid interests in ensuring that the courses and programs it offers are in fact available and accessible to its students. Many institutions include notions of institutional service and collegiality in their promotion and tenure policies. If the concept of a community of scholars is to be taken seriously, then some sharing among faculty members within a department seems reasonable. Would it make a difference if this were a one-time occurrence rather than a permanent switch, however? Should Professor Profit be compensated in some fashion when her materials are used in courses where she is not the instructor?

Another aspect to consider is the relative status of the faculty members involved. What if Professor Profit were not a full-time faculty member? If she were an adjunct, part-time, or non–tenure-track faculty member, for example, she might have little ongoing job security at the institution. She might also be teaching at other institutions simultaneously—perhaps on the same subject matter. Once again, university policies and practices in this area must be flexible enough to deal with the variety of faculty appointments.

The university joins a for-profit distance education venture. As part of the venture, the university provides courses that are created and supervised by members of the faculty. At the time that the courses are created, written agreements are signed between the university and the individual faculty members that cover revenue sharing and intellectual property issues. In all, about 10% of the faculty participate in the venture. Professor Profit, however, does not participate. Instead, a private publisher developing a series of online courses has approached her. The publisher will cover all of the development costs for a new course with all new material. No university resources beyond Professor Profit's participation will be used, and Profit will get an advance and royalties.

Can Professor Profit enter this arrangement? At first blush, it certainly looks a lot like other forms of scholarly work, many of which are funded by entities outside the institution. If the institution's policy considers such works to belong to faculty members for copyright purposes, if it is not a party in the funding arrangement, and if no unusual university resources are used, then it seems unlikely that the institution will have a claim to the material in terms of copyright.

Once again, however, copyright law and policy is not the only consideration. The company presumably has approached Professor Profit because of her reputation and expertise in the field in which she teaches and conducts research. It may want to display her university affiliation prominently in its advertising campaign, and perhaps even include a symbol of the university (such as a famous trademark) to take advantage of the institution's prestigious reputation. The university may have a legitimate interest in how its name and marks are used by other entities, especially when those entities are commercial enterprises. In fact, many institutions are now developing or revisiting policies involving use of their names or marks to protect their reputations.

Does the target audience of the private publisher matter? What if it is going after some of the same types of students as the distance education venture in which Professor Profit's home institution is participating? Does Professor Profit have a conflict of interest or perhaps a conflict of commitment?

As colleges and universities become involved in more of these types of ventures, and as more for-profit entities enter the distance-education marketplace, the lines between nonprofit higher education and for-profit corporate training or education are becoming harder to draw. As part of their scholarly activity, faculty members at most institutions are expected to be involved with the world beyond their campuses by engaging in consulting, outside lecturing, and other activities that enrich their experience in their fields of expertise. Institutional limitations on these activities usually take the form of general policies on conflicts of interest that focus on traditional notions of time and space. For example, such policies may limit the amount of time in a week or month faculty members can spend on outside activities or consulting, or they may require faculty members to get institutional permission to teach a regular course on another campus. But Professor Profit may be able to complete the requested work for this publisher without leaving her own home (e.g., by using her home computer) and without spending more than 20% of her time on the project.

The deeper problem is the possible conflict of commitment confronting Professor Profit. If she and other faculty members can make more money working with outside companies to develop online materials than they can make with their home institution, they will of course be tempted to give their time and attention to the outside entities instead of their own institutions. At the very least, this sort of activity can take time away from other university activities and service. As the outside activities look more and more like activities in which the university is itself engaged, it can also become a form of competition with the university. In the corporate sector, many companies (such as software manufacturers, for instance) require their employees to sign no-compete agreements as a condition of employment. Colleges and universities are now confronted with the same possibility, and some are revamping their conflicts policies to reflect this specter of competition from their own faculty.

It seems to us that the key to handling these types of situations lies in early disclosure. In many instances, a faculty member's outside work will not compete with the university or detract from the individual's institutional responsibilities. Indeed, a former dean at our university once remarked that what his college needed was more BMWs in the faculty parking lot— meaning that the institution often gains in reputation from the entrepreneurial activities of its faculty. Institutions and their faculty need to work together to create environments in which disclosure and discussion of such projects is encouraged and not overly burdensome in terms of the process or timing involved. Institutional policies must make clear what is, as well as what is not, permitted.

What Challenges Does Collaboration Bring?

Professor Cole Aberator

As an experiment, psychology professor Cole Aberator has his students participate in a web-based discussion. Their insights were stunning, and he decides to write a scholarly paper about the experience. As a precaution, Aberator removes all of the identifying information from the postings. However, his final paper includes many of the postings, reprinted in their entirety.

Can Professor Aberator use his students' work in this way? He probably cannot. In terms of copyright law, students own their own works unless they create them within the scope of employment as employees at the institution. In this instance, the students' expressions are clearly not part of any responsibility they have as employees of the institution. In fact, they pay to take the course!

Professor Aberator might be able to use their work in this fashion if he obtained permission to do so, but the power relationship between him and his students can certainly be an issue. As a pedagogical matter, he can probably require students to participate in a web-based discussion as part of the course. But he may not be able to require the students to give him permission to use their comments for a publication outside the classroom, because at that point the comments are being used for his personal (albeit professional) purposes rather than for the students' own educational purposes. The possible coercion involved would be exacerbated if the class was required or served as a prerequisite for other courses.

Does it matter if Professor Aberator eliminates all of the identifying information from the postings? From a copyright perspective, it certainly does not matter—like any other copyright owners, the students own their works from the moment they are fixed in tangible form. This ownership interest is not lessened merely because someone else removes the true author's identity. And from an ethical perspective, Professor Aberator's actions may constitute a breach of trust and professional responsibility—not to mention other rules pertaining to privacy protections or human participants research, for example.

> *A graduate student who is interested in doing a multimedia thesis project approaches Professor Aberator. Together, they decide on a project that Professor Aberator has wanted to pursue for some time. The final "work" will serve both as the student's thesis and as an education piece with possible commercial outlets. Professor Aberator provides some, though not all, of the funding, and university staff are involved to a significant degree in the preparation of the project.*

Who owns the resulting work? Collaborations among faculty, staff, and students within and across departmental and institutional lines are becoming increasingly common in the age of the Internet, bringing with them added layers of complexity for purposes of copyright law.

The first rule to remember is that ideas themselves are not protected, only tangible expressions. Nobody can claim copyright ownership merely because they had the original idea for a project, no matter how profound or original the idea might be. Thus, Professor Aberator cannot claim ownership of the project by virtue of any initial conversations with the student.

The second rule to remember, as discussed previously, is that students normally own the copyright to their own works, assuming they were not created as works for hire in the course of employment at the university. In this case, however, the student probably is not the only owner. The involvement of staff members who work for the university may, for example, give the university some ownership interest if those staff members were acting within the scope of their university employment. If the staff members actually participated by contributing tangible expression, the university might have a claim to their contributions. If the intent at the outset was for these staff members and the student to be joint authors (and if their respective contributions are difficult to pull apart), then the university and the student might both be able to claim to be joint authors of the resulting work.

Finally, the university's provision of funds should raise a yellow flag as a matter of institutional policy and practice. This scenario provides another example where a simple written agreement at the outset can avoid a lot of misunderstanding and hard feelings once a project is completed. Such written agreements do not need to be long documents with lots of small type and legalese; they can be relatively short and simple, using plain language to describe the rights and interests of the parties involved in the completed work.

What Materials Can You Use, and When?

Professor Ivanna Sharall

Professor Ivanna Sharall develops a website for her history course that includes her syllabus, some of her own scholarly articles, images and music she has found on the Internet, brief clips from movies she borrowed from the library, and links to other related sites.

Can Professor Sharall post all of these materials on her website? The website is associated with her course, after all, and she has been told that she can display all sorts of materials in her face-to-face classroom teaching. Congress recently passed an amendment to federal copyright law that essentially extends the classroom exemption to the display of many materials used in distance-education programs. That legislation applies only to nonprofit educational institutions and requires that access be limited. The Technology, Education and Copyright Harmonization Act of 2002 (TEACH Act, 2002) does not extend to publicly accessible websites.

What about the concept of educational fair use? If we think about the factors considered in the fair use analysis (as discussed previously), Professor Sharall can certainly argue that her website serves educational, nonprofit purposes. On the other hand, by making materials available and accessible on the Internet, Professor Sharall is making it easy for people to copy and use such materials for free. If any of these works are commercially sold or licensed, unfettered public access would seem to interfere with the potential market for the works. Yet many faculty members want such websites to be available to educators at other institutions and even to the public at large— not just to their own students—as part of their educational outreach mission.

Professor Sharall might assume that at the very least, she is on safe ground with regard to the posting of works she created. She is almost certainly on safe ground in posting her syllabus publicly. Whether or not her institution claims any ownership interest in it, it is unlikely that the institution would object to its public display. But what about her own scholarly articles? Before she posts them freely on the website, she might want to check the fine print in any publishing contracts she signed for such articles. Many publishing contracts require faculty members to assign copyright in their works to the publisher. If the contract does not reserve the faculty member's right to publicly display the article, then the professor may breach the contract by including her own article on the website. For this reason, faculty members should review such publishing contracts carefully to ensure to the extent possible that they reserve all of the rights that they want and need for their own teaching and research purposes. These rights might include, among others, the rights to display their own works, to reproduce them for scholarly conferences and meetings, and to share them with their own colleagues and students.

Music and movie clips present special complications on websites. When you use music from another source, for example, you may have to consider multiple copyrights—composers, lyricists, and performers (or the entities to whom they have assigned copyright) may all have copyright interests in a particular work. In the age of peer-to-peer networks, the music and film industries have been especially aggressive in policing the Internet and enforcing their copyrights. These industries also have developed sophisticated mechanisms for licensing use of many works, in whole or in part, in a wide array of settings. The relative ease of obtaining a license (albeit for a price) may be seen as making it less excusable for someone to use the material without permission.

Images taken from books, magazines, or other sources can also pose special challenges. Even if an image appears in a book or magazine, it may not be readily apparent to whom the copyright belongs (if anyone) for the particular image. As a history professor, Sharall might assume that she is safe using images of sculptures or other works that have long since passed into the public domain, but photographs themselves may be protected under copyright law—even if much of the subject matter in the photograph is not itself protected.

One thing Professor Sharall can most likely do is to provide links from her website to other sites where these works are located. So long as such links are not framed in a way that misleads the viewer into thinking that they are still in Professor Sharall's own website, the law to date has generally protected the right to provide links in websites to other sources.

RECOMMENDATIONS

As we noted in the opening, changes in copyright law, along with the growing tendency to see ideas and expressions as proprietary commodities with tangible value, pose serious challenges for academics, their institutions, and scholarly culture in general. Although there are no easy answers, we offer the following recommendations for consideration and discussion.

- Know your basic rights under copyright law, and think about which of those rights you really need (and which ones you are willing to give away or share) for any given work.
- Be aware of your institution's intellectual property policies and practices, and know who to contact if you have questions. Do not forget about potential resources on this subject such as the faculty handbook, collective bargaining agreement, university websites, and so forth.
- When dealing with publishers, pay special attention to the rights you are giving away. Make sure that you do not transfer rights that you might care about (such as the rights to create derivative works or to use works for your own teaching and scholarly presentations) or that publishers do not really need.
- When creating works in collaboration with other people in or outside the university, or works where substantial or unusual university resources are involved, get an agreement in writing at the outset of the project specifying the rights and responsibilities of the parties involved.
- Be aware of your institution's indemnification policies.
- When using works from other creators, think carefully about the extent to which you need to use or distribute the actual works. Do not be afraid to take advantage of fair use when appropriate. Likewise, do not hesitate to ask for permission when fair use is unlikely to apply.
- Get copyright permissions in writing whenever possible. Remember that permissions can be short and sweet—just be sure to get the party giving permission to sign and date a letter or form explaining what rights you have been granted with respect to their work.
- Do unto others as you would have them do unto you. Remember that the shoe could be on the other foot at any time—we are all creators, users, and distributors of intellectual property in many forms.
- In situations where you are a copyright owner, remember that ownership may also entail potential liability (e.g., for copyright infringement), as well as responsibility for granting permissions and enforcing other ownership rights.
- Do not let the law be the only driving force in how you deal with copyrightable works. As members of an academic community, we must also take into account ethical considerations

relating to trust and power in relationships (e.g., in dealing with students), rules regarding appropriate attribution, plagiarism, and so forth. Copyright law is not a license to forget about these other norms.

- Finally, always keep in mind that copyright is not a mere spectator sport. As in many other areas, the squeaky wheel often gets the attention when it comes to copyright policy. As these issues become more important on our campuses and in the world at large, you can play a role by helping to educate your colleagues and community, you can encourage discussion around these issues, and you can provide feedback to institutional representatives who help to develop and implement policies and practices, both on campus and nationally.

CONCLUSION

We realize that there is a strong sense of irony running throughout this chapter. On the one hand, we argue that the academic community must retain its tradition of sharing. The academy has thrived precisely because it is a place where ideas and expressions are freely exchanged. On the other hand, our advice consistently has a legalistic flavor. We suggest that contracts, policies, and written understandings are generally good ideas. How do we reconcile the spirit of free exchange with the pragmatics of negotiation? We think there are two routes to reconciliation.

First, we have become convinced that explicit agreements represent a fairly natural extension of good teaching and mentoring practices. To get back to our dental analogy, dealing with copyright issues does not have to be as painful as a root canal. Agreements do not have to be negotiated through attorneys or framed in legalistic language. At their core, they are agreements among collaborators about what a project entails, what outcomes are expected, and how they want to proceed. Just as syllabi emerged to clarify expectations in the classroom, we believe written agreements will emerge to clarify the expectations associated with collaboration.

Second, we have become convinced that explicit agreements offer the best hope for preserving the exchange of ideas against the backdrop of a popular culture in which ideas and expressions are treated as pure property. Consider one example that potentially foreshadows the university of tomorrow. We recently read an account of a student who required his professor to sign a nondisclosure agreement before submitting his paper for grading. Suffice to say that if we do not find ways to deal with the culture of property that today's students bring with them, that culture will become the culture of the academy going forward. In other words, you can run, but you cannot hide.

REFERENCES

Agreement on guidelines for classroom copying in not-for-profit educational institutions with respect to books and periodicals. (1976). H. R. Rep. No. 83, 90th Cong., 1st Sess.

American Association of University Professors (AAUP). (2001). *Policy documents and reports* (9th ed.). Baltimore: Johns Hopkins University Press.

Copyown policies: A resource on copyright ownership for the higher education community. (2003). Retrieved February 27, 2003, from http://www.inform.umd.edu/copyown/policies/index.html

Copyright Law of the United States of America and Related Law Contained in Title 17 of the United States Code. (2001). 17 U.S.C. §§ 101-803.

Crash course in copyright: Fair use of copyrighted materials. (2003). Retrieved February 27, 2003, from http://www.utsystem.edu/ogc/intellectualproperty/copypol2.htm

Definitions USC 101. (2003). 17 U.S.C. § 101 (2003).

Digital Millennium Copyright Act summary. (1998). Pub. L. No. 105-304, 112 Stat. 2860 (Oct. 28, 1998).

Gasaway, L. (2001). *When works pass into the public domain.* Retrieved February 27, 2003, from http://www.unc.edu/›unclng/public-d.htm

Gorman, R. A., & Ginsburg, J. C. (1993). *Copyright for the nineties: Cases and materials* (4th ed.). Charlottesville, VA: Michie.

Harper & Row, Publishers, Inc., v. Nation Enterprises. (1985). 471 U.S. 539.

Lessig, L. (2002). *The future of ideas: The fate of the commons in a connected world.* New York: Vintage Books.

Marchese, T. (1998). Not-so-distant competitors: How new providers are remaking the postsecondary marketplace. *AAHE Bulletin* [online]. Retrieved May 1998, from http://www.aahebulletin.com/public/archive/Not-So-Distant%20Competitors.asp

Remedies for infringement: Damages and profits USC 504(c)(2). (2003). 17 U.S.C. § 504(c)(2).

The Technology, Education and Copyright Harmonization Act of 2002 (TEACH Act). (2002). Pub. L. No. 107-273 § 13301.

IV

ORIENTATION TO THE ACADEMIC ENVIRONMENT

12

POWER, POLITICS, AND SURVIVAL IN ACADEMIA

ELIZABETH D. CAPALDI

Faculty members live in departments, small isolated worlds within the true political domain of universities. In this chapter we will give you some perspective on the forces outside your department that affect your professional life. You need to understand these forces to operate successfully as a faculty member, because you may frequently be called on to deal with your dean, provost, president, legislature, member of the board, or member of the public in your professional activity.

CLASSIFICATION OF UNIVERSITIES

The first crucial measure you must take is of your university's commitment to research. Not all universities have a commitment to research. American universities and colleges come in a multiplicity of forms, and the missions and structure vary in important ways. The leading classification of institutions of higher education is done by the Carnegie Foundation for the Advancement of Teaching, and is termed the *Carnegie Classification of*

Revision of chapter by Gerald R. Salancik.

Institutions of Higher Education. Begun in 1973, the most recent classification (2000; see Table 12.1) eliminated the familiar categories of Research I Universities and Research II Universities, substituting instead Doctoral/Research Universities—Extensive (during the period studied, they awarded 50 or more doctoral degrees per year across at least 15 disciplines) and Doctoral/Research Universities—Intensive (during the period studied, they awarded at least 10 doctoral degrees per year across three or more disciplines, or at least 20 doctoral degrees per year overall). For the classification see http://www.carnegiefoundation.org/Classification/. This new classification eliminated the consideration of research expenditures, one of the main criteria for Research I and Research II universities in the previous classification. Of the 148 universities in the Doctoral/Research Universities—Extensive group, 89 were classified as Research I institutions in 1994, 37 as Research II, 19 as Doctoral I, and 5 as Doctoral II. Many feel the new Carnegie classification has lost some important information—to what extent a university is a "research university."

So How Can You Know If You Are in a "Research University"?

One definition of a research university is that it has more than $20 million of federal research expenditures in a year. TheCenter, an independent research center located at the University of Florida, lists all the universities in the United States that fit this criterion and classifies research universities based on various quality measures (http://thecenter.ufl.edu). There are 154 institutions that fit this criterion in the United States, 106 public universities and 48 private.

If you are at a research university, the value placed on grants and research will obviously be higher than if you are at a university or college that is not research-intensive. Many faculty today at non–research-intensive universities received their doctoral degrees from research-intensive universities. This can cause a tension between the faculty desire for participation in research and the available support for research. One colleague in a non–research-intensive university had a paper accepted for presentation at the Midwestern Psychological Association but was forbidden to attend the meeting because all faculty were expected to attend graduation. Research universities understand and wish their faculty to have a guild mentality and to function nationally in their fields by attending conferences, serving on grant panels, and being editors of journals. Universities without such an emphasis on research value teaching and local university activities. Teaching loads are higher and commitment to campus activities as opposed to national activities is valued. To function appropriately in your university you first must understand what type of university it is and the values of your university. Indeed, the most important message of this chapter is that for you to succeed in your institution you must shape what you want and need into the structure

TABLE 12.1
The Carnegie Classification of Institutions of Higher Education

Type of institution	Definition
Doctorate-granting institutions:	
Doctoral/Research Universities—Extensive	▪ Offer a wide range of baccalaureate programs ▪ Committed to graduate education through the doctorate ▪ During period studied awarded 50 or more doctoral degrees per year across at least 15 disciplines
Doctoral/Research Universities—Intensive	▪ Offer a wide range of baccalaureate programs ▪ Committed to graduate education through the doctorate ▪ During period studied awarded at least 10 doctoral degrees per year across three or more disciplines or at least 20 doctoral degrees per year overall
Master's colleges and universities:	
Master's Colleges and Universities I:	▪ Offer a wide range of baccalaureate programs ▪ Committed to graduate education through the master's ▪ During period studied, awarded 40 or more master's degrees per year across three or more disciplines
Master's Colleges and Universities II:	▪ Offer a wide range of baccalaureate programs ▪ Committed to graduate education through the master's ▪ During period studied, awarded 20 or more master's degrees per year
Baccalaureate colleges:	
Baccalaureate Colleges—Liberal Arts	▪ Primarily undergraduate colleges with major emphasis on baccalaureate programs ▪ During period studied, awarded at least half of their baccalaureate degrees in liberal arts fields.
Baccalaureate Colleges—General	▪ Primarily undergraduate colleges with major emphasis on baccalaureate programs ▪ During period studied, awarded less than half of their degrees in liberal arts fields
Baccalaureate/Associate's Colleges	▪ Undergraduate colleges where the majority of conferrals are below the baccalaureate level ▪ During period studied, bachelor's degrees accounted for at least 10% of undergraduate awards
Associate's Colleges	▪ Offer associate's degrees and certificate programs, but with few exceptions award no baccalaureate degrees.[a]
Specialized Institutions	▪ Offer a variety of degrees ranging from the bachelor's to the doctorate and typically award a majority of degrees in a single field

[a]This group includes institutions where during the period studied, less than 10% of undergraduate awards were bachelor's degrees.

and needs and wants of those above you, the governing board of your university: your president, your provost, your dean, your department chair, and the other faculty in your department. In addition, those in state institutions must also understand your state legislatures. Most faculty do not think beyond their department chairs. This is a mistake.

State Legislatures

If you are in a state institution you should follow what is said about higher education in your state. You will then understand the pressures on your board and your president and your institution and understand how you can help generate increased funding for your school. Higher education competes against many other priorities in states, prisons, K–12, and social services. Why should the legislature fund higher education in the face of these seemingly more pressing needs? You can help by demonstrating the practical value of your research to the state, by cooperating in the need to demonstrate the productivity and quality of faculty work, and by understanding political realities in your own requests. Legislators do not enjoy being treated as a bunch of uneducated idiots by faculty any more than faculty enjoy being treated as irrelevant intellectuals by legislators. As a faculty member you should speak willingly when asked by the press about your work, so that the public and legislatures can understand its importance. You should understand the issues of the day in your state to apply your knowledge usefully where it is needed. You should in general realize that states fund institutions of higher education, in which case you actually work for the state. In all types of institutions, as a faculty member you should understand and pay attention to your governing board.

Governing Boards

All universities have governing boards. If you are in a state institution, the form of your governing board is determined by the state. You may have a local board, a state-level board, both of these, or some combination. If you are in a private institution, the institution will have its own governing board. The president of your university reports to some board, and the board has tremendous power to influence policy and procedures in universities. It behooves you to read what is available about your board and to determine how what you do fits within their priorities. Many boards are quite concerned with teaching, both in terms of quantity and quality. This should give you some perspective on the necessity for measuring quality of teaching. If you were a board member, would you not care about the quality of teaching in the institution for which you were responsible? Many faculty resist the idea that teaching quality should be measured or that these reports should be available to those outside the university. However, it is in faculty members' self-interest to demonstrate to those responsible that quality of teaching is high. All boards are interested in the financial stability of their institutions. This interest leads to a desire to know the faculty are productive and the institution is run well.

Presidents

The president reports to boards and needs to represent the university to outside constituencies. Presidents also usually have primary responsibility for fundraising and dealing with the local community. Presidents love good news and hate bad news. They receive enough bad news from the external world; internally they want to hear success stories they can use to generate funds from the outside world. This does not mean you should not complain to your president. It does mean you should go through the chain of command, which in turn means that you have to complain to a lot of people before you get to the president. In general, the best course is to send the president reports of your wonderful activities and those of your colleagues and send your complaints to your department chair.

Provosts

The provost reports to the president and your dean reports to the provost. Provosts typically determine how much money your dean will receive, and this is important in determining how much money your department will receive. You may indeed need to be involved with your provost, if you believe your college or school (dean-level) is underfunded and that this underfunding is interfering with the ability of psychology to function appropriately. This is not uncommon for psychology departments, which are often lost in the fabric of the university, misplaced for historical or other reasons. Psychology departments often have at least some portion of their faculty who require wet labs, expensive equipment, and who generate considerable amounts of grant money—functioning more like science faculty than like social science faculty. If they are in a social science college that reports to a dean without much funding, this can be an occasion for a discussion with the provost. We will say more on this later when we discuss power and money.

Deans

The dean is an important person for any faculty member, and it pays to know him or her personally if possible. Deans have many demands on their time, but they will process your tenure and promotion document, they are responsible for allocating your department's budget, they appoint your department chair, and they care about what you do. The general rule of fitting into the priorities of others holds with particular force in the case of your dean. Your dean should be worrying about fitting into the priorities of the provost and president, but you need to understand the dean's unique perspective as well. It is also wise to understand how much flexibility the dean has. This will tell you where power really lies on your campus. Does your dean have total authority to allocate departmental budgets? If not, who does? That is the person with true power over your department. Whoever that person is, you need to understand the basis for departmental budget allocation. That process may take into account credit hours taught, grant money brought in, quality of department, or other factors that are important for your university. Sometimes the process is also a matter of personal patronage and relationships. If the latter, it pays to have a personal relationship with the dean. This is not that difficult, but you must first assess the relationship of your chair with the dean and be sure you do not overstep your bounds. Personal relationships with any administrator are easy to establish by sending the administrator reports on your work in the press, or from other sources, or just sending pictures and easy to understand reports of your work. Invite senior administrators to your lab or to parties at your house. Faculty are often afraid to do this, but administrators like faculty and are flattered to be considered. Administration is a lonely job, and administrators like to see and hear about the work of faculty, which is after all the thing they are all working to support. Assuming your chair does not object, invite your dean to events and keep your dean informed, always copying your department chair on anything you send to the dean, and always invite your chair to any event where the dean is invited.

Department Chairs

Department chairs make the day-to-day decisions that affect your life—they are critical in your tenure and promotion, in your space allocation, and in the support you receive. You *must* have a good relationship with your department chair. You *must* understand the values of your department and how resource allocations are made. The possibilities are much like those we discussed for dean. Your department chair may allocate resources based on credit hours generated, grant money brought in, or some other objective factors. You should ask. Alternatively, you may be in a patronage system, where your relationship with the department chair is key. Or most common, the system will be some combination of these. You need to figure out what the rules for money allocation are. Talk to senior faculty, but more important watch how money is allocated.

STRUCTURE OF THE UNIVERSITY

Universities are typically organized into departments within schools or colleges. Departments typically represent faculty guilds and have their own rules for evaluating quality and productivity. The English department has its standards and methods, which are not the same as the physics department, which are in turn not the same as psychology's, and so on. We all know teaching loads vary by disciplines on a campus, but across the nation teaching loads for a particular discipline in a research university are fairly standard. This is because competition for faculty and students is within discipline at the graduate level—psychology departments compete with each other for the best faculty and students, not with other departments within the university. Deans, provosts, and presidents understand this structure. Faculty often do not. Thus faculty members in a psychology department may complain that their teaching loads are higher than those in the physics department and that they teach more credit hours. This is undoubtedly true, and it is true across the country. It is also irrelevant. Physics departments contribute to universities mostly by research and grant money, psychology departments as a whole contribute by producing credit hours and by bringing in grant money. The appropriate comparison group for your psychology department is other psychology departments in the same type of university, not the physics department in your university. In the framework of a university, psychology is also not at the very core. You cannot have a university without an English department but you can have a university without a psychology department.

Psychology departments, however, have a possibility of participating beyond their own department by interdisciplinary work with other units on campus. Indeed, psychologists can do this almost more than any other discipline. Psychology overlaps with sociology, political science, management, biology, mathematics, and many other disciplines. Depending on the priority given interdisciplinary work on your campus, this can give you leverage with the upper administration. Although your department may be housed in a college that receives little money, you as a faculty member could form or participate in an interdisciplinary center that could be forward-looking, generate lots of grant money, attract students, and bring fame and fortune to your university. It is well worth your while to keep your eye on interdisciplinary opportunities, particularly those well-funded by federal agencies, and start a center or institute on your campus in any fruitful area.

POWER AND MONEY

The most important principle to understand is that power is money, which can also be expressed as money is power. In universities, faculty generate money by teaching (via tuition and state funding, sometimes) and by research (grants). Teaching is a local market. Depending on how your university receives money for teaching and how it allocates money based on teaching, generating credit hours can be important as a source of power—or not important at all. If you are in a university that is not funded for enrollment, or that does not allocate budget based on enrollment, teaching may be not be a source of power. Practically all faculty teach, and most faculty members teach well. Knowledge of your teaching ability is customarily limited to your own university, and there is no national market for good teachers. This means the extent to which teaching a lot of credit hours or teaching well matters is dependent on how your university values these activities. Research talent is rare, however. Some faculty do no research, others do only a little, and only some do it very well. The market for research faculty is national, and your productivity and quality in research is demonstrable and known on a national market. Competition for the best research faculty is intense, and faculty who generate large amounts of grant money are powerful on campus. In the future, faculty members who can generate large amounts of income for a university via distance learning products or patents and licenses will also be powerful. This coincides with the general principle of fitting what you can do into your university's priorities. Because all universities need money, if you can generate money for your university you will be valued.

If you teach a lot of credit hours but do not receive rewards for this, you should probably reexamine this activity. If your department teaches a lot of credit hours but is not rewarded for this activity, your department chair should be discussing this with the dean. If your college teaches a lot of credit hours but is not rewarded for this activity, your dean should be having a conversation with the provost. This is because you are indeed generating revenue, which is important to any university.

POWER WITHIN DEPARTMENTS

Consider the case of a colleague at another university. We call her Janet. Janet was five years out of graduate school. When she finished her degree, the job market was, shall we say, soft. Janet was more fortunate than many of her friends, though, and got a job at one of the better schools, the only woman psychologist hired in its 60 or so years. Perhaps because she appreciated her fortune, Janet did not worry much about the details of the offer when she accepted it. Two details she should have been concerned about were the department's provision for summer salary and convention travel money. Both, it later turned out, were available and both were critical to Janet's future. Janet built up a fair-sized debt in school. When she neared the end of her first year, she asked about summer support so she could devote herself to research. The department head, leaning back in his chair, told her the department had committed its summer research budget already and had assumed she did not need any because she had not said so when she was hired. "But," said the head, "if you want to teach, we could at least get that for you." Janet took the teaching offer and, of course, abandoned much of the research she had planned.

The next few years saw similar exchanges. Each time there was some reason Janet could not get what she needed. Her most recent "surprise" came when she sought funds to go to a special conference in her research area. Again she went to her department head. He explained that the department's travel policy was to cover the complete expenses of one trip per year per faculty member and that she could choose any conference she wanted to attend in the United States. "Well," Janet interrupted, "I would like to go to the APA this year, because I'm going to present a paper. But I also need to go to this special conference, because it's very important for my work." Again, the department head told her the policy and pointed out that although he normally had some discretionary funds, they were committed already. "I wish I had known this earlier," he said as Janet left.

Janet was quickly behind in her work relative to colleagues who had entered the department with her. And comparisons between her and her colleagues were never more than a whisper away, whispers she heard clearly enough to realize she might not be promoted with them.

Janet's problems arose from her department's ordinary politics. Where is the power in this situation? The department head? Let us explore what makes the department head powerful. First is the fact that Janet, like others in her department, wants a particular resource. Second, neither Janet nor the others have what they want. Third, the department head temporarily controls its allocation, with discretion to dispense it any way he wishes. These conditions are necessary and sufficient for the creation of the department head's power. You want something and somebody else has the freedom and capability to provide it that you lack. If any of these were not true, there would be no power. If Janet and the others cared not a hoot for summer and travel moneys, the head would reign over an empty realm. If these funds were nondiscretionary and had to be allotted according to some incontrovertible standards, the head would be reduced to a keeper of books, tallying requests and dispersing funds.

In short, the department head is powerful because of the role his position plays in the department. Power concentrates into his position precisely to resolve conflicts of the kind embroiling Janet. Departments are not the same in this regard. Some do not concentrate power as much, and permit their heads little say. In universities, there are two types of departmental administrators. One is called a head; the other a chair. The choice of words is probably not accidental. A head is appointed with no fixed term. Its occupant authorizes all departmental educational, budget, hiring, promotion, and salary decisions. It is a powerful position and much like headships at other universities. The chair position, in contrast, has a fixed term. Its resident is obligated to attend to the advice of the elected "executive committee" of a department. This position does not concentrate power in the administrator but leaves it with the faculty.

How much power concentrates into organizational positions—chairs, heads, deans, grant administrators, committees—will depend on the extent of an organization's conflicting interests. The chair administrative form we described, for instance, arises when faculty are unable to resolve their conflicts into directions that all interests will support. Through an elective process, the contestants ensure their points of view will be represented in the executive committee where they can bargain and negotiate with one another. Often they shuffle back and forth between positions because no group is able to convince the others of its greater merit. This form arises in fields with less agreed on paradigms. It is more common in the social sciences; more rare in the physical sciences.

When power concentrates into formal positions, as it does in most academic departments, the concentration serves the needs of dominant interests in a department. A head can move a department in particular directions with vigor, neglecting some interests at one point in time and others at another. A department head, however, cannot long get away with consistently neglecting major interests in the department. Anyone who has seen a department head roll when it displeases critical faculty knows how trepidatious tenancy can be.

Power in a department, then, rests with a department's faculty, or at least some of them. Where, then, was the power in Janet's situation? To find out, Janet talked to associates about what else was going on in the department and who was getting the funds she needed.

The story quickly got sorted out. The department had been building its cognitive psychology group for the past few years and the money that Janet was not getting was going to newer faculty in these areas and, in some cases, older faculty. This happened with enough frequency on enough issues that a reasonable statistician would conclude it was not random.

At first Janet got annoyed. Later she thought about why the department head was leaning toward the cognitive group just then. The group was growing; its faculty were building a graduate program and were starting to fund it with a few large grants. The departmental budget had barely been keeping pace and, although the overall doctoral program had grown slightly, government cutbacks hurt the social, clinical, and experimental groups severely in the past two years.

Annoyance drifted to depression as Janet realized that what was going on was more systematic than a few unlucky lost opportunities. Although the head was powerful, his power only mirrored the faculty's. Yet it seemed all faculty were not equal. The cognitive group, as Orwell would have it, were more equal. Decisions reflected their interests the most. Why? Because the doctoral program of the rest of the department depended on the cognitive group's larger coffers. Although the details in other departments may differ from those in Janet's, the general situation is typical. Power organizes around those subgroups (departments, disciplinary groups, or individuals) in an organization thought to contribute its most critical resources.

Janet's situation shows us organizational power is not a personal quality of the fortunate or greedy. It is situational. The cognitive faculty were powerful not because of any particularly charming qualities they possessed. They were powerful because they contributed what the department needed just then. This role was more circumstantial than deliberate. It followed a few decisions of U.S. presidents and a developing industry in computer intelligence.

Ultimately, power in academic institutions originates outside them. We can see this easily in the growth of the physical sciences following President John Kennedy's decision to go to the moon, and in the growth of the social sciences following Lyndon Johnson's decision to end poverty. We can see this also in our own universities. Departments in universities, and the areas within them, represent different disciplines, each somewhat separate from the others. Each discipline has its own sources of funding, its own markets for faculty and students, its own journals, and its own definitions and markets for prestige. Although some intellectual strands link them, and although they compete at some level for funds, students, and public attention, disciplines for the most part operate independently. These facts form the bases for the distribution of power in universities and departments.

Departments are rarely equal in their power. Some command larger shares of resources, have an easier time getting their people hired and promoted, have lighter teaching loads or more teaching assistance distributed to them. Different groups dominate in different universities. Prestigious private universities are more likely than prestigious public universities to have outstanding law and business schools, and prestigious public universities are more likely to have outstanding engineering and agricultural schools. These differences reflect the historical flow of resources into the institutions. In a similar way, the distribution of power among and within departments results from the way resources come into them and the roles they play.

In one typical research university, the University of Illinois, the most powerful departments come from the physical sciences. It does not take much to see this. Most of the important committees in the university are peopled by faculty from the physics, mathematics, and engineering departments. The only well-represented behavioral science department is psychology. Curious about the dominance of these groups, a colleague and one of the authors of this chapter (Salancik) studied 13 years of the university's history, examining the budgets, grants, teaching loads, academic rankings

(ACE ratings), and such, of more than half of the departments in the university. The departments on key committees were allotted larger portions of the state budget relative to other departments and disproportionate to their teaching obligations to undergraduate or graduate students. The budget of one physical science department, for instance, correlated .73 with its 13-year growth in its undergraduate teaching, whereas a comparable correlation for one social science department was −.64. Allocations to the powerful were also disproportionate to their academic rankings, despite frequent claims that the limited funds of the university should go to the "better" departments. In these 13 years, a top-ranked psychology department was not quite worth as much as a top-ranked electrical engineering department.

It is not difficult to figure out what was accounting for the budget decisions. One need remember only that power distributes along the lines of critical dependencies. The University of Illinois is a major research institution. Research and graduate education are its primary goals. Talk about them invades every meeting and colors every issue requiring organizational attention. Recognizing this, it was easy to deduce that the most critical contributions the departments made to the university were the resources needed to run large-scale graduate programs. These did not come from the state of Illinois in the amounts required, either. They came from grants.

Grants are important in universities for two reasons. The less important reason is that they fund research. This, however nice for faculty and students, benefits mainly the department getting the grant, not the university as a whole. Grants would not be a basis for power in a university if that were all they did. The second, and more important, role of grants is that they contribute discretionary money in the form of overhead rebates.

Overhead funds play a key role in maintaining quality in educational and research programs throughout a university. They accumulate into piles of money available for activities unjustified by other budgetary categories. Their greatest value is that they are discretionary. They benefit research by providing seed money to projects awaiting grant support or groundwork for frontier areas that have not attracted government or foundation attention yet. They benefit teaching by funding innovations beyond the reach of the normal educational budget.

Discretionary funds also play a big role in managing a university. They can be critical in attracting and keeping talented faculty and students. A smart department head can promise the wavering support for special projects or summer research, competing more effectively than without such funds. And when the discretionary funds in one department are used up, a head in good standing with campus administrators can petition to dip into their much larger discretionary piles. The University of Illinois at one time amassed a million dollar funding and equipment package to attract the inventor of magnetic resonance imaging. Fifteen campus units cooperated, and much of the support came from discretionary money. Funding a major investment of this nature reflects not only a department that has already contributed overhead but also an investment that the university sees as likely to recover overhead in the future.

With grants generating such critical discretionary funds, it was not surprising to find a department's power was proportional to its contributions to the overhead pool. The major predictor of the differences between the power of departments was the grant money they provided. Seventy percent of the variance in power measures was associated with contract funds, and power in turn was the major predictor of state budget allocations. What this meant is that the small fractional discretionary funds provided by some departments promoted their control of the rest of the budget. With only slight hyperbole, 10% of the resources determined how 80% of the budget was spent!

One cannot simply extrapolate these results to other institutions. Universities differ in their goals, and more important, in the factors affecting their survival. For the University of Illinois, the quality of its graduate and research programs is important, and not an easy task given the constraints of its environment.

Other universities organize around other resources. The one generality is that power plays a role in every university and derives from the critical resources that shape that institution's success and ultimately its survival. Private schools, lacking the subsidies of a state appropriation process, operate differently than public universities. They survive by accumulating endowment, which depends on their graduates' wealth and willingness to part with it as they age. Not surprisingly, private schools pay a lot more attention to their undergraduates' experiences. They want their students to leave with warm feelings and fond memories. And this affects their decisions as much as grants do at the University of Illinois. It just affects them in different ways.

CONCLUSION

Money is key in understanding power and influence. Most academics prefer not to think about money, believing if they have a good idea it should be funded. However, those who run universities are confronted by many good ideas and must choose among them. To choose they must maximize the quality of the entire institution. The best way to have your idea funded is to understand the context in which you and your institution function.

13

MANAGING THE DEPARTMENT CHAIR AND NAVIGATING THE DEPARTMENT POWER STRUCTURE

LOUIS A. PENNER, JOHN F. DOVIDIO, AND DAVID A. SCHROEDER

The goal of this chapter is to offer advice to junior faculty members about the best ways to "manage" their department chair or other faculty members who occupy positions of power in their departments. From the perspective of junior faculty, who sometimes feel powerless and under the microscope, the concept of managing the department chair may seem alien and risky. Indeed, the term *manage* is a bit of a misnomer, because it suggests that a new faculty member might be able to cleverly manipulate or control the person who is his or her boss. As we will stress numerous times in the pages that follow, this is an inaccurate and counterproductive way of viewing your relationship with your chair.

Perhaps the best analogy for the relationship between junior faculty and chairs is the relationship between bright children and their tough but responsible and caring parents. Such parents love their children, feel a responsibility to help them to succeed, but demand and expect the best from them. When the children do achieve success, the parents derive great vicarious pleasure and satisfaction from this. Also, just as parents invest in their children (e.g., braces, college tuition), department chairs make substantial investments in new faculty members in terms of recruiting costs, start-up funds, research space, and equipment. It is clearly in a chair's best interests to show his or her superiors that these investments were wise ones, as evidenced by your success. Thus, even if a chair does not love you as much as your parents do, it will still make him or her happy if you are successful.

Our parent–child analogy also highlights another aspect of the relationship between a chair and a junior faculty member. As you may recall from your own adolescence, caring parents and talented children will frequently and honestly disagree about what is needed to become successful, or even about what constitutes success. Similarly, caring chairs and talented junior faculty members can have different perspectives on success. But the relationship between a junior faculty member and a department chair is really an interdependent one and should *not* be seen as a series of zero-sum exchanges. It is much more productive to see it as a cooperative effort to reach a mutually beneficial goal.

By the way, we hope our junior colleagues do not find the parent–child analogy demeaning or patronizing. We are not suggesting that chairs are invariably wiser than junior faculty (even more than parents are necessarily wiser than their bright children), but rather only that they usually do care about them *and* that they are typically older, more experienced, and always more powerful than new faculty members.

The chapter is intended to help junior faculty effectively and successfully manage their department chair, as stated initially. But it may be important for you to know that the three authors of this chapter have had among them about 30 years of experience as chairs of psychology departments. We admit that for some, this latter bit of information may conjure up the image of three smiling people saying, "We're from the government; we're here to help you." However, we see ourselves instead as aspiring angels, who want to earn their wings by helping others.

To do this, we first identify some basic assumptions about the nature of chairs and faculty members. After that, we outline formal and informal structures and sources of power within a department. Next we suggest ways that junior faculty members, who are initially in relatively low status positions, can gain status and become valuable members of the department. Then, recognizing that despite the best of intentions of all concerned, the relationship between a junior faculty member and a department chair can become strained, we suggest ways to help ensure fair treatment.

SOME BASIC ASSUMPTIONS

The advice contained in this chapter is predicated on three assumptions. The first is that the people who read this chapter are bright, competent professionals who are serious about their careers, have the potential to become successful academics, and are capable of being reasonably objective about their abilities, aptitudes, and aspirations. Thus, this chapter is not about "How to Succeed in Academics Without Really Trying"; it is for capable people who are highly motivated to succeed in their careers. The second assumption is that faculty members in most psychology departments are treated equitably and evaluated on the basis of their performance rather than on the basis of capricious whims. But it is important not to confuse effort with accomplishments. Success in academia (as elsewhere) is not determined by how hard people work but rather by how much they actually accomplish. The third assumption is that (and this may be awfully self-serving) most department chairs are basically decent individuals who have been selected because people who know them well trust them and because they see helping new faculty to become successful as one of their primary job responsibilities. Indeed, the power of a chair is often based largely on the support of the faculty that he or she serves.

FOLLOW THE LEADER, BUT FIRST FIGURE OUT WHO THE LEADER REALLY IS

At the risk of sounding like Machiavelli, we suggest that one of the most important things new faculty members should learn is how much power their chair actually has and what the bases of that power might be.

Chairs and Heads

Although this chapter is about managing the department chair, leaders of academic departments are not always designated as the chair. In a small but significant number of departments, the leader is a "department head." Head is not simply another name for a chair; they differ in important ways. A chairs is traditionally seen as being a faculty colleague who serves as the department's representative to the administration. A department head, in contrast, is viewed explicitly as part of the management; he or she technically administers the department as an agent of the university administration, and, at least on paper, a head's primary allegiance is to the dean. Because their power is based in their formal, delegated position, heads typically depend much less than do chairs on faculty support and consensus for their actions. Of course, there are heads who are exceptionally democratic and consultative, and there are department chairs who appear to have learned their leadership style from Joe Stalin. However, heads may not be as democratic as chairs, because they are seen as having different administrative roles and responsibilities in the university hierarchy.[1]

Less Tangible Sources of Power

There are other, less obvious aspects of a chair's situation that contribute to the amount of power he or she has. One of these is simply how long a chair is expected to serve and the processes whereby a chair is (or is not) reappointed. You can probably find this out by simply asking a colleague or checking the departmental constitution or bylaws. However, such formal guidelines may often be misleading. There are a number of departments in which a chair must be formally reelected or reappointed every three or five years. But, in many of these departments, the chairs have served multiple consecutive terms, and reappointment is more or less a *pro forma* matter for both the department and the dean.

Some other objective kinds of information regarding a person's status as chair concern whether the individual is an acting chair, interim chair, or permanent chair and whether the department has a tradition of rotating chairs. With regard to the last of these, some departments have a system by which senior faculty members assume the chair position for a fixed term and then, barring unusual circumstances, rotate out of the position. Obviously, an acting or interim chair has less power than a rotating chair, who, in turn, has less power than a permanent chair. Thus, negotiations about long-term commitments and goals with acting or rotating chairs may not be particularly worthwhile activities unless the negotiations result in formal, *written* agreements. As the legendary Hollywood producer Louis B. Mayer once said, "Verbal agreements aren't worth the paper they're written on."

Another important component of a chair's power is, ironically, how willing and able the chair is to walk away from the job. Chairs who want to continue in the chair position indefinitely or have aspirations of higher administrative positions are unlikely to go out on a limb for a junior faculty member. Their concern about staying in the job will make them much more likely to be swayed by the wishes of a dean or the demands of powerful senior faculty. One way to determine where a chair falls on this dimension is to examine how active the chair is in research or, to a lesser extent, in teaching. A chair who describes him- or herself as "a teacher and researcher who is chairing for awhile" may have significant power in dealings with others. However, if a chair is not active in either of these domains, then

---

[1]In addition to *head*, there are other terms to describe department leaders (e.g., *faculty representative*). However, from now on we will use the word *chair* as a generic term to describe the position of the person who leads the department.

this is probably a person who hopes to remain a chair for a long time or to move on to another administrative position.

Finally, quite independent of the chair's personal goals, it is important to know how the dean feels about the chair. At the simplest level, one needs to know whether or not the two get along and whether the chair has the dean's respect and confidence. But it is perhaps even more important to know how much autonomy the dean allows the chair. A chair with substantial autonomy can be a force for good or for evil but is a force that needs to be reckoned with in either case. A chair without much autonomy may be little more than a caretaker. But even if the chair appears to have relatively little autonomy, he or she is responsible for the administration of departmental affairs and should be your first contact when problems arise. Most universities are relatively "flat" (i.e., nonhierarchical) organizations, but there still is a chain of command, and there is little that one could do to alienate most chairs faster than going around them to the dean. Such tactics could also upset other department faculty members and will not be warmly received by a good dean.

No Chair Is an Island

A common misperception of new faculty members, which to a certain extent we might have perpetuated thus far, is that a chair is the sole decision maker in the department. Actually, this is rarely the case. Most departments have some sort of formal faculty governance. In small departments, critical decisions about the operation of the department may be made by consensus or a direct vote of faculty. In larger departments, a subset of the faculty may be given this responsibility. This could take the form of an executive committee elected by the entire faculty, a council made up of the directors of different subareas within the department, or some other decision-making body made up of faculty besides the chair. Among the critical decisions the members of this committee may make are resource and space allocations, teaching assignments, and the size of raises. In some departments these kinds of decisions are left entirely to such a committee; in others, the committee may serve only an advisory role for the chair. The most common arrangement, though, is some sort of power sharing. It is easy to learn about who sits on this committee (or committees) and what the various committees' formal responsibilities are; it is much harder to accurately judge a committee's power relative to that of the chair. Here again, there may be a difference between what is written and what are, to use a military phrase, the "facts on the ground."

Closely related to the issue of who really governs the department— and perhaps even more important—is who makes the tenure and promotion decisions. These are, after all, the most important decisions in a person's academic life (or death). In most institutions, a series of committees and administrators at different levels of the university review the cases sequentially, but the department recommendation is a critical first step in this process. Usually, chairs make an independent judgment and recommendation about tenure and promotion that becomes an official part of a person's tenure or promotion application. This is usually accompanied by a recommendation from a "promotion and tenure" committee and, in many but not all departments, some sort of faculty vote by the tenured faculty. We urge you to learn as much as possible about the exact tenure/promotion policies and procedures in your department and at your institution *as soon as possible* after joining the faculty. In fact, we outline these procedures in detail during job interviews, so the candidates can make informed decisions about how well they will fit into the system if a job offer is extended.

But once again, there is more than the formal rules. In some universities, the chair's recommendation regarding tenure or promotion is just one among equals, but in most institutions it carries much more weight than any other departmental recommendation. Two critical factors affecting the weight given to the chair's recommendation are the chair's relationship with the dean, mentioned earlier, and his or her reputation on campus with faculty from other departments who may serve on college-level or university-wide personnel committees. If the chair's relationship with the dean is strained at a personal level, if there are differences in their academic goals and values, or if the chair is not well regarded on campus, then the chair may have a diminished role in the final tenure decision.

Of course, if a department has rotating chairs or if the current chair is expecting to step down in the near future, then it is likely that the current chair will not be the one who will review your tenure or promotion application. It is thus important to learn all you can not only about the current chair's relationship with the dean but also about the likely future chair's standing within the university. Avoid making the common mistake of putting all your eggs in the current chair's proverbial basket. We know of too many instances where a junior faculty member essentially did all of the chair's bidding and worked to please the chair rather than other faculty or even him- or herself. Besides undermining the autonomy and freedom that is so central to an academic life, this is simply an inadvisable course of action. As we have suggested earlier, chairs rotate out, quit, leave, retire, or get forced out (or sometimes even simply disappear without a trace). If your future is inextricably intertwined with this person's, then you may find yourself in serious trouble if or when there is a change of power. However, if you clearly understand the core values and missions of the department and perform in ways that are consistent with them, you will have placed yourself in a good position, regardless of the idiosyncrasies of the individual occupying the chair position.

Before we leave the issue of power in a department, we want to make explicit something that has been implicit in the preceding paragraphs. It is not sufficient just to learn the written policies and procedures for the department and the university. You must also learn the local customs and norms and think about the future as well as the present. This may be a slow, painful, and difficult process, but it is critical to a full understanding of your department and university.

Knowing the department chair and understanding the institutional culture provide a solid foundation for successfully navigating the power structures within a department. Nevertheless, success in academia is not simply a function of being liked by the chair or being popular with key senior colleagues. As noted before, excellence in performance is essential. But it is also essential that you make the chair and other department faculty aware of your excellent performance. We now turn to this matter.

BECOMING KNOWN AND BECOMING WELL-KNOWN

In the play *Death of a Salesman*, the tragic protagonist, Willie Loman, laments that among his colleagues he is "known, but not well-known." Success in a good department often requires that junior faculty members make themselves well-known to all their colleagues.

Unless you are in a rather small department, it is likely that it, like the discipline, has divided (perhaps even compartmentalized) itself into subareas. Thus, colleagues, even those in the next office, may be unfamiliar with the area in which you do research. Here is one example. One of us, a social psychologist, has had a good personal and professional relationship with a colleague in neuroscience for the past 10 years. Indeed, he was chair when the neuroscientist was hired. The two were having lunch one day, and the conversation turned to evolutionary psychology. The social psychologist was telling the neuroscientist about a certain experiment designed to test some theories of kin selection. The neuroscientist found the results interesting but expressed surprise on learning that social psychologists actually conduct experiments! We fear this lack of familiarity and misunderstanding about the nature of our colleagues' research is not an isolated incident, and such misconceptions can be damaging to a junior faculty member's career.

Becoming well-known is difficult because of the centrifugal forces at work in psychology today, and it is compounded by the dramatic changes in how faculty members are currently able to do their jobs. When the three of us started our careers, faculty members worked almost exclusively in their offices. After all, that was where the people who typed your syllabi and manuscripts worked, where you received your mail, and where you chatted around the coffeepot to find out what was *really* going on in the department. Your office was the base of your professional activities. Today, powerful desktop personal computers, electronic mail, and the Internet make it quite possible to carry out a major portion of your job effectively without getting anywhere near your office. Most faculty now have equipment at home that replicates or perhaps even surpasses the equipment in our office, and, thus, some faculty spend more time working at their homes than at their offices on campus.

We do not really miss the good old days; we appreciate more than you can imagine the benefits of the technological changes that have occurred at almost all colleges and universities. But we would argue that for some faculty, especially junior ones, these incredible gains in time and efficiency are accompanied by potentially significant costs. Specifically, the isolation that can result from these changes have dramatically reduced the opportunities for informal but important contacts among junior faculty members and their senior colleagues. These informal contacts allow others in the department to learn about what kind of person you are and what you like to do and allow you to get to know them. True, faculty members submit annual reports of their activities ("brag sheets") to the chair and an evaluation committee, but the people who review this information may not even be allowed to tell others about an individual's performance or accomplishments. In addition, it is very difficult to provide information about one's collegiality in an annual report, but at many institutions such qualities are receiving increased consideration in promotion and tenure deliberations.

If the first time a senior faculty member is exposed to a junior faculty member's research interests and accomplishments is during a promotion or tenure review, this may be too little information, provided far too late. The reviewer may have already formed a impression (and a potentially biased one) about the faculty member's research area, and, as any social or cognitive psychologist will tell you, people often have difficulty processing schema-inconsistent information. First impressions are important, and the first impression you make on members of a promotion and tenure committee should not be when they look at your vita or read your articles, especially if the articles are in an area with which they are not familiar. Like Willie Loman, you should aspire to become well-known to your colleagues early in your career.

Make Yourself Available

One way to make a positive impression is to spend time in your office over and above the time you spend meeting with students. Simply being around the office creates the opportunity for colleagues to talk to you and learn about your work and vice versa. Many management consultants (e.g.,

Peters, 1985) recommend that effective supervisors use a "management by walking around" strategy to get first-hand information about what is happening in their departments. Junior faculty should heed similar advice and become known by walking around. For example, you should follow your mother's advice and "eat a good lunch." (Well, maybe she would say breakfast, but let us not quibble.) We suggest this because lunches with colleagues, especially colleagues from outside your research area, provide an excellent vehicle to tell others what you do and why you do it. And these exchanges also afford you with the opportunity to learn about them and their research. It is personally and professionally valuable for you to take a sincere interest in learning what your colleagues are doing and to benefit from their experiences. Besides providing opportunities to learn about what is expected within the department, informal exchanges about teaching and research are part of what make a department a stimulating and interesting place to be. We also suggest that you attend colloquia, brown bags, and other departmental events even when they are outside your primary areas of interest. The best reason for doing this is that you might actually learn something that you did not know, but such events also provide another opportunity to make you and your work known to others. Finally, as you engage in these social interactions, it is important for you to just *be yourself*. We mentioned previously the need for academics to be honest with themselves about their abilities, aptitudes, and aspirations; social honesty is also important to gain the respect of colleagues. Disingenuous attempts at impression management and self-serving ingratiation will be detected and are likely to backfire.

Make Yourself Valuable

To return to Willie Loman one more time, his professional failure was really a result of something other than simply not being well-known. Even among the people who knew him well, he was not considered to be much of a salesman and therefore not of much value to his employers. How do new faculty members avoid the fate of Willie Loman and make themselves valuable to their chairs and their departments?

Part of our answer to this question comes from recent work in industrial–organizational psychology. Walter Borman and his colleagues (e.g., Borman & Motowidlo, 1997) have argued that job performance has two distinct components: task performance and citizenship performance. We consider task performance first. It involves the technical and formal aspects of the job; good task performance requires certain kinds of professional knowledge, skills, and abilities. In the case of an academic position, teaching and research constitute the task performance component of the job. Obviously, the relative weight put on each of these two activities will vary across institutions and departments, but it is unlikely that people could succeed or even survive in a department if they were not good at one of these. Indeed, in most contemporary departments one has to be valuable in both areas.

How do faculty make themselves valuable with respect to teaching? Obviously, one should be a good classroom teacher (see chapters 5 and 6, this volume), but there is more to it. Following are a few things that may increase one's value as a teacher. First, teach courses that are needed by the department as a whole and that others cannot or will not teach. If you are only willing (or able) to teach a narrow range of courses that interest only you (and perhaps only a few students), your value to the department as a teacher is diminished. We are not suggesting that you commit yourself to a broad range of course preparations that fall outside your area of expertise, but rather that, within reason, you be willing to—or even volunteer to—teach the courses that the chair says need to be offered to meet the mission of the department. Learning new teaching technologies can also make you a valuable teaching resource for your colleagues (especially the older ones because they will use you to teach them). In addition to formal classroom activities, a valuable contributor to teaching in a department is someone who is willing to direct student research at both the undergraduate and graduate levels and who is willing to serve on and contribute in meaningful ways to graduate thesis and dissertation committees. Serving on thesis and dissertation committees also provides excellent opportunities to make yourself and your skills known to other faculty members.

We offer one cautionary note about being a valuable teacher. Although high-quality teaching has become much more important at universities in recent years, in a research-oriented department it will not compensate for a lack of scholarly productivity. Being an effective and popular teacher can be seductive. It provides more immediate and continuous gratification than does research. It then becomes easy to distort the relative value placed on teaching by the department and the university so that it conform to one's strengths. Regardless of how *you* feel about the relative importance of teaching and research, remember that promotion and tenure decisions will be based on the established criteria of the department and college, not what you might like them to be. It is crucial that you maintain a realistic view of the criteria for tenure through regular contact with the chair and other senior colleagues. You need to keep this in mind and again be objective as you evaluate your overall value to the department.

Turning to research, in our view a valuable researcher is someone who develops a coherent research program that involves students, results in publications in top-level professional journals, and earns the person a measure of professional visibility. At many universities, to be considered a valuable researcher you also need to be able to attract external funding for your research program. To the extent that your research brings overhead or turn-back money into the department and the university, your value to the department will be enhanced. However, universities vary in the emphasis given to extramural support, and it is important to know how such activities will be weighted during tenure and promotion considerations. Allocate your efforts accordingly. It may even be wise to have the chair include an explicit statement about the importance of extramural support in your annual reviews so that a paper trail will be established in the event that standards change before you come up for tenure–promotion.

Now we turn to the other aspect of job performance posited by Borman and his colleagues: citizenship performance. Citizenship performance involves behaviors that directly and indirectly support and facilitate the formal, technical activities of the organization. Most analyses of citizenship performance identify two major components. The first is altruism, which involves behaviors that are intended to help other members of the organization perform their jobs. This would include activities such as directly aiding a colleague in the performance of his or her job (e.g., providing statistical consultation or doing a guest lecture) and treating others with courtesy and respect. The other component is conscientiousness, which involves behaviors directed at helping the organization itself. Behaviors reflecting conscientiousness include doing more than is expected or required of you (e.g., agreeing to teach an extra course because of unusual circumstances or developing a new course) and being an informed and constructive member of the department. Borman and his colleagues, like many other industrial–organizational psychologists, argue that citizen performance may be as important as task performance to the success of an organization. We propose that this may be especially true in an academic department because they are highly interdependent entities and are often seriously understaffed. As a consequence, people who are willing to help out individual colleagues and the department itself are of considerable value. Of course, we must reemphasize what the industrial–organizational literature and common sense tells us: Outstanding citizenship performance will not make up for inferior task performance. However, given that a person's task performance is good, substantial citizenship performance makes the person much more valuable, and that value may make a difference in a difficult tenure or promotion decision.

In the context of citizenship performance, we also need to discuss service activities. In addition to teaching and research, most departments evaluate faculty on their service. The kinds of service that are evaluated are activities that benefit the department, the university, the profession, and sometimes the general community. Service in the first area most often means membership on departmental committees. In most departments, all faculty members are expected to serve on some departmental committee. You may not get many bonus points for doing this, but you can lose a substantial number of points on annual evaluations and in the eyes of colleagues if you are unwilling to serve. Nevertheless, there is a possible dilemma. Chairs do need help with department committees; they will honestly be grateful to you and may even reward you for this service, but promotion and tenure committees are rarely impressed by departmental service. This is a type of activity that can be immediately gratifying, but department service will not in any way make up for weaknesses in teaching or research. Although you want to be a good citizen, you have to guard against being intentionally or unintentionally exploited by the chair.

Service on university committees is also part of academic life, but our experience is that this activity is less valued by chairs than is departmental or professional service. The major reason for this is that such service is often of no direct benefit to the department and may even involve a net loss if it takes faculty members away from their primary duties within the department. Exceptions to this general rule would be when representation on a university committee will serve the interests of the department (e.g., Institutional Review Boards, Institutional Animal Care and Utilization Committees). The pressures to perform university service may be a special problem for minority faculty and women. Most universities seek diversity on campuswide committees, and if you are a member of an underrepresented group, you may be deluged with invitations to serve on such committees. You may feel some personal or social responsibility to do this, but remember that it counts for little in most chairs' evaluations of you. If it interferes with your teaching or research, it could be a net minus for you professionally.

In contrast to the department, university-wide tenure committees are likely to weigh university service more heavily than departmental service. Thus, it is important that you balance these different types of service activities. The appropriate balance between departmental and university service is typically a function of norms specific to your institution. For example, at smaller institutions, visibility within the university community may be important for tenure and promotion. Nevertheless, in general, our advice would be that, unless a university committee is addressing some issue that is intrinsically interesting to you, you should probably limit university service activities early in your career. (A useful hint: If you are being overwhelmed by extradepartmental service requests, you might ask your chair to step in to provide the excuse that will enable you to say no.)

Professional service involves activities such as reviewing articles for journals and grants for federal agencies and contributing one's time and effort to professional organizations or conferences (e.g., being a program chair). These activities are valued by most chairs because they increase both the faculty member's and the department's visibility in the field. Of course, such activities are also of direct professional benefit to the person who engages in them because they can help establish valuable professional contacts (i.e., networking) for a new faculty member.

Ultimately, the best measure of a faculty member's value relates to the answer to the question, "What would the department lose if the person left?" Chairs and departments value individuals who make important and unique contributions to the department. These contributions could involve the courses one teaches, the number of students one supervises, the kind and quality of research one does, or the types of service one provides. Different institutions, however, weigh these contributions differently, and it is critical that a faculty member clearly understands the institution's and the department's priorities. Thus, a junior faculty should look for ways to make unique contributions to the department, particularly in the areas most important to the department. But remember, contributions that are unique but irrelevant or even antithetical to the department's mission hardly make a faculty member more valuable.

THE ART OF SELF-DEFENSE: PROTECT YOURSELF AT ALL TIMES

Let us summarize what we have said so far: (a) Determine who has power in your department and how long these individuals are likely to maintain this power; (b) let powerful others know who you are and what it is that you do; and (c) make substantial and valuable contributions to your department in the areas of teaching, research, and service. Do these things and a straight and smooth road to academic success lies before you. Well . . . . Unfortunately, this is not always the case. In this section we examine how you might avoid certain potholes and bumps in that road and effectively deal with those that were not successfully avoided. Specifically, we discuss the importance of getting and keeping written documentation of agreements, the value of obtaining regular feedback, and some guidance for conflict resolution.

Please Put It in Writing

Remember what Louis B. Mayer said about verbal agreements? Even in the most benign and supportive of departments, there are certain things a person should know and do in case things go bad. Specifically, as a new faculty member, you should learn about and have easy access to the university's or department's written guidelines regarding how annual duties are assigned, performance evaluations are carried out, raises are determined, and faculty grievances are handled. More important, these documents should also clearly describe the processes for reappointments during your pretenure, probationary period and how tenure and promotion decisions are made. You should keep careful and complete files of all documents and correspondence you receive concerning policies, procedures, and decisions relevant to the performance of your job.[2] If a problem arises about some understanding you had about a course release or a promised piece of equipment and you are frantically looking for a two-year-old e-mail that the chair sent you about the matter and it is 10 minutes before a meeting on this matter, you are not in a position to protect yourself very well. Let us repeat this point with emphasis because it is the most important thing you can you do to protect yourself: *Get hard copies of all personnel documents and commitments for resources and support and keep them in a safe and accessible place.*

At the risk of scaring you, we must add one final cautionary comment to this discussion. Even with written copies of promises and commitments, there are still no ironclad guarantees that all agreements will be honored. Legislatures can cut budgets; endowments can lose money; university priorities can change; and departments may therefore be faced with substantial budget cutbacks. Because of such financial exigencies, well-intentioned and honest chairs may have to delay (or even retract) some promises and commitments. If the problems appear to be restricted to the short-term, you can probably ride them out and reasonably expect the promises to be fulfilled when times get better. But if the problems appear to be long-term, you may be faced with some difficult personal and professional decisions about your future at your current institution.

No News Is Not Good News; and Good News Can Be No News

Open systems, such as humans, survive in large part because they receive feedback from their environment and are able to modify their behavior accordingly. New faculty members also need feedback to survive in an academic environment. To be more specific, all faculty, but particularly junior faculty, need and deserve periodic feedback (evaluative and formative) about their contributions to the department from the chair and other sources to optimize their performance. What we suggest is difficult but important: Regularly solicit information about your progress, and seek out as many opportunities for constructive criticism as possible. If your department does not provide detailed and informative annual evaluations, request periodic meetings with the chair or other appropriate faculty members to discuss your progress. Afterward, you might also write up a summary of this conversation and then ask the chair to sign off on it to document the accuracy of the content. Almost all universities do mid-tenure (e.g., third-year) reviews, but if your department does not, it would be prudent to ask for one. Moreover,

---

[2] One such resource is your university's faculty handbook; it usually includes a full description of all personnel policies and procedures. Make sure you get a copy and keep up with any changes that are made in this document.

try to get input on your performance from people besides the chair. These people could include other senior faculty members, particularly those who are in line to become chair, or senior colleagues at other universities.

When you receive these evaluations, you must remember, however, that people are generally reluctant to transmit bad news, especially to someone with whom they will have continued close interactions. In addition, because people do not like to receive negative information, you may inadvertently steer the conversation toward your strengths and away from your weaknesses. As a consequence, you may have to take some of these evaluations with a grain of salt. We are not suggesting that you *invite or encourage* negative comments, and it might not be in your best interest to have some of your initial shortcomings become a part of your permanent record. Instead, we are strongly suggesting that you encourage honest and constructive feedback from multiple sources early on. It is better to get negative feedback when you have time to make appropriate adjustments and improvements than to get it when you are up for tenure and promotion and it is too late to take corrective actions.

WHAT TO DO WHEN THINGS "GO SOUTH"

This chapter would be incomplete without a discussion of what happens when things go awry between a faculty member and his or her chair. As we have implied several times, most academic departments are rational meritocracies, led by well-intentioned individuals (like us). But even under these conditions, it is possible for serious disputes to emerge between a junior faculty member and a chair or other senior faculty members. The fact that these problems may be the result of honest misunderstandings rather than someone's malevolence is largely irrelevant. Whatever the cause, you should have a strategy for dealing with such conflicts.

The first thing we would recommend is that when the conflict arises, no matter how upset you are, avoid any precipitous or dramatic actions. Remember, this is an unequal power relationship, and you do not want to make things worse than they may already be. These situations are also often complex, and reacting without all of the available information and a full consideration of alternative courses of action is not in your best interest. Your first move should be to seek counsel from others concerning the merits of your position and the best way to resolve the problem. The goal of this activity is not to gather allies but to seek advice. The best sources of advice would probably be people within the department who are more senior than you or at least who have a longer history of dealing with the chair or others who may be involved. Although it may be difficult, approach colleagues who are able to make a dispassionate and objective judgment of the situation rather than friends who might be more interested in providing you with social support. As we suggested at the beginning of this chapter, departments are like families. It is best to keep the issue within the department as long as possible and to seek resolution without bringing in people from outside the department, except as a last resort. Do not be embarrassed about disclosing your problem to others; academic squabbles are hardly rare. If it is simply a misunderstanding, it may be that there was, in fact, no problem at all. If the conflict is more substantive, input from others can help put the problem in a broader perspective and help determine the most effective course of future action to resolve the matter.

Once you have received advice from multiple sources, you need to plan a course of action. Here is something to keep in mind as you do this. Academic conflicts rarely, if ever, have a clear winner and a clear loser. If the conflict is resolved, it is almost always with some sort of compromise. This is important because you should know going in that whatever the relative merit of your position, it is unlikely that the issue will end with you standing victorious over a vanquished chair. But also remember that although the opposite is somewhat more likely to occur, it is still a low-probability event. We tell you these things not to frighten (or embolden) but rather to encourage a realistic assessment about the eventual outcome of the dispute. As wise sage Mick Jagger once said, "You can't always get what you want."

Turning to the resolution of the problem, we urge you not to begin this effort with an e-mail or any other form of written document. If a chair receives a written document—even an e-mail—that outlines supposed grievances, he or she will almost always respond with another written document (for reasons of self-protection). The two of you might then enter a phase of "dueling e-mails" (or memos). Such exchanges are unlikely to produce a lessening of tensions or a reasonable resolution of the issues at hand. Instead, they could cause even a simple misunderstanding to quickly become an unpleasant confrontation. Therefore, we advise you initially to try to address conflicts and misunderstandings in less formal ways. For example, you could begin with an informal meeting with the chair aimed at clarifying the points of contention and reconciling the conflict. Your goal in this meeting should be finding a solution for the conflict, not winning debating points. Therefore, you should have a clear idea of what you want the chair to do to solve the problem and present your proposal to him or her. Often academics are better at talking than listening, but try to begin this session by listening. Remember that it is usually in the chair's best interest to resolve any conflict as quickly as possible. Look for suggestions and statements from the chair that will end the conflict rather than those that might perpetuate it.

If a meeting with the chair fails to address your concerns, then the next step might be to ask a senior department member to mediate the disagreement. If that approach is also unsuccessful, then a formal memorandum or letter in which you outline your position and again ask for some resolution of the problem is probably in order. We would advise you to send this message just to the chair; do not copy it to anyone else (e.g., a dean) at this time. Taking your problem public at this stage would almost surely escalate the conflict, harden positions, and infuriate the chair—further diminishing any chances of a constructive solution. It is not a good idea to back the chair into a corner; rather leave him or her some room to move in a constructive direction. Remember, as you go through this process, you should be sure to carefully document what was done and said by you and by your chair. If all attempts at resolution have failed, then you have a critical decision to make. Do you drop the matter, file a formal grievance, or take it to the dean? Deans are typically loath to get involved in such disputes, and unless the issue involves clear violations of university rules or federal or state statutes (e.g., gender-based discrimination), he or she may simply refer it back to your chair. Alternatively, the dean may decide to refer the matter to the faculty grievance committee (or recommend that you do). You must carefully weigh the costs and benefits of taking such action, however. Using an established grievance process is most likely to be successful when a faculty member can *document* that a chair's actions have violated some *formal procedures* of the university. It may not seem right to you, but bad (or even unfair) decisions that do not clearly violate university policies and procedures are rarely remedied by grievance committees. Grievance committees primarily address the types of deviations that have legal or fiscal consequences for the university. Thus, it is important for you to distinguish between actions of the chair that you do not like and those that you do not like *and* that violate university procedures intended to ensure fair and equitable treatment. The point is that, under most circumstances, you should not expect the dean or other official university bodies to directly intervene on your behalf unless you have a strong and documentable case for procedural irregularities.

If the faculty members at your university are represented by a collective bargaining organization (e.g., union), then you might turn to that group or, in exceptional cases and perhaps as a last resort, you may want to seek the services of a lawyer. The problem may be serious enough to merit such actions, but obviously they are accompanied by some substantial costs, and you again must realistically consider what the likely outcome will be. That is, what are the most positive possible consequences of initiating formal or legal action, and do those consequences outweigh the personal, professional, fiscal, and psychological costs you might incur? Academia is a small world with many informal networks, and public actions can have long-term repercussions not only for the chair but also for you. As you might suspect, we have no final advice on this matter; the specifics of a particular case would have to be carefully weighed to determine the course of action most likely to achieve your goals.

CONCLUSION

As we close this chapter, we must confess something we perhaps should have mentioned at the beginning. There are no secret, foolproof strategies to managing a department chair and navigating your way through the power structures within the department. If your chair is an honest, reasonable, and competent administrator, he or she will treat you fairly. As we have said several times, it is in his or her best interest to do so. But notice that we said "treat you fairly" not "treat you well." You are entitled to fair treatment relative to other members of the department but not to treatment that favors you over other colleagues who are as valuable as you are. Keep in mind that fair treatment may not always make you happy. If the chair's resources are extremely limited, fair treatment may not provide you with all that you want or unfortunately even most of what you need.

In the same vein, a good chair is someone who operates on the principle of equity and rules of procedural fairness and who does *not* reward (or punish) people just because she or he likes (or dislikes) them. Arbitrary and capricious behavior runs counter to the long-term best interests of the department, the university, and certainly those who are the targets of these actions. Liking and valuing someone should not lead a chair to conclude that the person meets the departmental criteria for success and excellence. As one of the authors once told an unsuccessful tenure candidate, "I like you, but I love my mother. And I still couldn't recommend her for tenure either."

Thus, whether your chair is good, mediocre, or terrible, our final message is the same. To manage a department chair successfully, you must learn both the formal rules and the informal norms in your department and university, know who has power and how much they have, make people aware of who you are and what you do and why, and convince people (*because it is true*) that you are a valuable and trustworthy member of your department. From then on, it is a matter of faith and trust that good people with the right information will make correct decisions and treat you fairly and justly. Our collective experiences tell us that the odds are very much with you.

REFERENCES

Borman, W. C., & Motowidlo, S. J. (1997). Task performance and contextual performance: The meaning for personnel selection research. *Human Performance, 10,* 99–109.

Peters, T. (1985). *A passion for excellence.* New York: Random House.

14

WIRING THE IVORY TOWER:
THE INTERFACE OF TECHNOLOGY
AND THE ACADEMY

KEVIN M. CARLSMITH

Against the odds, you have finished your dissertation, survived the interviews, and landed an academic position. Hurrah! But as should be clear after reading the previous chapters in this volume, you will soon be asked to set up your lab, equip your office, prepare to teach, and establish yourself as an independent researcher. These tasks are all covered in other chapters of this volume, but cutting across each of them is the common thread of technology in academia. Although coping with these issues will be a constant in the years ahead, it is important to consider at this critical juncture of your career how the changing technological landscape will affect you specifically and academia generally.

The early 21st century is at the crux of a technological revolution. The technology associated with the heart of academia—teaching, writing, research, communication—has changed both quickly and dramatically. It is a safe guess that the near future will bring even more change; but change cuts both ways, and the modern academic's challenge is to discriminate between technological advances that enhance rather than inhibit productivity. The goal of this chapter is to examine how recent technological changes have affected various academic domains and to provide a speculative road map to identify technological promise, peril, and pitfalls.

There is a saying that only "fools and weathermen" make predictions, and it is with some trepidation that any author speculates about the future of technology. Like the weather, it is simple to describe the present, challenging to forecast tomorrow, and downright foolish to talk about next year. To not sound too hopelessly dated in the years following publication, much of the discussion will involve present conditions and recent trends and will only make rather broad speculation about future possibilities. The chapter is organized around the major themes of the academic life: teaching, researching, and disseminating information, with a final section of practical advice.

TEACHING

The transmission of information from one generation to the next has been the fundamental occupation of the academy for millennia. In the current period of change, there is enormous potential to harness new tools for improving the educational process. Likewise, however, there is also potential to be unwittingly harnessed by technology and thereby become a less effective teacher. The goal of this section is to identify some of the pedagogical domains most affected by recent changes in technology and to explore their benefits and downsides. For a more complete discussion of teaching and technology, the reader is directed to the Technology Source (http://horizon.unc.edu/TS/) or to chapters 5 and 19, this volume.

Access

Accessibility has been one of the great promises of the technological revolution. Within an educational context, the promise is that students will have access—at any time—to the syllabus, full-text readings, previous exams, student papers, lecture notes, and any other course material that the instructor chooses to make available. In addition to these materials, students also have (and increasingly expect) full access to the professor and teaching assistants. At many schools, office hours are expected to be augmented by rapid response e-mail, course-related chat rooms, instant messaging, and other methods of around-the-clock communication. Moreover, it is becoming increasingly possible (and therefore, one suspects, expected) to provide video coverage of the lectures, and to make these videos available to students through cable or computer interface. In all, one of the great promises of 21st-century education is that all of the resources traditionally available to the students should be accessible at any time, not merely at prescribed times and locations.

Students will certainly be in favor of these changes because they provide increased flexibility with few apparent drawbacks. But people often yearn for outcomes that are not in their best interest (Gilbert & Ebert, 2002; Schwartz, 2000), and this may be one such example. Students are notorious procrastinators, and the freedom to put off reading and attending lectures is likely to increase end-of-semester cramming. We know that spaced learning is more effective than massed practice, and it may be our responsibility as teachers to impose this structure for our students' own good. This tension between access and structure is similar to the long-standing decision of whether to distribute lecture notes to one's class; it differs only in scope and not in kind. So, despite the obvious advantages of a fully accessible classroom, each instructor will need to determine how the trade-offs will affect his or her particular students.

Distance Learning

As the previous discussion suggests, the logical extension of the fully accessible classroom is one that does not require the physical presence of either the instructor or students. The technology is already in place, and major universities are experimenting with distance-learning classes in which physical location of the students is limited only by their access to computers and Internet connections (U.S. Department of Education, 2000). Students read the text and watch the lecture on their own and then "assemble" in virtual classrooms at designated times for moderated discussions. Tests and essays are given remotely and can be graded entirely by computer. Once a course is developed, lectures can be recorded and the course repeated indefinitely with little or no additional effort on the part of the originating lecturer.

Such a scenario has some rather inviting implications. First, universities may be able to offer their services—at limited additional cost—to populations of traditionally underserved or geographically remote students. A second obvious benefit is that materials, indeed entire courses, can be recycled from one year to the next, ultimately yielding better classes with less effort. Such speculation, taken to its logical end, leads to the (admittedly pleasant) image of teaching via computer without the bother of getting dressed and going to school.

It remains to be seen, of course, whether these technological advances actually improve the caliber of education at colleges and universities. Certainly low-tech "correspondence courses" have been in place for years without causing much of a ripple in the academic community. The critical difference between traditional and correspondence education is the degree of personal interaction among students and between the student and instructor. If access to information was the sole critical component in education, then surely we would have seen this sort of academic revolution after the Gutenberg press; the hope for high-tech distance learning is that the online interactions will be of such high quality that the experience will be closer to the vibrancy of traditional classrooms than to the solitude of the correspondence course.

.EDU Economics

Members of the academy are rightfully concerned about the impact these technological advances will have on the business of education and on the structure of academia. On the one hand, it is likely that students will generally resist distance learning unless there is a compelling advantage to engage in it. If distance learning is reserved for those in particular circumstances (e.g., remote locations, certain disabilities, inflexible work or family commitments, etc.), then the overall impact may be negligible. On the other hand (and at the risk of sounding a bit like Chicken Little), a school in financial straits might find the notion of a one-time expense to develop a course with unlimited reproduction rights to be a fiscally savvy option. The overall teaching requirements for these schools in the long run would be greatly reduced, and one presumes that the faculty ranks might be similarly culled (Eamon, 1999). Under this scenario, courses taught "live" might become the prerogative of upper-level seminars or private schools that can charge handsomely for the privilege.

Alternatively, one can imagine entire courses being marketed and distributed in the manner of textbooks. Each publishing house might produce its version of "Cognitive Psychology" and "Introduction to Psychology," and it would be up to the individual department to decide whether to go with the prepackaged course or to hire a faculty member to assemble his or her own unique course. Large faculties across the country could be replaced with a few super-star "edutainers." The implications for such a change are profound and would obviously reverberate throughout the academy if it came to pass.

If such propositions sound far-fetched, it is probably because as academics we are well-acquainted with the importance of personal interaction in the teaching and learning process. We are rightly skeptical that prepackaged courses, even with the latest technology backing them up, can replace the dynamic interaction that comes from many active minds struggling with a particular question. But this is preaching to the pulpit. The issue in the future may be to convince nonacademics that good educational experience cannot be replaced merely with good educational technology.

RESEARCH

Research and technology have a symbiotic relationship; research is informed and enabled by technology, and technology is spurred and directed by the needs of research. In the midst of rapid technological change, it is no surprise to encounter vast potential changes in the research landscape.

For the new professor, technological advances represent one particularly effective means to advance a program of research, and any such advantage is critical in the competitive path to tenure. These advantages can play out in a number of ways. Consider, for example, the relative ease of running a cognitive reaction time study. Although the technique was introduced by F. C. Donders in 1868, the ease of such techniques was vastly improved with the advent of desktop computers, which in turn facilitated the cognitive revolution in psychology. Those who were among the early adopters of computer-aided research clearly maintained an advantage. It is worth noting, however, that although reaction-time studies became easier with newer technology, the accuracy of such studies actually declined initially because of untested, unreliable, or unstandardized computer equipment. In general, though, advances in technology often take the labor out of a well-established empirical technique, allowing broader, faster, and more frequent experiments.

Second, the processes underlying well-established phenomena can often be described, or described more fully, with the development of new technologies. Much of the research in social psychology in the 1990s, for example, focused on the cognitive processes associated with behavioral phenomena described in previous decades. Current trends suggest advances in functional magnetic resonance imaging (fMRI) technology will serve to localize the brain activity of these same phenomena (Kruglanski, 2001).

Third, open empirical questions become tractable as technological limitations recede. Consider the example of multivariate research: Although the mathematics of factor analysis was developed by the turn of the 20th century, it was not commonly used until mainframe super-computer systems made the calculations manageable. In recent years, as super-computers have made their way onto individual desktops, a profusion of studies (particularly in personality psychology) have been enabled exclusively because of increased computing power.

Fourth, new domains of research open with improved technology, and new questions can be brought to bear on old problems. The emerging field of social cognitive neuroscience is a case in point (see Ochsner & Lieberman, 2001). Researchers in this interdisciplinary field seek to understand phenomena at all three levels of analysis (neural, process, and behavioral) and generate hypotheses that are particularly effective at dissociating competing theories of process. The point is that although new technologies in neuroscience seemed largely irrelevant to social psychologists, recent advances in cherished social psychological domains (e.g., cognitive dissonance, person perception, stereotyping, etc.) have proven otherwise.

Ethical Considerations

Such speculation leads, one hopes, to concerns about privacy and other ethical issues associated with these possibilities. One of the fundamental implications of advances in science and technology is that ethical boundaries, once defined by practical rather than ethical limitations, must now be defined by explicit decision. Static adherence to an ethical code is probably insufficient in this period of transition. This is not to say that the ethical principles are changing, but rather that the application of those principles is in flux.

Research psychologists are necessarily concerned with protecting their participants' privacy. Ideally, all personal data is stored in locked filing cabinets with restricted access, and computer records are carefully locked and encrypted so that others can neither access the data nor connect the data to the individual participants. In practice, however, it is not uncommon to encounter "needle-in-the-haystack" security. That is, the information gathered (e.g., a need-for-closure score) is of such limited value to those with nefarious intentions, and the effort of sorting through thousands of pages of raw data so tedious, that the real likelihood of an individual's privacy being violated is functionally nil. As the quantity of information and the ease of storing it in permanent databases increases, however, so too does the risk to the individual participant. Moreover, as labs discover the ease and advantage of sharing participant information across multiple studies the real danger to the participant expands dramatically. Whereas 10 years ago a participant's privacy was somewhat protected by cumbersome and antiquated data storage procedures, a modern and well-organized lab today may ironically pose an increased risk to participant privacy. Although individual researchers may not fundamentally change their attitudes toward privacy, the ever-increasing power provided by their computer databases may well necessitate significant changes in their practices.

Caveats

The adoption of any new technology entails start-up costs that need to be carefully compared to the overall expected benefit. In addition to the monetary expense, you should consider the amount of time and effort that you and your staff will need to invest in the technology. Simple point-and-click software programs often have gentle learning curves and represent relatively safe investments. Mastering a computer language, by contrast, generally has a steep learning curve that qualifies the potential benefits derived from being able to customize your own software. These start-up costs are particularly relevant given the typical life cycle of cutting-edge advances. Technology is not an academic panacea; like any tool it must be evaluated in terms of its overall costs and benefits.

COMMUNICATION

At the time of writing, the most obvious change in communication has been the sudden and complete dominance of e-mail as the communication medium of choice. It sprang into existence for mainstream academia nearly overnight and has since become the ubiquitous form of communication among colleagues.

E-Mail

One reason for the popularity of e-mail is that it enables one to be well connected to many diverse sources of information. Many divisions of the American Psychological Association (APA) and other specialized academic groups provide listservs that allow individuals to e-mail all regis-tered members. The Society for Personality and Social Psychology, for exam-ple, provides a ready venue for professors, postdocs, graduate students, and interested others to converse, ask questions, post job announcements, and exchange ideas in a remarkable international forum. These listservs (or any modern variant of them) are increasingly essential for full participation in one's academic community.

For scholars at small or remote institutions, e-mail and other forms of electronic communication can facilitate the formation of a scholarly community in a particular field. Although you are unlikely to have colleagues with similar interests adjacent to your office, you can have daily correspon-dence with other experts in your field. This permits you to have an active voice in your field during the long periods between annual conferences, and substantially mitigates one frequently cited drawback to working at smaller institutions (see chapter 18, this volume).

Like most aspects of new technology, e-mail can be a double-edged sword. The simplicity of sending mass mailings means you are also liable to receive mass mailings. The convenience of e-mail comes at a cost of information overload, and one challenge for the future is to manage such a high volume of communication. At present, it is not uncommon for individuals to find 50, 100, or more e-mail messages waiting for their arrival each morning. One technique for reducing this onslaught is to become something of a virtual hermit through judicious dissemination of one's e-mail address. However, given that most students, departments, and journals *want* to provide access to you for their constituents, it may well be a losing battle. Thus, even if you are cautious with your e-mail address, you may still receive several hours' worth of e-mail each day from people and organizations, and managing this e-mail is essential. Most popular e-mail programs will allow you to set up filters and automatic sorting rules, and it is well worth your time to take advantage of these features. For example, one can set up a series of rules to place e-mail from a particular listserv into one folder (e.g., an APA folder), e-mail from a spouse into another, and flag those e-mails that were sent to you personally (as opposed to carbon copies or mass mailings). For more advanced users, mail with a certain subject line or return address can be automatically given a different priority ranking, forwarded to other accounts, or have a standard reply sent. This allows you to focus on the most important mail first and to read less urgent messages at your convenience.

These features get at the heart of why e-mail has become so popular. Unlike the telephone or face-to-face communication, e-mail permits the recipient to control to a much greater extent the flow of communication. Requests for your attention need not disturb the time you set aside for writing or research. In an interesting twist, this "protection" ironically enables lower status individuals to contact higher status individuals more freely. Imagine the graduate student, for example, who might open a productive dialogue with an eminent researcher by e-mail but who would never do so via telephone. The benefit of such contact, of course, depends entirely on one's perspective. For the young academic it is a tremendous resource to have open lines of communication with others in the field, but for the established expert it represents an annoyance that can develop into a significant time-management liability. The drawback of such accessible communication is that it permits people to easily violate established norms of scholarship. For example, it is now a simple matter to zap a question to the world's authority on an issue rather than do the academic legwork of finding and reading that person's published works. This problem is exacerbated when the questions occur to individuals who have not paused to read even a textbook summary but go instead straight to the source. It may be important that as a community we explicitly apply existing norms of scholarly research to e-mail communication.

For the academic seeking respite from the constant demands on his or her time, the overall advantages of electronic mail cannot be overstated. As communication becomes easier, it will also surely increase in volume. It is essential, therefore, to master the tools that enable you to filter unwanted communication (see chapter 19, this volume).

From Absent-Minded to Just Plain Absent

As remote access to all forms of information and communication increases, the necessity of working from one's academic office decreases. Indeed, many are finding that uninterrupted time to think and write are luxuries rarely found within their department. Accordingly, working from home (or a café or mountaintop) is becoming both possible and rewarding for some academics. The office, increasingly, is being perceived as a place to check mail and hold office hours between on-campus commitments.

Such absentee professors impose a cost on the collective department and university. Students note that their professors are difficult to find, departments note the loss of community, and the hallways lose the bustle of activity, opinion, and shared ideas. Instead, they echo with confused undergraduates and lonely graduate students. Some schools, particularly smaller liberal arts schools, are explicit in their expectation that faculty have a full-time campus presence (Wilson, 2001). This conflict, which is analogous to the individual consumption of any common resource (the so-called "tragedy of the commons"), is likely to become a common and contentious issue in the coming years. The junior academic may want to consider carefully the trade-off between the increased productivity that might come from working remotely and the image that will be projected to colleagues through increased absence. Most departments and chairs value departmental citizenship and expect faculty to contribute to the intellectual community of the department. There are clearly benefits and costs associated with these decisions, and the best advice might be to uncover the local customs and expectations in your department.

Dissemination

The ease of disseminating one's work has increased dramatically over the past decade. References, abstracts, and full-text articles are accessible through electronic databases, and reprints can be sent via e-mail as word-processing documents or in locked printer-ready formats (e.g., PDF files). Likewise, it is becoming acceptable to place preprints and reprints on websites, although authors must always check the current copyright guide-lines of the APA and the journals that might publish the article. (See chapter 10, this volume.)

This distribution issue is hotly debated, and it is unclear exactly when and how it will be resolved. At the time of this writing, we clearly have the technology in place to move from a traditional paper publishing paradigm to an entirely digital distribution system. The substantive arguments against such a transition are generally resolvable, though, and the primary obstacle appears to be the vested interests of current publishers (see Harnad, 1998, for a more detailed introduction to this issue). At the time of this writing, many prestigious journals are accessible on-line (as well as the traditional hard-bound copy), and the APA has expressed support for electronic dissemination of preprints (APA, 2001).

Preservation

It is ironic that the preservation of one's data and papers should be an issue given the recent development of sophisticated databases and memory devices. But visions of a clutter-free paperless office may yet be premature. Consider the example of portable file storage: In the mid- to late 1980s floppy disks were still floppy, and anyone with data in that format today will have a difficult time finding a disk drive that can read the disk. If one were successful in finding a drive, it is even more difficult to find a program able to read the files. When, for example, was the last time you encountered WordStar or ScreenWriter, two of the most common early word processors?

There is not yet reason to think that today's media and file formats will be any more durable. In 2000, Apple Computer omitted floppy disk drives from its entire line of computers in favor of CDs, DVDs, and Zip drives, suggesting that once again, the dominant portable storage medium is undergoing a transformation. Although these media appear to be physically durable, it is an open question whether they too will go the way of the 5¼ inch floppy disk. In the absence of stable electronic media and file formats, the prudent academic may want to embrace the Ludditic ideal of acid-free archival paper. If the time comes when documents should be digitized, the process will undoubtedly be quite simple—far simpler than trying to herd an electronic stable of manuscripts, materials, and data from one archival format to another. Thus, although the technology for safely and permanently archiving knowledge exists, we are not yet at the point where it makes sense to blithely enact this transition.

NUTS AND BOLTS

The preceding discussion intentionally avoided specific advice regarding technology. Given the rate of change in this area, advice given today will tomorrow sound antiquated at best, wrong and foolish at worst. This section offers some concrete suggestions for anyone in the field facing a transition from older to newer technologies. Like all of the advice in this volume, these recommendations should be modified to fit changing times and individual circumstance.

Computers, Hardware, and Software

The first thing to remember is whatever you buy today will almost certainly be obsolete tomorrow. When I entered high school some years ago, my father bought me a very fine calculator able to compute exponents and trigonometric functions. In pointing out its features, he commented that just a few years earlier he had purchased a computer system at Stanford University that filled two entire rooms, cost thousands of dollars, and was somewhat less powerful than the handheld marvel in front of me. Although strategic planning can perhaps mitigate such experiences, they can never be avoided entirely.

The first line of defense against such planned obsolescence may be a purely cognitive act—accept the inevitable demise from "top of the line" to "door-stop" that befall most newer technologies. The second line of defense is to buy the best equipment you can afford to maximize its likely lifespan. There are always two costs associated with equipment becoming antiquated: the (obvious) cost of replacement and the (obvious in hindsight) cost of transitioning from one system to another. Even in the ideal situation in which you are not changing computer platform, operating system, or brand, and you have competent tech support making the transition for you (conditions that seem rarely to occur together), there is still likely to be a productivity cost of days or weeks. Under less optimal conditions, there can be issues of file compatibility, degradation, or loss. In keeping with the advice from Taylor and Martin (chapter 19, this volume), an efficient academic is one who can spend time on important matters (however defined) and not on the details surrounding those matters. It is important to remember that although the computer—and technology more generally—is fast becoming essential to modern academia, it is only a means and not the end. Time spent worrying about it should not preempt the heart of what we do: teaching, research, and dissemination of our ideas. Thus, although it can be tempting to buy last year's model at a deep discount, it may be more economical in the long run to pay a premium up front for a system that will last longer and lead to fewer system upgrades throughout your career.

No discussion of computers would seem complete without reference to the often-heated debate over the relative merits of one platform operating system (e.g. Windows, Linux, Macintosh) over another. Fortunately, the clear trend over the past decade has been to move toward platform-independent document formats. That is, whereas it used to be that documents created by a particular program (e.g., manuscripts, spreadsheets, etc.) could only be opened by that same program, the onus today is on the authoring program to ensure that any other related program can read and manipulate the document. Assuming that this trend continues, the issue of compatibility should continue to decline, and the decision of whether to ally oneself with

Macintosh, PC, or other platforms can rightfully recede to one of personal preference and social identity rather than one of professional compatibility.

Electronic References

The days of poring through *Psychological Abstracts* to find relevant references have gone the way of computer punch cards and hand-calculated sums of squares: occasionally used for teaching, frequently used for war stories, but never used as a practical matter. Any researcher these days should quickly acquaint him- or herself with the numerous reference databases and on-line journal articles. Examples include PsycInfo, Lexis-Nexus, Social Science Citation Index, and numerous others. Bibliographic software programs (e.g., EndNote) can download references from these databases to your own computer, allowing you to maintain a personal repository of references that can simplify one aspect of the writing process.

A word of caution regarding databases is in order. Although *Psychological Abstracts* was bulky and inefficient, it was the primary repository of references and one could count on it to have the complete record of articles published in major psychological journals. The recent profusion of user-friendly but incomplete databases (including personalized ones just described, and also earlier versions of PsycInfo) can sometimes be an attractive nuisance. Although convenient, they can lead researchers to abandon a search without a comprehensive review of the literature.

Multimedia

Some advisors will suggest that graduate students learn to use a good digital camera during their training. Many areas of psychology can benefit from the simplicity of creating stimulus materials with digital camcorders and the like; I would only add that this sound advice could be usefully expanded to include new technology in general. Graduate school provides a critical opportunity to acquire cutting-edge skills, opportunities that are more difficult to come by as an assistant professor. The recurring theme of this chapter, however, is that all advice is qualified; investing in new technology and becoming an early adopter can be a professionally risky maneuver. Certainly an audience appreciates a slick, professional presentation with all the bells and whistles, but if the research underlying the presentation reflects technological prowess and little psychological insight, the student is unlikely to go far in the field. On the other hand, graduate students who resisted word processing and e-mail in the 1980s were at a considerable disadvantage relative to their peers. The best advice is to be aware of emerging trends and technologies, and to adopt those that enhance your scholarly and pedagogical pursuits.

PowerPoint

It has become common practice recently to give colloquia and other presentations with computer-aided displays such as Microsoft's PowerPoint. If you are not yet proficient with this type of program, let it become a priority. Several words of caution, however, are required with this advice. In the first edition of this volume, Darley and Zanna (1987) recommended that the savvy presenter come prepared with a spare bulb for the overhead projector in the event of a blown bulb. Although such advice is not specifically suited to computer projectors (because each brand calls for different bulbs and each tends to cost more than $100), the take-away message remains sound; anything that might go wrong eventually will go wrong. There is such an array of potential glitches with computer-aided presentations (particularly with unfamiliar equipment) that it is prudent to always bring a backup set of overhead transparencies and a set of lecture notes.

More substantively, whereas the pace of presentations was once governed by the necessity of explaining a concept, writing on a chalk board, or swapping transparencies on a projector, today these presentational speed bumps have functionally disappeared and the resulting tendency is to go too fast and present too many slides. Like a teenager behind the wheel of a muscle car, the inexperienced presenter will sometimes hit the accelerator instead of the brake, and the hapless audience can do little but stare in uncomprehending stupor as the presenter speeds into a spectacular pedagogical crash and burn.

Nobody wants such a result, but neither does anyone wish to be seen as a pokey Sunday driver. So how does one calculate a safe and sane SPH (slides per hour)? Clearly, the answer varies depending on one's particular talk and particular style, but there are some general rules to keep in mind. The goal for any presentation, of course, is that the audience understand and retain your pearls of wisdom. One of the clear findings from early studies in the psychology of learning and memory is the relationship between study time and memory: Up to some limit, slower is better. But it is up to the presenter to estimate this limit, and because the presenter is typically more familiar with the material than the audience, this limit is consistently underestimated. The slides should serve as supplement and emphasis for your words, and as an outline for the talk as a whole. Thus, it is generally poor form to read your slides verbatim or to present a graph and let it speak for you. If every point you make has its own slide, then your talk is liable to unfold like a series of disconnected facts rather than as a coherent story.

As an upper limit, one should rarely have more than one slide per minute, but the best advice is always to observe others in your research area and to use those norms as a reference.

CONCLUSION

There can be no simplistic summary that technology is "good" or "bad." Aspects of it can be variously useful, and the challenge is always to figure out the cost–benefit analysis for an individual's particular needs. Recent technological advances provide an amazing toolbox for teaching and research, and use of these tools can greatly facilitate these endeavors. Indeed, much of the research done today is possible only because of these advances. Nonetheless, the core of what we do—observe, theorize, experiment, write, teach—has not really changed as a result of new technology. Although each can be improved, deepened, simplified or otherwise enhanced, the fundamentals remain the same. In the rush to use the latest technology— whether it is web-based dynamic surveys or fMRI studies of social behavior— it is sometimes the case that fundamental issues of design or psychological interest get overlooked.

The core advice comes down to a low-tech but time-tested adage: Look before you leap. There are always start-up costs associated with being an early adopter of any technology, and those costs can easily overwhelm the benefits of the new technology. Take a careful look before acquiring a new technology, evaluate not only the surface pros and cons but also the deeper implications that might be relevant over time or as others adopt the same technology. After taking a long and careful look, do not be shy about taking full advantage of the many technological advances available to academia in the 21st century.

REFERENCES

American Psychological Association. (2001). *Posting articles on the Internet.* Retrieved May 10, 2002, from http://www.apa.org/journals/posting.html

Darley, J. D., & Zanna, M. P. (1987). The hiring process in academia. In M. P. Zanna & J. D. Darley (Eds.), *The compleat academic: A practical guide for the beginning social scientist* (pp. 3–20). New York: Random House.

Donders, F. C. (1969). On the speed of mental processes (Trans. W. G. Koster). *Acta Psychologica, 30,* 412–431. (Original published 1868)

Eamon, D. B. (1999). Distance education: Has technology become a threat to the academy? *Behavior Research Methods, Instruments, & Computers, 31,* 197–207.

Gilbert, D. T., & Ebert, J. E. J. (2002). Decisions and revisions: The affective forecasting of changeable outcomes. *Journal of Personality and Social Psychology, 82,* 503–514.

Harnad, S. (1998) On-line journals and financial fire-walls. *Nature, 395,* 127–128.

Kruglanski, A. W. (2001). That "vision thing": The state of theory in social and personality psychology at the edge of the new millennium. *Journal of Personality and Social Psychology, 80,* 871–875.

Ochsner, K. N., & Lieberman, M. D. (2001). The emergence of social cognitive neuroscience. *American Psychologist, 56,* 717–734.

Schwartz, B. (2000). Self-determination: The tyranny of freedom. *American Psychologist, 55,* 79–88.

U.S. Department of Education, National Center for Education Statistics. (2000). *The condition of education 2000,* distance learning in postsecondary education (NCES 2000-602). Washington, DC: U.S. Government Printing Office.

Wilson, R. (2001, Feb. 2). It's 10 a.m., do you know where your professors are? *Chronicle of Higher Education,* A10–A12.

V

DIVERSITY IN ACADEMIA

15

THE DIALECTICS OF RACE: ACADEMIC PERILS AND PROMISES

JAMES M. JONES AND EUN RHEE

Am I an African American psychologist or *just* a psychologist? Am I an Asian American female psychologist or *just* a psychologist? Are we judged more highly if we study race or if we do not? Is it presumed that we are capitalizing more on our experience as members of racial groups and less on our analytical and scientific capabilities if we study race? Do we need to prove ourselves by going beyond race? Choice and identity are closely related (Waters, 1990). However, categorical judgments close the dimensions of choice and frame the possibilities of identity in ever narrowing spheres.

ACADEMIC PURSUITS IN A CULTURED CONTEXT

These are not rhetorical questions. Each of us, at various points along the way, has faced these kinds of issues and had to make choices about whether and how we would develop our professional careers and identities around the subject of race. There are many illustrations, but two of the more salient ones follow.

As a graduate student in the late 1960s, the first author was given some advice: Do not work on race stuff because that would stereotype him and limit his range of opportunities. Companion ideas include the notion that "race" was not a variable (i.e., one's race was not manipulable, so the *scientific* utility of the concept was itself limited), and "we (social psychologists) are interested in variables not people!" If race is not a variable, and we are interested in variables, then where could he find his own place in this field? Critical in this set of early experiences is the sense of dialectical choice. Race and questions related to it were juxtaposed with mainstream questions and issues. He grants that this did not make race studies uninteresting, but they were perhaps lower on the rung of scientifically important pursuits. As a new assistant professor at Harvard in the early 1970s, the first author was counseled by a colleague and peer to focus on his work and not let the turmoil and social activism of the civil rights movement, Black power, and the university efforts to use him in a variety of roles deflect his efforts to create a tenurable record. He went to graduate school in social psychology to pursue a career modeled on the important work of Kenneth B. Clark on race relations. He felt strongly that he was not only identifiable by his uniquely personal qualities and experiences but was representative of African Americans who were seeking voice within higher education and academic circles. It seemed to the first author at the time that he needed a strategy that allowed him to plan a career that was rewarding and fulfilling, successful and meaningful. Moreover, he felt it would be a failure of responsibility if he worked exclusively for himself and failed to heed the needs of others like him. He wanted to help and he was willing to let the university use him. It was a conscious choice that he has made repeatedly since. The dialectics of race were prominent and have always guided his decision making in his career.

When the second author was a graduate student in the early 1990s, the most consistent advice she was given emphasized the importance of conducting sound "basic" research and ultimately obtaining an academic position. However, during her first year in graduate school she became interested in cultural influences on psychological processes and racial identity. These interests stem partially from her membership and experiences in two vastly diverse cultures and being a racial minority in American society. When she expressed these interests the response was far from enthusiastic. At that time, there were no faculty interested in these issues, and she was told, both explicitly and implicitly, that the study of "culture" was atheoretical, methodologically unsound, and "less" important in understanding how people, in general, thought and behaved. Culture was "noise" psychologists needed to control for, not studied for its own sake. Thus, the message she received was that her research on cultural influences was "interesting" but not as scientific as the study of basic psychological processes. So, she faced a dilemma. She felt that many of the studies she was learning about did not represent her "reality" or world view, and yet if she wanted to succeed in her chosen endeavor she might need to pursue questions that others viewed as more scientifically important. Her early experiences exemplify the issue of dialectical choice. Does she pursue her research interests because she found them to be meaningful, even if they may be perceived as less "scientific?" Is it better for her career aspirations to pursue research on "mainstream" questions and issues by learning as much as she could from the experts in the graduate program or does she pursue her more personally meaningful interests even if it means narrowing of opportunities? By focusing her research on "minority" issues, was she pigeonholing herself? If she does not pursue these issues, was she "selling out?" The irony underlying her experiences is that the field values individual initiative in research and yet the field may be less supportive of that independence if the research is not within "valued" areas.

These are just two stories. There are many more stories from those who have experienced the perils and promises of academia on multiple levels. In this chapter we attempt to address some of these academic challenges that are faced by graduate students and early career faculty of color (members of underrepresented groups) as they navigate graduate school and career development in an environment that may pose a conflict with the established goals and the personal values they hold. The dialectical analysis is framed by a bicultural synthesis of racial considerations that are defining and personally relevant, and mainstream possibilities within which the reward structure and academic promise is largely measured.

More ethnic and racial minorities are being hired for academic positions, but they continue to be underrepresented in psychology departments (making up only 9.9% of full-time faculty; Waters, 2001). This issue is becoming increasingly important because the demographic trends in the racial or ethnic composition of the U.S. population are clear: By 2050 "minorities" collectively will become the majority population, which highlights the need for more faculty of color in psychology. For faculty and graduate students of color, the promise and rewards of academia are numerous, including contributing and expanding psychological knowledge, enriching psychology's curricula, preparing students to meet the needs of an increasingly ethnically and racially diverse society, teaching a broader perspective to students, and interacting with other professionals. However, these rewards may also come with costs. Taylor and Martin (1987) pointed out many new professors "have virtually no idea of the powerful stresses and conflicting demands that are inherent in being an Assistant Professor" (p. 23). For some assistant professors these stresses and demands may be even more challenging because of their membership in certain social categories, such as race and ethnicity. They may find that their membership in these categories is implicated in every level of their academic endeavor, from topics of research to writing grants.

In this chapter we tell personal stories that provide a context for extrapolating the principles that come into play as a person of color considers and pursues an academic career in psychology. These issues include choice of research area, career choice and racial identity, teaching about racial or and ethnic minorities, outlets for research, and service. In each of the issues, there are choice points, dialectical possibilities that must be faced. Choices will vary depending on the person and type of institution, and we do not pretend to guide the readers in what choices they should make. We attempt to present the options that may be available.

PRINCIPLES OF DIALECTICAL DYNAMICS

The underlying principle of a dialectical analysis is the challenge of embracing or incorporating conflicted possibilities and viewpoints. We have framed these issues broadly in terms of culture, and a bicultural framework is perhaps the closest to our ideas (cf., LaFromboise, Coleman, & Gerton, 1993). In this section we outline specific dialectical possibilities that we have encountered in our own academic careers. You may think of others we have omitted.

Ethnic- and Racial-Relevant Versus "Generic" Research Topics

Traditionally psychology has assumed universal applicability of its theories, research procedures, and findings (e.g., Shweder, 1990), which has led to a paucity of knowledge about multicultural and racial issues and variations in human experience. In addition, there has been a lack of a clear understanding and appreciation of the value of diversity for the discipline and the significant contribution of ethnic or racial minority faculty.

Questions concerning the scientific merit of ethnic and racial-minority-focused research still persist. Why is it that when we study White, middle-class individuals we can generalize the findings to all human beings, but when the sample consists of people of color, the findings are not generalizable or limited to that particular ethnic and racial group? What are the implicit values underlying this assumption (Whites are the standard or norm; "the other" is deviant)? Thus, the implicit attitude that "mainstream" issues are legitimate topics to study, whereas ethnic- and racial-focused research is justified only from a social advocacy perspective and not from a scientific perspective marginalizes ethnic-focused research.

Even when the research focuses on race/ethnicity and culture, it has historically focused on Whites (cf., Jones, 1983). That is, this subject matter has focused on Whites as perpetrators of discrimination and bias. Group comparisons, when they occur, typically compare Whites to Blacks and other groups, but because so little of the research has elaborated the dimensions of the experiences of ethnic and racial minorities, the comparisons are typically on standards associated with Whites. Exceptions are usually when comparisons are truly cross-cultural.

So, there is a major need to learn more about the experiences of targets of racial or ethnic bias and how they cope with and respond to the real or imagined or potential threat of discriminatory treatment. We are beginning to round out this picture on all counts (cf., Crocker, Major, & Steele, 1998; Fiske, Kitayama, Markus, & Nisbett, 1998; Jones, 2003; Swim & Stangor, 1998), and opportunities for career success have never been better. Thus perils turn into promise.

When we tell other academics that our research involves culture or race-related issues, they nod in understanding. Maybe they perceive that our research interests "fit" with our racial or ethnic group membership. We are persons of color; therefore, it is not surprising to them that we would conduct research about our ethnic and racial groups. However, some may also assume that we are capitalizing on our experiences. That is, even if your research is considered good, the insights and perspectives that drive your research may be perceived to derive from privileged insider experience more than analytical acumen. We do not want to push this point too hard, but it does surface from time to time when one may not expect it.

Similarly, there may be times when you feel you are stereotyped by others about your research interests because of your ethnic or racial group membership. Although your choice of research area may not have anything to do with your racial or ethnic group membership, others may assume a relationship between your research topic and your racial or ethnic identity. For personal, career-related, or other reasons, some academics of color may choose to conduct research on ethnic or race-related issues, whereas some may choose to conduct generic research. However, if you conduct generic— in other words, nonethnic or non–race-relevant research—you may be questioned about your choice from both those in the mainstream and members of your ethnic or racial group. For example, someone from the mainstream may question why you are not studying "your own people" because you must have "special knowledge" about them, whereas members of your group may question why you are not studying "us" given that there are so few of us studying "us" and so many of "them" studying themselves. You might even be accused of selling out. Although the U.S. culture supposedly endorses personal choice and academic institutions are supposed to embrace academic freedom, you may have to face this issue.

For personal and career-related reasons, both of us chose to conduct research on topics that we found meaningful and interesting. We have both taken the view that our interest in culture and cultural comparisons is basic to understanding human behavior. The best evidence of scientific principles often is reflected in the boundary conditions for their expression. Knowing when a certain behavior will occur and when it will not is to truly understand it. Knowing the conditions under which certain processes will occur and in what ways is one crucial element of understanding behavior, and culture provides such a limiting condition. So we feel that our work is basic to a comprehensive and ultimately scientific theory of human behavior.

Whatever choice you make, ask interesting questions, and care about the answers. Set out to answer them with the best theoretical guidance and methodological rigor you can. You will succeed.

Career Choices and Ethnic or Racial Identity

Many of us are highly identified with our ethnic or racial groups. To what extent are career choices tied to such identities, sense of belonging, and membership? There is no simple answer to this question, but we feel that you should confront the issue head on. If it is important to you in your professional as well as personal life to be involved with people of your racial or ethnic group in a variety of ways, then that should be a major criterion for your career choices. And you should not if you feel it is an inappropriate criterion.

We have already considered the research you do, but that will be linked to the overall set of career and personal choices you make. For example, if you study racial identity; or poverty; or the intersection of poverty, cognitive development, and psychological well-being, your career choices will be profoundly affected by where you can find a job. If you are a single African American female, your social life may hang in the balance. How will you maintain equilibrium and deal with the inherently conflicted pluses and minuses? Get your career started and worry about your social life later? Focus on the broadest aspects and implications of your research, and build to the essence of your interests in the race/ethnic aspects? Any decision you make about direction and approach is personal. There are no generic guidelines that we can write that work for everyone. We simply advise that you recognize that such choices are common to people of color, and you may seek out others at various stages of their careers for advice or tips on how to make good choices and avoid bad ones.

Service to Whom, for What? Giving Back and Going Forward

The academic trilogy of service–teaching–research is an ascending pyramid of value within most departments. But for many of us, the pyramid may be inverted or more likely, better represented by a rectangle of balanced proportions. The freedom to pursue interesting questions is important, but so too is the felt obligation to be of service and relevance to other members of your group. This is a real pressure that students and faculty of color may face that is not shared by others. As a young assistant professor at Harvard, the first author was appointed to the prestigious Faculty Council of the University. He was the only similarly ranked person on the Council. He does not think for a minute that he was there for any reason other than the fact that he is African American and it was the early 1970s. Would that enhance his career? Almost surely not. Would he learn something about how the university works and perhaps contribute a perspective to the decision-making process that was missing? He wanted to believe so.

We give service all the time, by advising students, making presentations to student and community groups, reviewing for journals, granting agencies, publishers, serving on university committees, departmental committees, and community agencies. African American students in other departments seek the counsel of the first author and support in their research. African American and other minority faculty and their departments seek him out to write letters of recommendation for their promotions even when their work is not in the area for which he has specific identifiable expertise. At times he feels beleaguered and used, but as noted earlier, he also takes the responsibility to help seriously. When you are a member of an ethnic or racial minority group and you are a minority in a department, you often are called on and seek out numerous opportunities to be of service. When the judgment comes (i.e., tenure and promotion), your service is acknowledged, but your publications and grants are what are evaluated.

A word about mentoring is in order. We find that students of color often feel alienated from psychology because it seems to offer such negative images and to make such negative scientific claims. Students are offended by discussions of research whose essential conclusion is that members of their group are inferior on dimension X to others. Sometimes, it is problematic when you're in the group that is considered superior on dimension Y, too. Helping students to sort out the values from the beliefs is often an important mentoring role. The feeling that White faculty will be dismissive or more simply, "just won't understand" often traps students of color. It can be humiliating and feel personal. Helping students deal with this is important.

Another issue is helping students deal with the idea that they "represent" their race. Students of color are often expected to educate others in the classroom about their group, to have special insights about their group, and to help others better understand their group. If they do not want to do this, they are accused of stifling real intergroup and interpersonal harmony. They are believed to obstruct the possibility of better relationships. The student may feel used and abused. Recognize the frustration and stress that accompanies this role. In your classes, you may have to be careful not to fall into using students in this way yourself.

We both believe that when you find a student of color who is African American or Asian American, or even in many cases Latino or White American, they may gravitate to us because we have a different perspective or approach. Particularly for students of color, this can be an extremely important validation of their experience, their ability, and their potential.

One final point concerning graduate students of color is worth considering. There is always the push–pull to do something that is personally meaningful and to get it done in a timely manner. A student may want to go beyond extant paradigms to explore something that is meaningful—maybe even important scientifically and practically—but methodologically complex. Engaging the student and being supportive may take you far afield from your work or tie the student up for a long time. You must play an important role by guiding the student between these shoals of possibility while keeping your focus on your own work. So one of your important mentoring roles is to help your students to strike a balance between the dissertation as *self-expression* and the dissertation as an *exit strategy*.

It is important that you spend your time in ways that matter to you. Giving back is a common sentiment for people of color. That is fine and important, but recognize that you may be able to give back most from the research you do, the students you teach, and the organizational influence you exert. Think broadly about service and try to integrate your service responsibilities and desires with your broader career goals and sense of personal fulfillment and well-being.

You will also find that you may be sought out to handle "minority issues." Most departments and programs have few if any faculty of color and the graduate student body is almost always more ethnically and racially diverse than the faculty. You may be asked to "represent" or "advise" on minority issues across ethnic or racial groups. For example, in many universities, the Affirmative Action Office "requires" that any department faculty search has an ethnic or racial minority faculty member on the search committee. There you are, all alone, serving on three searches at once. Not a good idea. Or you may be the "minority" student advisor, or the recruiter for graduate student diversity. Apart from protecting yourself, you can also use the occasion to make a case for the need for more faculty of color. But pick your service carefully and evaluate it against your personal and career goals and do not be afraid to say *no*.

Target of Opportunity or Token?

In graduate school, some graduate students would tell the second author, "Of course you'll get a job. You are a double minority" (i.e., Asian American and female) without mentioning research productivity. Such statements clearly focus on one's group membership and not on one's qualification. They imply that getting an academic position for someone who is a member of an underrepresented group or a double minority is not based on qualification or merit but solely on group membership.

How many of us have been told by our well-meaning colleagues that, "We didn't hire you just because you are 'African/Asian American.' It was because you were the most qualified candidate." Whenever the second author hears this type of "reassurance" of her qualifications, she wonders how to interpret such statements. For instance, is the person implying that she was not a "target of opportunity?" Most likely, the person is attempting to be supportive, and yet a part of her cannot help but wonder if getting the job was based, to some extent, on being an Asian American and a woman and because she fills some need in the department or institution. It is fashionable these days to mount antiaffirmative action arguments on the belief that "attributional ambiguity" (Crocker & Major, 1989) may cause doubts in one's ability and have damaging effects on one's self-esteem. You must have a self-standard of your ability.

These types of comments and statements may seem innocuous in isolation, but when you are told or hear about them from various sources, they form an insidious pattern. Sometimes prejudice is expressed in subtler and potentially dangerous forms. These implicit prejudices may play a role in the evaluation of your research and adversely affect your promotion and tenure decisions. As noted by Iwamasa, you should "know that you are being closely watched—successes may be minimized, while perceived failures might be exaggerated (or even fabricated)" (quoted in Waters, 2001, p. 58).

You may also encounter blatant prejudice at your institution. Not everyone in an institution is supportive. We received the findings of a survey conducted by a faculty member in another department concerning the views of the faculty at the University of Delaware on the increased recruitment of ethnic or racial minority graduate students and faculty. The bottom line of the report was that graduate students and faculty of color were bringing down the "standards" of the university. Again, the author of the survey was making the assumption that people of color are accepted into graduate programs or hired for academic positions because of their group membership, not their qualifications. The findings were not persuasive given that the survey had major methodological shortcomings, such as biased sampling, but we are concerned about why such a report is even distributed among the faculty and what kind of impressions such findings give to other faculty members.

A few years ago, we were discussing the desirability of adding a person of color to our faculty. There was a generally positive sentiment for us to do this, but for reasons that varied greatly. One view was that a person of color should fit a departmental need (developmental psychopathology, cognitive science, and so on) and should not be specifically interested in race-related research. Others felt that having someone who was interested in race-related research was important for two reasons: One, it added the person of color we sought, and two, it broadened the overall department perspective in an arena that was almost nonexistent. Implicit in the former position was that a person of color who studied race issues was not as strong a candidate for prestigious visibility as one who fits a hot general topic area. This is a view from the other side—how will you be seen in the field and how do you want to be seen? Will you be discounted if you study race? Will you be augmented if you do not?

You may be the only person of color in the department. Are you a token? Whether you are token or not, keep in mind that you are qualified for the position whether your group membership was a relevant desideratum or not. Further, you need to know the importance of your contributions to the department and the field. If there are two candidates who are equally qualified, then the person of color (or a woman) may have the advantage because of the needs or goals of the department or institution. In addition, the hiring decision may not have anything to do with your ethnicity/race, but rather your research topic may have been the most important factor. If your research area is what is needed in the department for depth or breadth, then being an ethnic or racial minority may be a bonus.

Teaching About Us to Them! Content Coverage and Stereotyping

You may be asked or expected to teach a course on the psychology of whatever group you are a member of (of course you are an expert because you are a member of that group), even if the topic is unrelated to your area of specialization. What do you do in such a situation? Agreeing to teach such a course would mean preparing for a course for which you have no or little expertise, you have to invest a large amount of time, and you may have little interest in teaching. You need to ask yourself, "What role am I expected to fill in this department as a faculty member and which of these roles stem from my being an ethnic or racial minority? Which of these roles are of personal and professional interest to me?"

Like many assistant professors, the second author thinks about her effectiveness as a teacher. In addition, because she is a young Asian American woman, she is concerned about how she is perceived by her students, which could affect her effectiveness as a teacher. She possesses some personal characteristics that fit the stereotypes of Asian American women (e.g., quiet). This poses a dilemma for her. If she acts to counter these stereotypes, things may backfire and she will be seen as a "dragon lady," but by being herself she may inadvertently confirm or perpetuate old stereotypes.

One of the ways the second author has dealt with this is to use her experiences as an Asian American as "teachable moments." When she teaches undergraduates, she finds that she can use her group membership as a springboard to discuss issues concerning racism, prejudice, and discrimination. Consistently, she sees many uncomfortable faces when these issues are discussed. For example, when she teaches introductory psychology, she finds that many of these students have bought the "model minority" myth about Asian Americans. They assume that because the stereotypes about Asian Americans are generally positive, Asian Americans do not experience prejudice and discrimination. She tells her class about her experience at a store in which the manager tells the cashier that "She can't read English." Whenever she tells her students about this incident, the typical reactions are ones of disbelief (after all, she is their professor so she must be able to read English!), attempts to produce credible alternative explanations (she has an accent), or that she may be overly sensitive (maybe she has misinterpreted the statement). Such reactions from students exemplify the need to balance between objective presentation of research findings on ethnic- or race-related issues and being misperceived as biased or defensive because of one's group membership. That is, because of your group membership, what you have to say may be taken more seriously, or conversely, you may get "here we go," why do we need to cover this again? So if you teach a course on ethnic- or racial-related issues, especially if you are at a predominantly White institution, be prepared for various types of reactions.

This is not to say there are no rewards to teaching. We find that the ethnic or racial minority students in our classes and labs get excited about learning about their ethnic or racial group that may not be represented in their textbooks or other classes, and many White American students are given opportunities to think about these issues. For example, we have the experience of having White American students say to us, "Why do we need this multicultural stuff?" Because of our research and experiences in two cultures and racial group membership, we can give White American students new ways of thinking about multiculturalism and some level of multicultural competence. The second author finds that by the end of her course on culture, the students are less likely to react to differences across cultures as "exotic," "weird," or "wrong."

Publications and Grants: Where and What?

Just as you may face the dilemma of what topic to research, you may also face a dilemma when deciding where to publish your research. If you have a study that is making a contribution to the literature but the sample consists of people of color (i.e., no White comparison group), where do you publish? Do you publish in mainstream journals such as *Journal of Personality and Social Psychology* or other journals, such as *Journal of Black Psychology*. How do you decide which is the right journal? One way you may address this dilemma is to ask, "Who is the intended audience?" Are you interested in contributing to the general body of knowledge or to a target group who may be especially interested in your findings? You also need to consider whether your article will be considered a contribution in the mainstream journals. This may be especially true if you do not have a White comparison sample. Some people have framed this issue in terms of working within the mainstream to make changes or working from the outside or margins, such as the underground approach to research on prejudice that has been virtually ignored by mainstream psychology (Gaines & Reed, 1995).

What if you study racial or ethnic minority populations but you are at a predominantly White institution with no easily accessible racial or ethnic samples? Do you "compromise" and study White Americans? Do you conduct research on topics of less interest using the group that is available so that you can show productivity? One solution is to collaborate with colleagues at other institutions with accessible samples. Another solution may involve conducting research projects that will have a relatively quick turnover for publication (Waters, 2001) but also those that contribute to your program of research.

Another dilemma you may encounter is whether to publish your research in a book chapter versus a journal. In tenure decisions, journal articles tend to count more than book chapters. However, a chapter may be useful if you have some good theoretical ideas and provide an outlet for their development.

Finally, getting a grant provides more time to devote to research and adds to your status and professional standing. Take advantage of any training and funding opportunities that are available at your institution as well as state and federal agencies for ethnic or racial minorities. For graduate students, there is a minority fellowship sponsored by the American Psychological Association, as well as the Ford Foundation. But there are also generic predoctoral fellowships at the National Science Foundation and the National Institute of Mental Health (NIMH), among others. For junior faculty, the NIMH offers a mentored training grant (K01), as does the William T. Grant Foundation (developmental psychology). Also, take advantage of the experiences of the senior colleagues in your department; ask them about the ins and outs of writing a grant. (See chapters 8 and 9, this volume. See also www.nih.gov for more about grant possibilities.)

Environment

Many new assistant professors find themselves in a new place with few social connections. If you are the only person in your ethnic or racial group in your department, you may experience heightened feelings of isolation and lack of social support. If this is the case, it is important to seek mentors and supportive colleagues with whom you can discuss your concerns. The second author has found supportive senior colleagues, who advised her to say "no," that it is perfectly okay to say no, not to volunteer for committee work unless you have to, and so forth. So seek out sympathetic others, even outside the department, who can advise you on these issues. Colleagues may tell you that "this is not just a job, it is your life," but also keep in mind that a balanced life is just as important.

THE DIALECTICAL SYNTHESIS

Crocker et al. (1998) frame the question of racial or ethnic marginalization in terms of a predicament. Among the dynamic processes that operate in the predicament of marginalization are *stereotype threat* and *attributional ambiguity*. Stereotype threat (Steele & Aronson, 1995) creates tension and pressure induced by the apprehension that one's performance in a given domain (e.g., test-taking) may confirm a widely held negative stereotype about the group to which one belongs. Trying hard not to confirm it may undermine performance. An alternative to avoid the apprehension is to disidentify with the domain, by either leaving the field or removing performance in the domain as a source of self-esteem and self-worth. This is a critical element in the dialectical synthesis. Whose judgments do you value with regard to your personal well-being? Your personal synthesis needs to keep intact the psychological coherence and sense of well-being and meaning that makes you whole. For faculty of color, the academic arena may be inherently a stereotype threat environment. The discussion in the previous section was meant to alert you to many of the threatening dimensions and help guide you through possible strategies for navigating them.

Attributional ambiguity (Crocker & Major, 1989) identifies another potentially threatening predicament. How do you know if you have done well or poorly if biased perceptions borne of simple racial prejudice (Jones, 1997), aversive racism (Gaertner & Dovidio, 1986), or perhaps even more insidious cultural ignorance lead you to discount the evaluative outcome: You might say, "I didn't get tenure because they don't want a person of color or a person who studies identity from an Afrocentric perspective to get tenure." Is it the *content* of your work or the *quality* of methodology or theory that accompanies it that best explains the outcome? I heard from an administrator at the National Institutes of Health that a grant applicant rejected a negative review of a proposal on the basis that the reviewers were not capable of evaluating the Afrocentric analysis of personality. Perhaps in the applicant's mind there was no "ambiguity," but for most of us there is a concern that the antagonism or marginalization of certain ideas will not afford a fair and impartial review in many different academic contexts.

Finally, we note the analysis of bicultural adaptation by which a person acquires a second culture (LaFromboise et al., 1993). This analysis stems from a cultural competence approach by which one functions effectively within a given culture by (a) possessing a strong personal identity, (b) having knowledge and facility with the culture's beliefs and values, (c) displaying appropriate sensitivity to affective processes, (d) communicating clearly in the language of the culture, (e) performing socially sanctioned behavior, (f) maintaining active social relations with the group, and (g) negotiating the institutional structures.

Clearly academia is a culture. Entering academe from a racial or ethnic minority perspective may indeed be akin to a second culture acquisition. This cultural adaptation may begin with graduate school and for many leads one to drop out before moving up the academic career ladder. For those who persist, there are five models by which the adaptation may take place. *Assimilation* is a process by which one is absorbed into the culture and adopts its values and acquires the full range of competencies. *Acculturation* occurs by acquiring cultural competence, but one is always considered a member of his or her racial or ethnic group. This is a unidirectional process, and one's academic competence is all that matters, even though one's culture of origin is acknowledged and maybe even appreciated. *Alternation* describes a process by which one is fully competent in both cultures and is able to call on those competencies at any time as the situation arises or dictates. *Multiculturalism* maintains the discrete separateness of each culture wherein one then collaborates with members of the other culture or cultures. Finally, *fusion* assumes a complete melding of all people into the dominant culture that is representative of each contributing group.

The choices are yours, as are the consequences of them. Research suggests that the alternation strategy may hold the most promise for psychological well-being and instrumental success (LaFromboise et al., 1993). Recognizing the options, considering the consequences, and choosing from a position of personal integrity and well-being will maximize the chances of a long, productive, successful, and enjoyable career.

CONCLUSION

We framed this essay as a dialectical process. Mainstream versus ethnic- or race-specific issues, needs, goals, and outcomes. Knowing how they work and setting your own agenda within this context gives you the best chance for success. There is bias and discrimination in the system and there are individuals who have prejudicial views. There are individuals who are also ignorant. Our profession is a culture within a society that is racialized and conflicted in many ways. Your strategies for life are probably a good place to start in your strategy for successfully traversing the perils of academia. But the prejudices are offset in part by the growing interest in and concern about issues of race and ethnicity and culture. Psychology has a great potential to address these issues, and many of us are doing just that. It is a tremendous opportunity for each of you and we encourage you to pursue it with enthusiasm. The bottom line is that you can enjoy the benefits of academic life, its freedoms, its intellectual challenge, and its personal rewards. We hope that by sharing some of our experiences and perspectives, we have helped you to think about and plan your own careers. We both remain open and willing to engage you in your process, so feel free to enter a dialogue with us. We wish you well.

REFERENCES

Crocker, J., & Major, B. (1989). Social stigma and self-esteem: The self-protective properties of stigma. *Psychological Review, 96,* 608–630.

Crocker, J., Major, B., & Steele, C. (1998). Social stigma. In D. T. Gilbert, S. T. Fiske, & G. Lindzey (Eds.), *The handbook of social psychology* (Vol. 2, pp. 504–553). Boston: McGraw-Hill.

Fiske, A. P., Markus, H. R., Kitayama, S. & Nisbett, R. E. (1998). The cultural matrix of social psychology. In D. T. Gilbert, S. T. Fiske, & G. Lindzey (Eds.), *The handbook of social psychology* (Vol. 2, pp. 915–981). Boston: McGraw-Hill.

Gaertner, S. G., & Dovidio, J. F. (1986). The aversive form of racism. In J. H. Dovidio & S. G. Gaertner (Eds.), *Prejudice, discrimination and racism* (pp. 61–89). Orlando, FL: Academic Press.

Gaines, S. O., & Reed, E. (1995). Prejudice: From Allport to Du Bois. *American Psychologist, 50,* 96–103.

Jones, J. M. (1983). The concept of race in social psychology: From color to culture. In L. Wheeler & P. Shaver (Eds.), *Review of personality and social psychology* (Vol. 4, pp. 117–150). Beverly Hills, CA: Sage.

Jones, J. M. (1997). *Prejudice and racism* (2nd ed.). New York: McGraw-Hill.

Jones, J. M. (2003). A psychological theory of the African legacy in American culture. *Journal of Social Issues, 59,* 217–241.

LaFromboise, T., Coleman, H. L. K., & Gerton, J. (1993). Psychological impact of biculturalism: Evidence and theory. *Psychological Bulletin, 114,* 395–412.

Shweder, R. A. (1990). Cultural psychology—What is it? In J. W. Stigler, R. A. Shweder, & G. Herdt (Eds.), *Cultural psychology: Essays on comparative human development* (pp. 1–43). Cambridge: Cambridge University Press.

Steele, C. M., & Aronson, J. (1995). Stereotype threat and the intellectual test performance of African Americans. *Journal of Personality and Social Psychology, 69,* 797–811.

Swim, J. K., & Stangor, C. (1998). *Prejudice: The target's perspective*. San Diego, CA: Academic Press.

Taylor, S. E., & Martin, J. (1987). The present-minded professor: Controlling one's career. In M. P. Zanna & J. M. Darley (Eds.), *The compleat academic* (pp. 23–60). New York: Random House.

Waters, M. C. (1990). *Ethnic options: Choosing identities in America*. Berkeley: University of California Press.

Waters, M. (2001, Jan.). So many hats, so little time. *Monitor on Psychology, 32*, 56–59.

16

WOMEN IN ACADEMIA

DENISE C. PARK AND SUSAN NOLEN-HOEKSEMA

So what is it like to be a woman in academia? Does your gender matter? Women have achieved much in academia in the past few decades. For example, in psychology women represented only 23% of doctoral recipients from 1920 to 1974 but were 66% of doctoral recipients in 1996 (Task Force on Women in Academe, 2000). There is greater pay equity at the assistant professor level and a greatly increased presence among junior faculty, thanks to affirmative action programs. However, if you look around a bit, it probably will not escape your notice that after 25 years of affirmative action hires, the number of tenured women full professors in the academy are relatively small. Moreover, there is recent evidence to suggest that even at the most elite institutions, senior women experience salary inequities and have less laboratory space than men (Task Force on Women in Academe, 2000). If this chapter had been written 20 years ago, its focus almost certainly would have been on how to handle sexual harassment, cope with a largely male environment, and handle gross and obvious inequities.

Things have changed a lot, mostly for the better. Nonetheless, there are a number of issues that women face that limit their opportunities and success, only one of which is gender-based discrimination. The goal of this chapter is to provide women with issues to consider *now* that will permanently affect the trajectory of their careers. We see some of the defining features of academic life for women as overcommitment, which leads to less productivity and more stress, a greater focus on interpersonal issues in the workplace, which has both costs and gains, and finally, implicit expectations by administrators and colleagues that women will be happy to help and perform more service-oriented activities, to the detriment of their own scientific careers.

In this chapter we focus on six issues that seem to distinguish the professional experiences of women academics from their male counterparts: (a) the presentation of self; (b) common traps for women academics; (c) interpersonal relationships including sexual relationships and sexual harassment; (d) family issues; (e) career aspirations; and (f) determining if academia is for you. We firmly believe that it is equally important to be successful professionally and interpersonally happy, and offer advice on how to achieve both. In this chapter, we will not present a literature review on research on women in academia (but see APA CWP CEMRRAT, 1998; Caplan, 1993; Task Force on Women in Academe, 2000; Valian, 1998). Rather, we concentrate on advice that emerges from the research literature and from our personal experiences and that of our women colleagues. Our advice may not fit all women academics because of differences in circumstances or personal beliefs or styles. We hope our advice will at least provide food for thought and discussion about some important issues.

PRESENTATION OF SELF

What adjectives would your colleagues use to describe you—as smart, positive, productive, creative, a leader, firm, confident, and a great collaborator? Or would they describe you as cooperative, someone they can count on, kind, quietly competent, warm, and thoughtful? In an ideal world, you might hope that your colleagues would describe you as all of the above, but it is the first set of attributes that will get you tenure. At the early stages of your career, it is essential that you be viewed as an asset to the department and that your colleagues think of you as productive and smart and someone who will contribute to the intellectual life of the department over the long haul while doing her fair share of the departmental work. These three attributes are important dimensions to project to your colleagues. You should be careful not to appear insecure or obsessively worried about getting tenure, because these types of behavior will undermine positive perceptions. Never start conversations with self-deprecating remarks about your own competence, such as "I know I don't give good talks so I'm worried about my presentation" or "I'm not a very good writer so it always takes me a long time to write journal articles." This is not to say you should be boastful or self-promoting—just do not be your own worst enemy.

Much has been written in recent years about how women have humanized the workplace, making it more acceptable for employees to discuss personal issues on the job and admit to their stresses and weaknesses. This is probably true to some extent, but the reality is that people who are frequently stressed out at work over personal matters and who in turn discuss their personal lives at length with others are often not viewed favorably in business or in academia. On the other hand, people who can cope with their personal and professional stresses and appear hardy and optimistic are seen as leaders and as attractive colleagues. Thus, when you are beset by personal or professional stressors—your baby is sick, your partner has become unemployed, you have three manuscripts rejected in one-week's time—share these discreetly with your most trusted friends, but do not announce them publicly to anyone who will listen. If you find yourself feeling weepy in your office at the end of a long day, recognize that this happens to even seemingly invulnerable women occasionally. Try to focus on your goals and how to overcome your recent setbacks to attain them. If you find yourself truly overwhelmed with stressors and unable to manage your emotional reactions to them, you might consider talking with a professional to work out how you can make things better. Some universities have confidential human resource departments that will help you. Nevertheless, we believe that it is in your best interest to leave no footprint within your institution of problems until you are ready to present them in a formal manner to your department head, dean, or other authority for solution.

You will occasionally have nasty interactions with your colleagues and students. Women have a tendency to ruminate or brood over problems in their relationships with others (Nolen-Hoeksema & Jackson, 2000). Unfortunately, rumination only magnifies the problems and impairs your ability to generate good solutions to the problems. It is better to try to get a healthy perspective on conflicts with colleagues and students by talking with trusted colleagues and friends and resolving not to let another's nastiness sabotage either your emotional or professional well-being.

With respect to personal presentation, it is our belief that there are different implicit norms for attire for women and men in academia, with men not losing as much status as women for poor dress. In other words, men can get away with looking like impoverished graduate students, but women often cannot. It is our advice that you dress somewhat better than is normative, even for women in your department. This will give you confidence and add to an aura of competence and presence. Do wear professional attire for any important committee meetings, teaching, or your own laboratory meetings. At the same time, be yourself. If you have worn blue jeans and t-shirts through graduate school and a postdoc, do not necessarily show up in a navy blue suit with leather pumps. Develop your own style—you have infinite latitude on this dimension; looking stylish and put together will be a plus, however you choose to define it. Save the t-shirts and jeans for summer schedules or working in the evenings when you are on your own time.

At professional meetings, it is particularly important to present well. You should be well-groomed and professionally dressed, while at the same time giving confident, organized, and controlled presentations. Remember that the members of your audience are likely the people who are going to write your external tenure letters. If you are an anxious speaker, rehearse your talks until they are automatized, so that only you know how nervous you are. After a few successes, you will become a relaxed and confident speaker. Appearing timid in any context may lead to protective responses from men and even women colleagues, and although these may be reassuring in the short-term, they will not help you over the long-term.

A trap for women academics is the impostor phenomenon (Harvey & Katz, 1985), whereby the individual feels that she is not really competent and that she is pretending to be so. It is only a matter of time until someone will recognize the magnitude of her incompetence and she will be unmasked and shamed. The most important thing to recognize about the impostor phenomenon is its pervasiveness among women. This feeling of incompetence can be used to work for you. In early stages of your career, use these feelings to fuel a work ethic. In an academic setting, perhaps the best way to displace anxiety is by working quietly in your lab or office. Do not express your feelings of unworthiness to colleagues; express them to a partner, close friend not affiliated with your job, or even to a therapist. Also recognize that this sense of unworthiness may dog you for a long time and is something you may have to learn to live with. You will be surprised that as soon as you achieve your aspirations (e.g., getting tenured and promoted), some new gremlin of achievement will appear. When confronted with feelings of inadequacy, it is important to dwell privately on your successes in their corpus and objectively recognize that someone who did not know what she was doing could not have possibly achieved as many things as you have. Also recognize how demoralizing failures are at the early stages of your career. Highly successful senior people continue to have failures just as you are having; what makes them successful is their ability to focus on their successes and also the fact that they have a number of balls up in the air. The rejection of one article is not as devastating for someone who has 100 publications as it is for someone who has 3. You will get there. Just do not put that rejected article in the drawer—turn it around immediately and resubmit it (see chapter 10, this volume). Do not let feelings of low self-esteem obstruct your success. Recognize that just about everybody (even most of the men) is perennially afflicted with self-doubt and impostor feelings. Use these feelings to energize you to do good work.

THE DOWN SIDE OF COMPASSION AND COOPERATION

Women are both perceived as and may actually be more genuinely warm and compassionate toward others than men. Unfortunately, the tendency to be compassionate and cooperative can hold many traps for women academics.

The first is what we call the Mommy or Earth Mother trap. There are many manifestations of this trap. First, you may be sought out by students and colleagues wanting to share their personal problems. Being helpful to these folks can be satisfying, but you can become so responsive to other people's problems and needs that it can impair your ability to do your job. On the other hand, having a reputation for being top-notch intellectually as well as providing a supportive and positive environment for students can be a factor in recruiting some of the most talented people in the department to work with you. There are days when you may feel highly satisfied by the rich and caring network of students and colleagues with whom you work. But there are also days when this rich network can come to feel like a spider's web of needs, commitments, confidences, and concerns that limit your ability to do your real work—the things that will get you tenure.

A second consequence of falling into the Mommy trap is that a fragile student may expect you to be "easy" on him or her. Then when you make reasonable demands of the student, or criticize the student's work, you are perceived as violating expectations or some implicit contract that the student thinks he or she has with you. This can lead to conflict and unpleasantness, at best, public accusations against you for being unfair or "difficult" at worst.

We are in no way advocating that you be anything other than kind and compassionate. We are merely pointing out that the opportunities to be helpful to people are limitless as an academic, and that if you inhabit the Mommy/Earth Mother role, you will soon find that you will have to get a little tougher with respect to other people's needs—or you will not meet your own.

Another consequence of your trying to be cooperative and helpful on the job is that you can end up being exploited. Look around your department: You may notice that women are chairing a lot of committees and writing a lot of reports and handling virtually all of the socializing. Women may also be asked to teach more of the undergraduate service courses, because they are perceived as more interested in, or in tune with, the undergraduates. It is desirable to be viewed as cooperative and helpful, but the very people who are thanking you for all the things you do are the same people who will not think twice about voting against you for tenure if your teaching or scholarship is inadequate. It is your job to keep things in balance and recognize that no one will think you are a bad person or uncooperative if you decline to serve on the curriculum committee because you are already on the personnel review committee. Set limits on what you can do. Your male colleagues certainly do. You will get respect and you will get your work done.

Equally important, do not start feeling underappreciated for doing lots of things that you decide to do that are not valued. Go into situations with your eyes open. Determine what matters in your department—is it teaching, is it research, is it service? Most likely it is all three, but find out what really counts and excel at that as your primary goal. Do not expect people in a research department to be anything more than minimally grateful to you for chairing the undergraduate parents' open house or hosting a departmental party in a research institution, although this could be viewed as an extraordinarily positive thing at a teaching institution. If it gives you real pleasure to do things that are not valued too much and are gender-stereotyped, go for it, as long as you do not do these things in lieu of activities that are more highly valued in your institution. Some people would suggest that you should never perform gender-stereotyped tasks such as bringing cookies to a meeting or remembering birthdays. We agree that this is not a good way to present yourself the first few months on the job. However, if things are moving along well for you and you sense that you are respected as a scientist and a teacher, feel free to express yourself in this way, if you so choose. If, however, you receive feedback from your department head suggesting that your work is marginal and that you are vulnerable, you should focus on achieving intellectual status in the department first before celebrating birthdays and the like.

The final trap is the result of successfully negotiating the other traps, and that is the overcommitment trap. If you are doing great work and are viewed as competent, creative, and are valued by your colleagues, you are soon going to be overwhelmed with requests and opportunities. There will be prestigious committees to chair at the level of the college or university; there will be talks to give all over the country; there will be students and colleagues clamoring to work with you; funding agencies and journal editors asking for your help in reviewing. It is absolutely essential that you pick and choose among your opportunities and recognize that every time you say "yes" to an opportunity, you are saying "no" to some unknown and possibly more desirable opportunity that may arise in the future because you have used up all of your time. The overcommitment trap is something that women are particularly vulnerable to because of the need to achieve gender balance on various committees and panels. Also, women are less likely to set boundaries because of a greater tendency to focus on others' needs as well as to feelings of genuine pleasure at the opportunities available to them. The overcommitment trap creeps up on you. Be careful and be mindful of the needs you have to enjoy things besides work. The overcommitment trap is destructive of relationships, of pleasure, and can even be destructive of academic careers if you commit so heavily that you become unreliable. Being irrevocably committed to doing 20 exciting and interesting things turns into a nightmare when you can reasonably only accomplish 10 of them. Travel becomes a grind as you are always preparing for a future trip or catching up from a past one. The exciting meetings are a chore rather than stimulating; and the quantity of e-mail becomes like a house full of dirty dishes. Do not go there!

INTERPERSONAL RELATIONSHIPS

It is obviously important that you develop some close relationships both inside and outside of work. With respect to interpersonal issues at work, we will consider friendships with other women, with men, limits on work friendships, maintaining integrity when professional–personal conflicts arise, and sexual harassment issues.

When you first arrive in a department, it is wise to be somewhat restrained in developing intense personal friendships. You are vulnerable at this time and people may not be what they initially appear. Women often build intimacy through self-disclosure. Such disclosure early on to a colleague that you do not know very well and with whom you might work for the next 30 years can be a dangerous behavior.

It is great to have a senior woman as mentor and friend in your department. At the same time, do proceed cautiously and listen carefully to advice or comments that other people might make about the individual. All too often warnings or negative comments about a new friend that you are inclined to disbelieve early on turn out to have significant merit. With respect to women colleagues in particular as friends, the great limiting factor often turns out to be time. Women in academia have such a plethora of commitments in terms of work, travel, and family that, when two schedules are combined, organizing a simple lunch may require a wait of a few weeks. It is our experience that it is hard to have stable friendships with other women academics simply because of the overcommitment factor. Be aware of this, and if you develop a valued friendship, nurture it with fixed and routine commitments. Attending events sponsored by campus women's groups are a good way to get to know women in other departments and develop an important professional and personal network.

You may also develop lasting friendships with male colleagues who can be a wonderful source of camaraderie and friendship, in addition to your women colleagues. Again, developing a routine afternoon coffee break once a week or a breakfast or lunch meeting can help maintain friendships. Men often provide a construction of a work situation that is considerably different from women's. Male colleagues can help you see your department and university, as well as your own situation, through the lens of other men—and it is a lens that many people at the university will use when constructing your situation and talents, so it can be valuable to at least be aware of this perspective.

With respect to sexual involvement with colleagues, it is a bad idea in general and a terrible idea if one or both parties is married to someone else. If you do develop a dating or sexual relationship with a colleague, it is best to keep it a secret or relatively low profile until you are confident that you plan to be a couple for the foreseeable future. If you do become a professional, intradepartment couple, it is extremely important to maintain professional independence and to keep professional confidences about your colleagues and students to yourself. Always behave with courtesy to one another in public.

It goes without saying that you should never—that is, *never*—get involved with a student. The conflict of interest, the gossip, and the potential risk to your future in the department are real. Moreover, your ability to get other jobs could be limited by leaving an ugly situation behind. Recognize that if the situation goes bad, the student could make all sorts of accusations against you which might not even be true and could result in formal actions against you. Also recognize that it is likely that the view of a woman having a sexual relationship with a student will be harsher than that of a man in the same situation. Having said all this, if somehow you do get involved with a student and expect the relationship to be permanent and thus public, get the advice of an objective party who is outside the university, such as a therapist, about how to handle the situation.

Occasionally, you will find yourself in a situation where your friendships and your professional interests are in conflict. The advice for this one is simple. Simply do what it takes to maintain your integrity, giving neither your professional interests nor your friendship priority, no matter how bad it feels at the moment. Over the long haul, behaving with integrity will always come through for you.

With regard to sexual harassment, there are subtle and direct ways this can occur. Subtle harassment is difficult to deal with, and you might try discussing what to do about this with a trusted colleague or have a direct conversation with the harasser. Examples of subtle harassment might be a male colleague routinely telling off-color jokes in front of you or giving you an "unwanted" lingerie catalog he happened to have (these are real examples). Be cautious in accusing a specific individual of sexual harassment. Even a joking comment that someone is sexist is almost as serious as calling someone a racist in a university culture. A formal grievance procedure in a university is a complex and draining process that will drag on for a long time. Try to settle things informally first.

If you believe you are experiencing direct sexual harassment, your best bet might be to talk things over with your department head, if you consider him or her trustworthy and likely to believe you and be sympathetic. If that is not a likely route, or it is the head who is the problem, you might consider discussing your problems early on with an attorney who specializes in labor law and who has a reputation for integrity. The attorney is not likely to encourage you to litigate if it is clear that it is not in your interest. He or she may provide you with helpful ideas and strategies on how to deal with the situation. The university is going to be motivated to disbelieve your claims, and a local labor attorney will know the players within the university (from past litigation experience) and can give you straight advice about what to do. The attorney may know which administrator might be sympathetic to you and would help you settle your situation quietly. Do not advertise that you got advice from an attorney, because the university administration will become wary of you if they learn of this. Never threaten anyone about what you intend to do about any grievance you might have. Litigation is a painful route to go—but tolerating bullying and harassment is unnecessary. Deal with problems earlier rather than later and save any e-mails or other materials that are suggestive of harassment.

You are most likely to be subjected to gender-based discrimination that is not sexual in nature. You may be viewed with less credibility as a scientist by your male colleagues; you may be given sex-typed tasks to perform on committees; you may be excluded from important committees and meetings; you may be excluded from outings and athletic activities that involve male bonding. You may get a smaller start-up package when you are hired than your male colleagues. You may be more likely to be asked to share lab or office space than your male colleagues, based on perceptions that you are generous and cooperative. You may get lower raises than your male counterparts, particularly if you are married and viewed as less needy of compensation. This type of insidious gender-based behavior is rife in academia, and being firm about your situation, without becoming hypervigilant and resentful, can be effective. Making gender-based accusations about such subtle but real problems is not likely to be well-received in a department or university. Documenting inequities in salary, laboratories, assignment of courses and graduate students and other such domains in a dispassionate and accurate way can potentially be effective in seeking recourse, particularly if a group of women join forces.

FAMILY ISSUES

Family issues are perhaps the hardest issues of all for academic women to deal with. Women who have children, who want to have children, and who are single all have different issues to deal with. In addition, there are the complicated issues of intertwining your career with a spouse or partner. These are all issues that men face as well, but women face additional challenges in each of these areas because we bear children, we still do most of the childrearing, and we are more likely to be partnered with professionals in narrowly specialized fields. What follows is a brief summary of some of the most troubling issues in all of academia and perhaps the hardest issues you will ever have to deal with in your professional and personal life. Being an academic means the work is never done; being conscientious means being chronically haunted by the fact that the work is never done. When you add in a partner and children into the brew, the line between a rich, multifaceted life and a fragmented, unbelievably stressed-out existence becomes very thin.

When to Have Children

There is no bad time to have children and there is no good time. A growing number of young women think the best time is during the latter part of graduate school or during a postdoctoral fellowship when the demands on you are probably the least they will ever be. You will only have your research to think of—no course work, no teaching, no committees. Starting a new job with a new baby is obviously demanding, and there is the real risk that your graduate school or postdoctoral pregnancy will play a role in limiting job offers. Nevertheless, this view has merit.

The more traditional idea of waiting to have a child until one is tenured sounds great and practical. Once you are tenured, you have job security and your career and reputation are established. You will have more maturity and, it is hoped, more opportunity to attend to your child without the distractions and stresses of the pretenure years. Of course, some women feel this is not an option for them because they are older when the tenure clock begins and do not want to wait until after tenure to have children. Even if you can wait, there are some disadvantages to having children after tenure. If your career takes off as you hope, just as you are having opportunities to travel and give invited talks and get credit for your hard work, you will find yourself torn between your infant and your career. You may try to do it all, but this can be terribly stressful emotionally and physically, especially if you do not have adequate support from a partner or other resources (such as a nanny).

The authors' own experiences with children differ. One of the authors had two children one year apart as a new assistant professor. Although the timing did not seem ideal, this model actually worked well in that the children typically were going to the same schools and places at the same time, and it was not so much more work to care for two children compared to one child after the initial uproar. In retrospect, this was inadvertently a wonderful way to raise two children and then later enjoy considerable personal freedom at a relatively early stage of life for an academic woman. One unexpected downside of this model has been having less in common with women colleagues of a comparable age who are actively raising children and are more child-focused. The other author had a child after tenure and valued facing new motherhood with greater maturity, financial resources, and security than would have been true earlier in her career. Despite these different models, we are both delighted with our experiences as mothers and as academics. The bottom line is that your life circumstances and preferences will dictate when you decide to have children. There is less stigma associated with having a child and being an academic woman now than in the past, but the pressure of balancing child, partner, and job is real and substantial.

Now You Have Children

All of the women we encounter, and we mean all of them, find the demands of academic life combined with raising children stressful. At the same time, it is not so difficult to work at home and adapt your work time to the needs of your children—that is the best part of academic life with children. Guilt seems to be a constant—it seems there is time for two things (job and children; partner and children; partner and job) but three things really are over the top. There is the chronic sense of running as fast as you can, working as hard and as smart as is possible, and never quite doing things right for your children, your job, or your partner. In addition, women frequently comment about the strain the children–job combination puts on their relationships with partners.

On the other hand, children truly do add a richness to life that is worth the stress and help you keep your work and career in perspective. If you want children badly and feel that you cannot have them because of your workload, you need to rethink your work situation. The key to making things work is to manage the multiple demands on your time and attention so that your children and your career thrive. One critical attitudinal shift is to recognize that now that you have children, you have to be even more committed to setting your priorities and sticking to them. You simply cannot do everything for your colleagues and for your children, so you have to decide what is important and be firm about your priorities. For example, when one of us had her first child, she recognized that a huge portion of her day at work was being wasted by appointments with students who would show up late or not at all. She adopted a policy that students had to sign up in advance for a specific slot during her office hours, rather than just dropping by whenever they felt like it or making an individual appointment anytime during the week. Students instantly became more respectful of the faculty member's time and efficient in conducting their business during the slot.

Women almost universally report that they enjoy professional travel when they have children so they can get some time for themselves and be in a situation where they are protected from the myriad of stressors, so building in some professional travel is good for you both personally and professionally. Setting limits, forgiving yourself when you do not meet goals, and keeping focused on a few key deadlines is essential to being a successful woman academic with children. Think about taking a "research vacation." Negotiate with your partner so that you will have absolutely no responsibilities for a few days and that you can work as much as you want to finish a grant or a critical paper. If you have the financial resources, you might consider occasionally checking into a local hotel at personal expense to gather thoughts and complete important projects on time. It is a great feeling to have time to yourself with no structure and to get an important task done that has been dogging you for months. Determine what you need to get your work done and do it. Happy moms are more likely to have happy kids. Happy families are more likely to occur when the mom gets tenure and does not lose her job—remember this when you feel guilty about the time you are spending away from your child or children.

As children get older, it can be great to take a child with you on a business trip. Your child can learn what you do, listen to your talk, meet your friends, and pick up some fine dining skills in an exotic setting. This is a wonderful and relatively inexpensive treat for both parent and child and one that is memorable and meaningful to children.

With respect to your life in the department, it is much more acceptable for men to say they have to leave a meeting to go pick up a child than for women to do it. The man gets gold stars for being a good daddy but the woman reminds the group of her overwhelming responsibilities with respect to childrearing. In general, it is probably better to not bring up child-care responsibilities as a limiting factor for scheduling a meeting or teaching a class during weekday hours from 9 to 5. It is fine to set limits and say that you cannot meet in the evenings because you need to be with your family. It is equally fine to state you have an appointment and cannot meet at a certain time without elaborating, when that appointment is to stay home with your child every Thursday morning. Elaborating on how you use work hours to manage child-care responsibilities is not a good idea. Everyone knows you do it, but do not be too direct about this, even though it is okay, if not rewarded, for men to do this. In general, if you are secure about your situation, bringing the kids to work is not ideal. However, it is fine if that is what it takes to get your work done because of some complication that has arisen. If you are a single parent, you really have little choice when things break down. Speaking from one author's experience, it is possible to raise successful, happy children, be a successful academic, and be a single mother, but something has to give. From personal experience, the cost was having no time for dating and spending little time on conventional food preparation, although dating and a marriage did occur later, after the children were in college.

Stopping the Tenure Clock

Many colleges and universities now have policies allowing women (and sometimes men) to stop the tenure clock if they have a child before tenure. This may seem like a no-brainer—all benefit and no cost, right? There are some pitfalls you need to be aware of, even though they are unfair and sometimes even illegal. When you have had an extra semester or year before the tenure decision, tenure review boards, and especially external reviewers, may expect more of you than a faculty person who has come up for tenure on the traditional clock. This is never stated explicitly, but the implicit evaluation may be that "she had 7 years instead of the normal 6 before tenure, and she still only has X publications." This, of course, ignores the fact that it is tough to be highly productive during the early postpartum months, especially if your baby is not entirely healthy or does not have an easy temperament.

This does not mean, of course, that you should not stop the tenure clock or take maternity leave. You just have to be aware that the implicit tenure clock is still ticking in some of your evaluator's minds. It is important to be extremely strategic and planful before your baby arrives in getting your research and manuscripts to a stage that they can keep moving forward even in your absence. If you can find the resources, hire research assistants and others who can keep gathering data for you when you are not there. Get manuscripts into submission before the baby is due. Be realistic about timetables—do not forget that the baby could come early, or you could be forced to cut back on work in the last months of pregnancy. And be realistic about how long it may take you to come back to full-time work after the baby arrives. If you have a partner, negotiate with him or her about child care before the child arrives to ensure that you are not doing everything. If you have financial resources, find child care support long before your delivery date.

You Are Single With No Children

This is a little-explored topic, but if you are a single academic woman, you need to work hard not to become the person everyone in the department expects to do all the extra committee work and attend award luncheons and graduation ceremonies because you do not have kids or an obvious partner and therefore must have more time. Do not fall into the trap of doing these things and then feeling resentful and used. The requests will be relentless, and only you can stop them. You are not paid more than others in the department and might even be paid less. Focus on doing things the department values—whether it be outstanding teaching or superlative research. Invest your time just like every other savvy, successful person in the department does. Do things that give you pleasure and joy, and certainly investing in some of these requests may do that and enrich your life. But recognize that you have a choice, and there should be absolutely no cost to you whatsoever if you make an investment in work no greater than those individuals who have families.

Your Partner as a Spousal Hire

It is relatively recent that departments have been concerned about the partners of women they wish to hire, and departments vary tremendously in how progressive they are concerning partner–spousal hires. Even among the more progressive departments, senior women will enjoy much more aggressive efforts to find their partners jobs than will junior women.

If you are being hired as an assistant professor and finding your partner a job will be an important determinant of your decision whether to take the job, definitely do raise this with the chair of the department and perhaps the search committee. There are two points of view on this matter. We believe you should not raise this issue until you already have the job offer. Raising this before you have an offer can kill your chances of getting the offer, although legally it should not. If you are asked about your partner on the job interview (and believe us, this still happens), respond in a way that does not reveal your shock at the question nor the problems you see in relocating your partner. Work out some response before you go on the job interview that protects your privacy and moves the conversation away from this issue. An alternative view from ours is that mentioning this up front will allow the department head to work with the administration to make a package offer to the two of you or begin to work out arrangements so you can accept the job. It seems to us, however, that this question should still never be asked until an offer is made, because it might preclude an offer if there was a tough decision about who the best candidate was. The additional complications your partner represented could tip the offer away from you. Once the offer is made, departments will typically make every effort to provide you with necessary resources so that you will accept an offer.

Once you have the job offer, investigate whether the university or college has a program for partner–spousal hires. Sometimes there is an administrator in the dean's or provost's office, or in the human resources department whose job it is to find placements for partners and spouses of new faculty. Do not rely on these resources, however. You and your partner need to do your own research on possible jobs in the area for him or her.

Be aware that the positions that universities often create for partners or spouses are temporary positions—for example, two-year postdoctoral fellowships, research scientist positions that are contingent on soft money after a year or so of salary support or year-by-year teaching positions. This may be all you can get, particularly if you are hired in at the junior level, and sometimes these positions work out well. But they will require constant renegotiations with the university that can be painful and time-consuming. Once you are a senior woman with some clout, hold out for more permanent and secure positions for your partner or spouse if you can.

CAREER ASPIRATIONS

Let us now focus on a bigger picture. What is it that you like and do not like about academia? And what are you good at? There is enormous opportunity for talented women in academia, and it is important to recognize what your goals are.

Academia is wonderful in the sense that it gives you the opportunity to create different jobs without ever actually changing jobs. In a single career at a single institution, a woman could be a distinguished researcher, a founder of an institute in her research interest, a dean, a department head, a master teacher, and even a college president or provost.

Our first piece of advice is not to underestimate yourself and to aim high. Aim higher than you think you can really achieve to compensate for women's tendencies to minimize their abilities. Plan to break that glass ceiling. Aspire to be a member of the National Academy of Sciences or to be a provost or president of a college or university. The earlier you set these goals the more likely you are to achieve them. Such lofty goals deflect your attention away from the grind of the tenure process and focus you on a means to an end that is much more tangible and meaningful than getting tenure, yet paradoxically, will increase your chances of getting tenure.

Be absolutely certain that you conduct work that is your own and choose collaborators carefully. Recognize that if you collaborate with a male partner, you run the risk of the work being attributed more to him than to you. Similar outcomes will occur if you continue to collaborate with an advisor. It is important to show your independence and ability to manage your research and teaching program and get some publications in areas that are uniquely yours.

Consider in your early years if your long-term interests lie with research or administration or a combination of both. Your first goal should obviously be to get tenure. If you think you might be interested in being an administrator, try chairing a committee. Women have unique talents as administrators, and men can be enthusiastic supporters of women administrators. It is almost certainly the case that your advisor trained you to be a researcher, but do not hesitate to break that mold and do not worry at all about your advisor being disappointed. What do *you* want? What excites you? You are in a rich and complex environment that allows you to define your job in many different ways. Consider trying on some different hats and going after what you want.

IS ACADEMIA FOR YOU?

We think this is a question too few women ask. The years of work toward achieving your dream—getting an academic job—do not lend themselves to considering once you have achieved this dream if it is really working for you. Academic women work incredibly long hours for relatively modest pay and at quite a high stress level, given all the competing demands that are made on their time. If you have landed an academic job, you are a bright, talented person. We think it is important that you value yourself enough to recognize that you have alternatives, many of which likely involve shorter hours and higher pay and potentially interesting work. Like just about every other job in this country, it really is harder for women to succeed in academia than it is for men. Women fail to succeed not because of lack of talent but because of an unwillingness to work the extraordinarily long hours that are required to be successful as well as because of gender-specific discrimination issues. It is important to recognize that evaluation is not a one-way street. In the early years especially, you should be evaluating your place of employment as intensely as you are being evaluated. Is this college or university a good place for you and a good place for your family? Are things likely to remain stable? Do not assume you will be at a place you find undesirable for only a brief period of time and then move. Mobility within academia is relatively limited, and even more so when there are two careers involved. Do not be afraid to recognize that academia is not for you if you are not loving it. You should also recognize that you will have good semesters and bad semesters, and that contextual events, such as the birth of a child, a divorce, and a difficult supervisor can all color your perceptions about the future, when in fact circumstances will change and things will get better. Try to envision your career at your institution across the various stages of your lifespan and make decisions accordingly.

Having focused on the down-side of academic life, we can also reiterate the things you already know. Academic life is exciting, generative, rewarding, and ultimately satisfying. Besides being able to study just about anything you want, you can work at home; you can travel with your children; you can organize your work life around the lives of your family to some extent; and every semester you have a chance to start fresh. You will work with exciting, creative people—students, faculty, and staff. You have the ability to create and recreate your job; to try out different roles and jobs with little risk. As you become more successful, you will have the opportunity for almost unlimited travel to interesting and exotic places at little or no personal expense. Moreover, tenure confers the ability to make financial decisions with little concern that you will lose your job—this can become important, particularly if you are or become a single parent and face the costs of buying a house or educating your children alone. Knowing that your income is guaranteed gives you an enormous sense of security when faced with borrowing money for education and shelter and allows you to offer your children many things that you might not be able to do if you had a conventional job that you could lose and thus required a substantial financial buffer.

Certainly, men and women have different experiences in the academy, but universities are probably among the best places for women to work rather than among the worst. You will likely experience less discrimination and little overt sexual harassment in academia relative to many other work environments. The opportunities for women in higher education are unlimited, and the compensation for women at the top is excellent, particularly in administration. You have the potential to affect thousands of lives in a positive way over your career and make a significant contribution to society, not just through research but also through teaching.

CONCLUSION

Our main message is that you need to control the job rather than let the job control you. The price at the highest levels of success can be quite high, but the rewards are great, and there are many points in between that may be the right comfort zone for you. Finally, remember that work should be fun, and this is one job where you can wake up every single day and feel excited about the intellectual, social, and emotional content of the day's events.

REFERENCES

American Psychological Association Committee on Women and Commission on Ethnic Minority Recruitment, Retention, and Training. (1998). *Surviving and thriving in academia: A guide for women and ethnic minorities*. Washington, DC: American Psychological Association.

Caplan, P. J. (1993). *Lifting a ton of features: A woman's guide to surviving in the academic world*. Toronto: University of Toronto Press.

Harvey, J. C., & Katz, C. (1985). *If I'm so successful, why do I feel like a fake: The impostor phenomenon*. New York: St. Martin's Press.

Nolen-Hoeksema, S., & Jackson, B. (2000). Mediators of the gender difference in rumination. *Psychology of Women Quarterly, 25*, 37–47.

Task Force on Women in Academe. (2000). *Women in academe: Two steps forward, one step back*. Washington, DC: American Psychological Association.

Valian, V. (1998). *Why so slow? The advancement of women*. Cambridge, MA: MIT Press.

17

CLINICAL PSYCHOLOGISTS
IN ACADEMIA

RICHARD R. BOOTZIN

At first blush, putting this chapter in a section on the diversities of experiences in academia is odd for someone like me. I have spent my entire career in departments of psychology promoting psychology as a unified discipline, not as a collection of relatively autonomous areas. Psychology as a discipline flourishes through interactions at boundaries and across subareas, even though clinical psychology is often separated because of the curriculum and training requirements needed for an accredited graduate clinical psychology program. Clinical psychology plays a central role in these interactions,

I am indebted to a number of academic clinical psychologists with varying amounts of experience who read an earlier version of this chapter and made cogent suggestions. Included are John J. B. Allen, Varda Shoham, Alfred Kaszniak, Brian Carpenter, Desiree White, Jeannine Morrone-Strupinsky, and Shauna Shapiro. Thanks also to Susan Zlotlow, director of the Office of Program Consultation and Accreditation of the American Psychological Association, who provided information on the requirements that accreditation site visitors must meet, and to Emmanuel Donchin, Edward Katkin, and Paul Nelson, who provided information on the chronology of accreditation changes. I particularly appreciate the contributions made by Henry Roediger III, one of the editors of this book, who was a generous and thoughtful commentator and helpful editor. Finally, I am fortunate to have had the help of my own personal editor, my wife, Maris Bootzin, who read the outline and drafts of the chapter with blue pencil in hand and assisted in keeping the chapter in focus and improving the writing.

providing opportunities to test applications of theories from basic research and extending basic theories so that they apply to the hard, real-world problems found in the practice of clinical psychology.

There has been mutual benefit from this interaction; basic research follows the lead of practice as much as the reverse (Davison & Lazarus, 1995). Some of the most exciting advances in psychology, in both science and practice, occur through integration across areas both within and outside psychology departments. There are fruitful interactions between clinical psychology, cognitive and emotion science, and neuroscience as well as between clinical psychology, social psychology, and communication and family systems theorists. It is the clinical psychologist who is often the glue that keeps these interactions working. Researchers involved in the development of the science of clinical psychology have had to be both basic and applied researchers as well as able to seek out intra- and interdisciplinary collaborators with special expertise.

Why is there a chapter regarding the unique demands confronting clinical psychologists in academia? Clinical psychologists, even though they are held to the same expectations as other faculty with regard to research, teaching, and service, are separated to some extent by the additional needs and activities associated with professional practice. There is an additional layer of challenges for the clinical psychologist in academia that has an impact on all faculty activities. This chapter will explore those challenges and possible solutions to them.

There are many different academic settings in which clinical psychologists are part of the teaching mission. A partial list would include university psychology departments with a graduate PhD program in clinical psychology, university psychology departments with a master's program in clinical psychology, professional schools of psychology offering a PsyD or PhD, college departments that do not have graduate programs, and university departments and colleges that have teaching missions other than psychology, such as medical schools and schools of education.

Although there are specific requirements in each setting, there are commonalities as well. The training of clinical psychologists as scientist–practitioners has led to their being valued in widely divergent settings as individuals who can integrate science and practice, who understand the methodology of science, and who can contribute to the advancement of knowledge, the teaching of the discipline, and the application of knowledge in practice.

This chapter will focus primarily on the challenges facing faculty in psychology departments that have PhD programs in clinical psychology, but much of what applies to such departments applies to the other settings as well.

THE BOULDER MODEL

Even at the beginnings of clinical psychology, when Lightner Witmer founded the first psychological clinic at the University of Pennsylvania in 1896, science as well as practice was considered essential (Kihlstrom & Kihlstrom, 1998; Woody & Robertson, 1997). For Witmer, the laboratory was the clinic and the science was based on the accumulation of findings from single-case studies. Despite the emphasis on both science and practice, the tensions between academic and applied psychologists were present then, as now, and continued during the first half of the twentieth century (Woody & Robertson, 1997).

Clinical psychology in academia grew dramatically after World War II as a result of training initiatives from both the Veterans Administration (VA) and the National Institute of Mental Health (NIMH). Emotional and mental disorders accounted for more than half of the hospitalizations in the VA, and there was a shortage of clinical psychologists available to provide care (Routh, 1994). In response to training needs, a conference on Graduate Education in Clinical Psychology sponsored by the NIMH was held at the University of Colorado in Boulder in August 1949. The scientist–practitioner model of training was endorsed by the conference and has come to be known as the Boulder model. This model proposed a merging of both science and clinical training as part of the PhD program in psychology in which the prototypical curriculum would include both research training and clinical practica, a third year predoctoral clinical internship, and a PhD dissertation during the fourth year. Accreditation of graduate clinical psychology programs started soon thereafter as a means of designating those programs that were producing clinical psychologists according to this model. Both the VA and NIMH awarded fellowships and training grants to support universities in developing clinical psychology training within academia.

In the years that followed, the basic scientist–practitioner training model was accepted by almost all PhD clinical psychology training programs, although there has been a gradual lengthening of the program and repositioning of the predoctoral clinical internship to the end of training. During the 1960s, there was increasing dissatisfaction expressed with the scientist–practitioner model, because some viewed it as unrealistic for clinical psychologists in practice also to be researchers (Woody & Robertson, 1997). An alternative practitioner training model in which clinical psychologists would be taught to understand and apply research, but would not learn the skills needed to be a researcher, was proposed. This practitioner model, associated with the awarding of a PsyD, was endorsed along with the scientist–practitioner model, associated with the awarding of a PhD, at a conference held in Vail, Colorado, in 1973. Practitioner programs, recently called scholar–practitioner programs, are more commonly found in freestanding professional schools of psychology rather than in university-based programs. There is variation, even among professional schools, however, as some award PhDs and not PsyDs, and some describe their programs as scientist–practitioner, irrespective of the degree awarded.

The Vail practitioner model represented a swing of the graduate training pendulum toward service delivery and professional training. Clinical psychology faculty at major universities became concerned that the pendulum had swung too far away from support for the advancement of knowledge in clinical psychology. Guild issues, such as reimbursement for services and state licensing, seemed to be driving decisions that had major impact on the capacity of clinical psychology programs to train graduate students in the science of clinical psychology. There was concern that issues regarding funding for mental health research, career opportunities for students, accreditation of clinical science programs, accountability for clinical services, and the scope and knowledge base of scientific psychology were not being addressed adequately at the national level.

In response to the perceived movement away from a scientific base for clinical psychology, a conference was held at Indiana University in Bloomington, Indiana, in 1994. At the conference, the Academy of Psychological Clinical Science (APCS), a coalition of graduate training programs committed to advancing the science of clinical psychology, was formed. In 2003, the APCS is an alliance of 50 leading, scientifically oriented, doctoral training programs in clinical and health psychology in the United States and Canada, including 41 academic graduate training programs and 9 clinical psychology internships. The mission statement and list of member programs can be found on the APCS website (http://psychclinicalscience.org).

All clinical psychology graduate programs provide some degree of balance between research and clinical training. The fact that there are different models of training, such as the scientist–practitioner model and the practitioner model, does not mean that there are two different, legitimate ways of being a clinical psychologist or that practice need not be based on science (McFall, 1991). A profession that is licensed by the state and receives reimbursement for its services must provide services based on scientifically validated principles and techniques (Kihlstrom & Kihlstrom, 1998; McFall, 1991). Even advocates of practitioner models recognize that psychology derives its prestige and public acceptance through its scientific base.

In the domain of training within departments of psychology, the pendulum is swinging back to a stronger emphasis on developing skills in the methods of science, not just in being aware of the current status of research in clinical psychology. Our understanding of psychopathology and effectiveness of interventions changes as new knowledge is obtained, but the process of scientific inquiry is constant. The skills of keen observation, critical thinking, and methodological rigor combined with inventiveness when putting conceptualization to the empirical test, as well as following the lead of empirical evidence, are valuable in all clinical activities, not just in research (McFall, 1985). The use of these skills by clinical psychologists is the best assurance that clinical psychology will remain a strong, vibrant field no matter where clinical psychologists are located.

RESPONSIBILITIES OF FACULTY MEMBERS

The responsibilities of clinical psychology faculty members fall into four broad categories: research, teaching, service, and clinical practice.

Research

A program of research requires attention to a variety of issues, some of which have been discussed in other chapters. Included are setting up the space for your research; recruiting, training, and supervising research assistants; getting access to participant populations; acquiring funds; writing articles, chapters, and books; writing lab and treatment manuals; giving presentations and workshops; developing collaborative relationships; and so forth. Fortunately, new faculty have had previous experience in similar research laboratories during their training as graduate students and postdoctoral fellows. Many of these experiences are helpful in setting up a new program of research, but previous experience can also limit one's vision to an overemphasis on familiar solutions. These are not always the best solutions. In making decisions in any or all of these areas, it is wise to seek out suggestions from colleagues in your department and others who do the same type of research that you do.

Access to Patients for Research

Every faculty member confronts issues about what types of research participants are appropriate for the hypotheses being tested. At universities, introductory psychology students have often been recruited as research participants because they are available and there are many of them. College students are ideal participants to answer some questions such as those having to do with the nature of learning. But not all research questions are best answered by studying college students, and this challenge is not unique to clinical psychology. A clear limitation to the use of college students is that undergraduate samples may not be representative of populations of interest (Sechrest & Bootzin, 1996). For example, should we expect that college students on mock juries are representative of the general population regarding sensitivity to different kinds of evidence or in making assessments of witness credibility? Or, if investigators are exploring changes in cognitive functioning as one ages, would undergraduates reflect the variation in age and ability that are found in the general population? It does not seem likely that college students would be representative in either of these cases. Researchers in many fields have striven to recruit representative samples for their research studies.

Research on understanding the course, determinants, or treatment of a psychopathology such as schizophrenia or generalized anxiety disorder would be difficult to do with college students. So how does one find participants who will participate in clinical research? Among the different ways are (a) using college students, but selecting only those who have the disorder or problem of interest; (b) advertising for participants from the community or enlisting patient support groups; (c) using the clinical psychology training clinic as a research facility; (d) collaborating with individuals who have clinics that serve such patients; and (e) developing your own clinic to serve patients.

It may be necessary to use a combination of strategies, depending on the hypotheses being tested. For some tests of theory, using college students is sufficient. For example, many of the initial studies that evaluated the beneficial health consequences of writing about one's deepest thoughts and feelings for three or four 20-minute sessions were evaluated in experiments with college students in which health center visits were examined for the six months before and after the interventions (Pennebaker, 1997). Other studies with other measures and other populations followed.

Whatever arrangements or combination of arrangements are used for providing access to clinical patients, the pace of research for the academic clinical psychologist is often slower, by necessity, than it is for their nonclinical colleagues. Patients with specific disorders are not as available as college students, or even control adults or elderly individuals, and there may be delays because of administrative procedures in facilities and organizations from which patients could be recruited.

In therapy outcome research, if you aspire to be funded to do clinical trials either individually in your own lab or as part of multisite studies, you will have to demonstrate that you have access to the patient population needed. You may also have to do pilot research to develop interventions and to demonstrate the feasibility of measures. The National Institutes of Health offer funding opportunities for small grants and for grants to develop interventions that could be used for these purposes. If you identify the major researchers in the areas of your interest (e.g., depression, anxiety disorders, schizophrenia, alcohol abuse, insomnia, pain, personality disorders, clinical neuropsychology, and so forth), you will see that most of them have either developed their own specialty clinics or have excellent collaborative relationships with existing specialty clinics.

Developing collaborative relationships has some advantages for the assistant professor in that the infrastructure for the clinic already exists and does not depend on your efforts. This is a major advantage because considerations about space, equipment, liability insurance, support staff, the capacity to bill for reimbursement, and access to clinicians of other disciplines will already be in place. There are disadvantages as well that could outweigh the advantages. Your research interests may not be a priority for the directors of the clinic. Junior faculty members have to be concerned about developing their own program of research and related issues of authorship, not just in assisting the ongoing research of others.

It is helpful to investigate opportunities for collaboration at the time of hiring. You can ask the search committee chair to assist by setting up appointments during the interview visit with relevant individuals who might provide access to patient groups. Later, if you receive funding for your research as part of your start-up package or from external funding, providing partial support for a staff member in the clinic may help ensure that your research interests receive priority.

An attractive alternative for new faculty is to build a specialty clinic for research purposes within the clinical program's training clinic. This also has the advantage of an infrastructure that is either in place or that could be strengthened with less effort than it would take to develop a specialty clinic on your own. Also, your research could provide clinical training in assessment and therapy for graduate students in the program.

Parenthetically, administrators sometimes view the psychology clinic as a money-making opportunity. Even before the advent of managed care, psychology clinics were seldom in the black. The expense of the clinic, for space, equipment, and staff, should be justified as necessary for clinical training and research and as a service to the community. The more the clinic can be used for clinical research, the more opportunity there is to bring funded research into the clinic and to expand clinical training opportunities for graduate students.

An initiative to help training clinics develop common research procedures has been the establishment of a national Clinic Practice Research Network (PRN; Borkovec, 2001). The goals of the network are to use common core assessment batteries to facilitate scientific research, to share information about methods for enhancing scientist–practitioner training, and to create collaborative research efforts among training programs.

Licensing

State licensing is required for psychologists to provide or supervise clinical services. In many states (e.g., Arizona), there are no exemptions for either research or being an employee of a state university, although there may be a grace period to become licensed. States differ with regard to licensing laws and the extent to which they apply to the activities of university faculty, but many of them require that the faculty member either be licensed or be supervised by someone who is licensed if clinical services are being delivered. Because the agreement to supervise someone's clinical activities means that the supervisor accepts liability for the activities of the trainee, it is not a trivial matter to find a willing supervisor outside the context of the training activities of the clinical program. Becoming licensed is not required of other academics in psychology. It is an additional activity and expense necessary for clinical psychologists to carry out research and supervise practicum students.

Most licensing laws require two years of clinical experience, one of which can be predoctoral and is usually the predoctoral internship. There is considerable variability among the states as to what types of experiences count toward postdoctoral experience. Some provide credit for almost all activities of a clinical psychologist including teaching, research, and direct service; others focus primarily on supervised direct service.

For those clinical psychologists in academia, the postdoctoral experience requirement can serve as a substantial barrier to becoming licensed and participating in all aspects of the clinical psychology program. Even those who have taken a postdoctoral fellowship may not meet the experience requirement. The fellowship may have been a research position during which little time was spent in supervised direct service. A faculty position makes it extremely difficult to meet the experience requirements unless the state accepts the definition of clinical experience to include teaching clinical courses and engaging in clinical research in addition to supervised direct clinical service.

Some states have been willing to allow assistant professors to accumulate clinical hours over a few years, but it is not clear that this helps. Political action is needed to help change the way experience is defined and administered. Nevertheless, you, as an individual, may still need to become licensed. Clinical psychologists when choosing a postdoctoral fellowship must consider the extent to which there will be opportunities to engage in sufficient clinical activities for licensure. Those who are hired into faculty positions without a postdoctoral fellowship or a postdoctoral fellowship with insufficient clinical activities may have to choose among the unappealing alternatives of attempting to acquire supervised clinical experience while an assistant professor or delaying taking the position to acquire supervised clinical hours. No matter which choice you make, the earlier you fulfill the licensing or certification requirement of your state, the earlier you will be able to develop fully your research program and participate in all aspects of the clinical program.

As an aside, the issues of licensing and its importance in determining access to patient populations and reimbursement has led many with PhDs in nonclinical areas to respecialize in clinical psychology. If even clinical psychologists have difficulties with access to patient populations, it is more difficult for those with PhDs in nonclinical areas.

Teaching (2)

The teaching responsibilities of clinical psychology faculty members at the undergraduate level often involves courses such as personality, abnormal psychology, tests and measurement, and introduction to clinical psychology. There may also be courses that are more specialized and that represent the interests of the faculty such as sleep and sleep disorders, psychophysiology, or psychopathology (or seminars in specific disorders). Because many psychology departments have difficulty staffing basic courses, such as introductory psychology, statistics, and experimental methods, the clinical psychology faculty may be called on to help staff these courses as well.

In some ways, clinical psychology faculty members are well-suited for teaching basic psychology courses as they are the generalists of the department. They tend to collaborate and use principles from other areas of psychology more than psychologists in other specialty areas. Even though clinical psychologists may be well-suited for teaching basic courses, they also face burdensome advising and graduate teaching demands.

The teaching responsibilities of the clinical psychology faculty member at the graduate level include mentoring and advising graduate students in their research activities, including masters or other research projects, comprehensive exams, and dissertations; teaching graduate courses in the clinical program curriculum; teaching graduate seminars; and teaching and providing practicum or externship clinical supervision. The clinical psychology graduate curriculum is usually so extensive that the balance between undergraduate and graduate teaching must be tilted more toward graduate teaching.

Accreditation

There are more than 200 accredited programs in clinical psychology, of which more than 150 are located in psychology departments in colleges of arts and sciences (APA, 2000). In most psychology departments, the clinical program is the only graduate program that is accredited and required to meet accreditation guidelines. The Committee on Accreditation (CoA) is a semiautonomous accrediting body that is supported in its efforts by the American Psychological Association (APA). The accreditation process involves a scheduled self-study report and a site visit that may be as infrequent as every seven years for accredited programs or on a more frequent schedule if there were areas of concern during the previous evaluation. Annual reports from the program supplement the less frequent evaluations. The accreditation guidelines cover eight domains, including eligibility; program philosophy, objectives, and curriculum plan; program resources; cultural and individual differences and diversity; student–faculty relations; program self-assessment and quality enhancement; public disclosure; and relationship with the accrediting body (APA, 2002).

Although the CoA is often seen by many faculty as the enemy, there are advantages to having an accreditation process. As can be seen by the lists of domains, there are many opportunities to consider and implement training enhancements in all areas of clinical psychology. Graduation from an accredited program typically facilitates state licensure, as well. The department and the university understand the need to provide resources to maintain an accredited program, and as a consequence, the need for resources receives a higher priority than it might otherwise. On the other hand, guidelines for accreditation can be administered in ways that do not reflect the goals of the program but instead emphasize a list of courses that should be offered (P. Nelson, personal communication, Oct. 31, 2001). This is often referred to as a checklist mentality.

In the late 1980s and early 1990s, the accreditation process appeared to be so unfriendly to programs that emphasized clinical science that there were discussions about programs withdrawing from the CoA and setting up an alternative accreditation process under the auspices of the American Psychological Society (APS). As part of the reaccreditation process of the CoA by the U.S. Department of Education and in response to the unrest in the field, the CoA was reorganized and new accreditation operating procedures were approved in 1995 (E. Donchin, personal communication, Oct. 7, 2001; E. Katkin, personal communication, Oct. 30, 2001).

A primary change was that the checklist of courses was replaced by evidence about how competencies were acquired. It is often easiest to demonstrate by course listings that a student has learned particular subject matter such as the ethics of clinical practice or the developmental bases of behavior. Having a separate course for every desirable topic, however, can quickly create a bloated curriculum. Under the new regulations, it is up to the program to demonstrate how competencies are developed and evaluated, whether through course work or other means.

A danger from accreditation is the addition of new "desirable" requirements that have the inevitable effect of lengthening the training program and reducing time for learning to be a first-rate researcher. If the accreditation process remains sensitive to the needs of programs to develop scientific, as well as clinical, expertise and supports innovation in training as opposed to using a course-dominated checklist process of evaluation, then it can be a desirable tool for enhancing training. However, it is a constant struggle to keep the curriculum manageable so that graduate students have time to develop expertise in their research areas and are not overwhelmed with course work and clinical skill building.

Clinical Supervision

One teaching requirement that clinical faculty have that other faculty do not is providing supervision in the clinical practica. Some faculty who are unfamiliar with the curriculum in the clinical psychology program express mystification about how this need is different from teaching graduate students in the research skills of their laboratories. Clinical psychology faculty have the same need as other faculty to train their graduate students in research skills, but that is not what is being discussed. In addition to research skills, the clinical psychology students have to learn how to assess and treat psychological disorders, how to consult with other professionals, and how to help clinics evaluate the effectiveness of their services. There is also the challenge of helping graduate students balance clinical practice with research and teaching responsibilities at the same time that the faculty are trying to do the same. Clinical supervision and mentoring of the integration of science and practice require a unique and time-consuming commitment from clinical faculty.

In an ideal program, all clinical faculty would be involved in the supervision of clinical skills just as they are in the supervision of research skills. The faculty are scientist–practitioners and are the appropriate models for how to integrate science and practice. In some programs, all faculty supervise in the clinical practica and receive teaching credit, sometimes proportional to the number of students in the practicum. Financial and staffing practicalities in universities often preclude this solution.

As a result, in many programs clinical staff are hired to administer the clinic and provide a substantial portion of the supervision. If the program clinic is, itself, a research clinic, then the clinical staff can be good models for the integration of science and practice. Similarly, if clinical faculty use the program clinic for their specialty research clinics, the faculty can have a larger role in the training and supervision of students in those activities. Or if faculty develop their own specialty clinics (at the university medical center or in other community locations), program students can take externships and receive training and supervision from clinical faculty in the same way that they could in other community externships.

Service ③

There are many domains of service to which all faculty contribute. The need to provide service to the department, college, and university through committee and other aspects of shared governance falls equally on clinical psychology faculty and other faculty in the department. There are other domains of service, however, in which clinical psychology faculty are called on to provide some unique services.

Junior faculty from all programs frequently have to be protected from taking on too many service responsibilities for the program, department, and university despite their energy and new ideas. Service activities are time-consuming and may prevent the new faculty member from getting research underway or may delay the analysis and writing of the findings of their studies. No one gets tenure and is promoted because of their service to the university. Although service activities are important, it is critical that the first priority for the new faculty member be on advancing science and developing a national and international reputation in his or her area of expertise.

Service to the Program

Clinical psychology programs have directors, and sometimes assistant directors, who are drawn from the clinical psychology faculty. There are often committees for admissions and for clinical training, and there are likely to be meetings of the clinical faculty to evaluate students and discuss ways in which the programs can be enhanced. The best programs have faculty who are willing to contribute their time and effort to make the programs as good as they can be.

New faculty are expected to contribute to that effort, but need to be careful not to take on too much responsibility too quickly. It is wise for the director of the program to be a respected tenured faculty member so that the needs of the clinical program can be brought to the department, college, and university administration by a spokesperson who can speak with authority. Other positions, such as assistant director or member of the clinical training committee, are excellent opportunities for junior faculty to contribute to and learn more about the governance of the program.

Service to the Profession

In this area there are many activities that can help develop skills in writing articles, applying for grants, and in networking with those who can help with your research and in placing graduate students. Included are reviewing journal articles, serving on grant review committees, being active in professional societies, speaking for continuing education workshops, and being an accreditation site visitor.

Developing mechanisms for the clinical psychology program to be involved in providing continuing education offerings is a good way to keep a strong relationship between program faculty and clinical psychologists in the community.

It is time-consuming being an accreditation site visitor, but the task provides the opportunity to learn about how others meet the same challenges that are facing your program or department. Every clinical psychology program should have a couple of individuals who are eligible site visitors so there is a sufficient pool of potential visitors from similar programs. Clinical faculty interested in becoming CoA site visitors must have received a doctoral degree from an accredited program, have five years of professional experience, hold appropriate licensure or certification, and must take a training workshop. There is often a shortage of nonclinical faculty to serve as generalist site visitors. It is helpful to have colleagues who are generalist site visitors so that there are faculty in the department who are informed about all that is involved in having a strong, clinical program. Generalists must have received a doctoral degree from an accredited institution, have five years of professional experience, have involvement in a department or school that has a CoA accredited training program, and must take a training workshop (S. Zlotlow, personal communication, Oct. 17, 2001).

Service to the Community

Clinical psychology faculty members may be called on more than other faculty to provide community outreach because the topics of clinical psychology tend to draw interest from the community. There may be talks to community and school groups, pro bono clinical services, media interviews, and opportunities to be on governing boards of community agencies. Sometimes there are national efforts to provide outreach to the community such as the National Day for Screening for Depression. The participation of faculty and graduate students in such efforts provides outreach to the community as well as a public service.

Some community activities can help develop clinical training opportunities for the program or help recruit research participants. For example, someone doing research on depression in elderly individuals might seek out invitations to speak at community centers or retirement communities to inform the older adult community about the research as well as recruit future research participants.

Clinical Practice

University faculty are typically evaluated on research, teaching, and service, not on the application of their scholarship. Clinical psychology faculty, on the other hand, are often drawn to the field because of an interest in applying knowledge, not only in advancing knowledge so that someone else might apply it.

There are many different ways that clinical service is delivered. Some clinical psychology faculty maintain a small practice as a means of satisfying those interests; other faculty develop specialty clinics that serve as training and research clinics; and still others limit their clinical activities entirely to their research and supervision of the training activities of the program. Not all clinical activities follow the models of individual, couple, family, or group therapy. Some clinical activities involve interventions and evaluations in broader systems such as clinics in community mental health centers or in the courts or in state health and mental health programs.

What is common and exciting in clinical psychology, and less common in other areas of psychology, is that the application of knowledge is part and parcel of the defining characteristics of the field. This is an extra dimension to what it means to be in clinical psychology, and it is something of which to be proud. The application of knowledge, however, often appears underappreciated in faculty annual reviews or promotion and tenure procedures. Department chairs and other faculty often understand clinical activities as a type of service, but clinical activities make important contributions to the quality of research and teaching as well.

CONCLUSION

As can be seen from the discussion of the special challenges that confront the clinical psychology faculty member in research, teaching, service, and clinical practice, the professional life of the academic clinical psychologist is remarkably full. What has not been conveyed well by the preceding discussion is that it is also an interesting, intellectually challenging, and enjoyable life. As mentioned at the beginning of the chapter, it is the clinical psychologist who is often the glue at the center of the most exciting advances in psychology. Even considering all the challenges and barriers, being an academic clinical psychologist is a wonderful career.

One measure of whether this is the career path for you is whether you love the multiple challenges of research, teaching, and practice. If you would consider it a loss to leave out any of these elements, then it is likely that you will flourish as an academic clinical psychologist.

REFERENCES

American Psychological Association. (2000). Accredited doctoral programs in professional psychology: 2000. *American Psychologist, 55,* 1473–1486.

American Psychological Association. (2002). *Guidelines and principles for accreditation of programs in professional psychology.* Washington, DC: Author.

Borkovec, T. D. (2001, June 14). *The National Clinic Practice Research Network (PRN)*. Presentation given at the meeting of the Academy of Psychological Clinical Science, Toronto, Canada.

Davison, G. C., & Lazarus, A. A. (1995). The dialectics of science and practice. In S. C. Hayes, V. M. Follete, R. M. Dawes, & K. E. Grady (Eds.), *Scientific standards of psychological practice: Issues and recommendations* (pp. 95–120). Reno, NV: Context Press.

Kihlstrom, J. F., & Kihlstrom, L. C. (1998). Integrating science and practice in an environment of managed care. In D. K. Routh & R. J. DeRubeis (Eds.), *The science of clinical psychology: Accomplishments and future directions* (pp. 281–294). Washington, DC: American Psychological Association.

McFall, R. M. (1985). Nonbehavioral training for behavioral clinicians. *Behavioral Therapist, 8*, 27–30.

McFall, R. M. (1991). Manifesto for a science of clinical psychology. *Clinical Psychologist, 44*, 75–88.

Pennebaker, J. W. (1977). Writing about emotional experiences as a therapeutic process. *Psychological Science, 8*, 162–166.

Routh, D. K. (1994). *Clinical psychology since 1917: Science, practice, and organization*. New York: Plenum Press.

Sechrest, L. B., & Bootzin, R. R. (1996). Psychology and inferences about public policy. *Psychology, Public Policy, and the Law, 2*, 377–392.

Woody, R. H., & Robertson, M. H. (1997). *A career in clinical psychology: From Training to employment*. Madison, CT: International Universities Press.

18

VARIETIES OF COLLEGE AND UNIVERSITY EXPERIENCES

DEBORAH L. BEST

Most faculty members cling, consciously or subconsciously, to the Platonic ideal of an academic department, no matter what sort of department they are in (Tucker, 1981). In this ideal department, every professor is a superstar and every program and course is vital to the welfare of the institution, the nation, and humankind. The ideal department is well-funded, faculty have generous salaries, and the chair is the clerk of court, duly recording faculty judgments and seeking ways to improve those judgments. As with all ideals, however, the Platonic ideal is unattainable. Yet, in spite of having been undergraduate and graduate students in departments that were most likely not utopian, the ideal still exists in the minds of faculty members and in many cases is what led them to seek an academic career. This ideal lurks in the background of many of the arguments voiced in department meetings about issues of resource allocation, course assignments, program development, and promotion and tenure. Although the Platonic ideal may always be present, somehow the day-to-day realities of an academic department never quite achieve this lofty plane. Whereas chapter 12 explored the faculty experience at the university level, this chapter explores the faculty experience *within* the department, examining how the culture of the academic setting affects the new faculty member.

VENUE OF THE DEPARTMENT

First, and most broadly, the location of the department within the institution plays an important role in how individual faculty members, as well as the department as a whole, are treated. In the United States, most psychology departments are housed in colleges of arts and sciences (Singer, 1990). However, psychology departments are also housed in business schools, schools of education, divisions of humanities, social or behavioral sciences, natural sciences, life sciences, biological sciences, and medical schools. Furthermore, there are independent schools of psychology and departments of psychology in professional schools, such as medicine or dentistry. The location of a department is not indicative of its quality, but it may influence the value or reputation of the department with administrators and other faculty within the institution.

Departments that are central to the mission of an institution may garner more favors and resources from the administration than departments that are seen as peripheral. By joining a highly regarded department rather than a less favored one, a new faculty member may have access to more resources (e.g., start-up funds, travel money, student assistants) or may instantly assume the new department's prestige and reputation with new institutional colleagues (e.g., "She must be good if that department recruited her"). Sometimes the location of a department is a cue to how it is viewed. For example, if an institution favors the sciences (e.g., engineering school), it may be beneficial for the psychology department to be among the favored group. Of course, it is sometimes difficult for a department to compete with a discipline (e.g., physics) that is well-established and has a strong track record within the institution (see chapter 12, this volume, for additional discussion).

Strong professional schools within an institution sometimes dominate internal resource allocation (e.g., space) because they often bring in substantial outside funding from research grants, contracts, or support from interested businesses, foundations, and wealthy alumni. Successful revenue sports programs also may receive what appears to be an unfair share of an institution's resources because such programs maintain alumni loyalty and financial support as well as provide media exposure and advertising for the school. In these sorts of environments, academic departments, including psychology, may constantly compete for resources and appear to get the short end of the stick. To deal with these sorts of rivals, in some institutions chairs across a number of departments will meet regularly to discuss strategies to lobby for their needs. Departments generally cannot compete with professional schools or athletics—just cheer for the teams—but when departments work together and develop supportive relationships with other departments, the climate is likely to be a collegial one.

Faculty unionization began in the late 1960s as a way to increase the role of faculty in institutional governance (Baldridge, Curtis, Ecker, & Riley, 1978). Most unionized faculty members are at public institutions and two-year community colleges. Junior faculty, part-time faculty, and faculty who are among the protected classes, according to affirmative action laws, are the ones who most frequently join unions to make their voices heard. Indeed, collective bargaining has changed the landscape of academic governance and has become a major force in higher education, particularly when educational budgets are tight.

TYPES OF DEPARTMENTS

Institutions of higher learning have not always been organized into discipline-specific departments. Although there are certainly exceptions, academic departments did not begin to appear until the latter half of the eighteenth century (Hecht, Higgerson, Gmelch, & Tucker, 1999). As knowledge accelerated and intellectual specialization grew, departments arose out of the need to improve the organization and management of the academic process. As a result, faculty allegiance to the institution decreased as commitment to the discipline increased.

During the 1950s, many institutions established separate centers, institutes, and bureaus for specialized teaching and research, and these often cut across disciplinary lines. Today, interdisciplinary programs and departments again have moved into the center of colleges and universities, and faculty are often encouraged to work with colleagues from other fields.

Departments vary along a number of structural and organizational dimensions that are generally related to the institution's size, administrative complexity, and prestige.

Large Versus Small Departments

Departments vary both within and between institutions in terms of size. In small colleges, many departments may have as few as two or three faculty members, but in large research universities, it is not unusual to find departments with 75 or more faculty members, resembling a small college in many ways. Large departments may tend toward fragmentation and expansion of administrative hierarchies as responsibilities are delegated to associate chairs or committees. Size certainly influences the organization of a department and the style of management used. Size may also affect the nature of social interactions, the opportunities for research collaboration with colleagues, as well as the general climate of the department, and these issues will be addressed later in this chapter.

Pure Versus Mixed Departments and Divisions

Pure departments are generally found in larger colleges and universities. In smaller institutions where the number of faculty in any one discipline is small, for economic and administrative efficiency, faculty from several disciplines may be blended into one mixed department or division. Mixed departments may also reflect the growing movement toward interdisciplinary teaching and research in higher education. Divisional structure is found in some small to mid-sized liberal arts colleges, and it is common in community colleges (Hecht et al., 1999). Large divisions may be subdivided into departments, with the department chair reporting to the division director or dean.

Bureaucratic Versus Autonomous

Bureaucratic departments are those in which the lines of authority are clear, formal, and hierarchical. Administrative rules and regulations control most processes, and "standard operating procedures" are followed. Paper trails documenting departmental actions are common. Bureaucratic departments contrast with the more informal, less structured, more autonomous departments where faculty members have more flexibility and control over their own professional activities. Fewer administrative rules and regulations limit or control faculty activities. A new faculty member should look to see how the internal structure of a department affects the social interactions and research collaboration of faculty members. Are these patterns consistent with how you would like to work with your new faculty colleagues?

Mature Versus Immature Departments

Tucker (1981) defined a mature academic department as one in which faculty members have the experience and capacity to work together as a group, they set high but achievable goals, and they reach decisions as a group and readily accept responsibility for their decisions and assignments. Some departments may be more mature than others, but departments can also be more mature in some situations than in others. In contrast, an immature department has difficulty reaching consensus or in developing and implementing action plans, and its members are unable or unwilling to work together effectively. Young departments, those that have been in existence for fewer than 15 years, are by definition immature because it takes time and effort to learn to work together. Age, however, does not guarantee maturity.

USEFULNESS AND LIMITATIONS OF DEPARTMENTS AS UNITS

Because departments develop as administrative units generally based on the number of faculty and students that can be managed within the culture of the institution, they invite different sorts of problems according to size. In smaller schools with mixed departments, faculty may have few colleagues in their specific field or even in their discipline with whom to share their academic interests. In larger departments where faculty usually have at least one or two colleagues within their specialty area, faculty in different programs may vie for resources and splinter into competing factions, which reduces collaboration and collegiality across program lines. Of course size is not the sole determinant of harmony, and many larger departments operate without such congeniality problems. It is important, however, for new faculty members to identify potential problems and to recognize any undercurrents that threaten the agreeable climate they anticipated finding when they joined the department (Bensimon, Ward, & Sanders, 2000).

FACULTY CULTURE/CLIMATE OF THE DEPARTMENT

Independent of size, there are various aspects of a department's climate that may influence how a faculty member ultimately feels about being a member of the department. Departments differ in their academic, social, and administrative climate, as well as in the resources available and the expectations of faculty.

Academic Climate

Perhaps one of the most important reasons a new faculty member chooses to join a department is the intellectual, academic climate he or she perceives. From job interviews, visits in the department, and knowledge of faculty and student work and reputations, a new faculty member can often informally determine the work ethic of the department, the quality of the programs offered, the competitiveness of the students, and other indications of the level or quality of the intellectual work being done. However, most telling, and often overlooked, is the content of informal hallway gatherings, chitchat by the coffee pot, and cocktail party discussions. Are those conversations about an article in the latest *Current Directions* or *Psychological Review*, about a student struggling to graduate, about last night's basketball game, or all of those? Listening to such small talk can reveal a great deal about the faculty with whom one works: what they value, how they do their jobs, how they get along.

In some departments, faculty members have heated discussions over intellectual issues, never coming to consensus but later laughing and joking about their differences. In other departments, such discussions would lead to all-out war, so they are carefully avoided. Still, in other departments, such discussions just do not take place, and casual conversations center around family, nonacademic concerns, and personal issues. It is important for a new faculty member to "look before you talk." The intellectual climate in a department can often set the tone for the evaluations and expectations of faculty as well as the nature of the social interactions between faculty members.

Indeed, an important aspect of the academic climate concerns faculty attitudes toward collaboration and interdisciplinary work. In some departments, working alone on research is assumed to indicate intellectual independence—you can stand on your own two feet as a researcher. However, in other departments, collaboration is the norm. Collaboration is a way to increase scholarly productivity, and research has shown that faculty who collaborate publish more that those who do not (Whicker, Kronenfeld, & Strickland, 1993). However, one should pick collaborators carefully! Everyone can recall group projects that failed miserably or were unpleasant when there was a weak member of the team. If collaboration is your style and it fits the department norms, are there particular faculty members with whom you would like to work? How could you go about getting these collaborations started? Successful collaborations grow out of contacts with colleagues who share similar interests, who have work styles that fit together well but are not necessarily the same, and who respect and value the relationship. Usually, these sorts of relationships do not just happen—they must be carefully cultivated and nurtured.

In some departments, faculty members collaborate with colleagues from other disciplines or from other programs within the department, and this work, whether research or teaching, is valued by the faculty within the department. This sort of across the lines collaboration may be particularly worthwhile for faculty in small schools in which there are only one or two other psychologists who may represent different specialty areas of the discipline. In larger departments with several programs, collaboration between faculty members in different specialty areas can lead to interesting new projects or courses. There are, however, some departments that take a purist view of research and teaching, and faculty place higher value on research falling narrowly within their own discipline or chosen specialty while discounting interdisciplinary work as lower quality or simply as a distraction.

Collaborating with colleagues at other institutions who are from the same specialty area or who share an interest in a research domain can often provide the new faculty member with a useful support network. Many clinical faculty in academic departments maintain a private practice outside the academic domain that provides them with continuing contact with clients as well as with colleagues with whom they can share practice experiences and problems. For faculty at smaller institutions, an outside group can reduce the local isolation by serving as an invisible college of colleagues who meet or correspond regularly and who share an interest in a common problem or research area (Weber, 1989). Making connections with colleagues from other institutions at professional meetings is an easy, useful way to expand the collaborative network. Getting to know colleagues face-to-face gives a reality to research discussions that phone calls and e-mail simply cannot provide.

Another aspect of collaboration involves working with undergraduate and graduate students in joint research projects. In smaller schools, not only are faculty usually expected to engage students in the classroom but they also are expected to supervise them as research assistants, direct their honors and independent studies, as well as advise majors and student organizations. In larger institutions, graduate students usually receive the lion's share of a faculty member's supervision time, and they may even assist in the supervision of undergraduate research projects and advising. In some larger departments, student contact beyond the bare minimum, particularly with undergraduates, may be considered a distraction from the important aspects of the faculty job—conducting research, publishing, and competing successfully for grant dollars. In other departments, however, both undergraduate and graduate students are valued and treated as junior colleagues, and faculty make themselves available to students outside the classroom.

Sometimes, faculty attitudes toward students are indicative of the quality of the students—that is, how intelligent and motivated they are. It is certainly more gratifying to serve as a mentor for a bright, eager student than for one who is less capable and requires constant prompting and supervision. The academic quality and reputation of a program are jointly determined by faculty and students in the program; both are essential parts of the puzzle.

Many of the previously discussed aspects of the academic climate contribute to departmental expectations regarding the faculty member's role, workload, desired work ethic, and other contributions to the work of the department. For example, some departments equally value faculty efforts in teaching and research, and others consider teaching to be a necessary evil, particularly at the undergraduate level.

Yet the love of teaching is one reason some psychologists seek out smaller institutions with close faculty–student relationships and heavy teaching loads (three or more courses per semester). For these faculty members, time spent in class and with students is time taken away from research. Hence, many find it difficult to initiate or maintain an ongoing research program even though scholarship is now becoming a requirement for tenure at most institutions.

No matter how high the departmental expectations are, a new faculty member should develop work habits that foster scholarly work. Time for writing should be scheduled with the same seriousness as scheduling office hours or class preparation. Do not put it off. Write regularly and set small, obtainable goals (e.g., remember how daunting the dissertation in toto seemed!). Discuss your research with colleagues, ask them to read drafts and provide feedback. Because scholarship has become a central expectation at most institutions, a new faculty member simply must make scholarship an integral part of faculty life. If so, when tenure time rolls around, there will be no surprises and you will be proud of your scholarly track record.

In some institutions research is narrowly defined as publication in refereed journals, and there are quantitative expectations for tenure (e.g., two peer-reviewed publications per year). However, in other institutions, mere evidence of scholarly activity is acceptable, and institutional research is considered appropriate scholarship. No matter what the expectation is for scholarship, a creative faculty member can often find opportunities for research projects (e.g., class projects) or collaborations (e.g., colleagues with equipment who lack student assistants) that are consistent with their academic environment. Indeed, faculty members who have access to few research resources (e.g., lab space, equipment, research assistants) can sometimes maintain their scholarly contributions to the field through writing theoretical papers, literature reviews, and textbooks. Often these sorts of papers and books grow out of an advanced class or focused seminar developed to explore a topic in greater depth than is possible in a general survey course. Many successful textbooks have been pretested in draft form with student classes.

Social Climate

After academic climate, the social climate of a department is probably the other most important reason that a new faculty member chooses to join an academic department. It is hard to believe that anyone would want to go to work each day in a department in which faculty members ignore each other when passing in the hallways; compete continuously for resources; argue openly during department meetings; pose hostile, sarcastic questions to students and visiting speakers; always work with their office doors closed; and constantly place students in the middle of warring faculty factions. This sort of war-zone department does in fact exist, and certainly it is detrimental to those who work there. Most departments, however, do not offer such a hostile environment. Most are collegial and supportive in spite of philosophical or other differences between the faculty.

In many departments, faculty have close personal relationships that extend beyond the office. Often faculty with similar personal circumstances (e.g., single, married without children, married with young children) will socialize outside of work, sharing child care arrangements, sitting together at sporting events, or having a beer after work on a Friday night. In contrast to such socially close departments, faculty in other departments may be cordial but more reserved and choose not to socialize with work colleagues outside the office. Relationships at work are more formal and distant. Although on the surface the socially close departments sound more inviting, having such closely intertwined professional and personal lives can sometimes lead to unanticipated problems.

In most departments, both large and small, in addition to the formal organizational structure of the department chair or head, perhaps an associate or vice chair, and chairs of various important committees (e.g., faculty evaluation, development, promotion and tenure, curriculum, space, graduate admissions), there also exists an informal hierarchy that is important to recognize. Status may be based on seniority, amount of grant dollars, size of research laboratory, reputation with the administration, or other less obvious faculty differences. In general, having higher informal status leads to a larger portion of the resources, more influence on departmental decisions (e.g., sometimes even tenure and promotion), more desirable teaching schedules, and other perks. If the majority of the faculty are tenured, middle-aged, and perhaps looking toward retirement, the milieu of the department may be very different than if the majority are young, nontenured faculty who are worried about making tenure. For a young, new faculty member, the latter department may be more comfortable at first, but the possibility for cross-age friendships and informal mentoring may be more likely in the former. In any case, do not let age be deceiving—many young faculty members find that the "oldest guy/girl" in a department turns out to be the person with whom they share the most intellectually and personally.

Although the figures have improved considerably over the past few decades, both minorities and women are underrepresented in the halls of higher learning (Rheingold, 1994). Despite national efforts (e.g., AAUP Committee on the Status of Minorities in the Profession, APA Office of Ethnic Minority Affairs), the number of minority graduate students and faculty in psychology remains small. In some departments, combining motherhood and work amid a whirl of sometimes-conflicting demands can be quite challenging—but not impossible. Married women with children do publish as much as their single female colleagues (Cole & Luckerman, 1987), but family and work are more likely to pull women in different directions, which is not so for men (Rose, 1983). (See chapter 16, this volume.) Even if a young faculty member is female or minority (or both), being an "only" in a department may not be so bad. If the climate of the department is supportive and there are mentors and perhaps additional resources (e.g., special minority programs, maternity leave, institutional childcare), the unique contributions a minority or female faculty member can make could be substantial and appreciated. (See also chapter 15, this volume.)

One aspect of the social environment that should not be overlooked is the nature of the physical situation of the department. Is the department in an old, dark, overcrowded building with broom-closet offices with no windows, or is it in a new, airy, state-of-the-art, high-tech facility? Is it spread across several building at the far reaches of the campus, or is it crowded into a dreary basement of a building shared with other departments? Is there space for labs as well as offices? Do the graduate students have space to congregate and study? Is there a faculty lounge or other area for informal gatherings, such as a cup of coffee, a lunch break, or an after-colloquium reception? In spite of our best intentions to overlook the "ugly" in our physical environment, it does influence the way we feel about going to work each day. Indeed, social psychologists told us back in the 1970s (Schopler & Stockdale, 1977) that the structure of the physical environment also affects the nature of our social interactions. In "Holiday Inn style" rows of offices, faculty tend to pass each other while headed to other destinations rather than stopping in the hallway to chat. Office suites, hallway chalkboards, lounges with comfortable seating, and coffee pots tend to encourage informal interaction. If department members value social relationships but are not blessed with desirable physical space, they will often create spaces to invite more collegial interactions.

Among the important social relationships to sort out in a department is how faculty members relate to students. In some departments, the status differences between faculty and student are almost rigidly enforced (e.g., students are not on faculty committees), and students and faculty do not interact socially outside the confines of the classroom or lab (e.g., no happy hours together on Friday afternoons). In other departments, students, particularly graduate students, are viewed as faculty in training and are given positions of responsibility (e.g., voting membership on admissions committees, interviewing job candidates) and are included in most social events (e.g., holiday parties, potluck dinners, meals with visiting speakers).

Although these sorts of departments are easier to relate to for a new faculty member fresh out of graduate school or a postdoc, there is a hidden nemesis. In such open, amiable departments, it is not as easy for a young, new faculty member to shed the grad student identity and behavior and to assume the mantle of a bona fide faculty member. Although new faculty members are often closer in age to the students in a department, particularly the graduate students, they must assume the identity and attitudes of the faculty or eventually risk losing the respect of both colleagues and students. Indeed, young faculty members whose relationships with students appear to be too close or friendly often become suspected of immature behavior or sexual harassment (see chapter 6, this volume, for additional discussion of these issues). It is not worth worrying about the truth of the gossip about your relationships with students—it is simply best to avoid even the *appearance* of impropriety.

Administrative Climate

Often, the administrative climate is one of the least important aspects of a department that a new faculty member considers when accepting a job, perhaps because it is often the least obvious. However, the formality and professionalism of the administrative structure usually affect many aspects of the academic and social climate of the department.

In more structured departments, faculty must go through the appropriate channels when requesting resources, when deviating from department policies (e.g., changing course deadlines), or when carrying out various faculty activities. In these sorts of departments, there are generally clearly written policy statements, as clarification or addition to institutional policies, that cover most usual operating procedures (e.g., recruiting, faculty evaluation, criteria for promotion and tenure), and these are closely followed. Rules and procedures may be monitored by the chair or by various departmental committees.

In less structured, more informal departments, the policy statements that do exist are more casual and are loosely followed. Enforcement of the rules and policies is not of much concern, and most individual faculty members operate somewhat independently. In these sorts of departments the procedures are more laissez-faire, and the chair and committees are flexible in organizing departmental tasks.

The effectiveness of a department chair's leadership style varies according to type of department (e.g., maturity, composition) and the issues the department is facing. Tucker (1981) suggested that chairs' styles differ along two dimensions: how directive (e.g., authoritarian to democratic) they are and how supportive (personal and psychological) they are. Membership on departmental committees may be by election or appointment, with committees serving three functions: developing policies, performing administrative activities, and providing technical advice (Tucker, 1981). Most committees operate as advisory to the chair or to the department, but some may be perceived as having decision-making responsibility (e.g., graduate admissions). Both the chair and various committee members can play important roles in a new faculty member's activities and job satisfaction.

An additional aspect of the administrative climate of a department concerns external relationships, those with the institutional administration and with other departments. In highly structured institutions, administrators and staff in offices outside the department may be territorial, and can often throw roadblocks into faculty activities. Paper trails required for even the most mundane of activities (e.g., registering one's automobile, sending an overnight package, getting a travel reimbursement) may be long, full of red tape, and quite exhausting. When navigating such shark-infested waters, it is often best to ask the advice and help of an experienced hand (e.g., a faculty mentor, a well-connected administrative assistant) to guide you through. Many bureaucratic walls have crumbled when a well-connected administrative assistant paves the way with lunch buddies or mailroom friends. Moreover, most administrators have preferred ways of communicating and working with faculty (e.g., short e-mails, phone messages through administrative assistants, no surprises). A faculty mentor experienced in the ways of the administration can sometimes suggest ways to "package" a request to improve its chance of success. In dealings with administrators or staff members, a new faculty member should be careful not to build a reputation of being a pain to work with.

Resources Available

The amount of money a department has is never sufficient to support every desired activity. However, the general wealth of a department and its access to institutional resources can have an important impact on the climate of the department. Resources available for professional development (e.g., travel, student assistants) can have a profound impact on one's research productivity and professional reputation and growth. If ample funds are available, young faculty members, who generally have limited personal resources, can readily attend professional meetings, copy research materials, hire student assistants, and expand their research program goals. Unfortunately, in most departments not all of these activities are possible for all faculty members, and choices must be made.

In making choices, and in planning and monitoring departmental budgets, chairs generally dislike two things: surprises and hen pecking. Given the usual resource limits of departments, it is never a good idea to spring an unexpected expense on the chair. Too many surprises can make a chair gun-shy of asking how things are going. Similarly, stopping the chair in the hallway 20 times a semester with budget requests or soliciting at every social event wears quite thin. Most chairs prefer for faculty members to provide them with a reasonable accounting of their needs for the coming year so that resources can be managed fairly and efficiently (see chapter 13, this volume, for additional discussion of these issues). Squeaky-wheel behavior does not endear one to the chair, colleagues, or administrators.

In larger, research-oriented departments, faculty with external funding from research grants pay for many of their own research support activities, whereas those without funding must depend on the often scarce departmental or institutional financial resources. In some departments, over time the climate has evolved into the haves and have-nots, with great pressure on new faculty to gain external funding. In these institutions, there is usually support staff, perhaps in an office of sponsored programs, who can assist in grant-writing activities and can be invaluable in the process. In departments where grant writing is not highly valued, faculty members must live within the available means. It is important for a new faculty member to understand the availability of resources and departmental expectations regarding generating and accessing them.

Not only are research resources important to consider but also resources aimed toward teaching. The availability of teaching assistants, teaching resource centers, and teaching mentoring programs are among the many resources that can help a new faculty member succeed in the classroom. Good teachers are not born; they develop through conscious effort and experience (Dunn & Zaremba, 1997). With sufficient teaching support resources in an institution, new faculty members who want to become good teachers can work to refine their craft and their courses.

Expectations of Faculty

Both by formal channels (e.g., written departmental policies) and informal channels, new faculty members can determine the actual emphasis an institution and department place on teaching, research, and service (O'Meara, 2000). Even in research universities, formal policies usually emphasize both teaching and research, but the informal message is that research is all-important. In smaller institutions, teaching constitutes the primary faculty activity, although most schools now consider scholarship to be an essential part of the faculty role. Service is the third, and usually the smallest piece, of faculty work. However, service often has considerable significance in smaller institutions where faculty may be expected to play important roles both on campus (e.g., serve on committees, recruit potential students, advise student organizations) and within the larger community (e.g., speak at civic club meetings, serve on boards of social organizations).

One of the best ways to learn the ropes regarding faculty expectations is to find a faculty mentor who can explain both the written and unwritten rules and attitudes of the department and institution but be circumspect in the choice of mentors. Although there is usually some formal mentoring available (e.g., teaching centers, peer mentors) to help with the usual teaching and research questions that arise, many valuable lessons can be derived from more informal learning opportunities. Often the unwritten rules are more powerful than the written ones (e.g., be friendly with students, but not friends; being unknown in a small liberal arts college can hurt at tenure time). Indeed, the most critical expectations for promotion and tenure may be the unwritten ones (e.g., only publications in top-tier journals are considered; good departmental and institutional citizenship is crucial; too much time with students may decrease research productivity).

As with choosing research collaborators, be prudent in choosing an informal mentor to guide you through both the charted and uncharted waters of a department and the institution. Is there a departmental sage? What faculty member has the respect of other faculty, administrators? Who seems to get things done without ruffling too many feathers? Who can you ask for advice without feeling naive or stupid? To survive and flourish, a new faculty member should know the values that shape the department and the institution, but where academic freedom is respected, it may not be necessary to share those values.

CONCLUSION

A love for teaching, research, and the diversity of tasks involved in each are the reasons that many psychologists seek careers in academia. One important lesson to keep in mind in a new faculty position is to find a healthy balance among the many enticing activities that such a position offers. Thoughtful planning and organization are necessary to meet one's own expectations and those of department colleagues who may be crucial throughout the course of one's career. By carefully learning the lay of the land, one can navigate a successful course to a rewarding life in academia.

REFERENCES

Baldridge, J. V., Curtis, D. V., Ecker, G., & Riley, G. L. (1978). *Policy making and effective leadership*. San Francisco: Jossey-Bass.

Bensimon, E. M., Ward, K., & Sanders, K. (2000). *The department chair's role in developing new faculty into teachers and scholars*. Bolton, MA: Anker.

Cole, J. R., & Luckerman, H. (1987). Marriage, motherhood and research performance in science. *Scientific American, 256*, 119–125.

Dunn, D. S., & Zaremba, S. B. (1997). Thriving at liberal arts colleges: The more *Compleat Academic*. *Teaching of Psychology, 24*, 8–14.

Hecht, I. W. D., Higgerson, M. L., Gmelch, W. H., & Tucker, A. (1999). *The department chair as academic leader*. Phoenix, AZ: American Council on Education/Oryx Press.

O'Meara, K. (2000). Climbing the academic ladder: Promotion in rank. In C. A. Trower (Ed.), *Policies on faculty appointment: Standard practices and unusual arrangements* (pp. 141–179). Bolton, MA: Anker.

Rheingold, H. L. (1994). *The psychologist's guide to an academic career*. Washington, DC: American Psychological Association.

Rose, P. (1983). *Parallel lives*. New York: Knopf.

Schopler, J., & Stockdale, J. E. (1977). An interference analysis of crowding. *Environmental Psychology and Nonverbal Behavior, 1*, 81–88.

Singer, J. E. (1990). Program quality and program location: Two separate issues. In L. Bickman & H. Ellis (Eds.), *Preparing psychologists for the 21st century: Proceedings of the National Conference on Graduate Education in Psychology*. Hillsdale, NJ: Erlbaum.

Tucker, A. (1981). *Chairing the academic department: Leadership among peers*. Washington, DC: American Council on Education.

Weber, A. L. (1989). Teachers who research versus researchers who teach. In M. R. Leary (Ed.), *The state of social psychology: Issues, themes, and controversies* (pp. 111–118). Newbury Park, CA: Sage.

Whicker, M. L., Kronenfeld, J. J., & Strickland, R. A. (1993). *Getting tenure*. Newbury Park, CA: Sage.

VI

KEEPING YOUR EDGE: MANAGING YOUR CAREER OVER TIME

19

THE ACADEMIC MARATHON: CONTROLLING ONE'S CAREER

SHELLEY E. TAYLOR AND JOANNE MARTIN

As faculty at any institution can attest, academic careers can be stressful. When we were younger, we thought that many problems would disappear once we had attained a certain level of accomplishment. To our regret, we found out that was not the case. The problems simply change their form and urgency.

We have organized this chapter into three phases that roughly correspond to a marathon: getting started, hitting your stride, and hitting the wall (or the rest of your career). This may seem like a euphemistic paraphrase of "life's a bitch, then you die," and so to counteract this impression, we want to say at the outset: You went into this career for a reason. It is endlessly fascinating and challenging. Like anything important in life, however, it needs to be actively managed. In each of these sections, we will address readers as if they were at that stage; for those of you who are full professors, prepare to relive it all, starting with those glorious, nerve-wracking years when you were an assistant professor.

GETTING STARTED

As a graduate student, you may have looked forward to the years when you would have the freedom to choose your own direction, set your own agenda, and embark on your day-to-day activities with no tests, papers, or other evaluations hanging over your head. Those days, you thought, would come when you became a professor.

As a graduate student, you may be shocked to learn that being a graduate student is easy compared to being a professor. Within a month of entering your new role, you will have double, perhaps triple, the number of the demands that you had when you were a student. You have to cope with all these demands, maintain your sanity, and, during the next six or seven years, do enough fine research to earn yourself tenure at a place you would enjoy working.

Given the difficulty of these tasks, it is dismaying to realize how little most new professors know about the realities of the job. Most students leave graduate school with carefully developed research skills and some teaching experience. Most, however, have virtually no idea of the powerful stresses and conflicting demands that are inherent in being a professor.

You are probably living in a new place, where you know almost no one. If your spouse or partner has moved with you, he or she may be coping with unemployment, a less-than-satisfactory job, or, at best, a new and challenging position. If your spouse or partner has not moved with you, the problems of adjustment may be even harder to deal with. If you have no partner, you may be trying to establish a social life.

On top of all this personal strain, this period that you had anticipated with such delight is not going as smoothly as you expected. Instead of planning an exciting program of research or writing brilliant papers, you are swamped with teaching, committee work, and tasks that have little to do with research. You are working harder and longer, you leave work at night with vast numbers of seemingly crucial tasks undone. Another month has gone by and you still have not gotten any research started. With all these problems, it is no wonder that the first years are difficult to handle. The immediate environment can be extremely intimidating. Everyone else seems established. They know each other and have inside jokes. They have well-functioning labs, they have their own theories, they have written books, graduate students have stories about them, and they seem absolutely certain of how everything should be done. The new assistant professor may wonder whether he or she will ever be like these others. The answer is yes, with time, a lot of work, and a sense of priorities.

Managing Your Teaching Load

The time that goes into designing and teaching a course is enormous. If the course is new, the time demands are even greater. Most new assistant professors have to develop one, two, or even more new courses simultaneously. Even those presented with an existing curriculum can rarely resist the temptation to redesign it. Often much of the course material is outside one's areas of expertise. Most of the time before classes start has been spent finishing a thesis rather than preparing lectures and reading lists. To the extent that preclass preparation has been done, it often has to be redone as you learn how little students can learn in an hour or read in a week. Getting your courses in order and teaching them will occupy more of your time than you ever dreamed.

It takes a while to ease into the teaching role. Even if you taught as a graduate student, you will be nervous the first day. Every assistant professor who has faced a hall full of undergraduates taking a required course knows fear. Even the most skilled lecturers battle anxiety about teaching. Being nervous is nothing to be ashamed of; it will fade with time.

No matter how good a job you do in learning to prepare your courses, you may be fighting an uphill battle if you have too many courses to teach. Heavy teaching loads are an inescapable fact of life, but do not assume this without testing it. Your course load may be more negotiable than you think. Most universities give first-year faculty lighter loads (e.g., three courses instead of four), and you should explore if this option is available for you. Find out what is the norm for your department. If everyone else teaches four courses, there is no reason you should teach five.

Your teaching schedule should have trade-offs. If you have agreed to teach a heavy lecture course, you should not have to teach two. If you have taught a service course for three years, it might be time for someone else to pick it up. Discuss these issues with your department chair. The important thing is to make your teaching more enjoyable and negotiate a teaching load that fits with your interests yet helps the department meet its priorities.

Explore the possibilities of guest lecturers. Why should you spend days learning a new topic when the country's expert is down the hall or visiting for a few days? Punctuating a course with an occasional guest can be useful for you and the students. Eventually you will be expected to reciprocate with guest lectures of your own.

You can ease your load by involving graduate teaching assistants (TAs) in the course. They can assume grading responsibilities and should be expected to give an occasional lecture, especially if it is on a topic they know well. It is good experience for the graduate student, especially if you give feedback afterward.

Finally, after developing a course, plan to teach it for several years. All the front-end work pays off if you have good lecture notes to work from. You will want to update your notes each time you teach the course, but solid preparation when you first develop it will save valuable time.

Administrative Work

As a graduate student, you may have heard vague grumblings among the faculty about time-consuming administrative duties, such as committee work. Administrative work can take up every minute of your life that is not already consumed by designing and teaching courses.

No one ever got promoted because of committee work. This is important to understand because administrative work has a certain attraction. There is considerable responsibility and power involved with some of these tasks—for example, admissions. You can quickly feel like a real faculty member. Administrative work is highly visible, often appreciated, usually easy, and therefore unthreatening. If you are nervous about getting a research program started or writing up the results of a study, you can always use committee work as your justification for procrastination.

Although doing too much committee work is not a good idea, you should do your fair share. If you do not, you will be resented. The key is to find out what the norms are. Ask other faculty members how many committees they are on and how much time each one takes. Some faculty serve on large numbers of committees that meet only once a year. Some committees consume unbelievable amounts of time (e.g., admissions, faculty search), a fact that official descriptions may downplay.

Your administrative workload is negotiable. An individual who does a lot of committee work at the department level should not have to serve on large numbers of university committees. If you feel you are overburdened, it is possible that people who have requested your services are unaware of how much other administrative work you are doing. Sometimes problems can be alleviated or prevented by having a word with your department chair about your university obligations or by discussing your departmental obligations with the university official in charge of committee assignments.

Learn which committees or responsibilities are important and which are not. Faculty hiring is important. Graduate admissions is important. There are committees that are entirely unimportant. One of the authors sat on a library committee, with time-consuming meetings focusing on such issues as layout of rooms and numbers of study carrels. The architect was developing a plan for the library without input from the committee. If you cannot escape assignment to the equivalent of a library committee, remember that what is not worth doing is not worth doing well.

Research: You Remember Research?

Now you may be feeling like Katherine Anne Porter, who looked back on her years as a novelist and observed, "I think I've spent about ten percent of my energies on writing. The other ninety percent went to keeping my

366   *TAYLOR AND MARTIN*

head above water." Given the immediate imperatives of course work and administrative tasks, it is hard to remember that at most universities research is a top—if not *the* top—priority.

Given the harsh realities of your new job, allocate your limited research time carefully. A top priority is rewriting your thesis for publication. Your thesis committee should have given you a feel for whether the study is ultimately publishable. If it is, rewrite it and submit it, while it is still fresh in your mind. It will give you a sense of accomplishment and a solid empirical contribution to launch your career.

Consider submitting a paper for presentation at a professional meeting. Active involvement in these meetings is an excellent way to meet colleagues from other parts of the country. Perhaps you can slice off a piece of your thesis or present some preliminary data. The rule for writing these proposals is KISS (Keep It Simple, Stupid). Make only a few key points. Do not attempt to present complicated theoretical ideas or four-way interactions. Given the page limitations of the proposals, the time and space limitations of symposium and poster sessions, you will not be able to communicate complexities effectively. If you include complexities in a proposal, the reviewers will probably turn it down. Avoid the problem by writing a cogent, pared-down proposal.

Try to get some new research going this first year. Starting research requires the resolution of two issues: You have to decide what to study and how to pay for it. Here are some hints.

You do not have to continue working on your thesis topic. You can be fairly sure your department approves of work in your thesis area, because they did hire you. It is probably also true that you feel confident of your expertise in this domain. However, you may be bored by now with your dissertation topic. If your heart is not in it, do not do it. One of the most important benefits of being a professor is that you have the freedom to choose what problems you work on. In deciding what research to do, develop tests of, or tests of variants of, other people's ideas. This is relatively easy to do, often publishable, and gives you exposure. However, eventually you should test your own ideas. Be careful not to be too grandiose. Fledgling researchers are tempted by highly abstract, multivariate theories that supposedly encompass much of the previous research in the field. Such theories seldom live up to their promise, and the stars of the field will not be overjoyed to learn that everything they have thought of during the past 20 years can be subsumed by your theory. Instead, develop mid-range theoretical ideas that can be tested with convincing, sound, and interesting studies that build cumulatively on each other.

Before sending your manuscripts out for review, you should get feedback on them. Early on, your papers are likely to be too long, too detailed, and not clearly written. Your senior colleagues will almost certainly be willing to provide this feedback. Accept their offers or solicit their advice. You can cultivate a couple colleagues elsewhere, perhaps friends from graduate student days, your former advisor, or people in your research area with whom you have developed a working relationship. The reason these latter people will be willing to provide this service for you is because they expect you to provide it in return. Although time-consuming, it will be worth it. Often an exciting piece of research is rejected from a journal solely on the basis of how it is presented. (See chapter 10, this volume, for tips on writing an empirical journal article.) Once you have received a rejection, there may be no way of resubmitting to the same journal, even though you know that many of the flaws will be correctable. Revise and resubmit is an open door. Out-and-out rejection usually is not. Be sure you spend the time getting a manuscript in good shape before you submit it. Pick your papers carefully: There is no such thing as a quick and easy publication. Everything takes time, and time spent on one thing might be better spent on something else.

You are going to need research funds. If you have been fortunate, your institution has given you start-up funds. If not, they may be willing to do so. Many universities have faculty grants or access to specially funded programs that make small amounts of money available to faculty who fill out a brief application. This is an easy way to get started. If your institution does not offer sufficient funds to mount a longer term research program, you should, as soon as you can, write a grant proposal. This is a special skill. Take the guidelines seriously. Be sure you have someone at your institution who has received funds recently read your proposal draft. To write an article based on your thesis, submit a paper to a professional meeting, plan one study, and prepare a funding proposal—these may seem to be a modest set of research goals. If you can manage more, fine. But before you tackle other projects, be sure you have finished these four tasks. Few get that far in the first year. Besides, you need to save some time for other parts of your new life.

Reading: Staying on Top of the Field

A psychologist once said, "You can be a reader or a writer, but not both." He changed from being a reader to being a writer and shortly thereafter became more famous. The volume of research that is generated in the field is enough to keep one, maybe two or three, individuals reading full-time.

Reading the *Journal of Personality and Social Psychology* (JPSP) cover to cover is not a good use of your time. Focus on articles germane to your classes and research interests. Do not restrict your reading to published work. By the time a paper actually appears in print, its author is at least a year or two away from it and into other studies. Early in your career, write to the 8 or 10 most influential people in your area of interest, and ask for preprints of their most recent work. If someone writes a paper in your area that you think is impressive, ask to be put on his or her mailing list, so you will receive his or her prepublication manuscripts. Scan the programs of the professional meetings for exciting ideas and studies, but be selective. The overwhelming majority of meeting presentations may sound interesting but may not be worth your time.

When you read, read for a purpose. Such purposes include planning the introduction to an article or grant, teaching, deciding how to design a study, or conducting a review of the literature. It may help to keep files of papers you want to read, labeled with the task for which they will be relevant. Information is best learned and retained when there is something to hang it on. Otherwise, the information may not stick.

Faculty Colleagues

On a professional level, collegial relationships are both more and less than they are cracked up to be. It is a myth that colleagues gather regularly, or even irregularly, to debate weighty issues with intelligence and wit. On the other hand, colleagues can influence your work substantially, through such channels as casual conversations, coteaching, colloquium presentations, sharing papers, and working with the same doctoral students. Do try to learn from your colleagues. Many are brilliant, thoughtful scholars who have much to offer. If such a person is giving a talk, go! If he or she is giving a seminar on his or her current research, strongly consider sitting in. You may be rewarded with insight, profundity, and even friendship.

Sometimes a colleague will give you a paper to critique. Be flattered, but circumspect. Doing a lengthy critique for a colleague may help him or her and make you look smart. But perhaps the colleague did not want criticism—perhaps he or she wanted your flattery or gratitude. Try to discern the colleague's goal and temper your feedback with this knowledge.

Your colleagues will, in turn, give you feedback on your work. Do not accept all the feedback you get from colleagues uncritically. It is tempting to pitch your work to your colleagues, abandoning ideas met with skepticism and following up suggestions that are tangential to your interests. After all, your colleagues will be determining whether you will retain your present position. Ultimately, your stature in the field depends on a wider audience.

Junior faculty often have to decide whether to accept a senior colleague's offer of collaboration. There are obvious benefits to such collaboration. It is flattering to be asked and your work might well be enriched. There are risks as well. The results of your joint endeavors are likely to be credited to your senior colleague, even if the ideas are clearly yours. Even if the behavior of your senior colleague is exemplary, others in the field may fail to give you credit, recognition, and, ultimately, tenure for the work. Once you have established your reputation as a scientist, collaboration with colleagues, even eminent senior colleagues, is perfectly all right—even highly desirable. However, too much collaboration with senior people, too early in your career, places you at some risk.

Assistant professors often have the impression that their progress is being monitored on a daily basis by their colleagues. This is certainly not true. They may well be leaving you alone to give you a chance to get settled. No matter how fascinating you are, rest assured that you are not a major focus of their attention. Do not be paranoid.

Remember, though, that one of the reasons your colleagues hired you was that they felt you would be someone they would enjoy and get along well with. Do not prove them wrong. Be sure you take the time to have fun with your colleagues. Have lunch, go for drinks, accept and return invitations to dinner, or attend informal departmental gatherings. University business is conducted in these settings, so be there. A department that has a sense of community, marked by genuine camaraderie, is a special but attainable place, so work toward it. Build a life for yourself in your department. Get at least one really good friend, preferably more. Enough weird things happen in academic life that it is really good to be able to talk issues through with someone who cares about you. And you need to be able to do the same for others.

Early on, you should realize that there is a phenomenon called department and university politics. The collective history of everything that happened before you got there stays around in various formal and informal ways. Personality conflicts may be played out over seemingly objective issues like space allocation or faculty slots.

The main thing to be said about department politics is: Do not take strong stands on issues you do not understand immediately after arriving at the university. Keep your ear to the ground, listen carefully, ask questions, and figure out as much of the politics as you can. You do not want to offend people inadvertently. You may choose to offend them at some later point, when you understand the dimensions of the issue.

The Biggest Pitfall

The new assistant professor may be his or her own worst enemy. Temper the eager-beaver enthusiasm a little. You do not have to say yes to everything.

The best thing about the stressful first years is that eventually, they end. You lose your obsession with course work and committees. Panic at the amount of work you have to do begins to subside. You begin to feel competent and to remember all those reasons why you wanted to become a professor in the first place.

HITTING YOUR STRIDE

Hitting your stride in an academic career is primarily a matter of settling on a research strategy and learning to manage your limited time efficiently. Research strategy provides the foundation for your other activities.

Research Priorities: Or What Not to Publish

During the first few years, you need to move away from the work you did with your mentor and find your own voice. It is best to try to publish several pieces in one coherent area. Steadily broaden your perspective until you have insights of your own for which you can provide empirical evidence.

At middle age, some researchers are still churning out interesting journal articles that are unrelated to each other. Although there are rewards for this type of research in the first years of your career, those rewards eventually disappear. If you continue with this pattern of publications, you will get a reputation for being atheoretical. To prepare for tenure, you need to carve out a piece of the field as your own. So two or three years into your assistant professorship, you should be refining your own theoretical ideas and formally testing them through a series of interrelated studies.

Having chosen a theoretical area of concentration, select your publication priorities carefully. Focus on top-quality empirical publications in leading journals. You will be judged primarily by the quality of the research you do, and by empirical publications in particular. The payoffs from publications in secondary journals are much lower, but they may be worthwhile if you are committed to having a certain paper see the light of day or if your coauthors are students, for whom such a publication could be helpful.

Also, try to make a strong theoretical contribution to your piece of the field. The premier publication outlets for this kind of work are *Psychological Review* and *Psychological Science*. Such a publication typically includes data, as well as some careful and innovative thinking about a problem, thus testifying to your strengths as both a researcher and a theoretician. To publish an article in *Psychological Bulletin* is also good. Such a publication does not involve data collection, and the theoretical content is more likely a novel perspective on an established area rather than an innovative theoretical analysis of a problem.

Do not make your reputation as a whiner who complains about or attacks other people's work. That works once, twice tops. People will begin to wonder if you can think for yourself. Study people, not other people's articles. Insight comes from intelligent observation, not the next derivative study of the *JPSP* article you just read.

Book chapters are a mixed blessing. You have considerable freedom to say what you want to say, and editors will often agree to let you approach a topic in an unorthodox way. Book editors, in comparison to journal editors, often have less stringent or narrowly defined standards for accepting manuscripts. Everyone knows this, so they sometimes discount chapters as publications. Avoid doing too many chapters early in your career and pick the few you do with care. A chapter can be useful if you have some good theoretical ideas and no readily available outlet for their development. Select a book put out by a major publisher. The topic should be relatively broad and preferably hot. You will benefit far more from a chapter that reaches a relatively small group of researchers in your field than from exposure to larger numbers of undergraduates or practitioners. If you are going to write a chapter, make sure it is good and published in a good place. *Do not publish* slight variants of the same chapter in two (or more) places. People will notice and be unimpressed.

Edited books, like chapters, are a mixed blessing. You do not get to be a primary force in shaping the ideas in the book, and you may have to do a lot of intellectually undemanding and often unpleasant work (nagging, editing) to get it out. If you include chapters of your own, they may be discounted as publications because, after all, it is your book. And if you do edit a book, make sure it is a good one.

Writing

Learning to write well and to enjoy the process may be one of the most difficult obstacles you face. Writer's block is a tremendous problem for many fledgling and not-so-fledgling academics. Often the problem is not that writing is not getting done, but that no writing is perfect enough to be sent out. Endless revisions can result in a writing style that is crabbed and defensive. It is better to err on the side of sending things out prematurely than to hold on to a draft for months or years until is it out-of-date or stale.

Sometimes the problem is that you are not spending enough time writing. One method of getting going is to write up a study as a convention paper first. These are less threatening, and the feedback received can improve subsequent writing or alert you to the need for a follow-up study before you submit to a journal. Or you can get yourself to tackle a tough paper by thinking, "It's just a rough draft no one will ever see." Regardless of how we trick ourselves into writing, the fact is that we simply must write. Break the paper down into sections. Start on an easy section, such as methods.

It is important to figure out what conditions you need to establish the habit of writing. One of the authors needs long periods of full concentration, and so she schedules full days of writing time. This approach has the advantage of minimizing the amount of time that is lost during startups. The other author prefers to write for two or three hours every day. This method has the advantage of minimizing time lost on those inevitable bad days, when no words come easily. It is hard to discipline yourself to create specified times to write, but gradually writing on a schedule gives you a rhythm and teaches you how to write. It is the single most helpful thing you can do to improve both the quantity and the quality of your writing.

You should allocate a minimum of about 10 hours a week for writing. Treat your scheduled writing time as sacred. Finally, before you quit writing on any given day, outline the first half-hour of the next day's writing to help you get started again.

Dictaphones can help you write more efficiently. Start with short letters, memos, and comments to students on papers. Include punctuation and capitalization as you go. You may gradually work up to sections of papers. It takes at least two to three weeks of regular use to learn how to dictate effectively.

Getting Reviews

Once you learn to write and submit what you have written, you have opened Pandora's box. Inevitably, your work will be reviewed. Steel yourself; reviews can be an unpleasant experience. They are sometimes hostile, irrelevant, or illogical; more often, they are detailed and constructive. Believe the percentages that journals state concerning their high rejection rates, sometimes as high as 85%.

One of your first reactions may be fury. How could the reviewers and editor have missed seeing the brilliance of your work? Decide soon what you want to do next. It is smarter to take advantage of the criticisms you have received. Suggestions for revisions or replications will be well-taken and will foreshadow comments you will get from reviewers elsewhere. There is always the danger you will get the same reviewers, who will not be pleased to see their pearls of wisdom ignored.

If your paper has been rejected with encouragement to resubmit, do so soon. You should address every major criticism raised by the editor and the reviewers. Either modify the coverage in the paper or explain in a cover letter why you chose not to. In your cover letter, highlight briefly not only how but where each of the major problems was addressed. The editor will be extremely grateful, and your manuscript may be processed more quickly.

Do not keep resubmitting a manuscript indefinitely. If one journal has found a fatal flaw in your study, chances are that a reviewer at another journal will do the same. In any case, the payoff for publishing your article in an obscure place is probably not worth the time it would take for you to do another revision. Put the article in a file drawer and go on to something else.

Providing Reviews

Once you begin to publish, you will not only be getting reviews of your work but also be asked to provide them for others. At first, it is difficult to know how to review a manuscript. New reviewers tend to pick at grammar and spelling, ignoring the more important points. To see what kind of information goes into a review, read reviews. Ask your graduate student advisor if he or she would be willing to let you see other reviews, so you can get a sense of how good ones are written.

Once the new reviewer overcomes the problem of what to put in a review, he or she tends to turn nasty. Resist this temptation. Realize that the author has spent a great deal more time thinking about this problem than you have, and may well have thought of your criticism but not have written about it well. Point out the flaw in a way that does not impugn the writer's character. Think of a review as an opportunity for constructive feedback. How could the author improve the work or design a Study Two to remedy the flaws in the first study? View reviewing as an opportunity for anonymous scientific interchange.

As you advance in your career, you will find yourself increasingly asked to provide reviews. A good review takes at least several hours, even after one has a lot of experience,. A useful rule of thumb is not to accept more than two reviews at any given time. If you are providing more than 20 reviews a year, then you are probably reviewing too much.

Self-Promotion

If you have planned your research strategy and gotten out a couple of papers, and you are still waiting to be discovered, do not hold your breath. No one is going to discover you; you have to promote yourself. Your advisors hopefully have brought you to the attention of their colleagues by writing rave letters about you and by introducing you at conferences. Now they have other students they are introducing, and you are left on your own. It is standard operating procedure to promote yourself. So, how do you market your work?

First, if you have a paper you are proud of, send it out. Send it to people whose work is important and relevant to your own. These are the colleagues who are most likely to be interested.

Do what you can to increase the chances that people will read what you send them. Do not send out everything you write. Most people have little time to read. They will be far less interested in a large envelope containing four papers than in one, solid published piece. Accompany the paper with a short personal note explaining how the paper might be of interest to the recipient. Be aware that three quarters of the recipients will toss your beloved paper in the circular file. A few will read it. Send the paper to people in the research area, to people writing books and textbooks that will cover work like yours, and to authors of *Annual Review of Psychology* chapters or their equivalents. These strategies increase the chances that your work will be cited. Self-promotion is uncomfortable, but do it anyway. You have worked hard on those papers, and you want them to be read and appreciated. Others in your cohort will be doing the same thing.

When should you send out a paper? The preprint stage is a good time. A paper is "in press," has been peer-reviewed and revised, and as a consequence its rough edges are gone. Prepublication drafts are okay to send, if you want the feedback. Reprints are important to send; post it on a website and let people know it is there.

Talk about your work. Give brown bag lunches, colloquia, and conference presentations. Think up a symposium topic that would be well-timed and organize a symposium yourself. Invite panelists who are doing well-regarded work in the area. Invite senior scientists in the field to present papers. Famous people sometimes have to be on conference programs to get their expenses paid. Be prepared for the fact that they may want to be chairs or discussants rather than presenters. Simply by calling them you have increased the chances they will remember you and your work.

Give others opportunities to get to know you and to promote themselves by inviting them to give colloquia or brown bag lunches in your department. Invite prominent people who do work in your topic area. They will be flattered by your interest. Your own colleagues may think better of your work by seeing the exemplary work of the best people in your field. You may even be mentioned during the talk!

It may seem discouraging that in academia, a certain amount of self-promotion is done. If you do not participate in these activities, it will not be fatal, but it may impede the development of your career. Getting to know the people in your field and having discussions focused on your ideas can be a great pleasure.

Dealing With the Press

There are two kinds of contacts with the press. The first is when they contact you to comment on an issue. The second is when you contact them because you have an issue you want to get out to the general public. The journalists who work for the top media, major newspapers and magazines, act more like colleagues than reporters. They have typically done their homework; they do not want their time wasted any more than you do, so they ask their questions quickly and usually get it right. These outlets will send you the story or fact-check basic aspects of the information you gave them. The fears we once had that reporters would print our work hopelessly wrong are less valid than they once were.

The same cannot be said for the less visible publications. These reporters often have an unclear idea about the stories they are writing. The most banal quote you give may go through three or four iterations until they get it right. "Just say no" is a good rule in these cases.

When you want to publicize something you have done that you believe is important, start with the publicity department of your home institution. Write a press release. Together with the professionals on your university's staff, you should prepare a two- or three-page account of your work. A good press release is worth its weight in gold, not just because it gives you something to send to reporters about your work, but because it forces you to think about how the general public will receive it. Keep it short and sweet. Do include a line or two about how you intend to pursue your ideas in the future. Put in a couple of examples that a reporter might pick up and put into a story. Make sure it gets read by someone unfamiliar with your work, preferably someone who reads magazines and newspapers. They will be able to tell you where you have not expressed yourself well.

If your press release gets picked up, you will be inundated with press contacts for approximately a three- to five-day period. There will be a long tail of press contacts for weeks after, as reporters farther down the media food chain pick up your story later. If you have a press department at your university, let the staff help you manage these contacts. They are good at it. A good press officer will protect you from your own enthusiasm. He or she will help you decide which offers to accept, schedule appointments with multiple media, and make them come to you instead of vice versa. If you do not have a press officer, then discipline yourself.

Do not be disappointed if your press release is not picked up by the media. There could be lots of reasons, including breaking news, or just being out of synch with the types of stories reporters are looking for at that time. The press release will still benefit you because it will help you step back from your work to appreciate its more general relevance.

Psychologists do not do enough of this kind of advance work for their own science. We wait until the science has been picked up by someone else. When you do that, you are often in the position of having to react to someone else's interpretation, as opposed to getting your own interpretation out front. The well-written, well-timed press release is a preemptive strike, and it is well worth the time and effort you invest in writing a good one. It also does great things for the field. Each time one of us is featured well in a publication, it reflects well on all of us.

Making Ends Meet

An unhappy fact about our profession is that it pays very little, particularly in the early years. It barely supports a swinging singles lifestyle, and pushes the edge of the poverty line for a family. In fact, a colleague of one of the authors was informed that his children were eligible for their school's free hot lunch program because their family's income was so low.

When you are deciding whether or not to take on a moneymaking venture, think about three things: (a) How much money will it actually make you for the time invested? (b) How much time will it take? (c) Are there any professional advantages? Your discretionary thinking time in your job is low, perhaps no more than a fifth or a quarter of your total working time. To clutter it up with moneymaking tasks that bring you no professional rewards can do you a disservice.

Beware of the lump sum. Most people grossly underestimate the amount of time it takes to do any project. For example, a lump sum of $200 for reviewing a textbook may look great. A week later, when you are still organizing your comments, you may regret that you took on this task.

Consulting on an hourly or daily basis with a business organization is frequently lucrative. However, it may also be time-consuming and may take you away from your professional agenda. Your publication record may fall off, and ultimately, you may have gained short-term financial aid at the expense of long-term prospects for tenure.

Continuing education presents another temptation. Often you write a lecture that you then deliver all over the country for a reasonably good fee (sometimes as much as $1500 per lecture). This may seem like a way to make the extra dollars you need but it has disadvantages as well. There is lots of travel time. You do not set your schedule, the agency does, and so you are often pulled away at times when your colleagues are counting on your input for meetings. Your students may need you when you are not there. Typically the audience is not your peers, and their comments are not the discerning, provocative ones you get at colloquia.

A chance to write textbooks (or a section of a textbook) often comes one's way. The amount of time that goes into such an endeavor (initial writing, rewriting, going over copyedited manuscripts and page proof, and reference location) can be enormous. Be forewarned. The professional payoffs are few, and the royalty figure may be lower than was initially estimated. However, once you have written it, if it is good enough to get adoptions, all you have to do is update it every few years and the financial rewards will be the same. So, if you decide to write a textbook, it is worth it to take the time to make it good the first time. The main advantages of writing textbooks are the money, the chance to frame a field from your vantage point, and the enforcement of the need to stay current with the field, because you revise the book every three or four years.

Another way to supplement your income is by teaching courses in summer school. You may need to do this for financial reasons, but there are risks. Summer is one of the few times when the work pace slows down, when you have a chance to do some writing and thinking. If you fill up the summer with the same obligations you have during the year, you may burn yourself out.

If you can avoid moneymaking activities and still keep your head above water, you will protect your free time for high-quality thinking. But if you must take on moneymaking tasks, do try to make them ones that are truly lucrative, that can help rather than hinder your career, and that do not end up taking all of your discretionary time.

Organizing Your Time

As the previous sections attest, you need to plan your time carefully. Letting your workload get out of control can literally kill you. It can make your work life miserable, and it can make your personal life nonexistent. You can get control of your workload if you are willing to be ruthless about the way you use your time. Learn to plan realistically. When you have worked out priorities, plans, and a time schedule, you know just what to do. You are less likely to disappoint yourself, because you have realistic plans. You are also less likely to disappoint others by making commitments you do not keep.

The first step in effective planning is establishing your priorities. Your research plans should be your chief guide. Give your highest priority to empirical projects, supplemented by one or two theoretical pieces. The next priority is secondary projects that are near completion, which you feel irrevocably, morally committed to complete. Third-place priorities are projects that you might like to undertake sometime in the future but to which you have not yet made a formal commitment.

It is useful to have some kind of organizational device that keeps your priorities firmly in mind. For one colleague, this is simply a stack of 21 pigeonhole boxes with names of projects, students, and courses written on them. One of the authors keeps a manila file of goals, organized into high, medium, and low priorities. Develop a system that works for you.

Using the Pipeline

Organize your research life so that it has a continuous, temporal flow. You should have projects at all parts of the pipeline. Some projects will be in the formulative problem stage. Others will be in the design, data collection, data analysis, writing, or review phases. You may only have one project at each of these stages of development, but keeping the pipeline filled at each stage keeps all your skills active, enables you to be consistently productive, gives you a variety of research tasks to do, and gives a flow to your work. The pipeline approach is easy to use if you have developed an interrelated set of ideas on one general topic. As the findings from the first study become clear, you will know how to modify the theory and design for the second study. Results from completed studies can also enable you to refine your research priorities and eliminate projects that are no longer desirable or significant parts of your work. If one part of the research process is more fun for you than another, having a pipeline full can give you the opportunity to alternate more and less desirable tasks.

From Priorities to Task Statements and Time Estimates

Most poor planners make three kinds of mistakes. First, they fail to be specific enough, listing "write *JPSP* article," rather than "write methods section on Tuesday morning." Second, they are overly optimistic about time estimates. They fail to anticipate possible obstacles. As a result, they are repeatedly disappointed in themselves and in the planning process. Third, poor planners often fail to delegate. This problem is particularly acute for academics. As a group, we tend to be loners and do everything ourselves, rather than investing the time it takes to get help or train others, such as support staff, graduate students, and work-study students.

It is possible to avoid these mistakes. For each of your top priority projects, split the remaining work into tasks, such as designing a questionnaire, pretesting participants, or writing a methods section of a paper. Keep these tasks small and specific. Estimate the time it will take—in hours, not days—to do each task. Multiply this time estimate by two. If the task is completed in less time, you will feel wonderful. More likely, unanticipated obstacles will make this seemingly conservative time estimate quite accurate.

If you can delegate the task and have someone else do it, then do so. If you think you cannot delegate it, consider hiring or training someone. A task that will take more than 10 hours of your time should be subdivided, because it is not specific enough. Seek subdivisions that permit delegation to others. Budget time for recruiting, training, and supervising.

The next step is to mesh these tasks into your calendar, realistically allowing for nonresearch demands on your time. Mark your calendar in pencil, because unanticipated obstacles will crop up, making revisions essential. Besides, if you do not revise, you will not get the satisfaction of crossing off completed tasks.

Organizational Aids

The structure that you create for yourself on a monthly, weekly, and even daily basis must be made concrete. To begin with, you need an appointment book. You may want a Palm Pilot or a Day Timer. Some appointment books provide for a detailed week-at-a-glance. One of the editors of this volume uses a wall calendar with every day of the year shown. One of the authors chapter uses a month-at-a-glance appointment book. The square for each day is very small (about one-and-a-half inches), and it is thus difficult to schedule in many appointments. Accordingly, plenty of time is left for reading and writing. The month-at-a-glance is then supplemented with a detailed daily schedule.

Some people keep an appointment book only on a day-by-day basis. This has two risks. First, one tends to cram too many appointments into a day because there is so much space, and second, it focuses one's attention on only one day at a time. We favor a system that enables one to see the large picture (week, month, or year at a time, depending on one's preference), supplemented with a detailed daily schedule.

Scheduling a Day

You should schedule how you are going to use your time each day. Effective time management begins with an understanding of your circadian rhythms. Each of us has hours when we are at our best and hours when we are fit only for the most mundane tasks. Save your best hours for your high-priority research tasks.

Avoid checkerboard days with appointments at 10:00, 12:00, and 3:00, and nothing in between. Try not to organize your schedule around the preferences of others. It is reasonable to ask some other people, particularly students and research assistants, to accommodate their schedules to yours. You will work far more effectively if you bunch your meetings and appointments together. Ensure that meetings that could take 20 minutes do not expand into an hour. Lunches and after-work drinks can serve double duty, as can walks between meeting places. Plan your day in detail, thus keeping your research time safe from encroachment. Assign a research assistant or a secretary to protect you from interruptions. Find a hideaway place to do your work, whether your home, your lab, or a library carrel.

Make technology work for you. When the telephone rings, you do not have to answer it; that is what voice mail is for. Just because your screen tells you that you have mail does not mean you should automatically read it. Everyone e-mails now. Your mail may be up to 100 or more a day. Triage your e-mail the way you triage your "snail" mail. Put aside messages that can wait or require a longer, more thoughtful response. Life is short; do not spend it typing. We debated how curt to be in responding to e-mails. One of us is brief to the risk of rudeness, often using only her initials to sign off. The other of us is more wordy, particularly with European e-mail recipients, who sometimes consider brevity brusque, even rude. We each think the other's style has flaws, and probably a bit of both would be ideal, so find an efficient and happy medium that works for you.

Dealing With Students

When you first became an assistant professor, you were probably grateful for any student who darkened your door. Now you probably have more student demands for your time than you can manage. You must impose limitations on the number and kinds of students you supervise.

When you take on a student, you owe that student a certain amount of time and energy. Every additional student you agree to supervise takes time away from the first. Decide how many students or how many projects you want to cope with simultaneously. Say no when these limits are exceeded. Four or five graduate students are probably the maximum you can supervise well. To this, you might add four undergraduates only if much of their direct supervision is done by graduate students. Work with students who are interested in what you do. It is tough to learn a new area of work just because a student wants to do research in it. It is hard to avoid being seduced by a bright student with an interesting idea about which you know little; however, you will have to invest a lot of time learning about this new area. You may trust the student to know the topic thoroughly, but often, such trust is misplaced. The end result may be unpublishable and you will have wasted time. Here are some ways to say no that the authors do not use frequently enough:

- "I am already supervising seven students. Your project sounds very interesting, but I would be doing us both a disservice to agree to supervise it."
- "I don't serve as a thesis reader when I haven't been involved in the design of the study, as conceptualization and design are the areas where I have found I can be most helpful."
- "I'm sorry, but I don't feel I know enough about your subject to be of help. My work is in (give short description that sounds as different from student's topic as possible)."

What Not to Do

If your work life is like ours, then you need some rules about what not to do. Control the visitors who come to see you. If you live in an area where everyone wants to spend the winter months, you may have more visitors than you can handle. Visiting works best if you invite the people you want to see rather than having them decide they want to be with you. Respond to potential foreign visitors carefully. They often expect much time and attention, so be ready to give it or beg off. Serve on dissertation committees outside your university at your own peril. (If you have taken on an obligation like this, have a good reason.)

Pick your conferences carefully. They are advantageous primarily when you want to showcase yourself or your work. If the conference location is wonderful, it can be a reward for your hard work. However, many faculty adopt a nomadic existence, wandering from conference to conference. If you do this, you will not get your work done. While presenting at a conference or two in the early years of being an assistant professor is good because it gives you and your work visibility, continuing this plan long into associate and full professorhood is probably not the best use of your time.

Do not build a bottomless pile. Do not put anything in a pile to be gone through again and again. Get rid of it the first time. Do not keep things you will not need. One of our most eminent colleagues keeps a "not now" stack, saying "You would be amazed what doesn't really need doing, if it sits undone for three months." Review only journal articles that are directly in your field. Send back promptly those you are not going to review. One of us (the less disciplined one) has a "floor pile" of papers that she hopes to read. When it falls over, she goes through it for a maximum of two "saves" and throws the rest out.

One key to controlling your work life lies in how you approach your mail. The first rule is, never read anything you do not have to. Glance at the sender's name, the title, even the first paragraph or abstract if you have to. Then make a decision: to read or not to read. Your mail is largely composed of changes in policies, memos, descriptions of books from publishers, campus newspapers, and so forth. Read the absolute minimum of this material. Much of it will become obsolete on its own.

The second rule is, do not put manuscripts to review in your pile. They will get buried. Three or four months later an editor will write you an irritated letter asking whether you intend to review a particular paper. If you intend to do it, do so quickly. If you do not intend to review it, return it immediately with a plausible reason.

If you have followed these guidelines, then your pile should be composed virtually entirely of papers you want to read. Even this pile can and should be drastically shrunk. By "chronologizing," you can gear your reading to your teaching and research. For example, if an interesting paper comes in your mail, save it for the week you are teaching this topic. Put it in the file for that week of the course. When the time comes to prepare for that class, that file will contain papers that you can use to fill out your lectures. Simultaneously, you will be reading current literature in this area. A similar approach can be used with papers germane to your research. Keep a file of work relevant to each of your projects. Read through the abstracts and papers before you start designing or writing.

Chronologizing will reduce your pile of papers to those that you have no immediate purpose for reading. Throw many of these away too. Select a few to file. Do not save too many. It is amazing how quickly you can fill file cabinets. The only thing left in your pile should be four or five gems—that is, papers that have been written by people who make strong contributions to the field and whose thinking can enlighten your own.

At the same time that you are struggling to do all this, you need to keep your career vital and interesting. You might want to add a few flyers that have captured your imagination. You can give yourself these for dessert someday, after a particularly productive bout of writing. Take little breaks, vacations that are perhaps only a few hours long. Go to a talk just because it sounds interesting. Have lunch with a visitor from another university. Sit in on a colleague's course. We are in this field to learn. Activities like these will renew your intrinsic interest in the field.

Should You Move?

If you have done well, there is a good chance you will receive one or more requests to join a new university. The decision to move could become one of the toughest of your life. Can your family be easily uprooted? Are they happy to be uprooted? Can you leave the friendships you have worked hard to build?

On the purely academic side, certain conditions may make it advantageous to move. They include the prospect of good or better graduate students, the prospect of good or better colleagues, the ready availability of some important resource or technology, or a substantial upgrade in your quality of life.

There are a few pitfalls to avoid as you contemplate moving: If you are unhappy where you are, be sure you know why. It could be something about you. In this case, therapy or a change in attitude might do you more good than a move. Beware the appearance of the warm, stimulating collegial climate. Sometimes, this atmosphere prevails primarily because you are visiting; after you leave, everyone will go back into his or her office and close the door.

When you are thinking about a move, you often focus on the benefits of the new place and the liabilities of the place you currently are. Remind yourself what you like about your current job and ask yourself if you will be able to duplicate it at the new location. Ferret out the disadvantages of the new place. Does stiff formality go along with its greater prestige? Will you be able to dress casually (if this is something you value)? Is it a state university? If so, how bad is the bureaucracy and how much will it affect your life? Will your paycheck be held up if the legislature does not pass a budget? Can you afford to live near your new academic home? If not, what will it do to your quality of life to live far away?

If you decide to move, be sure it represents a major upgrade for you, because once you get there, the true costs of your move will be apparent. You will experience many of the problems of the new assistant professor all over again—loneliness, finding a dry cleaner, figuring out how to get a paper clip. The people who thought you were so wonderful when you interviewed are not going to engage in so much hero worship after you get there. Everything you thought would be easy about the move will be hard.

Yet in many cases, a move will be just the right thing. It can invigorate your thinking, give you previously unimagined opportunities for empirical work, provide new collaborators, and boost your ego. Just go into the decision with your eyes open.

Getting Time to Rest and Gain Perspective

The rhythm of the academic year provides natural opportunities for you to rest, think, evaluate your work, and change your course of action if you so desire. A few weeks before a new semester or quarter begins or during the summer are good times to reevaluate one's activities. Remember the research on incubation effects. Solutions to problems often surface at unlikely moments when the mind is seemingly at rest but actually liberated to solve a problem on its own. Free times, including extended free time during summers and sabbaticals, can provide you with this opportunity. To take full advantage of these times may require your getting away. In the summer, for example, it is useful to take some of that time off. When you come back to your work, your priorities may have changed, and trivial tasks that seemed so important when you left have faded into their rightful importance.

In most colleges and universities, you will be eligible for a one- or two-semester sabbatical, sometime every four to eight years. If you are fortunate enough to get a sabbatical semester or year, try to take it away from your university. For some, particularly those involved in dual-career relationships, this may be difficult to do. If you stay at your home university, you may be tempted to work with a few students or do a few administrative favors for the chair in your department. Soon you will discover that your sabbatical has been eroded by precisely the dross you were trying to avoid. Plus, if you stay at your usual university, you get none of the stimulation that comes from learning your way around a new environment. Try to pick a host institution that will not make formal demands on your time but that will provide you with office space and stimulating colleagues in your area. It will help if the university is located in a setting with exciting cultural opportunities, good food, and wine. Provence, we hear, is lovely in the spring. The London theater is breathtaking in winter. The sabbatical is a time when you can reward yourself for your hard work while simultaneously stimulating your mind in preparation for the work that is to come.

A sabbatical is most effective if you set yourself a plan and a schedule, otherwise there are too many temptations. Use it to clear a few things out, learn something new, and reinvigorate your life. If your chair or your dean says that you are the only faculty member who can possibly head up this committee, recognize it for the bull it is and do not cave. Sabbaticals are too rare.

Life Outside of Work

Yes, there is life outside of work. It is, however, probably not an accident that this section of the paper is short. The stressful first years eat up your energy, and hitting your stride almost always means regular, long hours of work. Despite the fact that it is hard to find room for it, the rest of your life is critical. After all, why are you working so hard and using your work time so efficiently, if not to enjoy your private life and your work? At times your work life will temporarily collapse around your ears. A grant proposal that you were counting on may not come through. An article that is particularly important to you may be rejected. When these things happen, it helps to have the rest of your life to fall back on.

Your private life is private. You know best what you need to thrive. Our parents and teachers were right when they urged us to eat well, exercise, sleep sometimes, and have a social life. The latter is particularly important, because social support is essential to cope successfully with the tension and time pressure of this career we have chosen. Many people find the most important source of support to be family and friends. Spend time with them now, or they will not be there when you need them. Schedule time for your leisure life, or it may go by the board in a crunch. Buy concert or theater tickets in advance, so you will have to go. Set up a regular tennis game. Have a regular biweekly dinner with a group of friends.

If you enjoy your work, the pleasures of the process will be evident to you. There may be some advantages and pleasures of your job that you may have overlooked. For example, as a faculty member your time is flexible; still, many professors treat their positions as 9-to-5 jobs. As long as you work enough hours, why hold yourself to a rigid schedule that may not be conducive to other needs in your life? If your writing is going well, why not write until dawn and sleep some other time? If it is not going well, why not go have some fun?

Academia also gives you the flexibility to choose where you work. You do not have to be in your office all the time—you can write outside, work at home, or go to a library.

You also have some flexibility in the tasks that you do. On one hand, you do not want to develop work habits that are positively weird in the context of your colleagues, but on the other hand, some deviation is clearly acceptable. Unlike most jobs, a faculty position also gives you considerable discretion in choosing what problems you want to study and what tasks you want to do next. If you have been writing a paper and the words are not coming, turn to something else. Make hedonistic decisions about what you are working on. If you always do what you think you are supposed to be doing and never try out something that you think might be unexpectedly absorbing, then you will ultimately feel robbed. You cannot blame your job for robbing you. You have robbed yourself.

HITTING THE WALL (AND THE REST OF THE RACE)

When you enter the ranks of professor and beyond, some of the previous problems have been solved, others are continuing, but a few new ones arise. The first concerns increasing demands on your time. You will be assigned to an increasing number of high-profile committees that are time-consuming but that require the experience and vision of a senior faculty member. These may include choosing or evaluating senior administrators at your university, planning curriculum changes or revamping the curriculum, evaluating candidates for appointments at all levels, meeting with community groups outside the university, serving as an advisor or on the board of an organization affiliated with the university, and so forth.

You will be asked to serve on dissertation committees outside your department and outside your university. Visitors from other universities and other countries will ask if they can join you for a semester or a year. High school students will track you down on the Internet for time-consuming interviews about how you chose your career and where you feel the field is headed. If you have any prominence in your field, you will also be swamped with conferences and your mailbox will be filled with invitations. Demands on your time for national service will increase, such as serving on a National Academy of Sciences panel, grant review panel, visiting committee to evaluate departments at other universities, and the like.

You have a choice: You can say yes to many of these things and stop doing research, or you can say no a lot, get people angry with you, and keep your research program active. There really is not a middle ground. The demands are too excessive for you to do both. The requests are flattering. They attest to the stature you have achieved and the esteem in which you are held by your field. Nonetheless, you need to recognize that you cannot do everything.

Your Biggest Problems

The first problem of full professorhood would have to be the number of evaluations you do. By the time you are a full professor, the sheer number of people in your professional life is in the hundreds, perhaps the thousands. Each year, you have to write letters for your own students as well as your former students. If you have gained prominence in a field, you will be asked to comment on candidates coming up for tenure and for full professor in your own university and at universities elsewhere. Each tenure review requires reading, recalling, or thinking about at least seven years of research; your colleagues who are applying for Guggenheims or other fellowships and junior faculty applying for Fellows status in professional organizations need thoughtful letters.

The only ones we turn down are requests to evaluate candidates who are not in our areas and whose work we do not know. It is much better for you and fairer to the candidate to comment on people whose work and stature you really do know. Once you have written a good master letter on a student or colleague, the chances that you will need to use it again are pretty high, so keep it in your active files so it can be updated.

The first tenure or full letter you write will take a while, but the requesting department will usually tell you what they want to know. Typically, you mention the person's standing in his or her particular research domain. Is he or she an identified leader? And how important *is* that domain? Where do the candidate's papers appear? Who are the papers with? Is the candidate free of his or her mentor? Has he or she attracted students? Is he or she first author? Has he or she gotten grant funding? What is the trajectory? Does it look like there is good stuff coming along? (The personal statement helps in this instance.) How does the person compare with others at the same career stage? Would the candidate get promoted at your school? This is what the department wants to know. Often only an excerpt of your letter will appear in the department report, so be sure you have a quotable quote!

A second problem is the sheer number of committees to which you may be appointed, especially university committees. When you are appointed to one of these it is a nod that you are senior, established, and valued by your community. They often take up hours of your prime time, and the consequences of your hard work may be minimal. The smaller your university the greater your impact may be. The larger your university, the more the solution to what appears to be a thorny issue has probably already been worked out, and the job of this shared governance is to convince the faculty to go along with it. This is not to say that you cannot have an impact on the policies that govern your university. But if this is important to you, then perhaps you should move into administration for a few years as a dean or even provost. In such positions, your policy recommendations may well carry weight and be implemented. But as a mere committee member, the fresh insights you bring to long-established, complicated problems may well fall on deaf ears.

The proliferation of committees is truly frightening. You have to say no to most, but you probably need to say yes to one or two. Once decided, do not be seduced by committees that look better.

For those of you with the power to decide, here is a request: Do not create committees. A couple of knowledgeable people with e-mail can often accomplish the same thing. A conference call can replace a meeting. Certainly some functions require excellent team work. But typically lengthy, meandering, and soporific academic committees are sometimes expendable.

However, the occasional visiting committee, review committee, or National Academy panel can sometimes be invigorating. Often these are interdisciplinary, and you get to meet some interesting people from related fields.

Is there anything you can reasonably turn down or cut back on at this point in your career, given how much certain of your obligations will increase? We debated about exactly what one should say no to and decided reluctantly that full professor is a point when you should scrutinize each request to evaluate journal articles quite carefully. At this stage in your career, you have probably burrowed into a particular problem or point of view and so your reviews may be quite opinionated and even cantankerous. Much of your reviewing time should go to evaluating the work you know best, which is work right in your field, often work that builds on your own. You may no longer have the breadth of expertise nor are you likely to be as current with all the recent literature as another reviewer might be.

So how do you finish the race when you have hit the wall and lost some of your zest for the marathon? We cannot help you with every one of these demands, but a few suggestions follow. Develop programmed solutions for problems: Most things happen more than once. Have a set of biographical materials that includes a reasonably up-to-date photograph that you can make available to people who want to know about your career. As part of this file you may want to put statements about your philosophy of science and your thoughts about where the field is headed. These materials can be quickly dispensed to high school students and undergraduates who ask for personal material, with a nice e-mail explaining that although you would love to answer their questions, you just do not have the time and hope very much these materials will suffice.

Handle requests quickly but cordially. The older you get, the more you will discover people you treated well remember their interactions with you. Be careful who you pass requests along to. When asked to review articles, talk with reporters on topics you know little about, or answer questions from someone outside the university, the temptation is to pass them off on a colleague. The more you do that, the more your colleagues will pass these kinds of requests back onto you. Better to develop a gracious way of saying no.

Many of the demands on your time cannot be turned down, and so the best way to handle them are first to bunch them, so you knock out a lot of them at the same time. Do so not during your prime time but during your tired time of the day. Try to keep your annoyance under control. Remember people have long memories. And if you are a senior person in the field, their memory for you will be far longer than yours for them.

Ultimately you are the one who has to decide what you are going to do, so take control over these tasks, set priorities, turn down the ones that are not essential, and do the tasks you choose well but quickly. Become a master of the "I would really like to but . . . " letter.

Keeping Your Career Vibrant

When we were getting ready to write this chapter, we read another book on the tasks of different stages of the academic career. In the section on full professors, the statement was made that often research assumes secondary importance at this time of a career in favor of service activities. To a degree this is true. Many people who reach their 50s and 60s are relieved to be able to cut back on their pace. It seems a good time to make use of hard-won wisdom instead of trying to create knowledge. Several of our colleagues have made this transition gracefully. Some have been able to give concrete form to a vision, such as establishing seed money for junior faculty or developing a new academic concentration for majors. Others have chosen to mentor the younger faculty. Junior faculty sometimes feel impatience or even contempt for those who have made this choice, because the good work they do is not as visible as a lot of publications. But senior colleagues have already been that route, they are largely done with it, and their contributions in the service role are important, too, if less immediately apparent.

Some people choose to take on the editorship of a journal during their full professorhood, for which the costs are clear: It is an extraordinary amount of work, and you make some people angry. The benefits are that you learn a lot, you get to shape the field (to a degree), and your visibility and stature in the field rise.

You may be asked to serve as president of a professional organization. It is not as bad as it might sound. The meetings are typically low-key, some of the other officers are friends, and the meetings are often held in nice places. There is an administrative structure, often with an executive officer, that was in place before you got there, which minimizes your workload.

Despite the fact that we all need to do some of this senior service, many of us resist and want to keep our research careers as vibrant for as long as possible. Perhaps we still think our best science is ahead of us. But this is the point where one will leave a legacy, if any is to be left.

Your legacy consists of your theories, your empirical work, the students you have trained, and the other ways you have shaped the field through reviewing and service. Ultimately, science is a collective endeavor. Your work will get used, mixed with other people's, change form. Realistically, your influence will last at best a decade or two. What if someone who should be citing your work is not? Usually, just let it go. You might send one relevant paper with a polite note indicating its relevance, but do not try to snarl and bully your way into someone's bibliography. What if you are misrepresented? Correct it politely. If you do not catch it now, someone else will make the same error later on.

As you get older, your ways of working with students and other collaborators may change. The gaps between what you know and what the students know gets bigger—and it is not always you who knows more. They will know the new literature, the latest technology, and the newest statistical techniques better than you. You will have a bigger view of the field and be able to see connections across fields much better. They will see the next analytical chess move in a narrow field. You will be impatient with this view and want to make a bigger move that may be unwise from your student's point of view. You are looking to say what you want, he or she is working for a *JPSP* paper.

How do you bridge this gap? And do you try to bridge it at all? It is good to try to strike a balance between what you want and what your students need. Do a few of their intense, empirical projects and pull them into a few of your more ambitious ones. Have a big grant, so you can break off manageable chunks for individual students to take on as empirical projects. But learn from your students as well. The fact that they now know things you do not can lead to better work. You may also find, though, that you are naturally working more with advanced students and postdocs or even assistant professors than used to be the case, because although they have needs for publications, they usually also have a broader perspective. You will find the balance that suits you.

One way to keep your interest in research vibrant is to branch into a new field. This is not to say that you necessarily make a complete switch in your career. More commonly, people add new skills to their research repertoire. This might include new statistical techniques or methodologies, expertise in the underlying biology of psychological phenomena, training in neuroimaging, and so forth. There are wonderful things about adding these skills and doing something new. But any such change may not be a whole-hearted and immediate success. Many of the new skills you will attempt to master are hard, and it takes some doing to get up to speed. When you are older it takes more doing than when you were younger. It is embarrassing to make the virtually inevitable mistakes when you are mastering some new technology. Recognize, too, that the field you are moving into may not be happy to see you either. There is often a harshness toward newcomers that may make it hard to get your new work funded or accepted for publication.

Another issue that arises at this stage in your career is how to achieve a balance of doing new work while defending your old work. The pull of exciting, new work is such that you may want to put the old work behind you, but as people misrepresent your work or attack it on grounds that you think are unfair, you are often put in a position of having to return to issues again. There are right and wrong ways to do this. Firing off stinging letters and rebuttals after each assault is not the way to defend your work. As always, the best way is to do it with better scientific evidence. This is a huge investment of time, and you have to balance how important it is to you to correct a misimpression against the time it will draw from your new and currently more involving endeavors. Yet one of the chief tasks of the late career stage is leaving a legacy, and sometimes defense of your early work is part of this task. If you believe you are right, then you would be doing your field and yourself a disservice not to defend your previous work.

How do you revitalize your teaching? Create a new course on something you have always been curious about; teach a freshman or honors seminar; coteach with colleagues in other departments; team teach a new course; teach a course on a book you want to write; or coteach with a junior colleague. If this does not work, seek ways to lighten your teaching load, at least temporarily, even if it means taking on some other, differently undesirable task.

Beware the Curmudgeonly End

In the later years of a career, there is a risk of getting jaded, growing impatient. You have heard every question, taught the same course a dozen times, read what seems like the same paper four or five times. Some of the "science" you read seems so small or meaningless. On the one hand, nothing moves fast enough—speakers take forever to make a modest point—but other things move too quickly: The assistant professors have seemingly boundless energy, but you feel like you need a nap.

Just as the risk of the assistant professor is the eager beaver, the risk of the full professor, particularly the advanced full professor, is the old curmudgeon. It will be difficult to create a legacy and retire with the respect of your colleagues if you spend much of your time complaining about the nature of the field. We know that your work is not read as much as it could be, is not valued as much as it should be, and is not even acknowledged when it is the intellectual roots of current thinking.

As you watch your incredible shrinking legacy slip away, realize that thousands of professors have been there before you. Do not torture your colleagues with your grumpy observations about this inevitable state. Think of it as the intellectual counterpart of arthritis, something that comes almost inevitably with age that you should try to control with a good diet, exercise, and cheerful thoughts.

CONCLUSION

Most of us chose to be professors because we thought we would enjoy the work, perhaps the satisfactions of research, the relationships to students, the process of teaching, the excuse for continuing to learn, or the freedom to decide what we want to study. In this chapter, we have discussed primarily the demands, rather than the joys, of academic life. The joys, however, are the primary reasons why this stressful, ill-paid line of work is worth pursuing. Personally, what drives us ultimately is the pure joy of research: "Those moments . . . when suddenly there is a synthesis of the human intelligence . . . and to know every day that it might happen again" (Gornick, 1983, p. 52).

REFERENCE

Gornick, V. (1983, August). Women in science. *Savvy, 4*, 44–52.

20

MANAGING YOUR CAREER:
THE LONG VIEW

HENRY L. ROEDIGER III AND DAVID A. BALOTA

The purpose of this chapter is to ask you to expand your time horizon and to think about (if not actually plan for) many years into the future. If you are like most people finishing graduate school or a postdoctoral fellowship and taking a job in academia, you are in your late 20s or early 30s. Your most immediate concerns—finding a job, beginning a program of research, setting up a lab, teaching courses, thinking about the tenure process and on and on—are dealt with in other chapters of this book. Given these more immediate pressing concerns, why should you bother to think further than five years into the future, if that far? Why not stick to the more serious and immediate problems of today?

We believe that having you think about your career for the long haul can pay dividends on at least three fronts. First, and probably most important, you may better situate yourself to reach long-term research or teaching goals. Developing a research career entails both short-term goals, such as completing the next experiment (and writing the next paper) and long-term goals, such as building a programmatic series of contributions that build on each other and (with luck) influence the direction of the field. A similar argument can be made for planning in teaching. One needs to

We thank Mark Zanna for comments that improved this chapter.

consider not only the current courses that you are teaching but also what you might teach in the future and how such teaching may fit within the goals of your department and your own personal goals. Second, you may think about some career goals and options that you would not otherwise consider. For example, could you ever imagine yourself becoming chair or going into university administration, as a dean or in some other capacity? If so, what should you do to prepare? Third, just thinking about the choices people make in academia may help you see the perspective of others with whom you will be interacting. Even if you never aspire to be a dean, you might consider why someone else would want to occupy such a position. After all, some dean in the future will be critical in making tenure and promotion decisions about you.

Planning for the future is a dangerous business. Our advice is to plan out possible scenarios for the future but do not necessarily become committed to any one of them. The reason is that long-term plans, even the most carefully laid, rarely become reality. You might decide that your research will be on certain topics and only those. But then what happens when an exciting new opportunity comes along for collaboration, where you and your field of expertise would fit right in and make you a natural player? Suppose you prepare your courses and decide that it was so much work that you will teach these forever, or as long as your department lets you. If you make this decision, you might again miss out by not teaching some new course when your interests develop and change. So, make a plan, but do not be locked into it. Keep your eyes open to changing situations and opportunities and take advantage of them.

THINKING ABOUT THE FUTURE

If you are entering academia in your late 20s, and if you retire at around age 70, you would have about a 40-year academic career. How do you plan for 40 years? Our advice: Make concrete plans for small chunks of time and more general plans for the more distant future. Books abound on long-range planning and how to do it for individuals and organizations. Our advice is to keep it simple. Some recommended planning exercises are so complex and unwieldy that you could spend all your time planning what you will do and not have time to accomplish the goals that you ultimately identify. We advise planning for chunks of time of varying length, revising your plans over time, and keeping your goals to be achieved in the form of simple lists (rather than long documents telling yourself what you will do). Let us consider short-term, medium-term, and long-term planning.

Short-Term Planning

Many organized people keep lists of things that they need to do and consult them frequently. The list should be hierarchical. What do you absolutely have to do this week? Prepare five lectures, attend two committee meetings, go to the departmental colloquium (which we believe is a must), and so on. The things that must be done obviously must have priority. In fact, you might just put them on your schedule and not on your list of things to do. Then the "to do" list can be devoted to more discretionary time. You could put writing the article that you need to write on the list, completing the manuscript review, and so on. Some people make a daily list of this nature, others a weekly list. These are the short-term things you need to get done. However, off to the side of even your short-term list, in a slightly different category, you might keep projects that take longer than a day or even a week to complete, such as articles you need to submit, a grant proposal you need to write, and so on. This keeps you mindful that you cannot fill up your short-term lists with only the daily affairs of academia—teaching, talks, meetings, committees, and so on. Yes, do all those things, as you must, but build time into your schedule for the other activities that make for success in the long run.

This brings us to time management in the short term. Given the work on circadian rhythms, it is clear that we do not function at the same level of energy, creativity, and productivity throughout the day or even the week. Allocate times accordingly. If writing is the most demanding task you engage in, set aside those times that are best for writing. For example, some people identify a specific set of hours (say 5 to 10 hours per week) during their most productive time to engage in writing. One of our most successful colleagues spends very early morning hours each day on theoretical analyses and developing experimental methods. Others isolate a day or two during the week to dedicate to their own research time. Some people find it useful to isolate themselves from outside distraction (possibly at a home office) during these dedicated times. Use other off-peak times to engage in less demanding but necessary tasks. Once you have built time for writing and research into your schedule, try to set it in stone and do not let anything except an emergency push it aside. We believe that identifying your best times for distinct activities and allocating them appropriately is a critical step in keeping on the most productive path.

We have covered short-term planning before we consider longer term planning, but really the process should be iterative. You may state lofty long-term goals as we suggest, but unless your daily and weekly plan builds in time to accomplish those long-term goals, you will not achieve them.

So make sure your daily and weekly schedules permit you to achieve these longer terms goals.

Medium-Term Goals

"Medium-term" can cover numerous time periods. We have found it useful to think of six-month chunks of time. One of us has a lab meeting twice a year in which each person in attendance says what major goals have been accomplished in the past six months and states their goals for the upcoming six months. A record is kept, so every six months the accomplishments for that period can be compared to the original goals. Success can be applauded and missed goals can be noted. Why did you not meet your goal? What can you change so that more goals can be met in the future? How should you change your daily or weekly plan so that these medium-term goals (submitting that grant proposal, writing that paper) can be accomplished? You might find this six-month review process useful for yourself, working alone, but do it honestly! It is probably easier if you and a close friend or colleague can get together and conduct the six-month review with each other, asking and answering the hard questions about unmet goals. In our experience, the process of explaining your past behavior and future goals to a public audience every six months is a good motivator. A lab group works well for this purpose.

Because of the nine-month teaching schedule, another natural unit of planning is the summer. People are often unrealistic regarding how much can be accomplished during a summer. Set reasonable goals, including vacation time, and stick to the schedule. Do not spread yourself too thin with too many goals over the summer. This can lead to the disappointment of not accomplishing any of them. Every academic we know has the experience of thinking that summer disappeared with amazing rapidity. At the beginning of the summer, it seems to stretch forever (in prospect) but then suddenly it is August or September and the new academic year has crashed into your plans. So, set goals for each month of the summer that are realistic and make sure to follow them as carefully as possible.

A year is another natural unit for planning, much as for making New Year's resolutions. Departments sometimes require individuals to specify goals and accomplishments on a yearly basis in annual reports. Unfortunately, goals and plans set for the year often meet the same fate as do New Year's resolutions: They are forgotten after a few weeks. That is why you need to make sure your longer-term goals (six-month or one-year) make it onto your daily and weekly lists of things you need to accomplish. Still, once a year (perhaps in August, before the new academic year begins), it is good to consider the question: "What do I want to accomplish in the next year?" and make a concrete list of goals.

Long-Range Goals

This type of planning is even more difficult, but you should do it. The ideas you produce in this context may range beyond concrete behavioral objectives to the category of dreams, hopes, and aspirations. Do you aspire to become a top researcher in your field? Do you hope to become an award-winning teacher? Would you hope to climb the administrative ladder, from department chair, to dean, to provost, to president? Do you hope to become a journal editor? Could you imagine serving in an organization that needs academic expertise but that is basically outside academia (say, working as an officer in a foundation or a federal agency)? Do you want to write a textbook? Do you think you will ever voluntarily retire early from academia and do something else with your life? You cannot do everything in life, so you must make choices. However, you need to consider the large range of options that are open to you within academia so you make informed choices and do not say, when you are 55, "Why didn't I ever consider doing X when I was 35?"

These long-range goals answer the question of what you want to do with your academic life during your 40 or so (possible) years in the field. One exercise that is somewhat morbid is to write your own obituary as you would like it to appear after a long and full life. What would you like it to say? How would you like to be remembered? What matters most to you? People differ markedly on these dimensions, and one can achieve greatness in being a wonderful teacher, a great researcher, an outstanding mentor of graduate students, a terrific administrator, or a great writer of books. Of course, some individuals appear to be able to do it all, but most people can attain excellence only in a subset of these areas. Often people take the approach of being good, but not excellent, in many dimensions instead of excelling in one at the cost of others. Look carefully at your skills and abilities, as well as what you really find rewarding, and choose accordingly. But keep in mind that you are making choices in whatever you do; by aiming at some goals, you are usually excluding others. Consider your full range of options and select wisely.

The foregoing remarks have been directed only at career paths. Of course, you will have many outside demands and interests, too. You should have separate goals and objectives there, too. You can be too focused on work. Many academics see their personal relationships fail when all their time and effort go into their careers. Workaholism seems at least as prevalent (and probably more prevalent) in academia as in other jobs in life, probably because "work" is ill-defined and there is always more reading to be done, more projects to work on, more writing to do. So the job can expand and take over one's life. We strongly urge you to prevent this from happening. Build in time that is sacrosanct for your personal relationships, family, exercise, or hobbies. Taking this time away from your academic work will probably help the quality of that work when you go back to it. Do not let your academic job take over your life, so that you wind up living and sleeping in your office and lab. You presumably went into your chosen field because you are intensely interested in it, but do not exclude all the other things in life. When the inevitable reverses come in certain aspects of your job, it is refreshing to have other sources of joy to which you can turn.

In the remainder of the chapter we consider possible career goals at various stages in your life. Our advice and thoughts reflect our own opinions and experiences, and all may not agree with them.

CAREER PLANS: EARLY CAREER

Most of this book is about how to manage your career early on, so we will be mercifully brief on this point and list items in bulleted format. Every point we make is considered elsewhere in this volume, sometimes in an entire chapter.

- If you are at a research institution, get your research going and publish papers, refereed journal articles. Remember, this is one of the primary criteria for earning tenure at most institutions. Do not publish, or attempt to publish, simple one-shot studies. That might build numbers, but careful, multistudy packages build reputations and careers.
- Teach courses your department needs and do it well. Teaching can consume your life, but do not let it. Be efficient in preparing your lectures. Early in your career, teach the same courses regularly to minimize new preparations (but keep working on the courses by improving them each time you teach). Keep your eyes open for excellent students who might want to do research with you. You will learn much from teaching, too, so the new information can feed into your research.
- Talk to people in your department about valued criteria. Often when we take our first job, or move to another university, we believe that the new department has the same values as at our previous position. This is not necessarily the case. It is useful to discuss such issues with other junior faculty, but we also recommend identifying a more senior faculty member within your department to help provide guidance, possibly as an academic mentor.
- Persevere! Academic life is full of reversals for everyone. Everyone has rejected papers, has some disgruntled students, and has

too much to do. Do not let it get you down. Taking a mental health day by phoning in "sick" when you are overwhelmed is not a sin, but do not overdo it. And never miss a class without having a good fill-in.

- Collaborate, but watch out. You can get sucked into collaborations that take an immense amount of time but do not lead to publishable products or, if the project is published, you do not get much credit. Watch out for colleagues to whom "collaboration" means "be my research assistant and carry out or oversee this project on which I'll be first author."

- Keep up with your field. Set aside time for reading journals. Skimming is a great skill. Use it to keep abreast of work that is in your general field but not your own more narrow area. Try to consistently work through each of the abstracts in a few critical journals in your area.

- Go to national and specialty meetings, as you can afford, and attend many of the talks. Some academics believe that they can avoid such meetings and let their publications do the speaking for them. Meetings are a great place to meet individuals who eventually may be writing letters for promotion for you. Consider organizing a symposium in your area at a national meeting. This will provide a venue to interact with leaders in your area. Give talks so that individuals will be able to see your best work before it is published. However, be sure to give practice talks before taking the show on the road.

- Be willing to perform service both for your department or your field, especially if the service will not take too much time or will benefit you professionally. Most department chairs will protect you from committees, so when she or he does ask you to do some (probably relatively minor) departmental chore, do not say you are too busy with your own work. Remember, the chair is giving up much more of her or his time to do "service" than you can imagine.

- When editors begin to find you and ask you to review papers, do so in a thorough but balanced manner. Do not look at every paper as hopelessly flawed and show the editor how smart you are by pointing out the flaws. Ask yourself: Is this an interesting paper that advances the field (despite whatever difficulties might be present)? No paper is perfect, even the best ones. Also, be prompt in reviewing. Establish a reputation as a good, reliable reviewer and you may find yourself asked to be on editorial boards.

- Learn to balance "yes" and "no" appropriately. As your career progresses you will be asked to take on more and more responsibilities. At first, it is easy to say "yes," but you need to ensure that this will not pull too much time from other more central endeavors. Likewise, it is useful to look beyond one's laboratory and take on responsibilities that benefit the department or the field as a whole. Again, a respected senior mentor can be invaluable in providing advice.

We could go on in this vein, but will desist. Just read the rest of this book to discover advice on what to do early in your career. Do not worry that not all the authors will agree in the advice they give. Consider their opinions and find your own way.

CAREER PLANS: MID-CAREER

Let us make the happy assumption that you are now seven or so years out of graduate school, have done well, earned tenure, and are facing the future. Tenure seemed like such a big hurdle. Now that you have it, the achievement may seem anticlimactic. After all, you may get a bit of a bump in your salary, but not enough to change your lifestyle. Everything else about academic life will stay the same except that you can put "associate professor" on your stationery and you may have to go to more committee meetings and be expected to contribute more to the life of your department and university. These sad facts can seem disappointing, but this is the time to look to the future. What do you want to do next?

Many people keep on much the same path, especially immediately after tenure. Old habits are hard to break. However, we believe that within a few years you should start considering other options than the business as usual model. In general, after tenure you may consider looking around and branching out, both in your research and in other activities.

Obviously, one of the most dramatic ways to branch out is to consider moving to a different institution. This can occur at any stage in one's career, but we decided to target this topic here because one most likely has just received tenure and may be a marketable rising star in the field. There is little doubt that moving to a new university can be energizing in one's professional career. The colleagues at the new institution often appear better, and one loses the old entrenched ways of doing business at the home institution. The intellectual climate changes dramatically, and this in itself can be invigorating. Everyone wants to be wanted, so being pursued by another university can be uplifting. Of course, caution is also necessary. Sometimes people do not wish to actually leave their home university but believe that an outside offer can better their current situation (e.g., increased salary or research support). The danger is that in some cases, the home university cannot match the external offer and so one is forced to move to a less desirable place or forced to stay with a bit of egg on one's face. The bottom line is that there is considerable energy expended by many parties when considering a move to another university, so it is important to ensure up front that a move is a real possibility before the process gets too far. One can easily lose a considerable amount of personal productivity and unintentionally upset many colleagues when engaged in protracted dances with other universities. However, when the move is indeed to a better situation, it can be worthwhile.

Now, let use assume that you are staying put, and you are still ready for some change. Let us consider research first. To gain tenure you might have used the strategy of publishing many empirical papers on a limited range of topics—on what you know well. You have made a name for yourself, as academics often do, by research and writing on a relatively narrow subject area. After you have received tenure, step back and take a look at your research program. Does it represent learning more and more about less and less? If so, consider branching out into other arenas that you find interesting. Read in related areas. Or maybe you just heard a colloquium that piqued your interest in something that is relatively far afield. Read up on it. Talk to people in that research area. Maybe you will strike up an interesting collaboration by bringing your knowledge, skills, and background to bear on a new subject area. Supervising an undergraduate honors thesis in a related area is also a good way to extend one's research perspective.

In addition, you might be due for a sabbatical, if your college or university permits them. If you can, attempt to go to an exciting university where your mental batteries might be recharged and where you might learn about exciting and different areas. Consider learning a new set of methods or analytical procedures that you can use in your work. Having new colleagues with different programs of research can start you off on a new path. Sabbaticals should also provide you with the opportunity to finish writing projects in an uninterrupted manner. A different style of sabbatical is simply to stay at home and attempt to use the time to catch up on ongoing projects. This can also be productive, and when there are family considerations this may be the only option. However, with this approach one can often be sucked back into the everyday routines of the department. So, when possible, it is useful to take a sabbatical at another university.

Besides new research arenas, you might consider different academic activities, too. In the paragraphs that follow we consider various paths you might consider. Certainly not all these suggestions will fit everyone, but they at least bear consideration.

First, if you have been writing mostly empirical papers reporting experimental results, consider making other kinds of contributions. One is to write synthetic review papers, of the sort that might appear in the *Psychological Bulletin, Psychonomic Bulletin & Review,* or *Advances in Experimental Social Psychology* (among many other possibilities). These papers can represent major and highly cited contributions if they help to summarize and crystallize research in a particular field. The same can be said for theoretical papers of the type that appear in *Psychological Review* and other journals. Once you gain some status in your field, you might be asked to write chapters for edited volumes that can also serve the same purpose. However, the huge number of edited volumes in all fields of psychology means that any particular volume or chapter may receive few readers and little attention, so publishing these kinds of synthetic contributions in refereed journals is a much better career move. Still, publishing chapters is often liberating, because the reviewing and editing are usually light and you are permitted to say what you want to say in the manner you want to say it, relative to the arduous process that most journal editors use.

You may also consider writing a book, a scholarly monograph, about your chosen field. Relative to edited volumes, there are fewer scholarly monographs, and they have the potential to make a greater contribution to the field. On a practical note, once you start thinking about being promoted from associate to full professor, many departmental and university committees start to look for a theoretical or synthetic contribution of some kind to document your status in the field, in addition to a series of empirical papers. Major review papers, theory papers, or a scholarly monograph will help to document your credentials on this front.

Suppose you have not established yourself as primarily a researcher but rather as a successful teacher, or possibly you are one of those individuals who is excellent at both. In either case, you might consider writing a textbook. If you teach the course, you are probably familiar with most of the books out there and you know their strengths and weaknesses. If you enjoy writing and others tell you that you are a good, clear writer, then you might consider writing a textbook. Writing a textbook might seem a daunting task to you, but do not be put off. After all, if you have taught the course for years and it is in a field you know, then writing a book about the topic should not necessarily overwhelm you. Textbook companies are always on the lookout for exciting new textbooks, and an outstanding textbook can set the standard for the field. Let us consider the pros and cons of writing textbooks in the next few paragraphs.

If you write a textbook for a fairly general course, you might make a bit of money. These courses include Introductory Psychology, Research Methods, Statistics, and the big survey courses taught in every department—Abnormal, Developmental, Social, or Cognitive, among others. However, most beginning textbook writers should consider writing a more specialized textbook before striking out in the big markets. Write an Attitude Change textbook if that is your field and then, if that experience is a good one for you, consider writing a Social Psychology textbook at some later point. Unfortunately, the more specialized the textbook, the less the market and hence the less the money you may expect to make. Yet even in the textbook market for larger courses, do not expect to make what the publishers tell you that you *might* make. They are always overly optimistic. Another advantage of writing a textbook is that you master your field in a way that you would not do without writing the textbook. To understand a subject well enough to write about it, you have to read deeply and synthesize your knowledge. Writing a textbook (like teaching a course) is a wonderful (and broadening) learning experience. In addition, your greater knowledge can produce a positive feedback loop to aid your own research, which may become better informed. In addition, writing a textbook that is widely used enhances your reputation in the field, as well as your name recognition.

There can be several downsides to textbook writing, too. For one thing, it is very time-consuming. Editors of publishing companies often sign professors to write textbooks with the mantra that "You have taught the course for years and you know the textbooks out there. All you have to do is write up your lecture notes." However, it is never that easy. It is one thing to know enough about a subject to give a lecture to undergraduates who know much less; it is an entirely different matter to write intelligently about a subject on which one is not well read where you will be judged by your peers at other universities. You simply must do your homework and immerse yourself in the field, at least to the extent of reading review papers about the topics on which you write. Another downside is that textbook writing is often underappreciated in universities, somewhat surprisingly. The attitude seems to be that scholarly monographs are to be taken seriously at the time of promotion and tenure but that authoring textbooks represents "writing to make money." Universities are increasingly emphasizing teaching, so this attitude toward writing textbooks may change. After all, a brilliant teacher on one campus can still only influence students there, but a brilliant textbook writer can educate a generation of students around the world. Textbook writing is certainly not for everyone, but if you are a good, clear writer and find that writing comes easily to you, you might consider writing a textbook.

Another direction that often affords itself during the mid-career period is becoming involved in national organizations, such as the American Psychological Association or the American Psychological Society, or more specialized organizations such as the Society for Research in Child Development or the Psychonomic Society. These organizations obviously do not run themselves but are dependent on the contributions from people dedicated to forwarding the goals of the discipline. Consider volunteering for some committee work or running for an elected position. Being involved in national organizations provides an excellent perspective on the diversity of the field and how large-scale organizations operate. These organizations also afford the opportunity to get to know the leaders in the field.

As a final suggestion, what about administration? Are you good working with people? Does your department call on you to chair committees because you are perceived as a leader and are known to be fair and to get things done efficiently and well? These kinds of talents are not necessarily plentiful in academia. In fact, some people seem to choose academia because they are quite bright and love ideas and research but do not have the practical or social intelligence to make it in highly collaborative, real-world environments. Academia still tolerates and sometimes encourages the lone scholar residing in the ivory tower, as well as the difficult personality. Because academia almost always chooses its leaders from within academia, the pickings are sometimes slim. For someone to become a department chair, dean, provost, or president means that the person is taking on a position for which he or she was not trained. These individuals have had to learn on the job. You might be one of these people who would find administration rewarding.

During your early mid-career period, you would probably be asked only to chair committees, but see if you like the experience of leading, of getting things done, of working with people. If you like them, you might consider administration at some later point in your career. The first step would be to be chair or head of a department. Of course, you do not choose this—your department and your dean do. Appearing too interested in being chair can, somewhat curiously, sometimes be the kiss of death in the selection process. Your department may see you as power hungry. Again, ask your colleagues about your potential administrative skills. You may be surprised to hear their responses. However, because many departments have a system of rotating chairs—one person does it for three to four years, then another, and so on—many members of the department will be chair or head at one point or another.

Very few people will go on in administration beyond the level of chair, but we hope some readers at least will consider this step. Of course, being chosen as a dean or provost or president of a university (among other posts) depends on being selected by outside search committees. But, why, you might wonder, would anyone want to take this step, which would remove the scholar from his or her chosen field and from teaching and research? This is a difficult question and depends on individual choices. However, every university needs outstanding academic leaders in these important posts. It is important for psychology (as a discipline) to produce academic leaders. At this writing, Richard Atkinson (a cognitive psychologist) is the recently retired chancellor of the entire University of California system of higher education; Judith Rodin (a social psychologist) is president of the University of Pennsylvania; William Gordon (whose field is animal learning and conditioning) was president of the University of New Mexico; and Nancy Cantor (a social/personality psychologist) is chancellor of the University of Illinois at Urbana–Champaign. These are only a few of the psychologists who hold important posts. Many others are provosts and deans. Each of them chose to give up outstanding careers in academic psychology to serve universities in these important posts. Members of their universities and psychologists at large should be grateful to them for serving in these capacities. Administration can be quite rewarding, as one helps to move a department, a division, or an entire university forward, but the jobs are demanding and provide their fair share of tough decisions and migraine headaches.

The mid-career period can represent a time in which you become immersed more deeply in your research and other scholarly activities, but as we have tried to indicate, we hope you will also consider it a time to look up from your work and to consider branching out. Academia offers a fair range of opportunities within its walls.

LATE-CAREER DIRECTIONS

What constitutes the late-career phase of a career, when there is no longer a mandatory retirement age in academia in the United States? (Other countries still have it. In Canada university professors are forced to retire at 65.) There is no fixed answer to this question, but because most people continue to retire around 65 to 70, we can consider late-career as beginning at perhaps 55. By this time, one's career path is usually relatively entrenched, although people can show dramatic shifts of interest even at this point. We have emphasized continual self-assessment, but around age 55 or 60 is another point to step back and to take a hard look at yourself. Are you still enjoying what you are doing? If so, great; look to the future and examine opportunities as they arise. But if you are burning out, if you feel you cannot bear to look at another new group of undergraduate faces and try to educate them about your field, if you are tired of research—then it may be time to reassess your options.

If you decide you no longer want to teach, do not simply hang on and teach with increasingly less effort and enthusiasm. Take the leap and get out of academia and let the younger generation take over. It is too costly to have students lose interest because of poor teaching. If you still enjoy your research, you might be able to become a research professor and support yourself. Some professors who have tired of teaching have officially retired and supported themselves from their retirement plan while still maintaining their laboratories. Others obtain external funding to support their research. However, some universities cannot afford to allow retired faculty members to continue to use their lab space, so this solution may not be an option. The point is that if teaching and academia no longer continue to excite you, our advice is to find something else for your abilities and not to stagnate on the job. You do not want to be considered dead wood.

There are other options for older faculty. We have already discussed departmental and university administration. Reinventing yourself by finding an exciting new direction and purpose to your research is always possible at this age. We have observed that many older scholars become more interested in the history of psychology in general and of their field in particular. Consider stepping back and writing an overview history of your field, tracing the fate of certain ideas and movements through the years. (The older you get, the more of the history you have actually lived through). Another extremely useful function for wise senior faculty is in mentoring junior faculty. In this way you can repay the department for the mentoring that you probably received (or you could give others the kind of mentoring you *wish* you had received). Every department needs a core group of experienced faculty on whom the junior faculty can depend for advice.

Many psychologists remain highly productive and make important contributions in research, in teaching and in service until late in their careers. There is no reason not to expect the same for yourself, if you put your mind to it. However, if you do find your enthusiasm ebbing, look around for a new direction and a new job.

RETIREMENT: PLANNING THE END GAME

The concept of retirement arouses different emotions in academics. In some fields, people look forward to the time when they can retire and often take early retirement so that they "can do things they really want to do." Our observation is that relatively few active academics feel this way. They are already doing what they really want to do—that is why they chose their field and their profession. So, retirement can seem a depressing or even dangerous concept: "If I retire I'll no longer be able to do what I want to do."

In the United States there is no mandatory retirement for college professors, as we have noted. However, there still appear to be informal expectations that one "should" retire at around 65 to 70, certainly no later than 75. If you do not, you might be considered a workaholic—and if not that, you would be perceived as blocking a job from some exciting young person just getting out of graduate school. However, there are many strategies for staying active past age 70, and "successful aging" is the watch phrase in the 21st century. Many academics who retire continue to be productive and can make important contributions. Some move to a retirement location near a university, where they may still have an adjunct appointment and do occasional teaching. Others continue writing and reviewing and may collaborate with younger scholars. Writing books or review articles, or editing books, can also be useful. Many individuals make good use of the wisdom acquired during the previous 40 plus years, such as serving in posts in national organizations.

One strategy for easing into retirement is phased retirement. You may go to half-time teaching for a few years before you retire, at reduced salary. This frees part of your time to look in other directions for new avenues. Some people find that they can even get more scholarly work done when their teaching load becomes lighter.

Another option, and often an admirable one, is to retire and not look back. You may have spent your 30- to 40-some years in academia. Now you will move on to some other phase of life and leave your old way of life behind, maybe just dipping into a journal once a year to see if there is anything breathtakingly new in your field.

Issues surrounding retirement, perhaps even more than other topics covered in this chapter, are highly personal, and no general rules will fit all cases. Each person must find his or her own way through these end-of-career issues.

CONCLUSION

This chapter has considered the long view of academic life. The main message is that there is life after tenure, and it should be lived to the fullest, but that the elements that constitute a full life will differ dramatically among individuals. Continue to assess your skills, your goals, and your situation to find your way through the variety of choices (inside and outside academia) that are open to you.

Index

ABOUT THE EDITORS

John M. Darley, PhD, is the Warren Professor of Psychology and a professor of psychology and public affairs at Princeton University, a former chair of the psychology department, and past president of the American Psychological Society. He graduated with a bachelor's degree from Swarthmore College and received his doctoral degree from Harvard University. His current research interests include examining the ways in which individuals construct their representations of the interpersonal world in which they find themselves and how that influences their behavior—a topic often called "conformity." He is also concerned with moral issues, particularly those concerning the intersections of legal codes and community morality. He has recently examined, with law professor Paul Robinson, the link and discontinuities between citizens' moral perceptions and the moral principles instantiated in legal codes and the consequences of those discontinuities.

Mark P. Zanna, PhD, is a professor and former chair of the Department of Psychology at the University of Waterloo. He received his bachelor's and doctoral degrees from Yale University. His area of research is the psychology of attitudes. Currently he is conducting research on overcoming resistance to change. He was president of the Society of Experimental Social Psychology and Division 8, the Society for Personality and Social Psychology, of the American Psychological Association. He coedits the *Ontario Symposium on Personality and Social Psychology* and edits *Advances in Experimental Social Psychology*. He is the recipient of the Donald O. Hebb Award from the Canadian Psychological Association and the Donald T. Campbell Award from the Society of Personality and Social Psychology, both for Distinguished Scientific Contributions. He is a Fellow of the Royal Society of Canada.

Henry L. Roediger III, PhD, is the James S. McDonnell Distinguished University Professor and department chair at Washington University in

St. Louis. He graduated with a bachelor's degree from Washington and Lee University and received his doctoral degree from Yale University. His research has centered on human learning and memory, and he has published 160 articles and chapters on cognitive processes involved in remembering. His recent research has focused on illusions of memory. He was editor of the *Journal of Experimental Psychology: Learning, Memory and Cognition* and *Psychonomic Bulletin & Review*. He is currently president of the American Psychological Society.